WIN

WINE BUYER'S GUIDE 2000

DORLING KINDERSLEY
London • New York • Sydney
www.dk.com

A DORLING KINDERSLEY BOOK
www.dk.com

First published in Great Britain in 1999
by Dorling Kindersley Limited,
9 Henrietta Street,
London WC2E 8PS

A CIP catalogue record
for this book is available
from the British Library.

ISBN 0 7513 0792 0

Printed in Italy by Graphicom

CONTENTS

HARDYS
YARRAMAN
chardonnay
1997
CHO
1935

INTRODUCTION

NO SOONER HAVE YOU focused your attention on one bottle, another barges its way into your line of vision, screaming "Try me!" The merchant's shelf is indeed a bitter and confusing battleground, where wines from around the world jostle for position and favour. Some rely on clever packaging and enticing label literature; others rely on reputation and word-of-mouth. The majority, however, are often an unknown quantity.

The citizens of many other nations, of course, never face quite such a dilemma. Their shelves are stocked mainly with national produce, providing little choice and even less scope for experiment. Britain, on the other hand, profits from little national bias and an innovative market, in which wines from around the world can be bought in the local high street. What method, then does one use to distinguish the good from the bad, the star performer from the pretender in the designer shirt but dirty vest?

REAPING THE REWARDS

Since its launch in 1983, WINE magazine's International WINE Challenge has become the world's largest, and most influential, wine competition. This year it brought together some 8,500 wines and over 550 finely-tuned palates. The results of those tasters' efforts appear on the following pages in the form of over 2,500 winners, descriptions of how they taste, where to buy them and how much they should cost. These must surely help you to find your way around all those shelves.

THE CHALLENGE

THE INTERNATIONAL WINE Challenge was created in 1983 by Robert Joseph, WINE's publishing editor, and Charles Metcalfe, associate editor, as the basis of an article which examined how English wine makers were doing compared to their counterparts in other countries. Neither had any idea at that stage that the Challenge would transform itself into the world's most international, most comprehensive and, increasingly, most respected wine competition. During the past 16 years, the number of wines entered into the Challenge has grown from 38 to 8,500. The number of professional judges has risen from 20 to 550.

WITH A LITTLE HELP FROM OUR FRIENDS

Broken down to a basic level, the Challenge's success lies in two essential factors. The first is the support it receives from both the wine trade in this country and the wine producers elsewhere in the world; the second is the ruthless impartiality and organisation with which it is run.

During the past fifteen years, wines appearing in the United Kingdom have become increasingly diverse. Wines from the former Soviet republic of Moldova now sit alongside Australian Chardonnay and German Gewürztraminer on the shelves, and each one tries to force its way into your field of vision and screams "Try me!".

WE CAN WORK IT OUT

The difficulty for retailers is that diversity is not enough; quality and value for money are the real selling points, especially to discerning British consumers. The same is true within the wine trade itself, where restaurateurs buying from importers are justly looking to make money from the wines they put on their lists. Consequently, both retail and wholesale merchants quickly recognised the need for a fair method of evaluating the wines on the market and, more importantly, for an effective mechanism to put across the results to the wine drinker.

CREATING AN INTERNATIONAL BENCHMARK

This simple method of guiding people through the minefield of wine buying has gained the International WINE Challenge its support from the trade. Companies ranging from retail giants such as Tesco, chains such as Unwins, to specialist merchants such as Justerini & Brooks all enter wines. Equally important is the support of such companies in the evaluation of Challenge wines, for it is their representatives who judge each and every wine. Buyers from these companies, renowned for their experience and accuracy, together with winemakers from all over the world and Britain's most respected wine writers make up the tasting team which works so hard for the two weeks of the Challenge. It is their involvement that generates the unique trust in the results, reinforcing the care with which every entrant to the Challenge is examined.

UNDER STARTER'S ORDERS

The process begins in January, when entry kits are distributed to thousands of companies worldwide, inviting them to submit their wines. Within a few weeks, the replies start pouring in, detailing information on every wine to be tasted, such as the principal grape varieties used and the regions in which the grapes were grown.

Once this information is logged in, the entire Challenge team descends to the venue to begin receiving the wines themselves. Some are delivered by local companies; others are samples brought in specially by courier.

GET READY

Next comes the 'flighting': placing entries into groups of 12-18 wines. Flights are grouped by origin, variety and retail price so that they can be evaluated fairly among equals. Bottles are then inserted into special 'co-extruded' wine bags, tagged with tamper-proof seals and boxed, ready for tasting - always a favourite job amongst helpers. Sparkling wines are chilled, vintage ports decanted and wines with distinctive bottles transferred.

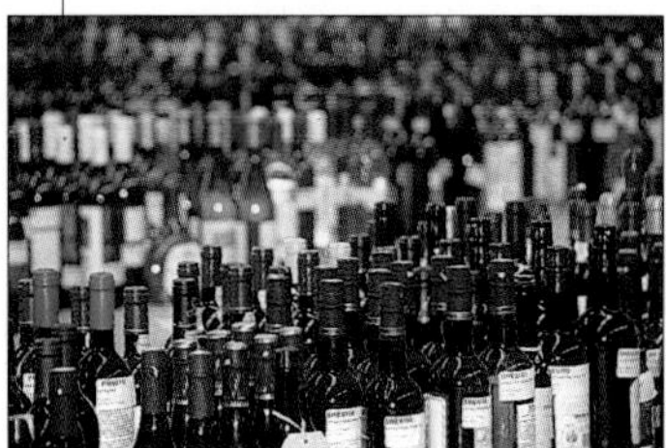

THEY'RE OFF!

It is now that the tasters arrive in droves, only to be split into tasting teams of five or six to tackle the wines. Flights are tasted, removed and recorded. Corked bottles are replaced within four minutes, and corks pulled at an alarming rate. Over 1,500 wines are tasted each day.

Attention to detail is meticulous: even the chlorine was removed from a nearby fountain to reduce the risk of contaminating smells! Lurking beneath is the less glamorous process of control. All results are double-checked; discarded wines are tasted once again by a 'Super Juror', an experienced and respected trade member or Master of Wine whose task it is to ensure no worthy wine slips the net. Tasting sheets proceed to the computer, the 'nerve-centre', where every result is recorded by helpers working in pairs, one reading, one inputting. The results are checked and double-checked by another pair to ensure that no errors are made. The second-round flights are born, wines are re-flighted, re-bagged, re-tagged and re-tasted by new judges.

WINES OF THE YEAR

ONE OF THE MAIN roles of the International WINE Challenge is to introduce the consumer to readily available, great-value wines. The Wines of the Year are the best Gold, Silver, and in the case of sparkling wines, Bronze, medal winners which fit two crucial criteria: widespread availability and reasonable price (under £8 for table wines and under £15 for sparkling). Wines were shortlisted by these criteria and then tasted by the trophy panel, who chose their favourite wines in each category.

THE FIZZ

The Fizz section this year entices the interest of all lovers of bubbles. From three different continents come the Sparkling Wines of the year, all holding the common thread of Champagne heritage. From Australia, **Green Point Vintage Brut 1995** displays a wondrous amalgam of pure fruit and yeasty complexity, taking advantage of the Australian forte of multi-regional blending. **Louis Roederer Quartet**

Anderson Valley 1995 offers fresh bread and refreshing citrus on a brilliantly complex palate. Champagne still offers remarkable value and quality, especially with **Alexandre Bonnet Brut NV;** this frisky little number offers a nose laced with limey and leesy characters and brilliant complexity for its price. These three fizzes will enable everyone to keep a little bit of bubble in their lives, while experiencing luxury at an inexpensive price.

Wines of the Year have been tasted by some of the finest palates in the world. We hope that you will enjoy trying these wines and discover for yourself the qualities recognised by our judges.

The White Wines

Antipodean Chardonnay shone through this year. From the English sounding town of Kingston-on-Murray in South Australia the Gold medal-winning **Banrock Station Chardonnay 1998** shows intense varietal character and lovely fresh zestiness. New Zealand chimes in with the luciously elegant **Montana Reserve Gisborne Chardonnay 1998** from her largest producer. The third wine

sees an old favourite emerge in a different guise, **La Domeque Tête de Cuvée Blanc VdP d'Oc 1998** offers a mouthwatering, floral blend of Muscat, Marsanne and Roussanne from the ever improving super region of the South of France. All three of these wines offer varietal integrity, typicity as well as fantastic value for money.

THE RED WINES

The Northern Hemisphere made a clean sweep of the reds this year, all showing wonderful diversity and great representatives of their styles. **Pepperwood Grove Zinfandel 1997** from California is a spicey, brambley monster of a wine. Portugal offers us the pleasantly tarry, smoky, blueberry-filled **DFJ Vinhos Ramada 1998,** which delivers astounding value from the Estremadura region north of Lisbon. France comes into play with the characterful **Noblesse de Sérénac 1997** from the picturesque Gaillac appellation in the South West, demonstrating slurpy dark fruit and an amazingly approachable structure. A diverse package of red wines for value hunters to enjoy.

THE TROPHIES

HAVING TASTED THE WINES and chosen the Gold Medal Winners, the final task is to select the supreme champions from each category: the Trophy winners. At this stage considerations such as price and volume of production are disregarded; wines compete against each other on their intrinsic qualities alone. Unlike any other competition, the judges were not obliged to award trophies in every category. From the start they were told to award trophies only where they thought they were deserved.

The following trophies were awarded by a selection of 14 of the UK's best palates, including 11 MWs. The first of which was to the **Louis de Belmance Vintage Champagne 1990** for the Champagne & Sparkling White Wine Trophy, followed closely by the young Australian upstart **Cockatoo Ridge Black NV** scooping the Sparkling Red Trophy.

The first Trophy awarded in the white wine section was to **Ernest and Julio Gallo,** who took the Trophy for their bold **Northern Sonoma**

Chardonnay 1996.

The New Zealanders then hit centre stage taking the Trophy for the **Isabel Estate Sauvignon Blanc 1998**.

Then from across the Tasman came the refreshingly elegant and understated **Tyrrell's Vat 1 Sémillon 1993** to scoop the Sémillon Trophy.

Not to be out done, the Italians came to the forc with a superb Verdicchio from Marches. The **Verdicchio dei Castelli di Jesi Classico Superiore Balciana, Sartarelli 1997** came out punching with a full asparagus and fruit nose to walk away with not only top Italian honours but also the overall White Wine Trophy - an impressive performance.

Then came the Germans, storming in to scoop the Riesling Trophies in their own inimitable style. The **Ruppertsberger Reiterpfad Riesling Auslese Trocken 1996** put forward a mighty herbaceous nose, while the **Serriger Vogelsung Riesling Auslese 1989** shared the trophy and the **Domaine Zind Humbrect Pinot Gris 1996** won over the judges to take out the Aromatic Honours.

And on to the reds where competition was equally if not more fierce. First off the mark was the Australian blockbuster - the **E&E Black Pepper Shiraz 1996**, winning dual honours for the Rhône and Grenache/Syrah Trophy and overall Red Wine Trophy. The Americans followed through with a double hit , scooping the Bordeaux and Cabernet/Merlot Trophy with the **BV Georges de Latour Cabernet Sauvignon 1995,** and the **Saint Francis Old Vines Zinfandel 1996** taking away the Zinfandel Trophy.

Not to be left out in the cold, the Austrians put on a sterling performance, winning the attention of the judges with the **Steinzeiler Kollwentz 1997,** which came seemingly from nowhere to make its mark with an Austrian Red Wine Trophy.

Other Europeans to join forces were the subtle yet powerful **Sergio Zenato Amarone 1990,** with all the finesse and elegance expected from an Italian Red Trophy Winner. The French also served well with the **Brouilly Domain J Tatoux 1998** rightfully taking the Beaujolais Trophy, while the Burgundy Trophy was awarded to the **Pommard Premier Cru Rugiens-Bas, Aleth le Royer-Girardin 1996** for its rich, meaty nose and remarkable velvet palate.

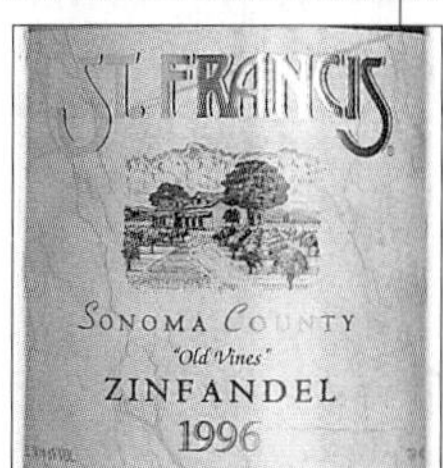

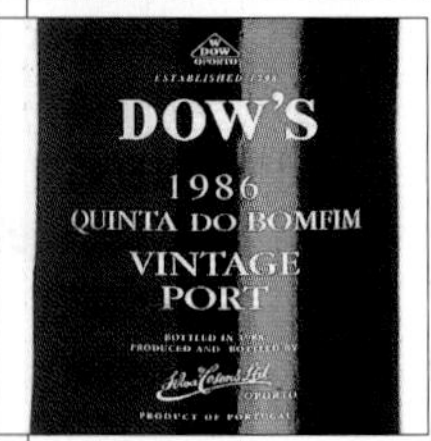

Another European success was the **Esporão Trinadeira Preta 1997** from Alentjo, Portugal, with overwhelming cedar and prune notes that drew the attention of the judges.

South Africa joined the trophy race this year by re-establicshing the Pinotage Trophy, presenting a superb **Cathedral Cellar Pinotage 1996** from the Coastal Region, showing all the grandeur of a truly mighty wine.

For the Overall Fortified and Sherry Trophies, Spain showed her true colours with the brilliant **Domecq Sibrata** from Jerez. The **Henriques & Henriques 15 Year Old Malmsey** took the Madeira Trophy and the **Dow's Quinta Bomfim 1986** completed the medley with the Port Trophy.

To round up, the **Feiler Artinger Klaus Neuburger Essenz 1997** collected the Dessert Wine Trophy, making it a double act for the Austrians, with the newly instated Austrian Red Trophy.

This year's WINE Challenge has demonstrated more than ever the diversity of the vinous world's offerings and proved that great wine can and is being made throughout the world, offering a wealth of new wine to discover.

WINES OF THE YEAR AND TROPHY WINES

SPARKLING WINES OF THE YEAR

Alexandre Bonnet NV (£10.00) *p133*
Green Point Vintage Brut 1995 (£11.50) *p92*
Louis Roederer
Quartet Anderson Valley 1995 (£14.40) *p233*

WHITE WINES OF THE YEAR

Banrock Station Chardonnay 1998 (£4.00) *p30*
La Domeque Tête de Cuvée
Vieilles Vignes Blanc VdP d'Oc 1998 (£5.00) *p155*
Montana Reserve
Gisborne Chardonnay 1998 (£8.00) *p246*

RED WINES OF THE YEAR

Noblesse de Sérénac 1997 (£6.00) *p169*
Pepperwood Grove Zinfandel 1997 (£6.00) *p235*
Ramada, DFJ Vinhos 1998 (£3.50) *p280*

TROPHY WINES

Champagne and Sparkling White Wine Trophy *p136*
Champagne Louis de Belmance Vintage 1990 (£17.80)
Sparkling Red Trophy *p91*
Cockatoo Ridge Black NV (£7.20)
Riesling Trophy
Ruppertsberger Reiterpfad Riesling
Auslese Trocken 1996 (£10.00) *p174*
Serriger Vogelsung Riesling Auslese 1989 (£6.00) *p173*

TROPHY WINNERS

Aromatic White Trophy
Domaine Zind Humbrecht Pinot Gris Clos St Urbain Rangen de Thann Grand Cru (£27.90) *p111*

Chardonnay Trophy
Northen Sonoma Estate Bottled Chardonnay, E&J Gallo (£20.00) *p223*

Sauvignon Blanc Trophy
Isabel Estate Sauvignon Blanc 1998 (£9.30) *p257*

Sémillon Trophy *p70*
Tyrrell's Vat 1 Semillon 1993 (17.30)

Italian White & White Wine Trophy *p212*
Verdicchio dei Castelli di Jesi Classico Superiore Balciani, Sarterelli 1997 (12.50)

Bordeaux & Cabernet/Merlot Trophy *p218*
BV Georges de Latour Cabernet Sauvignon 1995 (£40.00)

Italian Red Trophy *p195*
Sergio Zenato Amarone Riserva 1990 (£40.80)

Rhône & Syrah/Grenache & Red Wine Trophy *p88*
E&E Black Pepper Shiraz 1996 (£27.70)

Pinotage Trophy *p328*
Cathedral Cellar Pinotage 1996 (£8.90)

Beaujolais Trophy *p112*
Brouilly Domain J Tatoux 1998 (£8.00)

Austrian Red Trophy
Steinzeiler Kollwentz 1997 (£17.90) Not available in UK at time of print

Burgundy & Pinot Noir Trophy *p126*
Pommard Premier Cru Rugiens-Bas, Alet le Royer-Girardin 1996 (£23.90)

Portugese Red Trophy *p285*
Esporão Trincadeira Preta 1997 (£7.50)(50cl)

Zinfandel Trophy *p237*
Saint Francis Old Vines Zinfandel 1996 (£14.10)

Dessert Wine Trophy
Feiler Artinger Klaus Neuburger Essenz 1997 (£23.60) (37.5cl) Not available in UK at time of print

Sherry & Fortified Wine Trophy *p342*
Domecq Sibarita (£15.00)

Port Trophy *p275*
Dow's Quinta do Bomfim 1986 (£21.10)

Madeira Trophy *p266*
Henriques & Henriques 15 Year Old Malmsey (£20.50)

The Wines

HOW TO USE THIS BOOK

Every wine in this guide has been awarded a medal at the 1998 International WINE Challenge. The wines are listed by country and region, with up to seven wine headings in the following order: red, white, sweet white, rosé, sparkling, sparkling rosé and fortified.

Under each heading the wines are listed in price order, from the least to the most expensive. Wines of the same price are listed in medal order: Gold, Silver and Bronze. Each wine carries the same range of information: its name (and vintage where applicable), a tasting note, average retail price, three-letter stockist's code (see page 322), and the medal it was awarded. Below is an explanation of how wines are listed, using the Red Wine of the Year on the opposite page as an example.

The wine name, vintage, producer and region

The average retail price

*The Medal: **G** Gold, **S** Silver, or **B** Bronze*

NORMAN'S WHITE LABEL CABERNET SAUVIGNON L106 1996, NORMAN'S CLARENDON WINERY South Australia	*Smoky, tobacco and cigar box notes on the ripe plum nose with flavours of blackcurrant, vanilla, mint and spice.*	£6.00	ODD TBC	G WINE OF THE YEAR

A tasting note provided by Challenge tasters

Codes for stockists (see page 322)

Gold medal winning wines are shaded gold

These symbols indicate a Wine of the Year or Trophy Wine

Silver medal winning wines are shaded silver

Wines of the Year and Trophy Wines that don't have a Gold or Silver medal are shaded this colour

TROPHY WINE

AUSTRALIA

Once again Australia has proven her consistency with a whole swag of medals, trophies and Wines of the Year. These pages reflect the growing diversity of Australia's vinous offerings from warm, fleshy Shiraz to cool, acid Riesling. New regions are emerging such as Wrattonbully, Kuitpo and Orange pushing the envelope of this country's regional exploration and innovation. Look to regions like this or for different styles from those established to find your own undiscovered gem.

AUSTRALIA • CABERNET SAUVIGNON

Wine	Description	Price	Stockist	Award
Co-op Australian Cabernet Sauvignon 1997, Angove's South Australia	*Soft bramble fruits ooze from this easy drinking style that offers good grip and a cleansing finish.*	**£4.70**	CWS	B
Lindemans Bin 45 Cabernet Sauvignon 1998, Lindemans South Australia	*Young and fresh showing intense cassis and mocha, well balanced with nice chewy tannins to finish.*	**£5.70**	Widely Available	B
Cranswick Estate Dry Country Cabernet Sauvignon 1997, Cranswick Estate New South Wales	*Intense cassis nose, rich berry fruits, marked acidity and soft tannins. Simple with elegant balance.*	**£6.00**	AUS	B
Cranswick Estate Nine Pines Cabernet Sauvignon 1998, Cranswick Estate New South Wales	*Vibrant raspberry fruit and a lively sweet palate with nice tannins and good length.*	**£6.00**	AUS	B
Wrattonbully Cabernet Sauvignon 1998, Cellarmasters South Australia	*Currant and mint nose with eucalyptus and vanilla oak. Rich fruit, palate a little tight but elegant and long.*	**£6.00**	WTS	S

AUSTRALIA • CABERNET SAUVIGNON

Normans Bin 106 Cabernet Sauvignon 1998, Normans South Australia	*Plum red with glowing fresh berries and lavender tones the palate offers silky tannins and super length.*	**£6.50**	PLB	S
Bleasdale Mulberry Tree Cabernet Sauvignon 1997, Bleasdale South Australia	*Visually vibrant offering plum, mint and mocha characters and supported by a soft, rich palate.*	**£7.00**	ODF PLB	G
Kingston Print Wildlife Cabernet Sauvignon 1998, Kingston Estate South Eastern Australia	*Fresh youthful colour with a berried blackcurrant nose with firm but not astringent tannins.*	**£7.00**	VNO VNP	B
Wyndham Estate Bin 444 Cabernet Sauvignon 1997, Orlando Wyndham New South Wales	*Rich berry nose with blackcurrants on the palate and moderate tannins. Good length.*	**£7.00**	A&A BAB PEA CAX	B
Best's Victoria Cabernet Sauvignon 1997, Best's Victoria	*Youthful, jammy nose. Red fruit palate, slightly drying green wood tannins. Good fruit length and complexity.*	**£7.20**	SWS WCR JNW ADW	B
d'Arenberg The High Trellis Cabernet Sauvignon 1997, F E Osborne & Sons South Australia	*Stalky nose. Palate with spicy oak and moderate weight of fruit. A little stalky but nice and juicy.*	**£7.30**	BWL ODF	B
Miranda High Country Cabernet Sauvignon 1996, Miranda Wines Victoria	*A straightforward nose offering berries and beans followed by drying tannins and a clean finish.*	**£7.50**	QWW HOH AVB	B
Preece Cabernet Sauvignon 1996, Mitchelton Victoria	*Vegetal, blackcurrant nose with marshmallows. Soft currant fruit with evident complexity. Soft tannins, balance and length.*	**£7.50**	WCR JEF TOS	S

Wine	Tasting notes	Price	Stockists	Award
Diamond Varietal Cabernet Sauvignon 1998, Rosemount Estate South Australia	*Blackcurrants and plum sauce topped off with mint and aromatic cedar. Lovely palate weight and a good finish.*	£7.70	Widely Available	S
Plantagenet Omrah Merlot Cabernet Sauvignon 1997, Plantagenet Western Australia	*Hints of burnt toast and brambles on nose. Chunky, meaty palate. Lacks elegance, but has charm.*	£7.80	NYW GGW LIB	B
Wakefield Cabernet Sauvignon 1997, Wakefield Wines South Australia	*Straightforward but pleasant confected fruit nose with nice mouthfeel and structure and a persistant finish.*	£7.80	WCR NYW SWS ABT BAL BTH UNS SWS	B
Preece Cabernet Sauvignon 1997, Mitchelton Victoria	*Elegant mint, eucalyptus and currant aromas. Fruit driven palate. Balanced, long and elegant.*	£8.00	JEF	B
Tatachilla McLaren Vale Cabernet Sauvignon 1997, Tatachilla Winery South Australia	*Dark and brooding, intense and dense with fabulous extracted blackcurrant and vanilla chatacters. Great length.*	£8.50	D&D	S
Tatachilla Cabernet Sauvignon 1996, Tatachilla Winery South Australia	*Ripe, rich, blackcurrant nose with mint. Well-integrated fruit and tannins with good concentration and flavour.*	£8.70	ODD NIC WTS	S
Evans & Tate Cabernet Sauvignon 1997, Evans & Tate Western Australia	*Nice up front fruit complemented by a herbaceous tinge with a crisp acid finish.*	£9.00	GRA FRT	B
Pewsey Vale Cabernet Sauvignon 1997, Yalumba Winery South Australia	*Big, spicy cassis nose. Ripe, quite sweet fruit on silky soft palate, with firm tannins.*	£9.00	TOS JNW NEG YAL	S

AUSTRALIA • CABERNET SAUVIGNON

Rouge Homme Cabernet Sauvignon 1996, Rouge Homme South Australia	*Attractive cherry and blackcurrants with hints of sandalwood and cassis. Big tannin structure, hang on to it.*	**£9.00**	WTS PEF	(S)
Tatachilla Cabernet Sauvignon 1997, Tatachilla Winery South Australia	*Ripe and spicy glazed fruit, with delicate berry flavours and nice drying tannins.*	**£9.00**	BDR QWW	(B)
Vasse Felix Cabernet Sauvignon Merlot 1997, Vasse Felix Winery Western Australia	*Clean, rich farmyard nose. Soft, well-balanced palate. Big ripe plummy fruit. Medium weight with good length.*	**£9.00**	BWC CPW TAN L&W CHC NEG	(B)
Three Bridges Cabernet Sauvignon 1997, West End Wines South Eastern Australia	*Mint and mocha on the nose lead to a full bodied palate and a neat tail.*	**£9.70**	BDR	(S)
Jim Barry Cabernet Sauvignon 1997, Jim Barry Wines South Australia	*Minty, cassis nose. Rich, ripe minty fruit palate. Big, balanced tannins with dry earthy finish.*	**£9.90**	BWC TAN DIR ODF CHC IVV NEG	(B)
Geoff Merrill Cabernet Sauvignon Reserve 1993, Geoff Merrill South Australia	*Tobacco leaf aromas on well evolved bouquet. Good palate structure with nice grippy finish.*	**£10.00**	SAF	(B)
Mamre Brook Barossa Valley Cabernet Sauvignon 1996, Saltram Estate South Australia	*A full blown nose of blackcurrant and toasty oak. A full bodied chalky tannin palate carries the flavour.*	**£10.00**	SAF MWW BPW	(S)
Wynns Cabernet Sauvignon 1996, Wynns Coonawarra Estate South Australia	*Attractive red clay colour with a nose of cedar and spice and a lovely blackcurrant backdrop. Keep.*	**£10.00**	Widely Available	(S)

Wine	Description	Price	Stockists	Award
Best's Great Western Cabernet Sauvignon 1996, Best's Victoria	*Nose of black fruit and spicy white pepper. Spicy and complex and chewy with fine tannins.*	£10.30	Widely Available	S
Stonier Cabernet Sauvignon 1997, Stonier Victoria	*Some pastilles and curranty characters introduce a light but savoury palate with decent tannin structure.*	£10.40	MZC	B
Yalumba The Menzies Coonawarra Cabernet Sauvignon 1996, Yalumba Winery South Australia	*Sweet blackcurrant fruit on nose. Leathery, black fruit flavours with slightly vegetal edge. Full and ripe.*	£10.50	Widely Available	S
Hardys Coonawarra Cabernet Sauvignon 1996, BRL Hardy South Australia	*Runner bean and herb aromas on nose. Fruity, with well-integrated oak and sweet herbal notes. Classy and long.*	£10.70	VLW WCR HBR	B
Balgownie Estate Cabernet Sauvignon 1997, Balgownie Estate Victoria	*Inky, concentrated, jammy nose. Up-front blackcurrant fruit. Chalky tannin structure with acidity on finish.*	£11.00	BPW	B
Bowen Estate Cabernet Sauvignon 1996, Bowen Estate South Australia	*Rich, maturing nose from this tightly structured, jammy, dark cherry fruit laden wine.*	£11.00	AUC	B
Long Gully Irmas Cabernet Sauvignon 1996, Long Gully Estate Victoria	*Light summer berry and cream cheese nose. Smoky and herbal palate with sweet fruit behind.*	£11.00	REN	B
Penfolds Bin 407 Cabernet Sauvignon 1996, Penfolds South Australia	*An intense, tight blackberry nose introduces a long palate of fruit, rich and up-front, with excellent oak integration.*	£11.00	Widely Available	S

AUSTRALIA • CABERNET SAUVIGNON

YARRA GLEN GRAND CABERNET SAUVIGNON 1997, ANDREW GARRETT VINEYARD Victoria	*Plenty of ripe fruit with a pronounced curranty nose. A powerful wine wih great structure and a grippy finish.*	**£11.00**	T&T	S
KATNOOK CABERNET SAUVIGNON 1996, WINGARA South Australia	*Rich, floral, dark cherry nose with minty freshness. Firm tannins balanced by rich dark fruit with spicy notes.*	**£11.20**	VLW BWL NYW	B
GEOFF MERRILL RESERVE CABERNET SAUVIGNON 1994, GEOFF MERRILL South Australia	*Minty cassis nose. Rich soft currants in the mouth with soft, ripe tannins. Long, sweet fruit finish.*	**£11.50**	SAF TOS PLE	S
WOLF BLASS PRESIDENT'S SELECTION CABERNET SAUVIGNON 1996, MILDARA BLASS South Australia	*Fresh and lively fruit flavour, with a mineral vein and a deightful fruit tannin tail.*	**£11.50**	Widely Available	S
ALLANMERE CABERNET SAUVIGNON 1997, ALLANMERE WINES New South Wales	*Sweet currants lead to an acid, refreshing and full palate with a dusty finish.*	**£11.60**	WFD ALE HAF HDL HUL VRS	B
PLANTAGENET MOUNT BARKER CABERNET SAUVIGNON 1996, PLANTAGENET Western Australia	*Boiled fruit and herbal tones with a spicy oak influence meets a touch of green pepper.*	**£11.60**	GGW NYW LIB	S
MICHELTON CABERNET SAUVIGNON 1995, MITCHELTON Victoria	*Classic New World mint and cassis. Intense palate fruit. Good balance and structure.*	**£12.00**	JEF	B
NORMANS SIGNATURE CABERNET SAUVIGNON CABERNET FRANC 1996, NORMANS South Australia	*A basket of treats in a bottle. Mocha, spice, cassis, red fruit, and mint rise from a wine lover's oasis.*	**£12.00**	TOS PLB	G

CABERNET SAUVIGNON • AUSTRALIA

Ebenezer Cabernet Sauvignon 1996, BRL Hardy South Australia	*Minty, curranty nose. Hard, sweet fruit with tannic finish. Jammy, minty with well-integrated wood. Firm, excellent structure.*	**£13.00**	HBR	(G)
Geoff Hardy Cabernet Sauvignon 1996, Geoff Hardy South Australia	*Ripe cassis with a hint of cedar and spice on nose. Complex with fine tannins and good balance.*	**£13.00**	CTH	(S)
Geoff Merrill Reserve Cabernet Sauvignon 1995, Geoff Merrill South Australia	*Stalky, vegetal nose with blackcurrant. Sweet palate of soft fruit and lean tannins. Long complex finish.*	**£13.00**	TOS SAF PLE	(S)
Lindemans St George Cabernet Sauvignon 1995, Lindemans South Australia	*Ripe, minty cassis and spice on nose. Velvety fleshiness on palate. Nice spice hidden under fruit.*	**£13.00**	UNS TOS ODD MWW BTH WCR PEF	(S)
Vasse Felix Cabernet Sauvignon 1997, Vasse Felix Winery Western Australia	*Subtle ripe fruit lies beneath a mint and pepper nose and follows on to a smoothly textured palate of great balance.*	**£13.00**	NYW BWC TAN CPW CHH IVV NEG	(S)
Hardys Coonawarra Cabernet Sauvignon 1995, BRL Hardy South Australia	*Sweet pastilles, spice and tobacco notes lead to a full bodied, richly textured palate of great fruit concentration.*	**£13.80**	VLW WCR SAF CWS HBR	(G)
McGuigan Personal Reserve Cabernet Sauvignon 1996, McGuigan Wines South Eastern Australia	*Ripe plums and fig aromas lead to a palate of chocolate and plums with a clean tannin tail.*	**£14.50**	VNO WAC QWW VNP	(S)
Petaluma Coonawarra 1996, Petaluma South Australia	*An array of fruits on the nose and a rich minty follow through. Stylish and elegant.*	**£14.50**	NYW MZC	(S)

AUSTRALIA • CABERNET SAUVIGNON

Coldstream Hills Reserve Cabernet Sauvignon 1995, Coldstream Hills Victoria	*Complex oak, figs and chocolate. Elegant plummy fruit. Quite rich and balanced with structured tannins.*	**£15.00**	ODD PEF	B
Yalumba Reserve Clare Cabernet Sauvignon 1996, Yalumba Winery South Australia	*Cherry menthol nose. Rich and concentrated in mouth with spicy nutmeg. Sweet, rich, complex but restrained.*	**£15.00**	JNW ODD NEG YAL	S
Dalwhinnie Estate Cabernet Sauvignon 1997, Dalwhinnie Estate Victoria	*Savoury and minty characters on the nose with terrific palate weight peak to a fine cleansing tail.*	**£15.50**	VLW NYW J&B	S
Evans & Tate Margaret River Cabernet Sauvignon 1996, Evans & Tate Western Australia	*Plummy, Merlot-style fruit and herbs on nose. Soft but intense front palate with cedar and loganberry.*	**£15.70**	CTH NYW GRA	G
Evans & Tate Margaret River Cabernet Sauvignon 1994, Evans & Tate Western Australia	*Aromatic berry and oak bouquet. Quite warm with broad flavour progression, almost raisiny finish with tannin backbone.*	**£16.00**	CTH GRA GRA	B
Orlando St Hugo Cabernet Sauvignon 1993, Orlando Wyndham South Australia	*Integrated cedar and blackcurrant nose. Balanced raspberry fruit and oak on palate. Lively red fruit finish.*	**£16.00**	CAP PEA UNS CAX	B
Orlando St Hugo Cabernet Sauvignon 1994, Orlando Wyndham South Australia	*A myriad of chocolate, blackcurrant, violet and savoury notes which meet chalky tannins and great balancing acidity.*	**£16.00**	UNS CAP PEA CAX	G
Haselgrove H Reserve Cabernet Sauvignon 1997, Haselgrove South Australia	*Very sweet and ripe cooked blackcurrant and caramel nose. A superb concentrated, complex and stylish wine.*	**£16.30**	VLW NYW WTS	G

CABERNET SAUVIGNON • AUSTRALIA

SUMMERFIELD CABERNET SAUVIGNON 1997, SUMMERFIELD Victoria	*Rich leather, blackcurrant nose. Smooth, front palate with rich Christmas cake fruit under steadying tannins.*	**£16.50**	BBR	S
SHOW RESERVE COONAWARRA CABERNET SAUVIGNON 1996, ROSEMOUNT ESTATE South Australia	*Beautiful creme de cassis and eucalypt working with intergrated oak. Good length and memorable finish.*	**£16.60**	SAF BWC TOS ROS	S
PETER LEHMANN THE MENTOR 1995, PETER LEHMANN WINES South Australia	*A classy nose showing bright fruit, mocha and licorice. Complex with fine tannins and a generous finish.*	**£18.00**	PLE	S
ROSE LABEL ORANGE CABERNET SAUVIGNON 1996, ROSEMOUNT ESTATE New South Wales	*Rich, dark coloured wine with concentrated fruit flavours and a splash of cinnamon and spice.*	**£18.00**	BWC ROS	S
D'ARENBERG THE COPPERMINE ROAD CABERNET 1997, F E OSBORNE & SONS South Australia	*Luscious colour showing jammy fruits, coffee and licorice. A great example of modern winemaking.*	**£18.60**	BWL ODF ODD	G
HOLLICK RAVENSWOOD 1994, HOLLICK South Australia	*Excellent fruit intensity in a well balanced and rounded wine with a neat acid tail.*	**£19.00**	L&W NYW JNW JLW	B
KATNOOK ODYSSEY 1994, WINGARA South Australia	*Inky colour with a nose incorporating liqorice, sweet oak and vanilla. Nice firm tannins and great structure .*	**£20.00**	NYW BWL	S
LEASINGHAM CLASSIC CLARE CABERNET SAUVIGNON 1996, BRL HARDY South Australia	*An array of black fruits and eucalypt, with a remarkable persistance of flavour make this wine an absolute classic.*	**£20.00**	VLW WCR TOS HBR	G

AUSTRALIA • CABERNET SAUVIGNON

Wine	Description	Price	Stockists	Award
HENSCHKE CYRIL HENSCHKE CABERNET SAUVIGNON 1995, HENSCHKE South Australia	*Delicate, restrained fruit, with wonderful structure and length. Elegant, intriguing and immensely enjoyable.*	**£25.50**	L&W	S
THOMAS HARDY CABERNET SAUVIGNON 1994, BRL HARDY South Australia	*Upfront, sweet oak backed up neatly by ripe fruit and a good, firm structure.*	**£28.00**	VLW HBR	B
WYNNS JOHN RIDDOCH CABERNET SAUVIGNON 1996, WYNNS COONAWARRA ESTATE South Australia	*Young with dense fruit and a touch of eucalypt, this wine is still a little closed.*	**£35.00**	NYW VWE MWW SEL PEF	B

AUSTRALIA • CHARDONNAAY

Wine	Description	Price	Stockists	Award
BANROCK STATION CHARDONNAY 1998, BRL HARDY South Australia	*Fresh lime and lemon zest aromas rise from a balanced palate where fruit shines in abundance.*	**£4.00**	VLW SMF ASD MRM JSM HBR	G WINE OF THE YEAR
LINDEMANS CAWARRA UNOAKED CHARDONNAY 1998, LINDEMANS South Eastern Australia	*Attractive gooseberry fruit and subtle oak on a sweet palate exuding a plethora of fruit.*	**£4.60**	Widely Available	S
BANROCK STATION UNOAKED CHARDONNAY 1998, BRL HARDY South Australia	*Soft and delicate but warm nose of lemon meringue pie. Nicely textured palate with good length.*	**£5.00**	VLW HBR	B
HARDYS NOTTAGE HILL CHARDONNAY 1998, BRL HARDY South Australia	*Clean lemon aromas seep from a pleasant, crisp and well balanced palate.*	**£5.00**	Widely Available	B

Wine	Tasting note	Price	Stockists	Award
MIRANDA ESTATE CHARDONNAY 1998, MIRANDA WINES South Eastern Australia	*Bright with a full nose and a nice dose of peach and apples.*	**£5.00**	WCR HOH HSL LUC AVB	B
OXFORD LANDING CHARDONNAY 1998, YALUMBA WINERY South Australia	*Rich creamy aromas of vanilla pod and tropical fruits greet the nose before a cleansing finish.*	**£5.00**	Widely Available	B
SOMERFIELD AUSTRALIAN CHARDONNAY 1998, PENFOLDS South Australia	*Delightful peach fruit and lemons sing from a tight bed of crisply folded acid.*	**£5.00**	SMF	B
CO-OP AUSTRALIAN CHARDONNAY 1999, SOUTHCORP South Australia	*Attractive toasty, nutty oak on the nose, lovely texture with boneyed fruit slightly hot finish.*	**£5.70**	WCR PEF CRS	B
THE 1896 WINE CO. ECHO POINT CHARDONNAY 1998, THE 1896 WINE CO. South Australia	*Peachy hints of vegetal characters, abundant fruit on the palate, complex oak and a long finish.*	**£5.70**	TRO FTH	S
LINDEMANS LIMESTONE COAST CHARDONNAY 1998, LINDEMANS South Australia	*Medium weight palate with a touch of citrus and stewed asparagus with a clean finish.*	**£6.00**	JSM PEF	B
MCGUIGAN MALO CHARDONNAY UNWOODED 1998, MCGUIGAN WINES South Eastern Australia	*Butterscotch with attractive lime and peach characters coming through on the palate.*	**£6.00**	VNO WAC VNP	B
SAINSBURY CLASSIC SELECTION SOUTH AUSTRALIAN CHARDONNAY 1998, BRL HARDY South Australia	*Delightful citrus fruit on the nose, fresh balanced fruit with integrated oak, good finish.*	**£6.00**	HBR JSM	B

AUSTRALIA • CHARDONNAY

Wine	Tasting note	Price	Stockists	Award
Tesco McLaren Vale Chardonnay 1998, Maglieri South Australia	*Ripe fructose nose with a tangy fruit mouthfeel leads to a clean, mellow finish.*	**£6.00**	TOS	B
d'Arenberg The Olive Grove Chardonnay 1998, F E Osborne & Sons South Australia	*Buttery fruit and lime on the nose. Mandarin and lime flavours on the oily palate.*	**£6.50**	BWL ODF	S
Fox River Chardonnay 1998, Goundrey Wines Western Australia	*Creamy, buttery nose with full savory almost cheesy palate good fresh acidity and excellent finish.*	**£6.50**	ORB	B
Deen de Bortoli Vat 7 Chardonnay 1998, de Bortoli South Eastern Australia	*Hints of lemon and lime on the nose, ripe fruit with fresh citrus finish on palate.*	**£6.60**	GGW CTH QWW BOR	S
Yaldara Reserve Chardonnay 1997, Yaldara South Australia	*A wine of great length with lots of smoky vanilla oak and pleasant apricot fruits.*	**£6.70**	GRT SWS TPE ADW WON	B
Plantagenet Omrah Unoaked Chardonnay 1998, Plantagenet Western Australia	*Rose petal and lemon characters on a picquant palate with an exotic fruit tail.*	**£6.90**	NYW GGW LIB	B
Chapel Hill Unwooded Chardonnay 1998, Chapel Hill South Australia	*Tropical and floral notes abound in a pineapple haze before pear drop and melon flavours.*	**£7.00**	AUC TOS	B
Chateau Tahbilk Chardonnay 1995, Chateau Tahbilk Victoria	*Tropical fruit characters on the nose with full bodied fruit, good acidity and a rich, sweet fruit finish.*	**£7.00**	ODD PLE	B

Wine	Description	Price	Stockists	Award
KINGSTON ESTATE CHARDONNAY 1998, KINGSTON ESTATE South Australia	*Bright and polished, excuding fresh fruit and cream, rich mouthfeel of toasty oak, long silky finish.*	**£7.00**	VNO QWW VNP	B
KINGSTON WILDLIFE PRINT CHARDONNAY 1998, KINGSTON ESTATE South Eastern Australia	*Fragrant fruit with toasty oak on the nose, tangy citrus and peach characters on the palate.*	**£7.00**	VNO VNP	S
WAKEFIELD CHARDONNAY 1997, WAKEFIELD WINES South Australia	*Attractive floral nose with subtle fruit and a fine textured palate and long finish.*	**£7.00**	SWS UNS QWW BAL RAE RIC	S
WAKEFIELD UNWOODED CHARDONNAY 1998, WAKEFIELD WINES South Australia	*A toasty and nutty nose with sweet pastilles tones on the palate tapering to a crisp, clean finish.*	**£7.00**	SWS ABT BAL RAE MHA	B
ROSEMOUNT ESTATE DIAMOND VARIETAL CHARDONNAY 1998, ROSEMOUNT ESTATE South Australia	*Lemon and melon on the nose, creamy citrus fruit on palate with crisp, clean finish.*	**£7.20**	Widely Available	B
SALTRAM ESTATE MAMRE BROOK BAROSSA CHARDONNAY 1998, SALTRAM ESTATE South Australia	*Pale yellow with green hue, peach aromatic fruit and oak aromas, light creamy fruit on the palate.*	**£7.20**	SAF ODD MWW UNS CAC BPW	S
WARBURN ESTATE CHARDONNAY OAK-AGED 1998, COOPER COUNTY WINES New South Wales	*Attractive style with tropical characters, moderate acidity and good length peaking with a tangy tail.*	**£7.20**	BDR	B

Pinpoint who sells the wine you wish to buy by turning to the stockist codes. If you know the name of the wine you want to buy, use the alphabetical index. If the price is your motivation, refer to the invaluable price guide index; red and white wines under £5, sparkling wines under £12 and Champagne under £16. Happy hunting!

AUSTRALIA • CHARDONNAY

Wine	Tasting note	Price	Stockists	Award
Miranda High Country Chardonnay 1997, Miranda Wines Victoria	*Mandarin, honeydew melon and custard aromas shine, well supported by structural acidity and subtle oak, nicely done.*	£7.30	QWW HOH AVB	S
Goona Warra Black Cygnet Chardonnay 1997, Goona Warra Victoria	*Nice oak on the nose with tropical citrus fruit characters well-balanced with a good finish.*	£7.50	BBR	B
Leasingham Domain Chardonnay 1996, BRL Hardy South Australia	*A big citrus and peach nose heralds a finely balanced herb and stone fruit palate.*	£7.50	VLW WCR WTS	S
Serentos Soft Press Chardonnay 1998, Kingston Estate South Eastern Australia	*Perfumed passionfruit and marzipan, melts in the mouth with subtle oak and persistance.*	£7.50	VNO QWW VNP	B
Tatachilla McLaren Vale Chardonnay 1998, Tatachilla Winery South Australia	*Tropical fruit aromas with fine grain oak, high acidity and creamy malic characters, long finish.*	£7.50	D&D QWW NIC	S
Wynns Chardonnay 1997, Wynns Coonawarra Estate South Australia	*Rich peach and tropical fruit salad to start, lovely toasty oak complements the palate.*	£7.50	WCR NYW VWE ODD MWW BTH	B
Coldstream Hills Chardonnay 1997, Coldstream Hills Victoria	*Honeyed slightly nutty nose with subtle oak and full-bodied tropical fruit flavours with lovely elegant finish.*	£8.00	WCR PEF	B
Haselgrove McLaren Vale Chardonnay 1998, Haselgrove South Australia	*A honeyed lemon, oak tinged nose precedes an elegantly textured palate. Great finish.*	£8.00	VLW LIB	B

Wine	Description	Price	Stockists	Award
McGuigan Shareholders Chardonnay 1998, McGuigan Wines South Eastern Australia	*Nutty and toasty aromas with ripe simple fruit, straightforward wine with good length and finish.*	£8.00	VNO WAC VNP	B
Petaluma Bridgewater Mill Chardonnay 1997, Petaluma South Australia	*A rounded and soft wine full of ripe fruit, dry with nicely integrated oak.*	£8.00	JSM ROD MZC	S
Rosemount Estate Honey Tree Reserve Chardonnay 1998, Rosemount Estate South Australia	*Lemon butter and toasty oak on nose and palate, good clean finish with persistent length.*	£8.00	M&S ROS	B
Rothbury Estate Brokenback Chardonnay 1997, Mildara Blass New South Wales	*Rich nose of buttery oak, sweet melons and pears. layers of fruit and oak, zesty finish.*	£8.00	VLW WCR SEA	S
Yalumba Growers Chardonnay 1998, Yalumba Winery South Australia	*Tropical characters and a subtle oak influence are the hallmarks of this very complex and well composed wine.*	£8.20	JNW NEG YAL	S
Hardys Padthaway Chardonnay 1997, BRL Hardy South Australia	*Buttered croissants and tropical fruit characters combined with integrated toasty vanilla oak and moderate acidity.*	£8.30	VLW WCR SMF NIC HBR	B
Hill-Smith Estate Chardonnay 1998, Yalumba Winery South Australia	*Limey, citrus notes to the fore with creamy tropical fruit flavours on the palate.*	£8.30	BDR ODD NEG YAL	B
Evans & Tate Two Vineyards Chardonnay 1997, Evans & Tate Western Australia	*Lovely apples, pears and white peaches, flowing to abundant zesty citrus on the palate.*	£8.50	GRA FRT	S

AUSTRALIA • CHARDONNAY

Wine	Description	Price	Stockists	Award
Lindemans Padthaway Chardonnay 1997, Lindemans South Australia	*Delicate citrus and spicy fruit, elegant palate with lemon and lime and subtle oak balance.*	**£8.50**	Widely Available	S
Ninth Island Chardonnay 1998, Pipers Brook Tasmania	*Asparagus and vegetal notes on a clean palate of impressive length. Well balanced and complex.*	**£8.70**	GSH VLW NYW TOS CAC BPW	B
Wolf Blass President's Selection Chardonnay 1998, Mildara Blass South Australia	*Nutty approach developing into rich buttery melons and tropical fruit. Full bodied with a grippy finish.*	**£8.90**	UNS VLW ABY SEA ODD WCR	S
Bethany Chardonnay 1997, Bethany Wines South Australia	*Melon and vanilla oak characters on the nose with a rich ripe tropical fruit palate.*	**£9.00**	D&D	B
Chapel Hill Reserve Chardonnay 1996, Chapel Hill South Australia	*Creamy toasty nose with hints of chestnut, rich tropical fruit with complexity and length.*	**£9.00**	AUC TOS	B
Chittering Estate Chardonnay 1997, Chittering Estate Western Australia	*Gentle creamy nose with seductive tropical fruit characters interlaced with well measured oak and a fresh acid finish.*	**£9.00**	PAT	S
Highland Heritage Estate Chardonnay 1996, Rex d'Aquino New South Wales	*Soft white peaches on the nose lead to a crisp dry palate with buttery oak and cleansing acidity.*	**£9.00**	CHN	B

Pinpoint who sells the wine you wish to buy by turning to the stockist codes. If you know the name of the wine you want to buy, use the alphabetical index. If the price is your motivation, refer to the invaluable price guide index; red and white wines under £5, sparkling wines under £12 and Champagne under £16. Happy hunting!

Wine	Description	Price	Stockists	Award
Marienberg Reserve Chardonnay 1998, Marienberg South Australia	*Peaches with creamy new oak aromas, ripe fruit on the palate with an apple lift.*	**£9.00**	HFI	S
Michelton Chardonnay 1996, Mitchelton Victoria	*Lime, tropical fruit and toasty oak aromas, rich ripe fruit on palate resulting in elongated finish.*	**£9.00**	MAR VWE JEF	S
Shaw & Smith Unoaked Chardonnay 1998, Shaw & Smith South Australia	*A flowery nose with kind citrus aromas and a pleasant fruit palate.*	**£9.00**	VLW NYW JNW GGW LIB	B
Yarra Valley Hills Chardonnay 1998, Yarra Valley Hills Victoria	*Peach and melon with vanilla oak aromas rich fruit on palate with a slightly oily texture.*	**£9.00**	ODD	B
Jim Barry Clare Valley Chardonnay 1997, Jim Barry Wines South Australia	*Clean aromas of apricot and mango jam with rich tropical fruit flavours and a fresh finish.*	**£9.20**	QWW BWC TAN ODF CHC HER DIR NEG	B
Chateau Reynella Chardonnay 1997, BRL Hardy South Australia	*A fruit basket style with herb and bay notes and leads to a bone dry finish.*	**£9.30**	VLW WCR HBR	S
Nepenthe Unwooded Chardonnay 1997, Nepenthe Vineyards South Australia	*Hefty pineapple and honey nose introduces a complex palate of minerals with an underlying leesy character.*	**£9.70**	GRT SWS ODD	S
Nepenthe Unwooded Chardonnay 1998, Nepenthe Vineyards South Australia	*The perfect after work tipple, passionfruit and melon lead to a complex palate and crunchy finish. Home James!*	**£9.70**	SWS GRT ODD	B

AUSTRALIA • CHARDONNAY

EBENEZER CHARDONNAY 1997, BRL HARDY South Australia	*Tropical fruit aromas, full bodied, creamy peaches and banana palate, elegantly balanced with excellent length.*	**£10.00**	VLW HBR	G
MAXWELL CHARDONNAY 1997, MARK MAXWELL South Australia	*Full buttery oak aromas with a hefty dose of sweet fruit and vanilla oak on the palate.*	**£10.00**	SWS	B
WIRRA WIRRA CHARDONNAY 1997, WIRRA WIRRA South Australia	*Butterscotch and full fruit characters on the nose, excellent structure and a clean crisp finish.*	**£10.00**	WTS WST	G
ROSEMOUNT ESTATE SHOW RESERVE CHARDONNAY 1997, ROSEMOUNT ESTATE New South Wales	*Great fruit concentration from a still young, tight wine with great ageing potential.*	**£10.40**	Widely Available	B
STONIER CHARDONNAY 1998, STONIER Victoria	*Smoky oak and hints of tobacco aromas with lime, citrus and succulent apricot fruit characters.*	**£10.40**	MZC	B
CHAIS CLARENDON PADTHAWAY CHARDONNAY 1996, NORMANS South Australia	*Citrus and honey with toasted oak characters and a thick, fruit palate.*	**£10.50**	ODF PLB	B
BEST'S GREAT WESTERN CHARDONNAY 1997, BEST'S Victoria	*Nice fig and rockmelon combine with tasty oak on the nose, finishing crisply and cleanly.*	**£10.60**	SWS CTH GRT JNW CAC	S
LENSWOOD VINEYARDS CHARDONNAY 1996, KNAPPSTEIN LENSWOOD South Australia	*Lime and subtle oak aromas, soft round creamy palate, honey and high acidity,balanced finish.*	**£11.10**	BWC	S

CHARDONNAY • AUSTRALIA				
KATNOOK CHARDONNAY 1997, WINGARA South Australia	*Well measured toasted oak with a touch of oiliness on the palate and a clean acid finish.*	**£11.20**	VLW BWL BTH	(S)
VOYAGER ESTATE CHARDONNAY 1996, VOYAGER ESTATE Western Australia	*Rich, toasty oak dominates the nose and palate of this creamy smooth wine that offers ripe melon flavours.*	**£11.30**	NYW J&B	(B)
NEPENTHE CHARDONNAY 1997, NEPENTHE VINEYARDS South Australia	*Full frontal cashews and white peach attack, reinforced by delicious oak, funky fruit acid persistance.*	**£11.50**	SWS ODD GRT	(B)
DE BORTOLI YARRA VALLEY CHARDONNAY 1997, DE BORTOLI Victoria	*Complex, cashew aromas a hint of greenness. Forward fruit on palate with integrated vanillan oak.*	**£11.90**	QWW HHF GGW BOR	(B)
DROMANA ESTATE CHARDONNAY 1998, DROMANA ESTATE Mornington Peninsula	*Soft new oak and citrus fruit aromas with supple juicy fruit and soft creamy palate.*	**£11.90**	CAC CCW	(B)
PENFOLDS ADELAIDE HILLS CHARDONNAY 1997, PENFOLDS South Australia	*Slightly spicey fruit on the nose, buttery oak and balanced tropical fruit palate. A wine that requires patience.*	**£12.00**	ODD SEL ADS PEF	(S)
TATACHILLA ADELAIDE HILLS CHARDONNAY 1998, TATACHILLA WINERY South Australia	*Soft tropical fruit flavours with vanilla and bacon characters from new oak on the nose.*	**£12.00**	D&D	(S)
BLUE PYRENEES ESTATE CHARDONNAY 1997, BLUE PYRENEES ESTATE Victoria	*Inviting nose of white peaches and creamy oak. Soothing palate of lively acid and dovetailed soft wood.*	**£12.50**	TOS	(S)

AUSTRALIA • CHARDONNAY

Wine	Description	Price	Stockists	Award
Shaw & Smith Reserve Chardonnay 1997, Shaw & Smith South Australia	*Subtle yet powerful aromas with citrus and tropical fruit dry smooth palate with well integrated oak.*	**£12.60**	VLW NYW JNW GGW LIB	B
Brookland Valley Chardonnay 1997, Brookland Valley Vineyard Western Australia	*Clean apple and vanilla oak aromas, citrus fruit characters with very lively acidity and integrated oak balance.*	**£13.00**	BBR FWM	S
d'Arenberg The Other Side Chardonnay 1997, F E Osborne & Sons South Australia	*Lovely attractive buttery and fig aromas with creamy full body and good acidic clean finish.*	**£13.00**	BWL ODF	B
Mountadam Chardonnay 1997, Mountadam South Australia	*Rich fruit and walnut aromas soft round peaches and a nutty palate, finish is slightly coarse.*	**£13.10**	NYW WRC BUP MAR VWE THS JNW	B
Eileen Hardy Chardonnay 1996, BRL Hardy South Australia	*Rich buttery oak aromas and sweet ripe peachy fruit on a tight palate that has years to go.*	**£14.00**	VLW WCR HBR	B
Kingston Estate Reserve Chardonnay 1997, Kingston Estate South Eastern Australia	*Lime spice and toasty oak on nose with body and weight from fruit giving balance.*	**£14.00**	VNO QWW VNP	S
Howard Park Chardonnay 1997, Howard Park Western Australia	*Limes, fig and banana mingle with vanilla oak characters on the nose. Buttery, citrus palate.*	**£14.40**	NYW JNW ABA	S
Dalwhinnie Estate Chardonnay 1997, Dalwhinnie Estate Victoria	*Appealing flavours of melon and passionfruit with nuances of creamy vanilla and spice.*	**£14.70**	VLW NYW J&B	B

Wine	Description	Price	Stockists	Award
Petaluma Chardonnay 1997, Petaluma South Australia	*A lime and pear pool tinctured with elegant oak finishes with grace and elegance.*	**£14.90**	RBS QWW NYW ODD PAT MZC	S
Coldstream Hills Reserve Chardonnay 1997, Coldstream Hills Victoria	*Cashews and honeydew rising from the elegant nose, lovely structural acidity and fine grained oak.*	**£15.00**	NYW ODD FUL PEF	B
Hillstowe Udy's Mill Lenswood Chardonnay 1997, Hillstowe Wines South Australia	*Ripe soft fruit with buttery oak aromas, soft full round palate with slightly bitter finish.*	**£15.00**	MKV	B
Lindemans Winemaker's Reserve Padthaway Chardonnay 1997, Lindemans South Australia	*Tropical fruit and vanilla on the nose, the palate has ripe fruit and integrated oak.*	**£15.00**	WTS PEF	S
Vasse Felix Heytesbury Chardonnay 1998, Vasse Felix Winery Western Australia	*Rich ripe tropical fruit with vanilla oak, with moderate acidity perfectly balanced with sweet fruits and nutty characters.*	**£16.30**	RBS NYW BWC CPW EPO VDV PAG NEG	S
Stonier Reserve Chardonnay 1997, Stonier Victoria	*Buttery oak on the nose with loads of tropical fruit, straightforward structure and a tidy finish.*	**£17.00**	MZC	B
Tyrrell's Vat 47 Pinot Chardonnay 1997, Tyrrell's New South Wales	*Aromatic gooseberries and a hint of spice. This wine is subtle with a clean finish. Will improve with age.*	**£17.60**	UNS NYW BDR HVN FUL CPW TAN PRG	B

Pinpoint who sells the wine you wish to buy by turning to the stockist codes. If you know the name of the wine you want to buy, use the alphabetical index. If the price is your motivation, refer to the invaluable price guide index; red and white wines under £5, sparkling wines under £12 and Champagne under £16. Happy hunting!

AUSTRALIA • CHARDONNAY

Rosemount Estate Rose Label Orange Vineyard Chardonnay 1997, Rosemount Estate New South Wales	*Lots of grapefruit, fig and sweet oak on palate, which lead to a long, lasting finish.*	**£18.00**	BWC ROS	S
Tarrawarra Chardonnay 1997, Tarrawarra Vineyards Victoria	*A perfumed and ever so slightly confected nose with generous fruit and a gentle acid wash.*	**£18.40**	NYW HVN PHI LAW	G
Pipers Brook Summit Chardonnay 1997, Pipers Brook Tasmania	*Elegant and tight, this peachy number is just starting to blossom, lovely zesty finish, give it time.*	**£21.00**	VLW BPW	B
Rosemount Estate Roxburgh Chardonnay 1996, Rosemount Estate New South Wales	*Toasted biscuit, bacon and citrus characters on the nose. Complex palate of lemon fruit and oak.*	**£28.80**	UNS BWC ROS	G

AUSTRALIA • FORTIFIED

Wine	Description	Price	Stockists	Award
Mick Morris Liqueur Muscat NV, Morris Wines Victoria	*The palate is delicate with good length of honeyed oranges, marmalade, caramel and malt aromas.*	£5.00	MWW TOS JSM SEL CAX	S
Penfolds Magill Tawny NV, Penfolds South Australia	*Sweet caramelised aromas flow from theglass, a beautifully rich and slightly woody palate with good acidity .*	£5.60	Widely Available	G
Carlyle Muscat NV, Pfeiffer Wines Victoria	*Hot butterscotch, praline, caramalised fruit and a hint of salt. Big ripe fruit palate with structure and complexity.*	£6.80	REN	S
Seppelt Rutherglen Show Muscat DP 63 NV, Seppelt Victoria	*This wine cries excess. Complex, malty, maple syrup flavour and full ripe fruit with incredible length.*	£7.70	GRA NYW ODD GRA	S
Stanton & Killeen Rutherglen Muscat NV, Stanton & Killeen Victoria	*Older style muscat with some rancio characters on the nose and rich full raisin fruit palate.*	£8.20	WAW WAC HHF ASD FUL WSO WSG	B
Yalumba Museum Release Reserve Muscat NV, Yalumba Winery Victoria	*A deep dark concentrated fortified, with leather butter and treacle characters with a clean finish.*	£8.30	JNW ODD WRC THS BUP NEG YAL	S
d'Arenberg Nostalgia NV, F E Osborne & Sons South Australia	*Wonderful raisins and mocha, rancio on the palate cut by lively acidity, wrapped in sensual viscosity.*	£10.50	BWL ODF	S

AUSTRALIA • FORTIFIED

Brown Brothers Liqueur Muscat NV, Brown Brothers Victoria	*This sweet wine of wonderful rancio characters travel along the palate to finish with wonderfully balanced acidity.*	**£12.90**	WAC GRT NYW BRB	(G)
de Bortoli Black Noble NV, de Bortoli New South Wales	*Complex nose of toffee, orange peel and bitter treacle, nicely layered palate finishing with cleansing acidity.*	**£13.50**	QWW GGW CAC bor	(B)
Campbells Merchant Prince Rare Rutherglen Muscat NV, Campbells of Rutherglen Victoria	*Incredible concentration blesses the palate splaying caramalised prunes, lots of rancio and molases onto the tongue.*	**£30.00**	WSG WSG	(G)

AUSTRALIA • RED • OTHER

Badgers Creek Australian Shiraz Cabernet 1998, Buronga Hill Winery South Australia	*Vibrant plums and cassis are surrounded by a dusty tannin frame balanced with a vanillin oak climax.*	**£3.00**	ALD GCF	(B)
Asda Karalta Oak Aged Dry Red 1998, BRL Hardy South Australia	*A balanced soft easy drinking style with sweet cherry fruit and rich syrupy texture.*	**£3.30**	ASD	(B)
Angove's Nanya Vineyard Malbec Ruby Cabernet 1997, Angove's South Australia	*Attractive and approachable with tea leaf and sweet fruit characters. Ask it to dance.*	**£4.00**	WRC BUP MAR THS WTS	(B)
Banrock Station Mataro Grenache Shiraz 1998, Banrock Station South Australia	*Opulent warm fruit on a full palate of spicy plum notes lead to a clean finish.*	**£4.10**	Widely Available	(B)

Wine	Tasting note	Price	Stockists	Award
SAFEWAY AUSTRALIAN SHIRAZ CABERNET 1998, SOUTHCORP South Australia	*Minty ripe cherries on a soft fragrant nose while ripe fresh tannins lead to a lengthy finish.*	**£4.20**	SAF	B
TESCO AUSTRALIAN RED WINE NV, SOUTHCORP South Australia	*A nose with herbal notes leads to good fruit and warm spicy oak, creamy with a long finish.*	**£4.50**	BWL TOS	B
HARDYS STAMP OF AUSTRALIA SHIRAZ CABERNET 1998, BRL HARDY South Australia	*Nice black fruit notes on the nose of this silky textured wine that offers a clean fruit finish.*	**£4.90**	Widely Available	S
DEAKIN ESTATE MERLOT 1998, WINGARA South Eastern Australia	*Warm fruit nose with leather and spice. Bramble palate, quite rich with medium tannins.*	**£5.00**	NYW GGW BWL WR BUP	B
SAINSBURY AUSTRALIAN CABERNET SAUVIGNON NV, BRL HARDY South Eastern Australia	*Attractive fruit driven style with an underlying minerally current immersed in a sea of fine grained tannins.*	**£5.00**	JSM	S
SEPPELT MOYSTON CABERNET SHIRAZ 1998, SEPPELT South Eastern Australia	*Very easy to drink style showing attractive ripe fruit aromas and caramalized characters with fine balance.*	**£5.00**	UNS GSH GRA	G
SACRED HILL SHIRAZ CABERNET 1998, DE BORTOLI South Eastern Australia	*Nice soft fruit very approachable now with good tannins and a spicey finish.*	**£5.10**	CTH QWW WIN GGW BWC	B
MCLAREN'S ON THE LAKE GRENACHE SHIRAZ 1998, ANDREW GARRETT VINEYARDS South Eastern Australia	*Tight nose with good primary fruit leads to nice structure and length, ripe fruit underneath.*	**£5.30**	UNS T&T	B

AUSTRALIA • RED • OTHER

CONUNDRUM VINEYARDS SHIRAZ MALBEC 1998, CONUNDRUM VINEYARDS South Eastern Australia	*Toasty, tarry aroma, juicy fruit, pepper, licorice notes and a balanced, long grippy finish.*	**£5.50**	SAF	(S)
D'ARENBERG RED OCHRE 1997, F E OSBORNE & SONS South Australia	*Spicey fruits with a hint of vanillin oak and good weight and balance.*	**£5.50**	BWL ODF	(B)
HARDYS NOTTAGE HILL CABERNET SHIRAZ 1998, BRL HARDY South Australia	*Good wood meets ginger spice and summer fruits in this well made satisfier that drinks well now.*	**£5.50**	Widely Available	(S)
RAWSON'S RETREAT BIN 35 SHIRAZ CABERNET SAUVIGNON 1998, PENFOLDS South Australia	*Clean light and fruity on the nose this is a delicate well balanced wine with a clean fruit finish.*	**£5.50**	Widely Available	(B)
SANDFORD ESTATE CABERNET SAUVIGNON 1998, WINGARA Victoria	*Berry fruit nose. Crisp flavours with hints of juicy cassis. Lingering finish, pleasant soft, ripe tannins.*	**£5.60**	CAC CCW	(S)
SOMERFIELD AUSTRALIAN SHIRAZ CABERNET 1998, PENFOLDS South Eastern Australia	*A heady nose of chocolate and plum precedes a sweet fruit palate showing laid back wood.*	**£5.90**	SMF	(B)
TESCO MCLAREN VALE GRENACHE 1998, MAGLIERI South Australia	*Ripe berry fruit with earthy complexity, rich with deft handling of oak and a long clean finish.*	**£6.00**	TOS	(S)
YALUMBA ANTIPODEAN RED 1997, YALUMBA WINERY South Australia	*Funky fruit tart notes lay back on a silky bed of soft tannins before peaking with a sexy acid tail.*	**£6.00**	ODD JNW NEG YAL	(S)

Wine	Description	Price	Stockists	Award
McGuigan Bin 3000 Merlot 1998, McGuigan Wines South Eastern Australia	*Spicy mint and eucalyptus aromas. Rich, smooth tannins with blackberry fruit palate. Attractive texture with some vanilla.*	£6.10	VNO CTH WAC QWW VNP	B
Haselgrove Sovereign Grenache 1997, Haselgrove South Australia	*Sweet strawberry nose with warm fruit and spice. Good balance with firm tannins on finish.*	£6.40	RBS VLW NYW LIB	B
Bleasdale Malbec 1998, Bleasdale South Australia	*Dense nose of spice, ginger, leather and currants. Lively palate with more rich fruit and wonderful structure.*	£6.50	TOS PLB	S
Cape Mentelle Ironstone Shiraz Grenache 1997, Cape Mentelle Western Australia	*A pleasant fruit nose, leads to dpicey fruit, integrated tannins and a good finish.*	£6.50	JNW PLA UNS TOS MWW FUL PRG	B
Essington Cabernet Shiraz 1998, Essington New South Wales	*Fruity cedar aroma rising from a tight palate of rich tannins and nicely integrated oak.*	£6.50	GRA FRT	B
Evans & Tate Gnangara Shiraz Grenache 1997, Evans & Tate Western Australia	*Cassis and black cherries flow on to a fruit laden palate with a neat oak measure and fine tannin structure.*	£6.50	GRA	S
Samuel's Bay Grenache 1997, Mountadam South Australia	*Loads of peppery, spicey berry fruit, crisp acidity and nice full mouthfeel with a good grippy finish.*	£6.50	BUP MAR VWE THS HAS WRC	S
Samuel's Bay Padthaway Malbec 1995, Mountadam South Australia	*A silky and elegant wine with just a hint of a green edge. Nice fruit in the mouth.*	£6.50	BUP MAR THS HAS WRC	B

AUSTRALIA • RED • OTHER

Wine	Tasting note	Price	Stockists	Award
SEPPELT HARPERS RANGE CABERNET MERLOT 1995, SEPPELT Victoria	*Showing some age this heady blackcurrent scented wine shows good wood and length.*	**£6.50**	PEF GRA	B
WOOLSHED CABERNET SHIRAZ MERLOT 1997, WINGARA South Australia	*Lots of blackcurrant fruit with herbaceous tones cascade on to a palate of lush tannins and structure.*	**£6.50**	BWL SAF FUL	S
PENFOLDS BIN 2 SHIRAZ MOURVÈDRE 1997, PENFOLDS South Australia	*Lovely black fruits well integrated with judicial use of oak on a firm fruit palate of fine tannins.*	**£6.60**	Widely Available	S
TATACHILLA WATTLE PARK SHIRAZ CABERNET SAUVIGNON 1998, TATACHILLA WINERY South Australia	*An inviting wine of rich ripe berry fruit with cracked black pepper, lovely supple finish.*	**£6.80**	QWW NIC CAM D&D	B
BETHANY PRESSINGS GRENACHE 1998, BETHANY WINES South Australia	*Soft slightly confected fruit provides an inviting nose and well balanced a palate and grippy tannins.*	**£6.90**	UNS WCR D&D	S
ROSEMOUNT ESTATE DIAMOND BLEND SHIRAZ CABERNET 1998, ROSEMOUNT ESTATE South Australia	*Intense licorice and eucalyptus aromas flow onto a palate with excellent concentration and very appealing tannins.*	**£6.90**	Widely Available	S
BUCKLEY'S CLARE VALLEY CABERNET FRANC 1997, BUCKLEY'S South Australia	*A nicely balanced wine showing sporty spice, menthol and confected fruit flavours.*	**£7.00**	AUC TOS	B
BUCKLEY'S CLARE VALLEY MALBEC 1997, BUCKLEY'S South Australia	*Nice oaked character with a hint of green beans and a pleasant dry mouthfeel.*	**£7.00**	AUC TOS	B

Wine	Description	Price	Stockists	Award
ST HALLETT CABERNET MERLOT 1997, ST HALLETT South Australia	*Cherry oak hides stewed fruits with an initial burst of blackberry on the palate. Good length and balance.*	£7.00	AUC TOS	S
TALTARNI MERLOT CABERNET 1997, TALTARNI Victoria	*Mint and pepper with an ever so sublime touch of eucalypt follow onto a palate well ensconched in firm tannins.*	£7.00	SAF AVB WWS HOH	S
TATACHILLA PARTNERS CABERNET SAUVIGNON SHIRAZ 1998, TATACHILLA WINERY South Australia	*Fresh fruity aromas and well integrated oak on the palate releases good flavour and swells to a fine finish.*	£7.00	BDR	S
TYRRELL'S OLD WINERY CABERNET MERLOT 1997, TYRRELL'S New South Wales	*Sweet and plummy showing a hint of menthol lollies, soft acidity and confected tannins.*	£7.00	JSM UNS PLA LAK HSL PRG	B
WAKEFIELD SHIRAZ CABERNET 1998, WAKEFIELD WINES South Australia	*Mocha and mint lead to a smooth tannin palate with pepper notes and a generous smoky bushfire finish.*	£7.00	SWS BAL	S
YALDARA RESERVE GRENACHE 1998, YALDARA South Australia	*Lovely, round, ripe intense violet and blackcurrant notes, good crisp acid and integrated oak, nice length.*	£7.00	SWS WRT GRT TPE	B
IRONSTONE ZINFANDEL 1996, CAPE MENTELLE Western Australia	*Warm blueberry and plum aromas with smoky oak wit balanced acidity, and a firm finish.*	£7.10	Widely Available	B
BROWN BROTHERS BARBERA 1996, BROWN BROTHERS Victoria	*Concentrated fruits and zesty, fresh cherry flavours in this well-integrated wine that finishes with a clean, fruit acid blast.*	£7.20	GRT NYW BRB	S

AUSTRALIA • RED • OTHER

Wine	Description	Price	Stockists	Award
D'Arry's Original Shiraz Grenache 1997, F E Osborne & Sons South Australia	*Very fragrant with rich berries and smoky tarry complexity, lovely balance, character and an infinite finish.*	£7.30	BWL ODF	G
Mamre Brook Barossa Shiraz Cabernet 1996, Saltram Estate South Australia	*Luscious, dark colour and attractive nose give way to excellent fruit with redcurrants and blackberries to the fore.*	£7.30	TRO ODD JSM MWW BPW	S
Riddoch Cabernet Shiraz 1997, Wingara South Australia	*Big and juicy with a ripe berry nose and cigar box characters. Nice complexity and length.*	£7.30	Widely Available	B
Deen de Bortoli Vat 1 Durif 1997, de Bortoli South Eastern Australia	*Ripe and plummy fruit with a sprinkling of pepper leading to a ong textured finish.*	£7.50	HHF NIC GGW BOR	B
Knappstein Cabernet Sauvignon Merlot 1996, BRL Hardy South Australia	*A sweet fruit nose in this cheeky number offering hints of cedar and herbs. Generous finish.*	£7.50	ODD SAF MZC	B
Rymill Coonawarra Merlot Cabernets 1996, Rymill Coonawarra South Australia	*Luscious entry of seething black currants and crushed tomato leaf, with fine structural acidity and supple fruit tannins.*	£7.50	IRI PLB	B
Warburn Estate Merlot Oak Aged 1998, Cooper County Wines South Eastern Australia	*An attractive fruit nose of pastilles and new oak flows on to a palate with considerable length.*	£7.60	BDR	S
Four Sisters McLaren Vale Grenache Shiraz 1997, Mount Langi Ghiran South Australia	*Classic spicey raspberry nose leads to a juicy sweet fruited palate that builds and builds, nice warm stuff.*	£7.70	NYW JNW LIB	B

Wine	Description	Price	Stockists	Award
STONYFELL METALA SHIRAZ CABERNET 1997, MILDARA BLASS South Australia	*A minty, fruity nose and palate dominated by some funky fig, scary spice and ripe redcurrant. Great length.*	£7.70	GSH NYW SAF ODD TOS BPW	G
KINGSTON ESTATE MERLOT 1998, KINGSTON ESTATE South Eastern Australia	*Loganberry, cassis and mint dance amid layers of ripe fruit and herb characters. One to savour.*	£7.90	VNO QWW VNP	S
BROWN BROTHERS MERLOT 1996, BROWN BROTHERS Victoria	*Dusty blackcurrants with chocolate liqueur shine from a palate of complexity built around fine tannins.*	£8.00	NYW BRB	S
BUCKLEY'S MOURVÈDRE GRENACHE 1997, BUCKLEY'S South Australia	*Delicious, sweet fruit to start, the palate shows nice depth and complexity, finishing well.*	£8.00	AUC TOS	B
COLDSTREAM HILLS BRIARSTON CABERNET MERLOT 1996, COLDSTREAM HILLS Victoria	*Soft ripe minty nose. Meaty palate with soft, juicy fruit and soft tannins. Good acidity. Elegant and long finish.*	£8.00	WCR PEF	S
HASELGROVE MCLAREN VALE GRENACHE 1998, HASELGROVE South Australia	*The palate is abundant with concentrated flavours of smoked black fruits and white pepper spice.*	£8.00	VLW NYW LIB	S
JAMIESONS RUN CABERNET SHIRAZ MERLOT 1996, MILDARA BLASS South Australia	*Strong redcurrant fruit nose. Cigar box oak tones and raspberry sorbet. Youthful, well-structured and long.*	£8.00	ODD SAF WCR SEA	S
JAMIESONS RUN MERLOT 1997, MILDARA BLASS South Australia	*Concentrated blackcurrant nose. Spicey oak.with ripe fruit and a full, well-structured tannin finish.*	£8.00	SEA ODD	S

AUSTRALIA• RED• OTHER

KNAPPSTEIN CABERNET MERLOT 1996, BRL HARDY South Australia	*Rich and dense showing some development with notes of cherry, menthol and herb.*	**£8.00**	GSH SAF	B
OLD PENOLA MERLOT CABERNETS 1996, RYMILL COONAWARRA South Australia	*An inviting nose of black fruits, rhubarb and licorice cascade onto a firm and tasty palate with good wood.*	**£8.00**	TOS PLB	G
PENFOLDS CLARE VALLEY (ORGANIC) CABERNET SHIRAZ 1997, PENFOLDS South Australia	*Great up front fruit with lovely pepper and spice follows on to a well rounded palate.*	**£8.00**	NYW JNW VWE PEF	B
ROSMEOUNT ESTATE DIAMOND PINOT NOIR 1997, ROSEMOUNT ESTATE South Australia	*Elegant, fleshy style with perfume and restrained extraction showing a clean fruit and a tidy tail.*	**£8.00**	ASD ROS	B
WYNNS CABERNET SHIRAZ MERLOT 1996, WYNNS COONAWARRA ESTATE South Australia	*Brilliant purity of fruit with complexing cigar box characters flowing to firm chewy ripe tannins*	**£8.00**	NYW TOS PEF	G
MIRANDA ROVALLEY RIDGE CABERNET SAUVIGNON 1996, MIRANDA WINES South Australia	*A mocha and licorice nose leads to a pleasant tannin palate with blackberry notes and a hint of menthol.*	**£8.20**	QWW AVB HOH	S
PETER LEHMANN CLANCY'S RED 1997, PETER LEHMANN WINES South Australia	*Intense ripe fruit and spicey oak give complexity to a rich palate of pleasing tannins and fruit acid.*	**£8.20**	WCR JSM ODD EPO PLE	S
NINTH ISLAND PINOT NOIR 1998, PIPERS BROOK Tasmania	*A nose of primary berry fruit and loads of barnyard aromas. Flavours of nuts and touches of stewed fruit.*	**£8.40**	GSH VLW NYW TOS SAF BPW	S

Wine	Description	Price	Stockists	Award
D'ARENBERG THE CUSTODIAN GRENACHE 1996, F E OSBORNE & SONS South Australia	*Berries combine with rich spice, leather and tar to offer complexity finishing with a tidy tannin tail.*	£8.50	BWL ODF	S
D'ARENBERG THE TWENTY EIGHT ROAD MOURVÉDRE 1997, F E OSBORNE & SONS South Australia	*Rich and robust initially, leading to an aromatic, spicey, brambly dark fruit ,'built to last'.palate.*	£8.50	BWL ODF	S
HILLSTOWE BUXTON MERLOT CABERNET 1997, HILLSTOWE WINES South Australia	*Ripe plums and fruitcake aromas. Soft tannins and good acidity with lots of ripe, soft fruit.*	£8.50	MKV	S
ROVALLEY RIDGE BUSH VINE GRENACHE 1997, MIRANDA WINES South Australia	*Cloves, plum fruit and mocha complemented by a good measure of toasty oak.*	£8.70	NYW WCR HSL SOH AVB HOH	B
TATACHILLA CABERNET SAUVIGNON MERLOT 1997, TATACHILLA WINERY South Australia	*Blackcurrant bonanza with a ripe chocolate edge and cedar notes follow through to the palate with a chalky finish.*	£8.70	SAF WTS	S
YALUMBA CABERNET SAUVIGNON MERLOT 1996, YALUMBA WINERY South Australia	*Big minty, choc-chip nose. Rich cassis and tobacco palate, with good acidity and chewy tannins.*	£8.70	QWW MWW ODD JNW NEG YAL	S
YALUMBA BUSH VINE GRENACHE 1997, YALUMBA WINERY South Australia	*Cherry chup-a-chups lead to a warm and soft palate with soft tannins and a clean acid finish.*	£8.80	Widely Available	B
PENFOLDS BIN 128 COONAWARRA SHIRAZ 1996, PENFOLDS South Australia	*Brooding, sweet, ripe spicey fruit very long and elegant, finished with tight grained French oak.*	£8.90	Widely Available	G

Wine	Description	Price	Stockists	Award
Bleasdale Frank Potts Reserve 1997, Bleasdale South Australia	*Blackcherry colour with a licorice, nutty and ripe red berry nose complemented with a toasty cedar nudge.*	£9.00	ODF PLB	S
Cornerstone Clare Valley Grenache 1997, Cornerstone South Australia	*A ripe opulent, fruity, oaky wine offers a very pleasant tannin structure and long finish.*	£9.00	AUC TOS	B
Knappstein Cabernet Franc 1996, BRL Hardy South Australia	*Jammy, minty, stalky nose with eucalyptus hints. Good concentration of fruit flavour on the palate.*	£9.00	QWW WCR SAF	B
Madfish Bay Dry Red 1997, Howard Park Western Australia	*Crunchy cherries and bitter chocolate. Sweetness with a soft tannin finish. Drinks well now.*	£9.00	JNW ABA	B
Maglieri Merlot 1997, Maglieri South Australia	*Good colour with licorice, mint and clove on the nose. Good mouthfeel and some length.*	£9.00	PLB	B
Preece Merlot 1997, Mitchelton Victoria	*Ripe fruit here with hints of mint and cedar and a full bodied palate of chalky tannins finishes long.*	£9.00	JEF	S
Rouge Homme Cabernet Merlot 1996, Rouge Homme South Australia	*Ripe cassis fruit and chocolate on the nose with firm ripe fruit tannins, and a pleasant acid tail.*	£9.00	FUL PEF	S
Bethany Cabernet Merlot 1997, Bethany Wines South Australia	*An enticing plum jam nose with blackcurrant notes heralds a soft, blackberry palate with some herbal notes.*	£9.20	D&D	S

Wine	Tasting note	Price	Stockists	Award
Richard Hamilton Lot 148 Merlot 1997, Richard Hamilton South Australia	*Sherbet and fruit cake aromas with plummy notes. Good tannin structure but slightly astringent without fruit backing.*	**£9.20**	ENO	B
St Hallett Grenache 1996, St Hallett South Australia	*Warm red fruit coupled with coconutty oak flow to a spicy finish and good length.*	**£9.20**	AUC WRC BUP MAR THS	B
Devil's Lair Fifth Leg Red 1997, Devil's Lair Western Australia	*Strange but intriguing earthy meaty nose with a dollop of euclaypt finishes quite dry.*	**£9.50**	GRT NYW JNW ABA	S
Rymill Coonawarra Cabernet Sauvignon 1996, Rymill Coonawarra South Australia	*Superb blackcurrent and vanillin definition on the nose cascade onto a fruit laden palate peppered with spice and a touch of herb.*	**£9.50**	MMW PLB	S
Tim Adams The Fergus 1997, Tim Adams South Australia	*Stylish black fruits and After Eights storm into a rich concentrated palate with lots of fruit grip.*	**£9.50**	AUC WRC BUP MAR THS	B
Tim Adams The Fergus 1998, Tim Adams South Australia	*Charred, spicey Grenache nose with a warm glow of alcohol. A soft slightly fruit driven style.*	**£9.50**	AUC WRC BUP MAR THS	B
Mount Langi Ghiran Billi Billi Creek Shiraz Grenache 1997, Mount Langi Ghiran Victoria	*An inviting nose this wine has power, structure, equilibrium and a very good finish.*	**£9.60**	UNS VLW NYW GGW LIB	B
Best's Great Western Pinot Noir 1996, Best's Victoria	*Youthful berry fruit with toasty oak on the nose, strawberries and herbaceous characters on the palate.*	**£9.70**	CWS ABT HOT CAC SWS	S

Wine	Description	Price	Stockists	Award
Leasingham Domain Cabernet Sauvignon Malbec 1996, BRL Hardy South Australia	*Red berry fruit nose with violet and vanilla aromas. Good berry fruit on palate with a neat end.*	**£9.80**	Widely Available	B
Chapel Hill Cabernet Sauvignon 1997, Chapel Hill South Australia	*Showing intense blackcurrant and oak notes. A rounded palate and lasting finish.*	**£9.90**	AUC WRC BUP THS TOS	S
Amberley Cabernet Merlot 1996, Amberley Estate Western Australia	*A ripe fruit nose offers a hint of sandalwood and a touch of eucalypt, and a neat tail.*	**£10.00**	ADN CPW BEN HAS	S
Cornerstone Grenache Shiraz Mourvèdre 1997, Cornerstone South Australia	*A savoury nose leads to brambly, spicey flavours on the palate with a long sweetish finish with vanilla notes..*	**£10.00**	AUC WRC BUP MAR VWE THS AUC	S
Haselgrove McLaren Vale Cabernet Merlot Shiraz 1997, Haselgrove South Australia	*Bright and lively plum colour showing a sweet fruit nose with a touch of creamy mint.*	**£10.00**	VLW NYW LIB	S
Pirramimma Petit Verdot 1996, AC Johnston South Australia	*A clean, fresh nose introduces a soft, balanced palate, with sweet fruit and oak, and a light astringent finish.*	**£10.00**	TOS	S
Pirramimma Petit Verdot 1997, AC Johnston South Australia	*Ripe fruit and well integrated oak are the hallmarks of this huge wine offering intensity and punch.*	**£10.00**	PLB	B
Yarra Valley Hills Warrenwood Pinot Noir 1998, Yarra Valley Hills Victoria	*Succulent with lots of sweet berry fruit and sage notes, balanced acidity and good length.*	**£10.00**	ODD	B

Wine	Description	Price	Stockists	Award
D'Arenberg The Ironstone Pressings 1997, F E Osborne & Sons South Australia	*Concentrated, powerful nose of earth, pepper and plums. Fabulous length developing through fruit and wood.*	**£10.10**	BWL ODF	G
Mt Helen Cabernet Sauvignon Merlot 1997, Mildara Blass Victoria	*Lovely burnt berry nose. Sweet and round palate of chewy blackcurrent, a real mouthfiller.*	**£10.30**	BDR HWL WFB	S
Coldstream Hills Pinot Noir 1998, Coldstream Hills Victoria	*Lemon balm and sage characters on the nose, subtle oak and a lovely lingering finish.*	**£10.50**	BWC ODD SEL PEF	S
Penfolds Barossa Valley Old Vine Red 1996, Penfolds South Australia	*Smokey, dark, concentrated loganberries and mulberries over subtle oak,singing fruit tannins and gamey notes.*	**£10.50**	WCR VWE MWW TOS BTH PEF	S
Tatachilla Clarendon Vineyard Merlot 1997, Tatachilla Winery South Australia	*An elegant start, showing a complex bacon, plum and spice nose with a soft and subtle palate.*	**£10.50**	NIC NYW CAM D&D QWW	S
Tyrrell's Eclipse Pinot Noir 1997, Tyrrell's New South Wales	*Sensual red colour, rich berry fruit with meaty, leathery characters on the nose and a concentrated fruit palate.*	**£10.50**	RBS PRG	S
Penley Estate Shiraz Cabernet 1994, Penley Estate South Australia	*A swirling psychedelic appearance introduces a velvet nose of ea-de-cologne mint and plum before a very groovy palate.*	**£10.60**	L&W	B
Plantaganet Pemberton Pinot Noir 1997, Plantagenet Western Australia	*Rich with black cherry, burnt almond and mint flavours. A perfect partner to Peking duck.*	**£10.60**	GGW NYW LIB	B

AUSTRALIA• RED• OTHER

Wine	Description	Price	Stockists	Award
Cleveland Pinot Noir 1996, Cleveland Winery Victoria	*Gorgeous meaty approach leading to rich strawberries and deep, supple tannins, lip smacking finish.*	**£11.00**	REN	B
Katnook Merlot 1997, Wingara South Australia	*Fresh aromatic nose, with mint and baked summer fruit. Smooth black fruit palate.*	**£11.00**	BWL	B
Maxwell Cabernet Merlot 1997, Maxwell Wines South Australia	*Relaxed yet ripe berry fruits enveloped in a textured smooth palate offering lovely palte*	**£11.00**	SWS	B
Brokenwood Cricket Pitch Red 1997, Brokenwood South Australia	*Smoky, spicy nose with elegant peppery highlights.Well measured oak influence and delightful balance.*	**£11.10**	HHF NYW H&H	S
Voyager Estate Cabernet Sauvignon Merlot 1994, Voyager Estate Western Australia	*Cherry and raspberries contrast nicely with the rich plum fruit palate beautifully treated with oak.*	**£11.50**	J&B	S
Yalumba The Signature Cabernet Sauvignon Shiraz 1995, Yalumba Winery South Australia	*Inviting cherry wood bouquet with blackcurrant and cigar box notes lead to a soft tannin palate of good length.*	**£11.60**	RBS QWW JNW F&M HAR BDR NEG YAL	S
Chateau Reynella Cabernet Sauvignon Merlot 1996, BRL Hardy South Australia	*Rose petals and cassis with vanilla. Great, savoury fruit, integrated with subtle oak, strong acidity.*	**£11.70**	VLW CWS HBR	G
de Bortoli Yarra Valley Pinot Noir 1997, de Bortoli Victoria	*Ruby red colour, ripe strawberries and cherries on the nose with berry fruit on the palate.*	**£11.80**	QWW HHF GGW BOR	S

Wine	Description	Price	Stockists	Award
Dromana Estate Pinot Noir 1998, Dromana Estate Mornington Peninsula	*Lush chocolate and cherry aromas. Full bodied, the palate reflects flavours found on the nose.*	£11.90	CAC CCW	B
Stanton & Killeen Rutherglen Durif 1996, Stanton & Killeen Victoria	*Inviting black cherry and plum notes, very well balanced and deep with great fruit flavours.*	£12.00	NYW ACH PGS WSG	B
Stonier Pinot Noir 1998, Stonier Victoria	*Showing development on the toasty oak nose, but the palate is still packed down hard with plums and damsons.*	£12.00	MZC	B
Veritas Shiraz Mourvèdre Pressings 1996, Veritas Winery South Australia	*Lovely aromas of licorice and violets with a touch of VA lift. Well balanced and long.*	£12.20	L&W NYW JLW	S
Heggies Vineyard Merlot 1995, Yalumba Winery South Australia	*Sweet raisiny fruit with tarry notes on the nose lead to a full bodied palate.*	£12.60	NYW ODF LAY JNW NEG YAL	B
Cullen Pinot Noir 1998, Cullen Western Australia	*Amazing nose of ripe berries and funky, frisky acid leads down the velvety tannined palate.*	£12.70	NYW ADN HAS	B
Maglieri John Loxton Merlot 1997, Maglieri South Australia	*Attractive French oak on the nose with berry tones and a warm and ripe palate. Good length.*	£13.00	AUC	B
Michelton Mourvedre Grenache Shiraz 1995, Mitchelton Victoria	*Glorious colour with a sweet cherry nose, palate of elegant blackberries and vanillin oak finish.*	£13.00	JEF	B

AUSTRALIA • RED • OTHER

Wine	Tasting note	Price	Stockists	Medal
Penfolds Bin 389 Cabernet Shiraz 1996, Penfolds South Australia	*Nose shows concentrated berry and chocolate. A deep and spicy palate, one for a dark corner.*	£13.00	Widely Available	G
Skillogallee The Cabernets 1997, Skillogallee South Australia	*Ripe and minty on nose lead to ripe, soft fruit palate well-balanced with ripe tannins. Good length and complexity.*	£13.00	ENO	S
Springwood Park Pinot Noir 1997, Andrew Garrett Vineyard Estates South Australia	*A rounded, zesty wine with plenty of plum, damson, blackcurrant fruit and dusty tannin palate.*	£13.00	T&T	B
Torbreck The Steading 1997, Torbreck Vineyards South Australia	*Lovely nose of spiced raisiny fruit leading to a well structured palate and good finish.*	£13.00	AUC	B
Richard Hamilton Marion Vineyard Grenache Shiraz 1997, Richard Hamilton South Australia	*Nose has plenty of spice, bramble fruit, cherries and crispy bacon and leads to a lovely clean palate.*	£13.50	ENO	S
Blue Pyrenees Estate 1996, Blue Pyrenees Estate Victoria	*Minty, herbal nose.Concentrated and tannic with lots of mint and ripe extracted fruit with cigar box notes.*	£13.80	TOS	S
Frankland Estate Olmo's Reward 1995, Frankland Estate Western Australia	*Ripe fruit soaked in carefully selected spices slides onto a slippery long palate.*	£13.90	CTH NYW H&H HHF	G
Chapel Hill The Vicar 1996, Chapel Hill South Australia	*Ripe plums and blackcurrants with a wiff of eucalypt lead to a seamless vanillan finish.*	£14.00	MAR VWE THS AUC WRC BUP	S

Wine	Description	Price	Stockists	Award
Kingston Estate Reserve Merlot 1997, Kingston Estate South Eastern Australia	*Ripe nose of fresh blackcurrants introduces a juicy fruit palate with great oak integration and structure.*	**£14.00**	VNO QWW VNP	S
Rosemount Estate Traditional 1996, Rosemount Estate South Australia	*Integrated, rich nose. Elegant and rich curranty fruit, subtle with good acidity, very fruity long finish.*	**£14.10**	WRC BWC FUL ROS	B
Joseph Cabernet Merlot 1997, Primo Estate SOUTH AUSTRALIA	*Rich and full coffee and mocha nose with underlying small berried fruits and a touch of mint.*	**£14.30**	AUC NYW	S
Devil's Lair Margaret River Cabernet Merlot 1996 , Devil's Lair Western Australia	*Warm blackcurrant nose with vegetal notes. Supple blackcurranty palate with intense dry tannins.*	**£14.40**	NYW ABA	B
Rosemount Estate GSM 1996, Rosemount Estate South Australia	*Full of spice and tangy red fruit mixed with orange peel and subtle cedary oak.*	**£14.50**	Widely Available	G
Evans & Tate Margaret River Merlot 1996, Evans & Tate Western Australia	*Groovy fruit, ripe and up for it intermingles with exotic herbs. Great fruit concentration meets satin tannins.*	**£14.90**	CTH NYW GRA FRT	G
Nepenthe Pinot Noir 1997, Nepenthe Vineyards South Australia	*Inviting berry fruits with a well measured touch of vegetal and meaty characters flowing to a soft, rounded palate.*	**£15.00**	SWS ODD GRT	S
Nepenthe Pinot Noir 1998, Nepenthe Vineyards South Australia	*Like climbing into bed with an old friend, warm, frisky and inviting. Luscious fruit and slippery tannins.*	**£15.00**	SWS ODD GRT	B

Wine	Description	Price	Stockists	Award
Nepenthe "The Fugue" Cabernet Merlot 1997, Nepenthe Vineyards South Australia	*Elegant nose displaying lashings of restrained berries and leafy, slippery tannis and cool acidity stretch the persistence.*	**£15.00**	ODD GRT SWS	B
Coldstream Hills Reserve Pinot Noir 1997, Coldstream Hills Victoria	*Closer and closer, this still restrained wine is showing many dimensions on its feral, fruity nose. Elegance personified.*	**£15.70**	BWC ODD PEF	B
Hillstowe Udy's Mill Lenswood Pinot Noir 1997, Hillstowe Wines South Australia	*Mild berries on the nose with raspberries and strawberries on the palate and a clean velvety finish.*	**£16.00**	MKV	S
Jamiesons Run Reserve 1996, Mildara Blass South Australia	*Still resting but showing hints of earth, minerals and black fruits. A taste of things to come.*	**£16.00**	BDR SEA	B
Redbank Sally's Paddock 1997, Redbank Winery Victoria	*Intense blackberry and spice on the nose showing richness and elegance before a beautifully structured palate.*	**£16.30**	QWW NYW BWC NEG	G
Tyrrell's Vat 8 Shiraz Cabernet 1996, Tyrrell's New South Wales	*A superb nose leads to mulberry, white pepper and sweet vanilla palate with integrated oak and tannins.*	**£16.70**	VLW NYW UNS FRN PWY PRG	G
Yaldara Farms Merlot 1997, Yaldara South Australia	*Ultra concentrated fruit flavours and generous sweet oak. Plenty of length and firm tannins.*	**£17.70**	BDR SWS	S
Yaldara Farms Merlot Cabernet 1997, Yaldara South Australia	*Fantastic, very concentrated and extracted fruit flavours commented the tasters of this ripe, ready-to-drink Australian number.*	**£17.70**	SWS BDR	S

OTHER• RED• AUSTRALIA

Wine	Description	Price	Stockists	Award
Tarrawarra Pinot Noir 1997, Tarrawarra Vineyards Victoria	*Mushroom and spicy, peppery characters flow on to a well defined fruit palate with soft tannins and lovely acidity.*	**£18.00**	PHI HVN LAW	S
Stonier Reserve Pinot Noir 1997, Stonier Victoria	*Abundant aromas summer fruits with pleasant creamy vanilla oak on the palate and a clean finish.*	**£20.00**	MZC	S
Cullen Cabernet Merlot 1997, Cullen Western Australia	*Cedar, violets and spice with blackcurrant aromas lead to a well balanced palate of chalky tannins and crisp acidity.*	**£20.20**	NYW HVN ADN SHB HAS	G
Howard Park Cabernet Merlot 1996, Howard Park Western Australia	*Great colour with aromas of mint, cassis, cedar and luscious black fruit. Beautifully balanced, emminently drinkable.*	**£21.40**	JNW ABA	S
Vasse Felix Heytesbury 1997, Vasse Felix Winery Western Australia	*Big and round and full of jammy fruit, the wine captures eucalypt and rich earth flavours.*	**£25.60**	Widely Available	G
Rosemount Estate Mountain Blue Shiraz Cabernet 1996, Rosemount Estate New South Wales	*Ripe fruit characters of blueberries and damson with a luscious vanilla vein and creamy fruit finish.*	**£35.00**	BWC ROS	S

Pinpoint who sells the wine you wish to buy by turning to the stockist codes. If you know the name of the wine you want to buy, use the alphabetical index. If the price is your motivation, refer to the invaluable price guide index; red and white wines under £5, sparkling wines under £12 and Champagne under £16. Happy hunting!

AUSTRALIA • RIESLING

Wine	Description	Price	Stockists	Award
Jacob's Creek Dry Riesling 1998, Orlando Wyndham South Australia	*A sherbet, gooseberry and citrus nose leads on to a fresh grapefruit palate.*	**£4.70**	Widely Available	B
Bethany Riesling 1998, Bethany Wines South Australia	*Bright fresh style with soft zingy fruit and lively acidity spilling across the palate.*	**£5.50**	WCR D&D	B
Basedow Riesling 1998, Basedow South Australia	*Delicate floral aromas and flavours of honey-suckle with a refreshing lime zest finish.*	**£6.20**	BWL GGW	B
D'Arenberg The Dry Dam Riesling 1997, F E Osborne & Sons South Australia	*A peachy, honeyed nose cascades gracefully onto an austere apple fruit palate with a crisp, acid tail.*	**£6.50**	BWL ODF	S
Knappstein Riesling 1997, Mildara Blass South Australia	*Elegant nose of limes and elderflower leads to sacks of attractively tart green fruits and a fresh, floral finish.*	**£6.50**	WCR EOR MZC	S
Wolf Blass Silver Label Riesling 1998, Mildara Blass South Australia	*Fresh lively citrus and melon fruit with tingling spangle acidity with amazing length and feel.*	**£6.50**	VLW SEA VWE WCR	S
Marienberg Cottage Classic Riesling 1998, Marienberg South Australia	*Fresh lemon green fruit on the nose, with super acidity with sherbet and apple nuances.*	**£7.00**	HFL HFI	B

Wine	Description	Price	Stockists	Award
PETALUMA RIESLING 1998, PETALUMA South Australia	*Elegant and restrained, exhibiting stylish florals along the citric structure, mouthwatering acidity promises a bright future.*	**£7.50**	NYW ADN HHC MZC	B
ST HELGA RIESLING 1998, ORLANDO WYNDHAM South Australia	*Clean floral nose with soft varietal fruit and coconut tones, good citric acid and attractive spritziness.*	**£7.50**	THS CAP PEA CAX	B
TIM ADAMS RIESLING 1998, TIM ADAMS South Australia	*Intense limes and floral talcum powder to start, lively acidity carries the fruit through to the intense finish.*	**£7.50**	AUC TOS	B
WAKEFIELD CLARE RIESLING 1992, WAKEFIELD WINES South Australia	*Lovely maturing nose of citrus and wiffs of kerosene, lively acidity keeps things fresh.*	**£7.60**	BDR SWS ADW BAL	S
HEGGIES VINEYARD RIESLING 1998, YALUMBA WINERY South Australia	*Attractive fruit characters of gooseberry and lime. Clean acidity with a fresh and zippy mouthfeel.*	**£8.00**	LAY ODF JNW NEG YAL	S
POLISH HILL RIVER VINEYARD RIESLING 1998, MILDARA BLASS South Australia	*Very tight to start with refined citrus nose and some blossom, zingy acid cut refreshes the palate.*	**£8.00**	SAF	B
ST HALLETT EDEN VALLEY RIESLING 1998, ST HALLETT South Australia	*LIfted floral and lime nose leading to steel acidity and an endless refreshing finish. Will last.*	**£8.00**	AUC WRC BUP	B
WIRRA WIRRA RIESLING 1998, WIRRA WIRRA South Australia	*Lovely lemon blossom and limes mix with the rigarous palate finishing with cleansing acidity.*	**£8.00**	ODD WST	B

AUSTRALIA • RIESLING

Wine	Description	Price	Stockists	Award
Best's Great Western Riesling 1998, Best's Victoria	*Full nose displaying strength of character and very good fruit, balanced acidity on a rich and full palate with length.*	**£9.00**	JNW SWS	S
Brown Brothers Family Reserve Riesling 1995, Brown Brothers Victoria	*Developing riesling showing great concentration on fruit on the palate and finishing with a very fine acid tail.*	**£9.50**	NYW BRB	S
Skillogallee Riesling 1998, Skillogallee South Australia	*Lively nose with loads of lemon and lime. Strong palate with high acid and restrained fruit on a good finish.*	**£9.80**	ENO	B
Howard Park Riesling 1998, Howard Park Western Australia	*A complex array of aromas on the tight nose, lovely acid structure on the mineral and mixed fruit palate.*	**£9.90**	NYW JNW ABA	B

AUSTRALIA • SEMILLON

Wine	Description	Price	Stockists	Award
Wyndham 1828 Semillon Chardonnay 1998, Orlando Wyndham New South Wales	*Lifted fruit nose with a hint of spice, balanced fruit palate with good depth and length.*	**£4.00**	PEA CAP CAX	B
Hardys Stamp Of Australia Semillon Chardonnay 1998, BRL Hardy South Australia	*Delicate floral nose, zesty citrus fruit palate which is fine and long, fairly high acid.*	**£4.50**	Widely Available	B
Penfolds Bin 381 Semillon 1998, Penfolds South Eastern Australia	*Full fleshy fruit palate with bitter almond characters, good acidity and a long finish.*	**£4.50**	M&S	B

Wine	Description	Price	Stockists	Award
McLaren's on The Lake Colombard Semillon Chardonnay 1998, Andrew Garrett South Eastern Australia	*Peachy aromas, the palate is full bodied with good balance and fantastically good length.*	£5.00	T&T	B
Peter Lehmann Semillon 1998, Peter Lehmann Wines South Australia	*Nice rich lemony fruit, good oak support on the good round palate, good example of its style.*	£5.70	WCR SAF ODD ASD G&M PLE	B
Penfolds Barossa Valley Semillon Chardonnay 1998, Penfolds South Australia	*Lovely aromatic citrus and white peach, quite rich with a good dollop of creamy oak.*	£6.00	WCR THS MWW UNS TOS ASD PEF	B
Tatachilla Wattle Park Semillon Chardonnay 1998, Tatachilla Winery South Australia	*Smooth pineapple and vanilla accompianed by toasty oak, displaying nice acid for a balanced finish.*	£6.00	QWW CAM D&D	B
Cranswick Estate Barrel Fermented Semillon 1997, Cranswick Estate New South Wales	*An initial offering of soft fruit flavours give way to a balanced, vanilla palate.*	£6.50	AUS	B
Yalumba Semillon 1998, Yalumba Winery South Australia	*Delicate lemon merangue approach, lovely nutty oak on the palate showing restraint and finishing crisply.*	£6.50	JNW NEG YAL	B
Cape Mentelle Ironstone Semillon Chardonnay 1998, Cape Mentelle Western Australia	*Elderflower, blossoms and mineral overtone with a good dose of acidity and a long clean finish.*	£6.80	Widely Available	S
Leasingham Domain Semillon 1997, BRL Hardy South Australia	*Lovely crisp lime characters combined with moderate acidity and some complexity, good length.*	£7.00	VLW WAV HBR	B

Wine	Description	Price	Stockists	Award
PENFOLDS BAROSSA VALLEY OLD VINE SEMILLON 1998, PENFOLDS South Australia	*Elegant, delicate nose displaying blossom, citrus and necterines. Good oak handling and lovely acid balance.*	**£7.00**	MAR ODD VWE TOS PEF	S
SIMON HACKETT SEMILLON 1997, SIMON HACKETT South Australia	*Creamy notes and lemon meringue flavours pervade a well structured palate with a clean, acid finish.*	**£7.70**	AUS	S
BETHANY SEMILLON 1998, BETHANY WINES South Australia	*Heady fresh fruit salad entices the nose and carries onto the palate with balanced acidity.*	**£7.80**	D&D	B
GRANT BURGE OLD VINE SEMILLON 1997, GRANT BURGE South Australia	*A soft, ripe entry of fragrant lemons and limes, palate showing a little too much zing and wood.*	**£7.80**	CTH VLW GGW UNS FSA	B
DRIFTWOOD SEMILLON 1997, DRIFTWOOD Western Australia	*Delicate fresh fruit characters, lively acidity and herbaceous tones brought together with a touch of oak.*	**£8.50**	BBR FWM	B
MCWILLIAMS MOUNT PLEASANT ELIZABETH SEMILLON 1994, MCWILLIAMS New South Wales	*A inviting nose of peach and pear pie laced with cinnamon and spice flow on to a lush palate with a neat fruit finish.*	**£8.50**	BHW C&H LAW	S
TIM ADAMS SEMILLON 1997, TIM ADAMS South Australia	*Lovely, subtle lemons and blossom aromas and fantastic fruit acidity. The finish is lithe and persistant.*	**£8.50**	AUC WRC TOS BUP	S
WILLOW'S SEMILLON 1997, WILLOW'S VINEYARD South Australia	*Dead serious wine here. Big oaky entry giving way to intense honeyed lemons. Lovely depth and structure.*	**£8.50**	MAR VWE THS AUC WRC BUP	S

Wine	Description	Price	Stockists	Award
Tim Adams Semillon 1998, Tim Adams South Australia	*Slippery primary fruit to start, leading to a pleasing palate displaying creamy oak structure.*	**£8.80**	MAR THS AUC WRC TOS BUP	B
Chittering Estate Semillon Sauvignon Blanc 1997, Chittering Estate Western Australia	*Fairly closed on the nose, the palate has apricot characters with a lovely rich, slightly oily texture.*	**£9.00**	PAT	B
St Hallett Semillon 1997, St Hallett South Australia	*Lovely honeyed fruit leading to integrated oak on the palate and a seductive finish. More please!*	**£9.00**	AUC	S
St Hallett Semillon 1998, St Hallett South Australia	*Sharply focused, showing Granny Smiths, straw and lemon water with quality, spicey oak. Complex and elegant.*	**£9.00**	WTS AUC	S
Devil's Lair Fifth Leg White 1997, Devil's Lair Western Australia	*Slightly closed mineral nose with citrus fruit palate, moderate acidity and a clean long finish.*	**£9.60**	GRT NYW aba	B
Amberley Semillon 1997, Amberley Estate Western Australia	*Ripe lemons and lime with floral aromas precede a well judged fruit palate with well measured acidity.*	**£10.00**	NYW WRC BUP MAR VWE THS HAS	S
Rosemount Estate Show Reserve Semillon 1996, Rosemount Estate New South Wales	*Offering glimpses of exotic fruits, the palate offers fresh fruit which is balanced with pleasing acidity.*	**£10.00**	WSO ROS	S

Pinpoint who sells the wine you wish to buy by turning to the stockist codes. If you know the name of the wine you want to buy, use the alphabetical index. If the price is your motivation, refer to the invaluable price guide index; red and white wines under £5, sparkling wines under £12 and Champagne under £16. Happy hunting!

AUSTRALIA • SEMILLON

TYRRELL'S LOST BLOCK SEMILLON 1997, TYRRELL'S New South Wales	*Intense lime fruit characters combined with soft fruit and a hint of oak.*	**£10.00**	PRG	(B)
VOYAGER ESTATE SEMILLON 1996, VOYAGER ESTATE Western Australia	*Intrigues from its intense vinous nose, river pebble texture and fruit laden palate before a classic, crisp tail.*	**£10.50**	J&B	(S)
VASSE FELIX SEMILLON 1998, VASSE FELIX WINERY Western Australia	*Aromatic lemons with a refreshing grassy cut, mouth watering acid adds structure with a pure persistance.*	**£11.10**	RBS NYW BWC CHH IVV CPW NEG	(B)
CULLEN SAUVIGNON BLANC SEMILLON 1998, CULLEN Western Australia	*Fresh grass and citrus, showing good flinty acid with nice structure, finishes well with a kiss of oak.*	**£12.00**	WRC ADN HAS	(B)
NEPENTHE SEMILLON 1998, NEPENTHE VINEYARDS South Australia	*Lovely stuff, still a baby. Complex lashings of lemon, peach and smoky bacon, chewy and long.*	**£12.00**	ODD GRT SWS	(B)
TYRRELL'S VAT 1 SEMILLON 1993, TYRRELL'S New South Wales	*A restrained herbal nose expands in the mouth to lively lemon, lanolin and buttery characters with superb texture.*	**£17.10**	NYW TAN F&M SAN HAR HAC PRG	(G) TROPHY WINE

AUSTRALIA • SHIRAZ

MHV AUSTRALIAN SHIRAZ NV, REDELLO WINES New South Wales	*Blackcurrants and spice notes with a delightful mouth feel and a clean finish.*	**£4.20**	MHV	(S)

Wine	Description	Price	Stockists	Award
Safeway Australian Shiraz 1998, BRL Hardy South Australia	*Showing lifted rasberries with some nice gaminess and flesh. Lots of character, balance and poise.*	£4.50	SAF	S
Tesco McLaren Vale Shiraz 1997, Maglieri South Australia	*Excellent fruit structure with minty, peppery overtones. Spicy acidity and well developed tannins lead on to a good finish.*	£4.70	TOS	B
Wellwood Shiraz 1998, Highland Heritage Estate New South Wales	*Ripe plums combine with damson fruit and dried currants flavours and a finely textured, tannin palate.*	£5.00	CHN	S
Banrock Station Reserve Shiraz 1998, BRL Hardy South Australia	*Easy to drink style offering hints of blackcurrant and plum nuances with a wiff of oak and well defined finish.*	£5.50	VLW JSM ASD ODD CRS HBR	B
Wynns Shiraz 1997, Wynns Coonawarra Estate South Australia	*A berry fruit nose with a warm jammy palate and excellent tannin structure.*	£5.70	Widely Available	S
Essington Shiraz 1998, Essington New South Wales	*Rich ripe berries merging with dark plums, evident new oak with a concentrated fruit palate.*	£5.80	GRA FRT	S
Tesco Australian Shiraz NV, Simeon Wines South Eastern Australia	*A savoury, woody nose. Overtones of leather and spice with ripe berry fruits. Clean finish.*	£5.90	TOS	B
Balgownie Black Shiraz 1995, Balgownie Victoria	*A serious tarry nose with a deep colour. Very concentrated spicy palate, balanced and fine.*	£6.00	PLB	B

Wine	Description	Price	Stockists	Award
Barramundi Premium Shiraz 1998, Cranswick Estate New South Wales	*Raspberry nose, super ripe fruit and a soft tannin finish.*	**£6.00**	TOS AUS	B
McWilliams Hanwood Shiraz 1998, McWilliams New South Wales	*Lighter style but bursting with fresh, vibrant fruit, peppery spice, ripe tannins and oak notes.*	**£6.00**	CSC MFS LAW	B
Tatachilla McLaren Vale Grenache Shiraz 1998, Tatachilla Winery South Australia	*Shows complex berries, cinnamon and spices leading to a full ripe palate and oak finish.*	**£6.00**	WRC BUP MAR VWE THS D&D	S
McGuigan Millenium Shiraz 2000 1997, McGuigan Wines South Eastern Australia	*Rich and deeply coloured with lovely plum and black fruit characters and a spicy, clean finish.*	**£6.10**	VNO CTH WAC QWW VNO	S
Salisbury Shiraz 1997, Salisbury Victoria	*Cigar box nose with sweet bramble fruit, some plum and spice on the palate. Soft tannins and a lengthy finish.*	**£6.20**	VLW NYW ENO	S
Haselgrove Sovereign Shiraz 1998, Haselgrove South Australia	*Good fruit with a moderate dose of oak, clean tannins and a delicately balanced finish.*	**£6.30**	VLW NYW LIB	B
Evans & Tate Gnangara Shiraz 1996, Evans & Tate Western Australia	*A well-balanced wine with dry berry fruits and fine tannins and lovely balancing fruit acidity.*	**£6.50**	GRA EPO FRT	B
Deakin Estate Alfred Shiraz 1996, Wingara Victoria	*A good concentration of ripe red fruit on the palate, finishing smoky and sweet.*	**£6.60**	BWL NYW GGW PHI BWL	S

Wine	Description	Price	Stockists	Award
Deen de Bortoli Vat 8 Shiraz 1998, de Bortoli South Eastern Australia	*White pepper on the nose backed by spicy fruit flavours on a well structured lingering palate.*	**£6.60**	QWW GGW BDR	S
Cellarmaster Eden Valley Shiraz 1998, Cellarmaster Wines South Australia	*Well integrated ripe fruit flavours. Velvety oak and spice usher in a fruit laden finish.*	**£6.70**	SAF IWS	G
Lindemans Bin 50 Shiraz 1998, Lindemans South Australia	*Very fresh with a rich fruity palate, a spicy balanced wine with a good texture.*	**£6.70**	Widely Available	B
Kingston Estate Shiraz 1998, Kingston Estate South Australia	*Lovely menthol and oak notes on the nose, this is a juicy, ripe wine with fine tannins.*	**£6.80**	VNO QWW TOS VNP	S
Baileys Shiraz 1996, Baileys Of Glenrowan Victoria	*A fragrant nose leads to sweet fruit with jammy, liquorice tones upfront. Nicely balanced with a long finish.*	**£7.00**	WCR NYW TOS ODD BPW	S
Bleasdale Bremerview Vineyard Shiraz 1997, Bleasdale South Australia	*This wine is warm and long with good fruit, excellent structure and good use of oak.*	**£7.00**	PLB	S
J J McWilliam Shiraz 1997, McWilliams South Australia	*This wine offers fragrant berry fruit, sandalwood and teatree notes and a hefty burst of fruit on the palate.*	**£7.00**	C&H MFS LAW	B
Wildlife Print Shiraz 1998, Kingston Estate South Eastern Australia	*Plummy fruit, good acidity and complexity. A powerful, elegant wine.*	**£7.00**	VNO TOS VNP	S

Wine	Description	Price	Stockists	Award
Lindemans Limestone Coast Shiraz 1998, Lindemans South Australia	*A lighter style and structure with pleasant summer fruit flavours and a good finish.*	£7.00	JSM PEF	B
Penfolds Koonunga Hill Shiraz Cabernet 1997, Penfolds South Australia	*Smoky black fruits on a spicy palate with rich tannins forming a velvety mouthfeel with a great finish.*	£7.00	Widely Available	S
Peter Lehmann Seven Surveys 1997, Peter Lehmann Wines South Australia	*A spicey nose rises from swirling purple as supple tannins caress the mouth and hints of herb and plum escape.*	£7.00	SAF ODD ASD PLE	B
Tyrrell's Old Winery Shiraz 1996, Tyrrell's New South Wales	*A very well structured wine of good weight, deeply coloured with spicy fruit and tannins.*	£7.00	MWW WCR DEN JUS PLA PRG	B
Wolf Blass Green Label Shiraz 1997, Mildara Blass South Australia	*Delightful spicy fruits with firm tannins in support. A very long sweet, juicy finish.*	£7.00	UNS VLW SEA ODD TOS WCR SEA	B
Wyndham Estate Bin 555 Shiraz 1997, Orlando Wyndham New South Wales	*Rich ripe fruit with a dusting of spice, a succulent palate, well structured with amazing silkiness.*	£7.00	MWW A&A BAB PEA CAX	S
Yaldara Reserve Shiraz 1997, Yaldara South Australia	*Quite a poweful nose introduces a pleasant basket of fruit on the herb tinged palate.*	£7.00	SWS PLA BTH GRT WON SWS	B
Hardys Bankside Shiraz 1997, BRL Hardy South Australia	*Approachable style offering clean and ripe fruit with good mouthfeel and a clean finish.*	£7.20	VLW WCR SAF ASD HBR	B

Wine	Description	Price	Stockists	Award
THREE VALLEYS SHIRAZ 1997, MIRANDA WINES Victoria	*Ripe plum and blackcurrent flavours lead to a firm palate of minty chunks with intense fruit flavours.*	**£7.20**	BDR	S
D'ARENBERG THE FOOTBOLT OLD VINE SHIRAZ 1997, F E OSBORNE & SONS South Australia	*Ripe style, nice vanilla fruit and rich chocolate nose, firm and juicy on the lingering finish.*	**£7.30**	BWL ODF	B
DAVID WYNN SHIRAZ 1998, MOUNTADAM South Australia	*Lightly spiced withrich, ripe plums and nice balance on the fruit driven finish.*	**£7.30**	NYW JNW HAS	B
WILDERNESS ESTATE SHIRAZ 1997, WILDERNESS ESTATE New South Wales	*Warm and generous wine, with a rounded mouthfeel and lovely tones of herb and plum fruit.*	**£7.30**	WOW	S
TATACHILLA KEYSTONE GRENACHE SHIRAZ 1998, TATACHILLA WINERY South Australia	*Intense summer berries show good depth, complex with lovely structure, top New World stuff!*	**£7.40**	BDR	G
WARBURN ESTATE OAK AGED SHIRAZ 1998, COOPER COUNTY WINES New South Wales	*Well made, dark in colour and rounded in the mouth showing nicely integrated oak and fruit characters.*	**£7.40**	BDR	S
MIRANDA HIGH COUNTRY SHIRAZ 1995, MIRANDA WINES South Eastern Australia	*A nose of raspberry fruit and oak aromas lead to a black berry fruit and boiled sweets palate.*	**£7.50**	AVB HOH	B
PREECE SHIRAZ 1997, MITCHELTON Victoria	*Attractive style with a concentrated fruit character. Clean strong pepper and blackberry fruit flavours.*	**£7.50**	JEF	B

AUSTRALIA • SHIRAZ

Wine	Description	Price	Stockists	Award
TEMPLE BRUER SHIRAZ MALBEC 1996, TEMPLE BRUER South Australia	*Great balance, intense fair fruit and structure in the mouth with blackcurrant and liquorice flavours.*	**£7.50**	TOS PLB	B
HERITAGE ROAD SHIRAZ RESERVE 1997, HERITAGE ROAD WINERY South Australia	*A buxom style offering plenty of mocha and mint, dark intense plummy fruits and creamy oak.*	**£7.60**	ROD BKI	B
BEST'S VICTORIA SHIRAZ 1998, BEST'S Victoria	*A lovely perfumed nose with good, ripe, sweet fruit flavours in ascendency and a generous length.*	**£7.70**	QWW JNW SWS HOT GRT FUL CAC SWS	B
ROSEMOUNT ESTATE DIAMOND VARIETAL SHIRAZ 1998, ROSEMOUNT ESTATE South Australia	*Peppery nose with notes of blackcurrent and damson fruit. Lovely palate with some savoury notes and a fined finish.*	**£7.70**	Widely Available	S
PLANTAGENET OMRAH SHIRAZ 1997, PLANTAGENET Western Australia	*A beautifully structured wine with a peppery nose and good ripe concentrated black earthy fruit.*	**£7.80**	NYW GGW LIB	B
BROWN BROTHERS SHIRAZ 1996, BROWN BROTHERS Victoria	*Toast and spicy pepper, raspberry and earthy flavours develop on the palate. Finish is almost smoky.*	**£7.90**	UNS WAC GRT TOS BRB	S
ROVALLEY RIDGE SHIRAZ 1997, MIRANDA WINES South Australia	*Ripe, juicy fruit mixes with toasty oak leading to a well balanced, warm palate.*	**£7.90**	HOH BDR	B
ANNIE'S LANE SHIRAZ 1997, MILDARA BLASS South Australia	*Mild spice aroma with varietal character on the palate gives way to a mushy fruit finish.*	**£8.00**	WFB	S

Wine	Description	Price	Stockists	Award
Buckley's Clare Valley Shiraz 1997, Buckley's South Australia	*Very ripe concentrated fruits dominate a vibrant palate. A well balanced wine with a lingering finish.*	**£8.00**	TOS AUC	S
Capel Vale CV Shiraz 1997, Capel Vale Wines Western Australia	*Mocha earth and spice at the front with black olives and expansive creamy vanilla flavours.*	**£8.00**	WCR SAF MWW BTH AHW	S
Chateau Tahbilk Shiraz 1996, Chateau Tahbilk Victoria	*Great up front fruit here with a layer of welcome spice and a palate of great depth.*	**£8.00**	PLE	B
Hill Of Hope Reserve Shiraz 1997, Hill Of Hope New South Wales	*A pleasant fruit nose meets pepper and tobacco tones on a fine tannin bed.*	**£8.00**	UNS SWS	B
Inglewood Show Reserve Shiraz 1996, Inglewood South Eastern	*Succulent and fresh with hints of white pepper backed by ginger and spice.*	**£8.00**	AMW SVT CFP GRO HWL	B
McGuigan Shareholders Shiraz 1997, McGuigan Wines South Eastern Australia	*Fresh berries with a touch of herbs on a firm tannin palate and clean fruit finish.*	**£8.00**	VNO WAC QWW VNP	G
Rosemount Estate Honey Tree Reserve Shiraz 1998, Rosemount Estate South Australia	*An easy drinking style offering blackcurrant and plum notes from a softly structured palate.*	**£8.00**	M&S	S
St Hallett Barossa Shiraz 1997, St Hallett South Australia	*A chewy, elegant wine that engages the mouth and nose. Well measured oak with menthol flavours.*	**£8.00**	MAR THS BUP WRC AUC	B

AUSTRALIA • SHIRAZ

Wine	Description	Price	Stockists	Award
St Hallett Faith Shiraz 1997, St Hallett South Australia	*Great depth and a lovely, smokey, leathery, spicy nose. A lively spicy fruit palate leads to a clean finish.*	**£8.00**	TOS AUC	S
Wakefield Shiraz 1998, Wakefield Wines South Australia	*Soft red berries lead to richly stewed plums and obvious coconut and vanilla oak. Balanced and long.*	**£8.00**	UNS ODD SWS	G
Bridgewater Mill Shiraz 1996, Petaluma South Australia	*Powerful fruit characters run into a luscious tannin structure full of pepper and spice.*	**£8.50**	MGN CLA PSC MZC	B
Knappstein Shiraz 1997, Mildara Blass South Australia	*Excellent fruit and flavours of cinnamon, plums and woody vanilla notes precede a finely tuned palate.*	**£8.50**	ODD MZC	B
Lindemans Padthaway Shiraz 1996, Lindemans South Australia	*Up for it fruit flows to a palate with velvety tannins and a clean fruit finish.*	**£8.50**	TOS ODD ADS PEF	S
Rovalley Ridge Shiraz 1994, Miranda Wines South Australia	*Pleasant savoury nose introduces a warm vibrant fruit pallate with plenty of pepper and a neat finish.*	**£8.50**	QWW BDR WCR LUC SOH AVB HOH	B
Yalumba Barossa Shiraz 1996, Yalumba Winery South Australia	*Chinese five spice and bok choy with a chunky redcurrent component introduce a grainy peppery palate.*	**£8.50**	JNW MWW ODD NEG YAL	B
Basedow Shiraz 1996, Basedow South Australia	*A luscious red colour and subtle nose with a fruity and spicy tobacco palate.*	**£8.70**	SAF SMF GGW BWL	B

Wine	Description	Price	Stockists	Award
Maglieri Shiraz 1997, Maglieri South Australia	*Big on blackfruits and green pepper with fruit and mint undertones emerging on the palate.*	**£8.70**	UNS TOS EPO PLB	B
Water Wheel Shiraz 1997, Water Wheel Victoria	*Super ripe plums and blackberries with a lovely vanillin vein. A clean tannin finish does the mopping up.*	**£8.70**	NYW AUC AUC	G
Basedow Shiraz 1997, Basedow South Australia	*A herbaceous nose with lots of sweet fruit on the palate and a pleasing finish.*	**£8.80**	GGW BWL SAF SMF NYW	B
Campbells Rutherglen Bobbie Burns Shiraz 1997, Campbells of Rutherglen Victoria	*A real show stopper with ripe fruit dressed up to the nines in pepper and spice.*	**£9.00**	NYW ODD WNS CPW GNW STE WSG	G
Essington Reserve Shiraz 1997, Essington New South Wales	*Mocha, earth and spice at the front with black olives and expansive creamy vanilla flavours.*	**£9.00**	FRT GRA	S
Marienberg Reserve Shiraz 1996, Marienberg South Australia	*A rich bouquet of black fruits with lovely vanillin oak characters. A firm tannin structure and a harmonious mouthfeel.*	**£9.00**	HFI	S
Mitchelton Goulburn Valley Shiraz 1995, Mitchelton Victoria	*Dense, big and minty, this wine is well-balanced with great tannin structure.*	**£9.00**	JEF	S
Penfolds Bin 28 Kalimna Shiraz 1996, Penfolds South Australia	*Terrific fruit on the nose and hints of eucalypt. Well measured oak gives sweetness to the fruit laden palate.*	**£9.00**	Widely Available	S

AUSTRALIA • SHIRAZ				
Richard Hamilton Gumper's Block Shiraz 1997, Richard Hamilton South Australia	*A complex nose of black spiced fruits with hints of leather and tobacco and a well rounded, satisfying palate.*	**£9.00**	NYW ENO	G
Rymill Shiraz 1996, Rymill Coonawarra South Australia	*Fruitcake, sweet fruit and spice aromas, smooth and supple on the well structured lingering palate.*	**£9.00**	CRS MWW PLB	B
Wirra Wirra Original Blend 1996, Wirra Wirra South Australia	*A big fruit and herb nose leads to a luscious tannin palate offering well integrated oak and a clean finish.*	**£9.00**	ODD WST	B
Montara Shiraz 1997, Montara Estate Victoria	*A round, rich and ripe wine. Its big but supple with a long juicy finish.*	**£9.50**	ADN HAS	S
Seppelt Chalambar Shiraz 1996, Seppelt Victoria	*Peppery spice on a nose of touch of mint leading to a palate of rich fruit cake flavours.*	**£9.50**	UNS NYW ODD GRA	G
Simon Hackett Anthony's Reserve Shiraz 1997, Simon Hackett South Australia	*Delicious ripe fruit merging with dark cherry fruits, evident new oak with concentrated fruit palate.*	**£9.50**	AUS	S
Tim Adams Shiraz 1997, Tim Adams South Australia	*Peppery notes with big ripe fruit and nice oak characters. Finely tuned fruit acidity balances the firm tannins.*	**£9.50**	TOS AUC	S
Reynolds Shiraz 1998, Reynolds New South Wales	*Cassis, stone fruit, black pepper and cloves flow to a palate laced with vanillin oak.*	**£9.80**	L&W JLW	S

Wine	Description	Price	Stockists	Award
BAILEYS 1920'S BLOCK SHIRAZ 1996, BAILEYS OF GLENROWAN Victoria	*Fresh and vibrant showing plum fruits and good wood, making for a chunky characterful red.*	£10.00	WCR MWW ODD BPW	B
BEST'S GREAT WESTERN SHIRAZ 1996, BEST'S Victoria	*Well defined oak and spicy pepper with a hint of eucalypt lead to a plum and earth palate of impressive length.*	£10.00	NYW JNW UNS GRT CAC SWS	S
CHAPEL HILL SHIRAZ 1997, CHAPEL HILL South Australia	*Almond hints and rounded in the mouth. It shows nicely integrated oak and fruitcake characters.*	£10.00	MAR THS WRC BUP TOS AUC	S
FERNHILL ESTATE SHIRAZ 1996, FERNHILL ESTATE South Australia	*This rich and up for it red offers a ripe and rich bouquet of blackcurrants and plum pudding.*	£10.00	HFI	S
GEOFF MERRILL SHIRAZ 1997, GEOFF MERRILL South Australia	*Deep inky red with intense spicy leather and soft ripe fruit nose. Firm tannins and bramble fruit finish.*	£10.00	ENO	S
GOUNDREY RESERVE SHIRAZ 1996, GOUNDREY Western Australia	*A herbaceuous nose and tones of truffles. Brambles and loads of ripe fruit flavours.*	£10.00	BLN EHL	S
HANGING ROCK HEATHCOTE SHIRAZ 1997, HANGING ROCK Victoria	*Plump fruit and some savoury flavours on the nose flow to a spicy fruit palate immersed in fine tannins.*	£10.00	MRN WLI	B
HASELGROVE MCLAREN VALE SHIRAZ 1998, HASELGROVE South Australia	*Great white pepper notes leading to spicy black fruits with tarry tannins and a long finish.*	£10.00	VLW LIB	S

Wine	Description	Price	Stockists	Award
Pertaringa Shiraz 1997, Pertaringa Vineyards South Australia	*Beautifully coloured this wine has nice ripe fruit characters, rich and deep with a long finish.*	**£10.00**	CTH	S
Rothbury Estate Brokenback Shiraz 1996, Mildara Blass New South Wales	*Nice plums and berry fruit flow to a palate of good acidity and tannins, long finish.*	**£10.00**	VLW ODD SEA	B
Tyrrell's Brokenback Shiraz 1996, Tyrrell's New South Wales	*Lovely ripe fruit dominated nose showing great concentration and spicy characters with a neat tail.*	**£10.00**	PRG	B
Willow's Shiraz 1996, Willow's Vineyard South Australia	*Intense chocolatey, oaky palate with raspberry fruit and rounded tannins in support. Great length.*	**£10.00**	WRC BUP AUC	S
Woodstock Shiraz 1997, Woodstock Wines South Australia	*Soft and oaky on the nose,vibrant spicy fruit flavours on the palate and a long finish.*	**£10.00**	WFD ALE FVM HAF MHW BDR VRS	S
d'Arenberg The Dead Arm Shiraz 1997, F E Osborne & Sons South Australia	*Very intriguing, deep and dark, this wine has delicious concentrated fruit and oak flavours in a long finish.*	**£10.10**	BWL ODF	S
Grant Burge Filsell Old Vine Shiraz 1997, Grant Burge South Australia	*Rather big good wood with intense licorice and eucalyptus aromas, boasting excellent concentration and appealing warmth.*	**£10.20**	UNS CTH BDR GGW FSA	S
Mt Ida Shiraz 1996, Mildara Blass Victoria	*A juicy, rich wine with lots of fruit, smooth tannins, lovely pepper flavour and a smoky finish.*	**£10.40**	QWW NYW BDR HWL WFB	S

Wine	Description	Price	Stockists	Award
Balgownie Estate Shiraz 1997, Balgownie Estate Victoria	*Fresh and aromatic, this wine has a good pepper spice palate and lingering finish.*	**£11.00**	BPW	B
Bethany Shiraz 1996, Bethany Wines South Australia	*Great earthy, farmyard nose, juicy blackberry fruit. Finishes well with some taut wood tannins.*	**£11.00**	WCR D&D	B
Miranda Family Reserve Old Vine Shiraz 1996, Miranda Wines South Australia	*Attractive cherry aromas with jammy fruit. Sweet oak mingles with red fruit in a lovely well-balanced wine.*	**£11.00**	MTC AVB HOH	S
Wolf Blass President's Selection Shiraz 1996, Mildara Blass South Australia	*A lovely spicy nose, big palate, burnt characteristics of spice and leather and a silky finish.*	**£11.30**	CTH VLW ODD WCR SEA	S
Allanmere Shiraz 1997, Allanmere Wines New South Wales	*Cassis, lavender and roses on the nose with flavours of dry and bitter cherries.*	**£11.60**	QWW WFD ALE FVM HAF VRS	S
Sorby Shiraz 1997, Tim & Simon Adams South Australia	*Attractive aromatic violets and ripe berry fruit. Good acidity adds to the fruit structure. One to age.*	**£11.70**	AUC	S
Tatachilla Foundation Shiraz 1996, Tatachilla Winery South Australia	*Cigar box nose with sweet bramble fruit, some plum and spice on the palate and a lingering, complex finish.*	**£11.70**	QWW BDR ODD NIC NYW CAM D&D	S
Tim Gramp Shiraz 1997, Tim Gramp South Australia	*Deep plum colour with warm Shiraz fruit and spicy, warm vanillan character leading to a long finish.*	**£11.80**	NYW JNW HAS	G

AUSTRALIA • SHIRAZ

Wine	Description	Price	Stockists	Award
Chateau Reynella Shiraz 1996, BRL Hardy South Australia	*Nice complex soft fruit and eucalyptus, brilliant crunchy acid and tight structure. Deft winemaking here.*	**£12.00**	VLW WCR HBR	S
Hillstowe Mary's Hundred Shiraz 1997, Hillstowe Wines South Australia	*Plump, round ripe fruit with nice use of oak and a clean tannin tail.*	**£12.10**	MKV	B
St Hallett Blackwell Shiraz 1996, St Hallett South Australia	*Nice pepper and spice riding with the plummy fruit. Elegant and poised on the palate, good stuff.*	**£12.50**	MAR THS BUP WRC AUC	B
de Bortoli Yarra Valley Shiraz 1996, de Bortoli Victoria	*Lovely integrated herbs, ripe fruit and oak, pleasing tannins and good acid structure. Nice persistence.*	**£12.60**	QWW HHF GGW BOR	S
Seabrook & Seabrook Barossa Shiraz 1997, Seabrook & Seabrook South Australia	*Firm, rich, clean fruit with good grated dark chocolate on the nose. Yummy wine.*	**£12.80**	SKW	S
Elderton Shiraz 1995, Elderton South Australia	*Racy, strawberry hot nose whilst dry, ripe and concentrated. Excellent fruit palate and fine tannins*	**£13.00**	FWM BBR	B
Geoff Merrill Reserve Shiraz 1995, Geoff Merrill South Australia	*A rich chewy wine showing complex peppermint and mocha notes with big tannins and a long finish.*	**£13.00**	TOS ODD PLE	B
Maxwell Ellen Street Shiraz 1997, Mark Maxwell South Australia	*A stewed fruit nose leads to a complex fruit and oak palate and a pleasant finish.*	**£13.00**	NYW SWS	B

Wine	Description	Price	Stockists	Award
Skillogallee Shiraz 1997, Skillogallee South Australia	*An intense blackberry nose with nice fruit, tannins and acidity on the palate. A hint of smoke and spiciness.*	**£13.00**	ENO	B
Bremerton Old Adam Shiraz 1996, Bremerton South Australia	*Plum and leathery characters and has a long rounded finish well supported by a firm tannins structure.*	**£13.20**	NYW QWW	S
Ebenezer Shiraz 1996, BRL Hardy South Australia	*Massive nose of ripe mulberries, chocolate and lashings of white pepper. Wonderful depth, almost endless finish.*	**£13.20**	VLW WCR HBR	G
Yaldara Julians Shiraz 1997, Yaldara South Australia	*A minty, spicy nose leads to a well balanced fruity and peppery palate tinctured with vanillin oak.*	**£13.30**	BDR DIR SWS	B
Difabio Bush Vine Shiraz 1997, Difabio South Australia	*Deep licorice and blackberry aromas with a full black fruit palate awell intergrated with pleasant sweet oak.*	**£14.00**	AUC	S
Steve Maglieri Shiraz 1997, Maglieri South Australia	*Ripe and luscious exotic spice and black fruit characters. Earthy with rich fruit and pepper.*	**£14.20**	UNS TOS EPO PLB	G
Kingston Estate Reserve Shiraz 1997, Kingston Estate South Australia	*Marvelously inviting wine, rich chocolate and coffee laces with the ripe truffles and fruit.*	**£14.30**	VNO QWW VNP	S
Wirra Wirra RSW Shiraz 1996, Wirra Wirra South Australia	*An attractive sweet, ripe, fruit driven wine that is well-balanced and rich, offers an elegant finish.*	**£14.50**	ODD UWM WST	B

Wine	Description	Price	Stockists	
McGuigan Personal Reserve Shiraz 1998, McGuigan Wines South Eastern Australia	*A delightful berry fruit and cassis nose. Loads of fruit and really easy to drink.*	**£14.70**	VNO WAC QWW VNP	B
Stonyfell Metala Original Plantings Shiraz 1996, Mildara Blass South Australia	*A herbaceous nose carries through to the palate and meets peppery, violet tones and light oak.*	**£14.70**	GSH NYW UNS BPW	S
Geoff Merrill Reserve Shiraz 1994, Geoff Merrill South Australia	*Juicy fruit, spicy pepper with a touch of clove lead to a full flavoured palate of stupendous length.*	**£15.00**	TOS ODD PLE	B
Meerea Park Estate Alexander Munro Shiraz 1997, Meerea Park Estate New South Wales	*Green peppercorn and ginger spice on a rich, smoky nose with creamy new oak and a brisk tannic finish.*	**£15.00**	UNS THW	B
Yalumba Reserve Clare Shiraz 1996, Yalumba Winery South Australia	*Rich spicy notes of freshly ground pepper with ripe fruit and a creamy oak finish to wrap up.*	**£15.00**	JNW ODD NEG YAL	B
Yaldara Farms Shiraz 1997, Yaldara South Australia	*Spicy fruit aromas point to a palate offering blackcurrant pastilles and aniseed characters peaking in a long silky finish.*	**£15.20**	BDR DIR SWS	S
Woodstock The Stocks Shiraz 1996, Woodstock Wines South Australia	*A deeply coloured, oaky wine pleasing to the eye. Warm and rich with good fruit and tannins.*	**£15.40**	WFD ALE MHW BDR VRS	S
Jim Barry McCrae Wood Shiraz 1996, Jim Barry Wines South Australia	*Up for it fruit to the fore with pronounced notes of wild blackberries with figs and dates, lovely grippy finish.*	**£15.50**	QWW DIR ODD TAN BWC BDR NEG	S

Vasse Felix Shiraz 1997, Vasse Felix Winery Western Australia	*Sweet and spicy flavours meld with rich fruit cake in this deliciously full bodied wine.*	**£15.50**	NYW BWC TAN CPW IVV NEG	B
Charles Cimicky Shiraz 1996, Charles Cimicky South Australia	*Generous spice aroma leads to a palate where beetroot and runner bean lead to a clean finish.*	**£16.00**	QWW SWS	S
Dalwhinnie Estate Shiraz 1997, Dalwhinnie Estate Victoria	*Nutmeg and pepper in a fruit pie before a fine, long and super fruity rounded finish.*	**£16.20**	NYW J&B	S
Rosemount Estate Show Reserve Shiraz 1996, Rosemount Estate South Australia	*Developed fruit and savoury notes on the nose flow to a mysteriously complex fruit and oak palate.*	**£17.10**	BWC ROS	S
Tyrrell's Vat 9 Shiraz 1994, Tyrrell's New South Wales	*This is an intriguing style offering plum fruits with a strong herbal vein and mineral component.*	**£17.20**	CPW HAR VHW PHI TPE PRG	B
Seville Estate Shiraz 1997, Seville Estate Victoria	*Attractively coloured with dark fruit, leather and tar flavours. A ripe and peppery wine with many dimensions.*	**£17.50**	H&H HHF	S
Tim Adams Aberfeldy Shiraz 1997, Tim Adams South Australia	*Fruit and mint flavours follow on to a palate with notes of vanilla and a clean, fruit finish.*	**£17.50**	NYW AUC AUC	S
Mount Langi Ghiran Shiraz 1997, Mount Langi Ghiran Victoria	*Attractive, spicy notes of pepper and nutmeg with meaty nuances of smoke carries onto the full bodied palate.*	**£18.30**	VLW NYW BDR JNW GGW LIB	S

Wine	Description	Price	Stockists	Award
Haselgrove H McLaren Vale Reserve Shiraz 1997, Haselgrove South Australia	*Plum and blackcurrent with a streak of white pepper on the noseover a spicy lingering palate. Huge!*	£19.60	VLW NYW LIB	S
Capel Vale Kinnaird Shiraz 1997, Capel Vale Wines Western Australia	*Luscious black cherry, spice and leather aromas. Fruit, mint and a warm liquorice palate with good tannins.*	£20.00	MWW RAC AHW	S
Leasingham Classic Clare Shiraz 1996, BRL Hardy South Australia	*Fruit and oak flavours on a fine tannin palate beautifully balanced by clean fruit acidity.*	£20.00	VLW TOS HBR	S
Stonewell Shiraz 1994, Peter Lehmann Wines South Australia	*Big and inky style with loads of fruit and mintiness and nice oak. Lay back on it.*	£20.00	ODD G&M BWL BDR PLE	B
Stonewell Shiraz 1993, Peter Lehmann Wines South Australia	*Pandora's box of aroma's encompassing open coconut, jammy fruit, licorice and fresh blackcurrant. Could be a classic.*	£20.20	BDR ODD G&M BWL BBR PLE	G
Brokenwood Rayner's Vineyard Shiraz 1997, Brokenwood South Australia	*Still a baby, yet releasing overwhelming touches of tar, chocolate and tea leaf tainted fruit. Elegantly powerful.*	£21.00	NYW H&H HHF	S
Fox Creek Reserve Shiraz 1997, Fox Creek Wines South Australia	*Attractive cherry aromas with jammy fruit. Sweet oak mingles with red fruit in a lovely well-balanced wine.*	£22.00	NYW	S
Penfolds Magill Estate Shiraz 1995, Penfolds South Australia	*Superb fruit basket on the nose with a vein of oak, white pepper and nutmeg. Needs time.*	£25.00	NYW ODD PEF	B

Wine	Description	Price	Stockists	Award
Henschke Mount Edelstone 1996, Henschke South Australia	*A dense wine with well balanced acidity, fruit and tannins with lovely vanillin sweet oak and a clean finish.*	**£26.30**	RBS NYW JNW L&W	S
E&E Black Pepper Shiraz 1996, BRL Hardy South Australia	*Deep, dark and brooding showing currants, leafy mulberries and a dusting of spice. Rich and multi-dimensional.*	**£27.70**	UNS VLW CWS HBR	G TROPHY WINE
Eileen Hardy Shiraz 1996, BRL Hardy South Australia	*Spicey plums and brambly berries with hints of eucalypt, layered oak and silky fruit tannins. Amazing.*	**£28.00**	VLW JSM DIR FUL HBR	G
Brokenwood Graveyard Shiraz 1997, Brokenwood New South Wales	*Angry and brooding, a cacophony of leather, truffles and leafy plums flow to the operatic tannin structure.*	**£29.00**	NYW H&H HHF	S
Yalumba The Octavius 1995, Yalumba Winery South Australia	*Smoky, sweet ripe flavours of baked black fruits lay back on a balanced, clean finish of good length.*	**£29.20**	QWW NYW JNW HAR BDR NEG YAL	B
Yalumba The Octavius 1993, Yalumba Winery South Australia	*Still a tad closed with a terrific mineral vein running through a dense fruit forest.*	**£30.00**	JNW NEG YAL	B
Yalumba The Reserve 1992, Yalumba Winery South Australia	*Sweet fruit bathing in American oak with great structure, good length and a pleasant finish.*	**£30.00**	NEG YAL	S
Wynns Michael Shiraz 1994, Wynns Coonawarra Estate South Australia	*Spearmint, plum and candied orange before a rounded palate of luxuriously and soft tannins matched.*	**£33.00**	NYW WTS	S

Wine	Tasting note	Price	Stockists	Award
Wolf Blass Black Label 1994, Mildara Blass South Australia	*Ripe and intense with nice rich cedary and fruit characters. The tannin structure suggests it may improve yet.*	**£33.50**	VLW AWB SEA	S
Rosemount Estate Balmoral Syrah 1996, Rosemount Estate South Australia	*A frisky nose of nuts, flesh and silk with great follow through to a voluptuos body showing superb use of wood.*	**£35.00**	UNS ROS	S
Wynns Michael Shiraz 1996, Wynns Coonawarra Estate South Australia	*Slightly closed at this stage, but a huge, well structured palate with big fruit characters and tannins.Give it time.*	**£35.00**	BDR NYW WTS VWE MWW SEL PEF	B
Clarendon Hills Liandra Shiraz 1997, Clarendon Hills South Australia	*A concentrated warm and confident wine, intensly fruity it develops wonderfully in the mouth. Very well-structured.*	**£44.00**	NYW J&B	S

Pinpoint who sells the wine you wish to buy by turning to the stockist codes. If you know the name of the wine you want to buy, use the alphabetical index. If the price is your motivation, refer to the invaluable price guide index; red and white wines under £5, sparkling wines under £12 and Champagne under £16. Happy hunting!

AUSTRALIA • SPARKLING

Wine	Tasting note	Price	Stockists	Award
Carrington Brut Rose NV, Orlando Wyndham South Australia	*Tantalising fresh strawberry nose with a slightly sweet palate balanced by a lively bead and crisp finish.*	**£6.00**	SEL CAP PEA CAX	B
The Peppermint Paddock Sparkling Chambourcin 1997, d'Arenberg South Australia	*Summer pudding topped with fresh blackberries on the nose leading to a creamy palate with a blueberry ice cream tail.*	**£6.50**	BWL ODF	S
Seaview Brut NV, Seaview South Australia	*A heavier style sparkling with a hint of mineralness on the nose and fresh simple fruit on the palate.*	**£6.60**	Widely Available	B
Nottage Hill Sparkling Chardonnay 1997, BRL Hardy South Australia	*Full ripe style with subtle yet developed characters, crisply balanced with a lengthy finish.*	**£7.00**	Widely Available	B
Jacob's Creek Sparkling Chardonnay Pinot Noir NV , Orlando Wyndham South Australia	*Biscuits and cream sing from a deep pool of strawberry flavoured bubbles immersed in a fresh bread palate.*	**£7.00**	Widely Available	S
Cockatoo Ridge Black NV, Yalumba Winery South Australia	*This wine has rustic dry fruit aromas with soft supple fruit on the palate.*	**£7.20**	NYW NEG YAL	G
Seaview Pinot Noir Chardonnay Brut 1995, Seaview South Eastern Australia	*Ripe soft stone fruit aromas before a finely beaded palate with a crisp, acid tail.*	**£7.70**	Widely Available	S

AUSTRALIA • SPARKLING

Wine	Description	Price	Stockists	Award
Orlando Trilogy Brut NV, Orlando Wyndham South Australia	*Full ripe citrus flavours spring from a full mousse palate with a pleasing acid finish.*	**£9.00**	CAP PEA CAX	B
Seppelt Sparkling Shiraz 1994, Seppelt Victoria	*Raspberries and strawberries party with farmyard aromas and delicate integrated oak.*	**£9.10**	Widely Available	B
Yellowglen Vintage 1995, Mildara Blass South Australia	*Yeasty aromas escape ahead of lime notes while the palate is refreshed by crisp acidity.*	**£10.00**	SEA ODD	S
Berrys' Australian Sparkling Wine NV, Taltarni Tasmania	*Meaty vegemite aromas, the palate is slightly chalky with a lovely zippy freshness.*	**£10.80**	BBR	B
Seppelt Show Sparkling Shiraz 1987, Seppelt Victoria	*Seductive cool climate characters sing with warm oak and delicious juicy berry fruit on a moussy palate.*	**£11.20**	UNS WCR NYW TOS GRA	G
Green Point Brut Vintage 1995, Domaine Chandon Victoria	*The palate confirms some bottle age followed by a brush of refreshing and lively acidity.*	**£11.50**	Widely Available	S
Miranda Show Reserve Barossa Old Vine Sparkling Shiraz 1994, Miranda Wines South Australia	*Great plum pudding and biscuit tones on a fruit laden palate with a surprisingly dry finish.*	**£12.00**	QWW HOH NYW AVB	S

Pinpoint who sells the wine you wish to buy by turning to the stockist codes. If you know the name of the wine you want to buy, use the alphabetical index. If the price is your motivation, refer to the invaluable price guide index; red and white wines under £5, sparkling wines under £12 and Champagne under £16. Happy hunting!

AUSTRALIA • SWEET

Wine	Description	Price	Stockists	Award
MIRANDA PIONEERS RAISINED MUSCAT 1998, MIRANDA WINES South Eastern Australia	*A touch of honeyed botrytis, a good rich balanced palate, finishing with a good burst of acidity.*	£4.50	WCR BDR GRP MTC HOH	B
LINDEMANS COONAWARRA BOTRYTIS RIESLING 1997, LINDEMANS South Australia	*Petrol and kerosene aromas with crunchy honey, figgy fruit and lemon acidity.*	£5.90	UNS SMF MHV ODD VWE FUL PEF	B
WELLWOOD ESTATE "STICKY" 1997, D'AQUINO New South Wales	*Flavours of caramel and ripe fruit flood the mouth in this full-bodied intensely sweet wine.*	£6.00	CHN	S
MAGLIERI BOTRYTIS GEWÜRZTRAMINER 1998, MAGLIERI South Australia	*Golden colour with marmalade and butterscotch An elegant spicey complexity, balanced with lemon fresh acidity.*	£7.00	EPO PLB	B
HEGGIES VINEYARD BOTRYTIS RIESLING 1998, YALUMBA WINERY South Australia	*Straw in colour with grapey honey, tight citrus fruit and underlying vegetal tones.*	£7.70	JNW ODF FUL NEG YAL	B
YALUMBA BOTRYTIS SEMILLON SAUVIGNON BLANC 1997, YALUMBA WINERY South Australia	*Unusual meaty aromas with fresh sultana, coconut and tropical fruit backed up by a pleasant fruit acidity.*	£7.70	JNW ODD MWW JNW NEG YAL	B
BROWN BROTHERS NOBLE RIESLING 1996, BROWN BROTHERS Victoria	*Golden colour with grapey aromatics and vegetal complexity. Fresh and racey with a lengthy herbal finish.*	£8.00	NYW BRB	G

AUSTRALIA • SWEET

Wine	Description	Price	Stockists	Award
McWilliams Riverina Botrytis Semillon 1994, McWilliams New South Wales	*Baked fruit, botryitised sultana, richly textured with balancing acidity and finish of treacle and barley sugar.*	**£8.00**	LAW	B
Vasse Felix Botrytis Riesling 1996, Vasse Felix Winery Western Australia	*Golden yellow with pronounced botrytis complexity, zesty citrus fruit, marmalade, honey and round soft mouthfeel.*	**£8.80**	Widely Available	S
d'Arenberg The Noble Riesling 1997, F E Osborne & Sons South Australia	*Deep golden colour intense limey marmalade honeyed aromas with smokey sultana fruit and a funky tail.*	**£9.00**	BWL ODF	B
d'Arenberg The Noble Riesling 1998, F E Osborne & Sons South Australia	*Hints of lavender, brown sugar and orangey complexity, herbal clean, almost minty citus fruit with a full finish.*	**£9.00**	BWL ODF	B
Tim Adams Botrytis Riesling 1998, Tim Adams South Australia	*Straw yellow, dried nectarines peaches, lychee and dried exotic fruit inviting a delicate floral finish.*	**£9.00**	AUC	S
Tim Adams Botrytis Semillon 1998, Tim Adams South Australia	*Youthful green colour with restrained nose, rich honeyed citrus fruit background with balance, complexity and apricot finish.*	**£9.00**	AUC	B
Cranswick Estate Botrytis Semillon 1996, Cranswick Estate New South Wales	*Golden colour with melon and orange peel on the nose, sweet honeyed fruit and telltale marmelade that standout on the palate.*	**£9.50**	BDR ASD AUS	G
de Bortoli Noble One 1995, de Bortoli New South Wales	*Vibrant rich gold colour, full concentrated botrytis aromas, extra ripe tropical and citrus flavours, complexity and balance.*	**£13.30**	QWW HHF GGW TOS CAC BOR	B

AUSTRALIA • WHITE • OTHER

Wine	Description	Price	Stockists	Award
JARRAH RIDGE DRY WHITE 1998, KINGSTON ESTATE WINES South Eastern Australia	*Mineral fruit nose with good middle palate weight and moderate acidity.*	**£4.20**	VNO QWW TRO VNP	B
OXFORD LANDING SAUVIGNON BLANC 1998, YALUMBA WINERY South Australia	*Flavoursome green apples, beans and herbs show with the ripe full palate. Nice, clean finish.*	**£5.00**	Widely Available	B
ST HALLETT POACHERS BLEND 1998, ST HALLETT South Australia	*A lively crisp apple liquid which has a touch of honey and a long clean finish.*	**£5.00**	AUC TOS	S
TESCO LANGHORNE CREEK VERDELHO 1998, BLEASDALE Langhorne Creek	*Full bodied tropical fruit nose combined with an oily complex and forth-coming palate.*	**£5.00**	TOS	S
DAVID HAMMOND TREBBIANO CHARDONNAY 1998, RIVERINA WINES South Eastern Australia	*Intensely perfumed and fruity with a palate that has integrated acidity, elegant complexity and structure.*	**£5.20**	BDR WAV	G
D'ARENBERG WHITE OCHRE 1998, F E OSBORNE & SONS South Australia	*An off dry style wine with a glossy texture and light citrus, apple fruit characters and a groovy acid tail.*	**£5.50**	BWL ODF	S
HARDYS CHARDONNAY SAUVIGNON BLANC 1998, BRL HARDY South Australia	*Grapefruit, lime and minerals married with a fairly full tropical fruit palate and moderate acidity.*	**£5.60**	WCR SMF CWS JSM SMF WAV DIR HBR	B

OTHER • WHITE • AUSTRALIA

Wine	Description	Price	Stockists	Award
YALUMBA ANTIPODEAN WHITE 1998, YALUMBA WINERY South Australia	*Lemon and limes with herbaceous overtones and nutty complexity, its an any time wine.*	**£5.90**	JNW ODD NEG YAL	B
MITCHELTON THOMAS MITCHELL MARSANNE 1998, MITCHELTON South Eastern Australia	*Apples and ripe William pear aromas the palate is creamy slightly chewy with good length.*	**£6.00**	WRC BUP MAR THS jef	B
OXFORD LANDING LIMITED RELEASE VIOGNIER 1997, YALUMBA WINERY South Australia	*Lovely lifted spice mixes sweet and sour on the nose of this rich wine with good texture.*	**£6.00**	UNS THS WRC BUP SAF JNW NEG YAL	B
BEST'S VICTORIA COLOMBARD 1998, BEST'S Victoria	*Buttery ripe melon and green peppers on the nose lingering fruit with a soft round structure.*	**£6.40**	WIN TOS HOT TPE ROD JNW CAC SWS	B
CHATEAU TAHBILK MARSANNE 1998, CHATEAU TAHBILK Victoria	*Lovely honey suckle and citrus to the fore flowing to an intensely balanced palate with remarkable length.*	**£6.50**	ODD G&M TOS PLE	B
SUMMER HILL VERDELHO CHARDONNAY 1998, COOPER COUNTY WINES South Eastern Australia	*Buttery ripe fruit nose with melon fruit characters, the palate is smooth, creamy with moderate acidity.*	**£6.60**	BDR	S
BLEASDALE SANDHILL VERDELHO 1998, BLEASDALE South Australia	*Stone fruit and honeyed characters, moderate concentration of fruit on the palate with balanced acidity.*	**£7.00**	PLB	B
CHATEAU TAHBILK MARSANNE 1997, CHATEAU TAHBILK Victoria	*Lychees, asparagus and green olive aromas with soft rounded fruit and an exceptionally well balanced finish.*	**£7.00**	WTS	S

Wine	Description	Price	Stockists	Award
Rothbury Estate Verdelho 1997, Rothbury New South Wales	*Rich ripe fruit combined with buttery aromas, the mouth is charged with lovely full bodied fruit.*	**£7.00**	VLW SAF	S
Rymill Coonawarra Sauvignon Blanc 1998, Rymill Coonawarra South Australia	*Lovely grassy approach, nice full palate balanced by mouthwatering acid, poised, elegant and persistent.*	**£7.00**	TOS IRI PLB	B
Taltarni Sauvignon Blanc 1998, Taltarni Victoria	*Excellent nose featuring classic ripe gooseberries and nettles, showing depth and complex raciness to the finish.*	**£7.30**	QWW HOH SAF AVB HOH	S
Bridgewater Mill Sauvignon Blanc 1998, Petaluma South Australia	*Pungent asparagus and tropical fruit salad exhibating classy acidity and depth. Well balanced and persistent.*	**£8.00**	WCR CLA MZC	S
Shinus Sauvignon Blanc 1998, Garry Crittendon Victoria	*Clean grassy nose, great explosion of fresh fruit in the mouth, lean acidity and reasonable length.*	**£8.00**	CAC CCW	B
Ninth Island Sauvignon Blanc 1998, Pipers Brook Tasmania	*Nicely perfumed nose of tropical fruit and cut grass. Good complexity and voluptuous mouthfeel.*	**£8.50**	GSH VLW SAF BW BPW	B
Michelton Marsanne 1994, Mitchelton Victoria	*Lush full fruit and vegetals riding shotgun, nice concentration with good acid to finish.*	**£9.00**	JEF	B
Allanmere Verdehlo 1998, Allanmere Wines New South Wales	*Zesty orange citrus fruit on the nose; fresh fruit driven palate with balanced acidity.*	**£9.20**	WFD ALE HAF HDL VRS SMF	B

AUSTRALIA • WHITE • OTHER

Wine	Description	Price	Stockists	Award
Shaw & Smith Sauvignon Blanc 1998, Shaw & Smith South Australia	*Clean floral and gooseberry aromas to start, lovely depth on the palate with a citrussy finish.*	**£9.40**	RBS VLW JNW GGW NYW LIB	B
Vasse Felix Sauvignon Blanc Semillon 1998, Vasse Felix Winery Western Australia	*A rich and generous style offering complementary herbaceousness and honeyed fruit characters..*	**£9.70**	BDR BWC CPW TAN IVV CHC NEG	B
Nepenthe Sauvignon Blanc 1998, Nepenthe Vineyards South Australia	*Intense passionfruit with pleasing grassiness, lovely palate of lush tropical fruit and well balanced acidity.*	**£10.00**	SWS ODD GRT SWS	B
Yalumba Growers Limited Release Viognier 1998, Yalumba Winery South Australia	*Ripe apricot fruit characters on the nose with a rich creamy texture and balancing acidity.*	**£10.00**	JNW MWW NEG YAL	S
Lenswood Vineyards Sauvignon Blanc 1998, Knappstein Lenswood South Australia	*Nice grapefruit and nettles style, showing nice crispness in the mouth around the crunchy fruit finish.*	**£10.40**	BWC BNC WRC	B
Heggies Vineyard Viognier 1998, Yalumba Winery South Australia	*Fresh clean nose with melon fruit characters hints of white pepper and balanced acidity.*	**£12.40**	RBS NYW ODF LAY BWC JNW NEG YAL	S
Michelton Viogner Roussanne 1996, Mitchelton Victoria	*Clean floral fruit characters consisting of apricots and peaches, attractive balance and feminine subtleness.*	**£13.00**	JEF	S

Pinpoint who sells the wine you wish to buy by turning to the stockist codes. If you know the name of the wine you want to buy, use the alphabetical index. If the price is your motivation, refer to the invaluable price guide index; red and white wines under £5, sparkling wines under £12 and Champagne under £16. Happy hunting!

AUSTRIA

The eclectic array of wines offered by this country reflects the enthusiasm and experimentation of its makers. Sweet wines continue to shine picking up a coveted trophy. A pleasant surprise was that a special trophy was awarded for an outstanding red wine. The wide range of sweet, red and white wines are becoming increasingly more available in the UK as experimenting consumers ask their retailers for wines offering value and flair. Austria continues to impress with her tradition, and innovation.

AUSTRIA • SWEET

Wine	Description	Price	Stockist	Award
GERHARD NEKOWITSCH EISWEIN SCHREUBE WELSCHRIESLING 1997, GERHARD NEKOWITSCH Neusiedlersee	*An extremely seductive, perfumed nose followed by refreshing grapefruit on the palate with a crisp finish.*	**£11.00**	NYW	B
NEKOWITSCH SCHREUBE BEERENAULESE 1997, GERHARD NEKOWITSCH Neusiedlersee	*Yellow gold, fresh peach and rose petal on the nose with long citrus overtones and pineapple and lemon finish.*	**£12.00**	NYW	B
ALÖIS KRACHER CUVÉE EISWEIN 1997, ALÖIS KRACHER Neusiedlersee	*Rich and creamy, full of intense ripe fruit, this wine is deliciously sweet with powerful acidity.*	**£13.00**	NYW	B
ZWISCHEN DEN SEEN TROKENBEERENAUSLESE No.3 1996, ALÖIS KRACHER Neusiedlersee	*Aromatic melon nose, creamy and nutty with good intensity. Mid palate structure overshadowed by a great finish.*	**£14.50**	J&B NYW	B
TRAMINER BEERENAULESE NOUVELLE VAGUE NO.1 1996, ALÖIS KRACHER Neusiedlersee	*Somewhat oxidative nose with burnt caramel and citrus flavours, rich and complex, the palate finishes with good acidity.*	**£17.00**	NYW	B

AUSTRIA • SWEET

Wine	Description	Price	Stockist	Award
Hammer Pinot Cuvée Ausbruch 1995, Weinbau Hammer Nuesiedlersee	*Sweet marmalade and honey greet the nose and introduce a luscious palate with a dollop of cleansing acidity.*	**£17.30**	HMA	S
Bouvier Muskat Trockenbeerenauslese No.2 1996, Alöis Kracher Neusiedlersee	*Lean, crispy nose, complex with a balance of fresh acidity. Attractive nutty depth and excellent citrus fruit length.*	**£18.20**	J&B NYW	S
Schilfwein Tradition 1997, Gerhard Nekowitsch Neusiedlersee	*Intense citrus fruit appears on the well-balanced full palate, which has immense length. Excellent!*	**£20.00**	NYW	G
'The Red One' 1997, Gerhard Nekowitsch Neusiedlersee	*A deep rosé wine with hints of rose and jasmine intertwined with an intense sweetness.*	**£20.00**	NYW	S
Kracher Muskat Ottonel Trokenbeerenauslese No.6 1996, Weingut Alöis Kracher Neusiedlersee	*Yellow, orange gold, rich ripe honeyed fruit. Soft mid palate moving to a strong fruity finish of good acidity.*	**£22.50**	J&B NYW	S
Kracher Grande Cuvée Trockenbeerenauslese No.7 1996, Weingut Alöis Kracher Neusiedlersee	*A fresh nose of citrus, grapefruit marmalade and pineapple follow onto the palate.*	**£24.00**	J&B NYW	S
Rose Nouvelle Vague Trokenbeerenauslese No.5 1996 Weingut Alöis Kracher Neusiedlersee	*Luscious apricots on the nose become further concentrated on the palate. The alcohol level gives a powerful kick.*	**£24.00**	NYW	S
Willi Opitz Bouvier Trockenbeerenauslese 1995, Willi Opitz Neusiedlersee	*Lemon and daisies on the nose with barley sugar sweetness makes a rich and approachable wine.*	**£24.10**	ASD T&W	S

Wine	Description	Price	Stockists	Award
Kracher Chardonnay Welschriesling Nouvelle Vague TBA No.4 1996, Weingut Alöis Kracher Neusiedlersee	*A sherbet lemon nose with an intense citrusy palate followed by an outstanding finishing.*	**£26.50**	J&B NYW	G
Willi Opitz Pinot Gris Trockenbeerenauslese 1995, Willi Opitz Neusiedlersee	*The aspects which shone through here were its floral orange nose pierced by the high acidity.*	**£31.70**	T&W	S
Willi Opitz Welschriesling Trockenbeerenauslese 1996, Willi Opitz Neusiedlersee	*With the appearance of sunrise, the excellent acid, balances this simply superb luscious style of wine.*	**£31.70**	T&W	S
Kracher Chardonnay Nouvelle Vague Trockenbeerenauslese No.8 1996, Kracher Neusiedlersee	*Kumquats and other citrus fruit aromas on the nose with a spicy sugar palate.*	**£33.00**	NYW	B
Welschriesling Zwischen den Seen Trockenbeerenauslese No.9 1996, Kracher Neusiedlersee	*A golden haze with lemons, clean fruit, balanced acidity and a long lingering finish.*	**£33.00**	NYW	B
Willi Opitz Goldackerl Trockenbeerenauslese 1995, Willi Opitz Neusiedlersee	*Fresh baked citrus fruit on the nose and palate with soft lemon acidity and long lasting sweet finish.*	**£34.40**	RBS T&W	S
Willi Opitz Eiswein 1997, Willi Opitz Neusiedlersee	*Well balanced, with intense flavours of honey and tropical fruit and a rich lingering finish.*	**£35.10**	RBS T&W	S

Pinpoint who sells the wine you wish to buy by turning to the stockist codes. If you know the name of the wine you want to buy, use the alphabetical index. If the price is your motivation, refer to the invaluable price guide index; red and white wines under £5, sparkling wines under £12 and Champagne under £16. Happy hunting!

EASTERN EUROPE

Some of the oldest wine producing regions in the world continue to benefit from the injection of capital and expertise after privatisation. Incredible diversity can be found from rich Bulgarian Merlot to aromatic Hungarian Gewürztraminer. The overall quality of wine continues to rise offering wine drinkers some exceptional value opportunities as well as diverse wine styles to choose from. This year's WINE Challenge proves that all bodes well for the future continuation of this trend.

BULGARIA • RED

SAFEWAY BULGARIAN COUNTRY RED 1998, VIVI SLIVEN Bulgaria	*Light fruits and violets on the nose introduce a full bodied wine with a big tannin struture.*	**£3.00**	SAF	B
SAFEWAY BULGARIAN CABERNET SAUVIGNON RESERVE 1995, VIVI SLIVEN Bulgaria	*A pleasant red showing small berry fruits and ripe tannins. Nice acidity and well balanced.*	**£3.70**	SAF	B
BOYAR ORIACHOVITZA CABERNET SAUVIGNON RESERVE 1995, MENADA STARA ZAGORA Stara Zagora	*Spicy, licorice nose. Soft weight of good ripe fruit with vanilla. Soft tannin and good length.*	**£4.00**	SMF FUL EUR CRS ASD WOW DBO	B
LOVICO SUHINDOL MERLOT RESERVE 1995, LOVICO SUHINDOL Suhindol	*Light, bright cherry nose. Soft sweetness on palate with gentle tannins and good length.*	**£4.00**	CWS JSM LUV	B
LOVICO SUHINDOL MERLOT RESERVE 1995, LOVICO SUHINDOL Suhindol	*Light, bright cherry nose. Soft sweetness on palate with gentle tannins and good length.*	**£4.00**	CWS JSM LUV	B

Wine	Tasting note	Price	Stockists	Award
Domaine Boyar Premium Cuvée Cabernet Sauvignon 1998, Domaine Boyar Eastern Region	*Brambles and blackcurrant on the nose. Rich, grainy tannins and a grippy finish.*	**£4.50**	WOW DBO	B
Azbuka Rousse Merlot 1996, Vinprom Rousse Rousse	*A curranty nose swims in vanilla and stewed fruits offering mature characters of aged pudding and weathered oak.*	**£6.00**	BVC	G

BULGARIA • WHITE

Wine	Tasting note	Price	Stockists	Award
Vinprom Rousse Reserve Chardonnay 1997, Vinprom Rousse Rousse	*An elegant creamy nose with a pleasant lees influence leading to a rich fruit palate.*	**£3.70**	SAF BVC	S

HUNGARY • RED

Wine	Tasting note	Price	Stockists	Award
Spice Trail Red 1997, Hungarovin Eteyeki	*Vibrant raspberry fruit on the nose following on to a clean, fresh palate.*	**£4.60**	WCR SAF MYL	B
Balatonboglar Chapel Hill Cabernet Sauvignon Barrique Aged 1997, Del Balaton	*Delicate, light nose. Balanced, mineral palate with good cassis fruit intensity and moderate finish.*	**£5.00**	SAF MYL	B

Pinpoint who sells the wine you wish to buy by turning to the stockist codes. If you know the name of the wine you want to buy, use the alphabetical index. If the price is your motivation, refer to the invaluable price guide index; red and white wines under £5, sparkling wines under £12 and Champagne under £16. Happy hunting!

HUNGARY • ROSÉ

Wine	Tasting note	Price	Stockists	Award
Balatonboglar Chapel Hill Pinot Noir Rosé 1998, Balatonboglar Winery Del Balaton	*Simple fruity and clean an attractively coloured wine with good texture and acidity.*	**£3.70**	ASD TOS MYL	B

HUNGARY • SWEET

Wine	Tasting note	Price	Stockists	Award
Hungarovin Tokaji Aszú 5 Puttonyos 1994, Hungarovin Tokaj	*Golden marmelade, floral complexity with botrytis citrus characters and caramelised fruit. Unctuous acid tail.*	**£11.40**	WAC JSM SAF MYL	S
Waddesdon Tokaji Aszú 5 Puttonyos 1993, Royal Tokaji Wine Co. Tokaj	*Amber with lifted apricot, oily nuttiness and citrus fruit, raisin, hints of honeyed complexity and velvety finish.*	**£11.70**	CAC WDM	S

HUNGARY • WHITE

Wine	Tasting note	Price	Stockists	Award
Safeway Mátra Mountain Oaked Chardonnay 1998, Nagyrede Mátra	*Ripe tropical fruit and zesty limes lead to a well balanced palate offering toasty oak.*	**£3.70**	SAF	S
Asda Private Reserve Sauvignon Blanc 1998, Neszmely Tök	*Pungent tinned peas and asparagus, well constructed palate, nicely balanced with reasonable length.*	**£3.80**	ASD	B

Wine	Description	Price	Stockists	Award
Hungarian Private Reserve Gewürztraminer 1997, Interconsult Mór	*A surprise packet, lemon yellow in colour showing aromatic notes and with a sweetish full palate.*	**£3.80**	ASD	S
Safeway Matra Mountain Unoaked Pinot Grigio 1998, Szoloskert Co-Operative Nagyrede	*Baked apples and fresh peachy aromas. Excellent middle palate weight finishing long and clean.*	**£3.80**	SAF	S
Hilltop Castle Ridge Sauvignon Blanc 1998, Hilltop Neszmély Tök	*A grassy nose interspersed with fresh fruit aromas lead to a luscious fruit palate of great length.*	**£3.90**	BGL	B
Hilltop 2000 1998, Hilltop Neszmély Hungary	*Intense apricot nose with a hint of gooseberry, luscious tropical fruit palate combined with racey acidity.*	**£4.00**	VER BGL	S
Hilltop Neszmély River Duna Chardonnay Barrique 1997, Hilltop Neszmély Tolna	*Lemon and banana on the nose with lots of heavy vanilla oak characters, zingy finish.*	**£4.00**	MRN BGL	B
Hilltop Neszmély Tolusi Oaked Chardonnay 1997, Hilltop Neszmély Tolna	*Citrus fruit with good flavor and length, nice oak treatment and a generous finish.*	**£4.00**	MRN BGL	B
Hilltop Sauvignon Blanc 1998, Hilltop Neszmély Sopron	*Quite a restrained herbaceous nose leads to a well weighted palate showing fine balance and persistence.*	**£4.00**	JSM BGL	B
Safeway Mátra Mountain Sauvignon Blanc 1998, Hilltop Neszmély Mátra	*Strong, ripe tropical fruit and nettles are apparent, a round full palate, finishing fresh and long.*	**£4.00**	SAF	B

Wine	Tasting note	Price	Stockists	
SPICE TRAIL WHITE 1998, SZOLOKERT COOPERATIVE Eteyeki	*Lovely sweet melon and floral aromas dance to the proboscis, the palate displays green linear acidity and persistence.*	**£4.00**	WCR MYL	(B)
HILLTOP BIN AK 28 SAUVIGNON BLANC 1997, HILLTOP NESZMÉLY Bataszek	*Sweet, perfumed slightly apricot nose leads to a zesty palate rounding out nicely on the finish.*	**£4.80**	WRC BUP MAR THS VWE BGL	(B)
BALATONBOGLAR CHAPEL HILL BARRIQUE AGED CHARDONNAY 1997, BALATONBOGLAR WINERY Del Balaton	*Apple spiced nose with creamy oak. Banana and custard palate cut by moderate acidity.*	**£5.00**	SAF MYL	(B)

MONTENEGRO

Wine	Tasting note	Price	Stockists	
MONTE CHEVAL PRO CORDE 1997, PLANTAZE AGROKOMBINAT PODGORICA South Montenegro	*Fruitcake and farmyard flavours with high acid and tannins to match. Nice length.*	**£5.20**	WEX MUK	(B)

ROMANIA

Wine	Tasting note	Price	Stockists	
IDLEROCK ROMANIAN PINOT NOIR 1998, THE HANWOOD GROUP Dealul Mare	*Deep colour with good purple tinges. Agile fruit complexity with good length, agreeably different.*	**£3.80**	MHV HAG	(B)

Pinpoint who sells the wine you wish to buy by turning to the stockist codes. If you know the name of the wine you want to buy, use the alphabetical index. If the price is your motivation, refer to the invaluable price guide index; red and white wines under £5, sparkling wines under £12 and Champagne under £16. Happy hunting!

FRANCE

In response to increasing competition from New World wine producing regions, a paradigm shift in wine producing thinking is sweeping the country. New generation winemakers are introducing modern techniques to improve overall quality without compromising the integrity and style of centuries old traditions. While the top Burgundies and Champagnes continue to set the benchmark for the wine world, the lustre of lesser known varieties and styles are really beginning to shine. Enjoy the journey.

FRANCE • ALSACE • SWEET

Wine	Description	Price	Stockists	Award
Riesling Altenberg de Bergheim Grand Cru Vendages Tardives 1990, Charles Koehly et Fils Alsace	*Intense honeyed apple fruit flowing through to the palate with a delicate octane aftertaste. Twangy!*	**£18.00**	HWL	S
Tokay Pinot Gris Rotenberg Vendange Tardive 1996, Domaine Zind Humbrecht Alsace	*Honeyed nose full of floral nector and sweet apricots, vibrant structural acidity sings to the mouth.*	**£23.30**	ABY DBY GON	S
Cuvee Caroline Tokay Pinot Gris Vendange Tardive 1997, Kuentz-Bas Alsace	*Exotic pineapple fruit on the nose, fresh and lively with good acidity and structure.*	**£25.00**	UNS WBU JEH BBR WSO PNA	B
Furstentum Gewürztraminer Selection de Grains Nobles 1994, Domaine Weinbach Faller Alsace	*A remarkably hedonistic blend of honeyed fruit and botrytis infused floral aromas.*	**£63.70**	J&B NYW	S
Tokay Pinot Gris Vendanges Tardives 1995, Domaine Weinbach Faller Alsace	*Excellent balance of rich fresh fruit and acidity with a lingering, yet not cloying, sweetness.*	**£81.00**	J&B	B

FRANCE • ALSACE • WHITE

Wine	Description	Price	Stockists	Award
DOMAINE MATERNE HAEGELIN TOKAY PINOT GRIS 1997, DOMAINE MATERNE HAEGELIN Alsace	*Limey fresh fruit salad with a hint of spice on the nose before excellent acidity and length.*	**£7.60**	VLW ABY MWW	S
CAVE DE TURCKHEIM HEIMBOURG RIESLING 1996, CAVE VINICOLE DE TURCKHEIM Alsace	*Deep nose with hints of apple and a touch of gooseberry. Good long finish with fine balance.*	**£8.00**	DBY BPW	B
CAVE DE TURCKHEIM VIEILLES VIGNES GEWÜRZTRAMINER 1997, CAVE VINICOLE DE TURCKHEIM Alsace	*An exotic, aromatic and spicey nose leads to an oily, peachy palate with a rich mineral vein.*	**£8.00**	BPW	S
DOMAINES SCHLUMBERGER PINOT BLANC 1997, DOMAINES SCHLUMBERGER Alsace	*Off dry style with fairly intense fruit acid to boot and a touch of honey to finish.*	**£8.00**	MMD	B
DOMAINE GRUSS ET FILS RIESLING LES PRÉLATS 1997, DOMAINE GRUSS ET FILS Alsace	*Nuances of turkish delight in this wine. Well textured with residual sweetness and a very long spicey palate.*	**£8.30**	3DW	B
KLEVENER DE HELIGENSTEIN RESERVE 1998, JEAN-LOUIS & NOELLE BACHERT Alsace	*Lemon citrus fruit characters with a creamy palate and perfectly balanced palate oozing with luscious fruit.*	**£8.40**	ABY	S
GUSTAVE LORENTZ RESERVE GEWÜRZTRAMINER 1997, GUSTAVE LORENTZ Alsace	*Sweet fruit on the nose with a good dose of spice, some pineapple fruit and a dry finish.*	**£8.50**	TRO FTH	B

Wine	Description	Price	Stockists	Award
KUENTZ-BAS CUVEE TRADITION GEWÜRZTRAMINER 1998, KUENTZ-BAS Alsace	*Almighty spiced peach aromas followed by light and subtle fruit and a big burst of acidity to mop up.*	**£9.00**	UNS WBU JEH BBR PNA	B
KUENTZ-BAS CUVEE TRADITION TOKAY PINOT GRIS 1998, KUENTZ-BAS Alsace	*Attractive floral, slatey aromas, full bodied fruit brimming with citrus characters and fabulously long.*	**£9.00**	UNS WBU JEH PNA	B
FRANÇOIS BAUR HERRENWEG GEWÜRZTRAMINER 1996, VIGNOBLES FRANÇOIS BAUR Alsace	*Bales of hay and straw with touches of residual sugar on the palate and refreshing acidity.*	**£9.40**	3DW	B
DOMAINES SCHLUMBERGER RIESLING SAERING GRAND CRU 1997, DOMAINES SCHLUMBERGER Alsace	*Fragrant spice aromas, with a well defined palate offering good acidity and excellent length.*	**£9.50**	CAC MMD	B
CAVE DE TURCKHEIM RIESLING BRAND GRAND CRU 1997, CAVE VINICOLE DE TURCKHEIM Alsace	*Blossoming florals and zesty limes rip through to the cutting acidity. Astoundingly complex.*	**£9.60**	GSH AMW BPW	S
GEWÜRZTRAMINER FURSTENTUM GRAND CRU 1996, KIENTZHEIM-KAYSERSBERG Alsace	*A funky aromatic nose with crisp acidity, sappy fruit flavours and a spicey aftertaste.*	**£10.00**	BDR ABY	B
GEWÜRZTRAMINER GLOECKELBERG GRAND CRU 1996, CHARLES KOEHLY ET FILS Alsace	*An inviting herbaceous nose, excellent sweet fruit and matching acidity with some residual sugar.*	**£11.00**	SVT HWL	B
DOMAINE OSTERTAG RIESLING HEISSENBERG 1996, DOMAINE OSTERTAG Alsace	*Pale yellow tinges, soft style riesling with hints of development. Savoury and refreshing with a stonefruit palate.*	**£11.10**	M&V	S

Domaine Zind Humbrecht Pinot d'Alsace 1997, Domaine Zind Humbrecht Alsace	*Warm spiced aromas mingled with nutty characters all brought together on a broad soft fruit palate.*	**£11.70**	RBS ABY WRC BUP DBY	B
Wunsch et Mann Gewürztraminer Hengst Grand Cru 1996, Wunsch et Mann Alsace	*A viscous chewy mouthfeel complimented by luscious ripe fruit flavours and a stylish finish. Well mannered acidity.*	**£11.80**	MKV	S
Wunsch et Mann Riesling Hengst Grand Cru 1996, Wunsch et Mann Alsace	*Hints of minerals entwined with subdued fruit on the nose, richly palated and dry in style.*	**£11.80**	MKV	S
Wintzenheim Gewürztraminer 1997, Domaine Zind Humbrecht Alsace	*A powerful aromatic style showing intense aromas of lime and mineral with a richly textured river pebble mouthfeel.*	**£12.80**	ABY WRC GON DBY	G
Domaines Schlumberger Riesling Kesler Grand Cru 1997, Domaines Schlumberger Alsace	*Complex spices and green fruits. A rich yet clean palate with well-balanced fresh acidity.*	**£13.00**	MMD	S
Domaines Schlumberger Les Prince Abbés Pinot Gris 1996, Domaines Schlumberger Alsace	*Pleasant petal and lychee flavours with a groovy oily feel and a dry, spicey palate.*	**£13.40**	MMD NIC JNW	B
Gewürztraminer Hengst Grand Cru 1997, Domaine Zind Humbrecht Alsace	*A maturing subtle oak nose with well integrated, rich, crisp fruit sauteed in gentle spices.*	**£13.60**	ABY GON DBY	S
Herrenweg de Turckheim Gewürztraminer 1997, Domaine Zind Humbrecht Alsace	*An incredible pineappley nose with rich appley flavours topped with cinnamon and spice showing exceptional length.*	**£15.60**	ABY	S

Wine	Description	Price	Stockists	Award
Paul Blanck Riesling Schlossberg Grand Cru 1996, Domaine Paul Blanck Alsace	*Peachy floral fruit with a slightly waxy texture of tropicals on the palate and finishing with frisky acidity.*	**£17.00**	ADN JBF	B
Kientzheim-Kaysersberg Riesling Schlossberg Grand Cru 1996, Kientzheim-Kaysersberg Alsace	*Restrained youthful nose with a light grapey fruitiness and fresh acidic backbone. Finishing strongly with great length.*	**£19.20**	ABY	B
Leon Beyer Comtes d'Eguisheim Gewürztraminer 1990, Leon Beyer Alsace	*A spicey and aromatic nose, rich with toasty notes offering a palate of perfectly balanced acidity.*	**£21.00**	AVB HOH	B
Domaine Zind Humbrecht Pinot Gris Clos Windsbuhl 1996, Domaine Zind Humbrecht Alsace	*Full bodied fruit with honeyed tones on the nose, good structure and mouth watering acidity.*	**£21.40**	VLW JNW GON DBY ABY	S
Gerwürztraminer Goldert Grand Cru 1997, Domaine Zind Humbrecht Alsace	*A nose of rich mineral and stone fruit characters blends harmoniously on a spicey, viscous palate.*	**£21.70**	ABY DBY	G
Domaine Zind Humbrecht Heimbourg Gewürztraminer 1997, Domaine Zind Humbrecht Alsace	*Bags of spicy flavours vaporise from a fruit laden nose with great follow-on to a luscious, viscous palate.*	**£21.70**	GON DBY ABY	S
Domaine Zind Humbrecht Clos Jebsal Pinot Gris 1996, Domaine Zind Humbrecht Alsace	*Full bodied ripe fruit characters on the nose and palate, balanced acidity and excellent length.*	**£22.10**	VLW WRC ABY DBY	B
Domaine Zind Humbrecht Riesling Brand Grand Cru 1997, Domaine Zind Humbrecht Alsace	*Citrus and floral nose showing a round complexity of talc, minerals and brilliant texture.*	**£23.60**	VLW DBY ABY	S

FRANCE • ALSACE • WHITE

Pinot Gris Clos St Urbain Grand Cru Rangen de Thann 1996, Domaine Zind Humbrecht Alsace	*Funky, rich and powerful. Lush peach fruit mixes with stream lined acidity resulting in excellent structure.*	**£27.90**	ABY GON DBY	G TROPHY WINE

FRANCE • BEAUJOLAIS

Domaine Manoir du Carra Cuvée Non Filtre 1998, Jean-Noel Sambardier Beaujolais	*Lovely, banana toffee nose ushers in a rich honeyed, plum fruit base with great mouthfeel and length.*	**£6.50**	FCA	B
Brouilly Lionel Bertrand 1998, Eventail Beaujolais	*Big spicey aromas and flavours with mint and creamy vegetal notes from this finely tuned wine.*	**£7.00**	EPO PLB	B
Fleurie Vieilles Vignes Domaine de la Madone 1997, Jean-Marc Desprès Beaujolais	*Sweet fruit with warm strawberries and a pleasant, zingy, palate structure lead to a clean fruit acid finish.*	**£7.00**	3DW	S
Juliénas Paul Boutinot 1997, Paul Boutinot Beaujolais	*A lightly perfumed nose with a touch of herb leading to a red fruit palate with a light mineral vein.*	**£7.00**	BPW NRW HOL	S
Morgon Paul Boutinot 1998, Paul Boutinot Beaujolais	*Sweet jammy fruit with gentle tannins, matching soft acidity and a succulent finish.*	**£7.00**	BPW	B
Moulin Á Vent Georges Duboeuf 1996, Georges Duboeuf Beaujolais	*Concentrated fruit nose with some tannin, leads to a full palate of damsons and plums.*	**£7.70**	Widely Available	B

Wine	Description	Price	Stockists	Award
MOULIN À VENT CHRISTIAN FLAMY 1998, EVENTAIL Beaujolais	*Lightly spiced fruit flavours and showing some savoury gamey notes. Lovely tannin and fruit acid balance.*	**£8.00**	PLB	S
MORGON CÔTE DU PY 1998, EVENTAIL Beaujolais	*Ripe raspberries and summer fruits on a light fruit structured palate with well defined tannins and finishing clean.*	**£8.00**	PLB	S
FLEURIE DOMAINE DE MONTGENAS 1998, EVENTAIL Beaujolais	*Soft red fruits sing with herbal notes in this gentle easy drinking style with neat balancing acidity.*	**£8.00**	HOL DIR PLB	B
JULIÉNAS EVENTAIL "LES ENVAUX" 1998, EVENTAIL Beaujolais	*Lovely cherries on the nose give rise to a fresh palate of crushed red fruit.*	**£8.00**	CHH PLB	B
DOMAINE BROUILLY J TATOUX 1998, EVENTAIL Beaujolais	*A classic style, showing fresh summer fruit characters with herbal undertones which flow onto the palate with grace.*	**£8.00**	WOC PLB	G TROPHY WINE
FLEURIE GRILLE MIDI 1998, ANDRE VAISSE Beaujolais	*Luscious flavours of ripe cherries, strawberries and raspberries. A soft, smoothly balanced finish.*	**£8.00**	PLB	B
MOULIN À VENT JEAN BRIDAY 1998, EVENTAIL Beaujolais	*Fabulous nose with ripe strawberry fruit and gooseberry aromas precede a chunky mouthfeel.*	**£8.00**	DIR PLB	S
JULIÉNAS LES FOUILLOUSES 1998, EVENTAIL Beaujolais	*Excellent rich fruit on this wine backed by a perfumed elegance on a fine tannin palate.*	**£8.00**	VWC EPO WRC PLB	B

Wine	Description	Price	Stockists	Award
Château des Deduits 1998, Georges Duboeuf Beaujolais	*Strawberry cheesecake on the nose with a bright cherry palate of lovely balance and length.*	**£8.20**	JNW BWC WTS	B
Fleurie Château des Labourons 1997, Château des Labourons Beaujolais	*Lovely fresh red fruits lead to a sensual palate with soft tannin highlights.*	**£8.90**	ROG ENO	B
Beaujolais Morgon Cuvée Jeanne 1997, Domaine Calot Beaujolais	*An orchestra of berries and the strawberry is conducting. Great clean final sonata ends the virtuoso performance.*	**£9.20**	ABA	S
Saint Amour Domaine Des Billards 1998, E Loron & Fils Beaujolais	*Like rose water filtered through a strawberry coulis served on a camomile lawn on a summers day. Devine.*	**£9.40**	NIC	S
Moulin à Vent Chateau des Jacques 1997, Louis Jadot Beaujolais	*Light and zesty with a sweet berry palate and a gentle caressing finish.*	**£10.00**	WTS HMA	B
Moulin à Vent Clos des Rochegres 1996, Louis Jadot Beaujolais	*Lovely strawberry characters with minty notes flowing on to a mouthfilling palate of light summer fruits.*	**£10.00**	WIM HMA	B

FRANCE • BORDEAUX • RED

Wine	Description	Price	Stockists	Award
Safeway Claret NV, Vinyrama Bordeaux	*A big pepper nose with berry tones leads to a medium weight palate with a pleasant finish.*	**£3.80**	SAF	S

Wine	Tasting note	Price	Stockists	Award
TESCO RESERVE CLARET 1997, YVON MAU Bordeaux	*Full rounded nose, spicy wood and bitter fruit flavour, clean on palate. Chocolatey finish.*	**£4.30**	TOS	B
L'ABBÉ DE BREYAC CÔTES DU MARMANDAIS 1998, YVON MAU Bordeaux	*Fresh slightly confected nose with a pleasant fruity palate. Light style with some oak and firm tannins.*	**£4.50**	STG YVM	B
DOMAINE JEUNE VDP DU GARD 1998, PAUL JEUNE Bordeaux	*A superb wine with tobacco box notes on the nose with a silky, figgy palate of currants and berries.*	**£4.50**	M&S MIS	S
CHÂTEAU LA CROIX DAVIDS 1997, ANNIE ET DIDIER MENEUVRIER Bordeaux	*Young spiced fruit on nose introduce a good grip of fresh tannins and herbaceous fruit, showing potential.*	**£5.50**	HMS	S
DOMAINE LA TUQUE BEL AIR CHÂTEAU DE CASTILLON LAVAU 1997, JEAN LAVAU Bordeaux	*Sweet, slightly cooked berries on nose. Ripe flavours with green tannin drying on finish.*	**£5.50**	SMF	B
CHÂTEAU DUCLA BORDEAUX ROUGE 1998, YVON MAU Bordeaux	*Deep purple in colour the nose shows sweet fruits while the palate is full bodied.*	**£6.00**	UNS SOH YVM	B
KRESSMANN MONOPOLE 1997, KRESSMANN Bordeaux	*Earthy, cedar character on nose. Classically structured, with firm tannins and medium body. Concentrated and long.*	**£6.00**	DOU	B
YVECOURT PREMIUM 1997, YVON MAU Bordeaux	*A striking oaky nose overlays a veil of fruit and oily seed tannins on the palate.*	**£6.00**	YVM	B

Wine	Description	Price	Stockists	Award
Yvon Mau Premius 1996, Yvon Mau Bordeaux	*Aromas of plummy fruits and hints of herbs. Firm tannins with nice balancing acidity and great length.*	**£6.00**	ODD SAF UNS STG YVM	S
Cordier Collection Privée Médoc 1997, Cordier Bordeaux	*Restrained fruit aromas lead elegantly on to a palate of fruity tannins and lovely texture.*	**£6.80**	TOS VDO	B
Domaine du Grand Mayne Cuvée Millennium NV, Andrew Gordon Bordeaux	*Spicey and steely with a very impressive structure offering terrific length with a lovely acid tail.*	**£7.00**	WSA	S
Numéro 1 de Dourthe 1997, Dourthe Bordeaux	*Understated cedar nose showing some development and notes of vanilla and spice. Drying tannins on the palate.*	**£7.00**	DOU	B
Château de Seguin 1997, Château de Seguin Bordeaux	*Blackcurrant nose with creamy, red pepper tones. Good fruit weight and balance with a fine tannin structure.*	**£8.20**	BDR	S
Chateau Plaisance 1996, Bordeaux	*A lifted floral nose introduces a pleasant fruit driven wine with nicely integrated lively acid.*	**£8.90**	SMF	B
Safeway Margaux 1995, Henry Lurton Bordeaux	*A mature wine showing some developed fruit cake characters with a touch of herb and neat finish.*	**£9.00**	SAF	B
Château Brisson 1997, Château Brisson Bordeaux	*Smoky, toasty oak on the nose. Ripe, cassis fruit and rich, chocolatey tones on a smooth palate.*	**£9.50**	BDR	S

Wine	Description	Price	Stockists	Award
CHÂTEAU HAUT BAGES MONPELOU 1995, BORIE MANOUX Bordeaux	*Woody, barky, slightly green nose. Elegant and restrained and sitting well on the palate.*	**£9.50**	CDT WAV	B
CHÂTEAU VILLA BEL AIR GRAVES 1996, COMPAGNIE MEDOCAINE DES GRANDS CRUS Bordeaux	*Perfumed nose with rhubarb and runner bean notes. A soft, pleasant structure gives rise to a clean finish.*	**£9.50**	ABY	B
CHÂTEAU LYONNAT 1996, D MICHADE ET FILS Bordeaux	*Herbaceous and minty with underlying berry fruits. Soft and rich fruit in the mouth.*	**£9.70**	CTH RBS	B
M&S EXCLUSIVE MARGAUX 1996, HENRI LURTON Bordeaux	*Mellow fruits lay in the luxury of gentle oak with dusty tannins while generous length completes the pleasant picture.*	**£10.50**	M&S	B
MOULIS CHÂTEAU LA GARRICQ 1995, CHATEAU GARRICQ Bordeaux	*Smoky nose with truffle aromas. Sweet, rich fruit intensity on palate. Smooth and well balanced.*	**£10.50**	GGW P&R M&V	B
CHÂTEAU PALOUMEY 1995, CHÂTEAU PALOUMEY Bordeaux	*Attractive young tannic nose. Stewed blackcurrant fruit palate with green watery tannins. Good without great distinction.*	**£10.70**	RBS NYW SEL SHB M&V	B
CHÂTEAU PALOUMEY 1996, CHÂTEAU PALOUMEY Bordeaux	*Good intensity of blackcurrant aromas with truffly oak. Complex cherry fruit with lovely tannins, finishing well.*	**£11.00**	RBS NYW M&V	S
CHÂTEAU BEAU SITE 1995, BORIE MANOUX Bordeaux	*Aromatic freshly cut coconut nose with a herbal touch leading to a full bodied palate.*	**£11.80**	ABY CDT WAV	B

Wine	Description	Price	Stockists	Medal
Château Cadillac-Branda 1997, Jean-Jacques Lesgourues Bordeaux	*Sweet, aromatic fruit bouquet. Palate of soft blackcurrant, herbaceous with an elegant mid-palate. Strong oak finish.*	£12.00	PAT	B
Château Liversan Cru Bourgeois 1996, Château Liversan Bordeaux	*Cedar, licorice and peppers lead to a palate of ripe fruits with some herb supported by firm tannins.*	£12.60	NIC	S
Château Clement Pichon 1996, Clement Faya Bordeaux	*Cinnamon and spice, the fruit rich palate offers fine grained tannins with good length.*	£15.50	BDR TOS	S
Château Haut Beauséjour 1996, Louis Roederer Bordeaux	*Blackcurrant pastille nose, balanced fruit, tannin and acid with lovely weight and length.*	£15.60	QWW MMD	B
Château la Commanderie Saint Emilion 1997, D Cordier Bordeaux	*Firm, smoky nose with bright berry tones. Soft, easy fruit palate, nice acidity and good finish.*	£15.60	JNW MMD	B
Château Lilian Ladouys 1996, Lilian & Christian Thieblot Bordeaux	*This is an elegant wine with fine grained tannins, a minerally palate and good length.*	£17.00	BDR TOS	S
Château de Pez 1996, Louis Roederer Bordeaux	*Fine, youthful colour with upfront fruit and a hint of spice on the nose. Nice flow onto the persistent palate.*	£18.00	MMD JNW	B
Frank Phélan 1996, Chateau Phelan Segur Bordeaux	*A beautifully balanced wine offering layers of fruit complexity, showing great sophistication and finesse.*	£18.10	VLW NIC	G

Wine	Description	Price	Stockists	Award
Château Jordi 1989, Guy Coubris Bordeaux	*Mature menthol and violet aromas with luscious tannin structure and a fine finish.*	**£18.40**	GSH JNW DLA	S
Château Canuet 1996, Château Canuet Bordeaux	*Deep colour offering an array of berry fruit and spice characters. A truly complex and elegant wine .*	**£19.90**	ABY	G
Château Trotte Vieille 1995, Borie Manoux Bordeaux	*Fascinating wine offering cigar box and black berry characters. Great structure and finesse, an elegant wine.*	**£20.50**	CDT WAV	G
Château Villemaurine 1996, Robert Giraud Bordeaux	*A lighter style with fine fruit character, mid weight palate of good length. Elegance.*	**£21.00**	HOH AVB	B
La Roseraie de Gruaud Larose St Julien 1994, D Cordier Bordeaux	*Curious off-beat nose with a light and easy palate with good length. Drinking well now.*	**£22.70**	MMD	B
Château Maucaillou 1995, Domaine du Château Moucailleu Bordeaux	*Nice depth of character here with good fruit tannins and length. Will travel well.*	**£23.00**	TOS	B
Château Grand Mayne 1994, JP Nony Bordeaux	*Lovely plum nose with spice. Soft, fruity palate. Balanced tannin and high acidity.*	**£25.00**	BDR WTS	S
Château Haut Marbuzet Cru Bourgeois St Estèphe 1997, H Duboscq Bordeaux	*Restrained fruit yet complex and intriguing with underlying layers of flavours waiting to be teased out.*	**£28.00**	WCR NIC BPW VWC	S

Wine	Description	Price	Stockists	Award
TROPLONG MONDOT 1995, Bordeaux	*Rose petals, minerals, rich jams and a hint of beefiness precede a silky tannin palate with structural length.*	**£43.50**	WCR J&B	G
CHÂTEAU PALMER 1990, SC DU CHÂTEAU PALMER Bordeaux	*Lifted violets and rich, sweet fruit, elegant, multidimensional with lithe structure, finishing long with a silky tail.*	**£44.60**	JNW CAC	G
CHÂTEAU PICHON LONGUEVILLE COMTESSA DE LALANDE 1990, Bordeaux	*Lovely richness and finesse. Fine, velvet tannins, superb texture and balance leave a lasting impression.*	**£98.00**	RBS	S
LE DÔME 1996, JCP MALTUS Bordeaux	*Tight, displaying a gently herbal, spice and subdued fruit nose interspersed with tasty oak with terrific length.*	**£117.50**	J&B	S

FRANCE • BORDEAUX • SWEET

Wine	Description	Price	Stockists	Award
CHÂTEAU ST LES LARMES DE CATHERINE CADILLAC 1997, CHÂTEAU ST CATHERINE Bordeaux	*Wisps of honey with rich apricot flavours, wonderful round texture with a clean long finish.*	**£9.00**	VEN	B
CHÂTEAU LIOT BARSAC SAUTERNES 1996, CHÂTEAU LIOT Bordeaux	*Floral aromatics, lychee and dried fruit on the palate, herbaceous clean acidity with a good intergrated nuttiness.*	**£9.80**	WTS	S
CHÂTEAU FILHOT 1989, CHÂTEAU FILHOT Bordeaux	*A hint of marmalade on the nose, a long finish and an excellent partner for a candle lit dinner.*	**£23.80**	JNW WTS	S

Château Coutet 1996, Baron Philippe de Rothschild Bordeaux	*Complexitities of fat, flowery, vanillin oak on the nose with fine follow through to a deliciously long palate.*	**£31.50**	J&B	G
Château Coutet 1995, Baron Philippe de Rothschild Bordeaux	*This wine is one for the cellars with rich boneyed tones and ripe fruit balance.*	**£33.20**	WDM J&B VWC LLV UNS THS C&H PRG	S
Château Lafaurie Peyraguey Sauternes 1995, Ets D Cordier Bordeaux	*Fresh, sweet fruit with a lovely depth of character and elegant touches of apricot and marmalade fruit.*	**£33.50**	MMD	G

FRANCE • BORDEAUX • WHITE

Four Corners Bordeaux Sauvignon Blanc 1998, Four Corners Consultancy Bordeaux	*Tropical fruit and citrus characters leading to a soft palate with zippy acidity and a dry closing.*	**£4.50**	TOS EHL	B
1725 Réserve du Fondateur Blanc 1998, Barton & Guestier Bordeaux	*Nice nutty biscuits with a green bean edge, chalky acidity balances well, finishing long.*	**£5.00**	SEA	B
Ginestet Barrique Fermented Sauvignon Semillon 1996, Ginestet Bordeaux	*Ripe, fragrant, fruit aromas, underlying minerallines and backseat oak finishing cleanly.*	**£5.00**	MRN IWS	B
Domaine du Grand Mayne Late Picked Sauvignon 1998, Andrew Gordon Bordeaux	*Ripe tropical fruit matched with light buttery oak offers a clean nicely balanced palate.*	**£5.20**	WSA	B

FRANCE • BORDEAUX • WHITE

Domaine du Seuil Bordeaux Blanc 1997, Château du Seuil Bordeaux	*Pronounced elderflower and citrus fruit characters blended with a touch of oak on the palate.*	**£6.00**	CDS	(B)
Château Timberlay Cuvee Prestige 1998, Robert Giraud Bordeaux	*An array of root vegetables here, zippy acidity, quite long and intense with a nut husk finish.*	**£6.90**	WCR AVB HOH	(B)
Château du Seuil 1996, Château du Seuil Bordeaux	*Lush, ripe nose offering grassy apricots, lightly oaked with good structure and a clean finish.*	**£8.80**	FRT GSJ	(B)
Château du Seuil 1997, Château du Seuil Bordeaux	*Good aromas of tropical fruit and passionfruit, nice acid structure finishing off with subtle oak.*	**£9.00**	J&B CDS	(B)

FRANCE • BURGUNDY • RED

Hautes Côtes de Nuits 1998, Domaine bertagna Burgundy	*A touch oxidised giving a complex earthy style with strong fruit and good structure.*	**£7.00**	RSS JSM	(B)
Henri La Fontaine Brouilly 1997, Faye & Cie Burgundy	*Ripe berries and mushrooms on the nose before a silky palate with a clean, long finish.*	**£7.20**	MHV	(B)
Côtes de Beaune 1996, Jean-Michel Jacob Burgundy	*Plummy jammy nose with long, lean cherry fruit. Good complex style with simple ripe finish.*	**£7.80**	3DW	(B)

Wine	Tasting note	Price	Stockists	Award
Laforêt Bourgogne Rouge 1997, Joseph Drouhin Burgundy	*Slightly closed but managing to show dark ripe plums and cherries. Taut with restrained acid showing much potential.*	**£8.00**	JNW CLA FSW RML MZC	B
Mercurey Premier Cru Sazenay Pillot 1996, Jean-Michel & Laurent Pillot Burgundy	*Fantastic confected plum and stonefruit nose. Good mouthfeel developing into a subtle long palate of pleasant weight.*	**£8.30**	3DW	B
Saint Amour Guy Patissier 1998, Eventail Burgundy	*Delightfully juicy with light berry fruit, onto a palate of seductive warm fruits.*	**£8.50**	SHJ PLB	B
Côte de Nuits-Villages Ropiteau 1996, Ropiteau Freres Burgundy	*Elegant and quite austere on the fore-palate coming together with firm fruit over a light oak finish.*	**£9.00**	CDT WAV	B
Hautes Côtes de Nuits Tastevin 1997, Yves Chaley Burgundy	*Light cherries with hints of farmyardy aromas on a full palate of ripe fruit, soft tannins and sweet acidity.*	**£9.20**	UNS PEC	S
Maranges sur lie Chêne 1996, Domaine Chevrot Burgundy	*Ripe berry fruit on the nose with spicey peppery characters, and a luxurious palate.*	**£9.20**	3DW	S
Mercurey Château de Mercy 1994, Antonin Rodet Burgundy	*Soft and round spicey nose, showing some maturity. Nice fruit balance with firm tannins and acidity.*	**£9.20**	FRT GSJ	B
Mercurey Château de Santenay 1997, Chateau de Santenay Burgundy	*Crisp cherries and complexing earthiness and wild mushrooms meld on the taut palate.*	**£9.30**	ABY	B

FRANCE • BURGUNDY • RED

Wine	Description	Price	Stockists	Award
Beaune Rouge 1997, Vaucher Burgundy	*Beautiful cherry aromas. Fine texture and integration with a burst of fruit on the back palate.*	**£10.00**	SMF	S
Château de Marsannay Rouge 1997, Noémie Vernaux Burgundy	*A flirty wine with warm fruity tannins and burning scents of tar. Weighty and warm.*	**£10.00**	SGL NAD	B
Mercurey Domaine Marguerite Carillon 1997, Domaine Marguerite Carillon Burgundy	*Lovely vegetal and savoury characters on the nose, with a velvety mouthfeel before a very silky finish.*	**£10.00**	SPR BKI	S
Santenay Premier Cru Clos Rousseau Château de la Charrière 1996, Yves Girardin Burgundy	*Up for it oak and cherry fruit characters on the nose, complex fruit on the palate and good length.*	**£10.40**	LCD	S
Beaune Premier Cru Les Avaux 1997, Jean-Michel Jacob Burgundy	*Aromatic cedary nose, dry fruits on the palate with upfront tannins and a long fruit finish.*	**£10.80**	3DW	B
Auxey-Duresses 1995, Louis Jadot Burgundy	*Herby black cherry aromas come to the fore, with just a sprinkling of black pepper.*	**£11.00**	WRC MAR TSR VWEBUP HMA	B
Auxey-Duresses 1996, Louis Jadot Burgundy	*Gentle sweet strawberry nose, with red currants and oak flavours. Tannins are softening so drink now.*	**£11.00**	TSR VWE WRC BUP HMA	B
Fixin 1996, Maison Louis Jadot Burgundy	*Cherries on the nose, delicious balanced fruit with integrated fine tannins and long finish.*	**£11.70**	WRC MAR THS TSR VWE BUP HMA	S

Wine	Description	Price	Stockists	Award
MERCUREY EMILE VOARICK 1997, DOMAINE PICARD Burgundy	*Violet red, mushroomy vegetal nose, touch sweet with great bite and intensity finishing well with good balance.*	**£12.40**	PLB	B
BEAUNE PREMIER CRU CLOS DU ROI CHÂTEAU DE SANTENAY 1997, PHILLEPE LE HARDI Burgundy	*Big cherry ripe fruit nose, a little confected with good flavours and length on the finish.*	**£12.80**	ABY	B
ALOXE-CORTON LES BRUNETTES ET PLANCHOTS 1997, CHÂTEAU DE SANTENAY Burgundy	*A moderate use of oak adds richness and finesse to an already full, fruity palate.*	**£13.30**	ABY	B
CHOREY-LÈS-BEAUNE 1997, DOMAINE MAILLARD Burgundy	*A floral and berry start before a textured palate of impressive length and depth. Very enjoyable.*	**£14.50**	NIC ENO	S
VOLNAY TAILLEPIEDS 1996, DOMAINE CARRE-COURBIN Burgundy	*Full of summer fruits tinted with violets. Rounded by well structured, soft tannins.*	**£15.50**	SAN BEN M&V	B
POMMARD PREMIER CRU BOUCHEROTTES 1996, DOMAINE FIEF DE MONTJEU Burgundy	*Dark berry fruit with smoky bacon characters on the nose, full palate of complex fruit with gamey tones.*	**£17.00**	SAF	S
VOUGEOT "LE VILLAGE" CLOS DU PRIEURE 1997, DOMAINE PONNELLE Burgundy	*Rich fruit aromas with meaty characters on the nose, smooth palate with full-bodied fruit.*	**£17.30**	BAB HAY	S
BEAUNE PREMIER CRU 1996, LOUIS JADOT Burgundy	*Pungent, slightly leathery oak with masses of spicey fruit aromas. Soft and spicy blackcurrant flavours.*	**£18.00**	TOS HMA	B

FRANCE • BURGUNDY • RED

Wine	Description	Price	Stockists	Award
Nuits-St-Georges Bouchard 1997, Bouchard Pére et Fils Burgundy	*Raspberry and strawberry nose with subtle hints of mushroom and forest floor. Fine tannin balance and good length.*	**£18.00**	H&B	S
Nuits-St-Georges Domaine de l'Arlot de Smet 1996, Jean Pierre de Smet Burgundy	*Light, florally perfumed fruit on the nose. Well reflected in the well structured, rounded palate.*	**£18.40**	L&W ABY WRC CAC	B
Aloxe-Corton 1996, Capitain-Gagnerot Burgundy	*Beetroot and ripe berry fruit on the nose. Quite complex palate with ripe fruit characters.*	**£18.50**	CAC CCW	S
Pommard Premier Cru Les Arvelets 1996, Domaine Parent Burgundy	*Slight prickle on the tongue gives way to rich orange peel and concentrated dark cherries.*	**£19.00**	H&D ESL CHN	B
Beaune Premier Cru les Cents Vignes 1996, Château de Meursault Burgundy	*Some slightly oxidised, gamey fruit adds to the luxurious feel of this full-bodied wine.*	**£20.00**	PAT	B
Volnay Premier Cru Clos des Chênes 1996, Château de Meursault Burgundy	*Personable wine offering idiosyncratic fragrances of violets and porcini mushrooms before a velvet textured palate.*	**£20.00**	PAT	S
Vougeot Premier Cru Clos de La Perrière 1997, Domaine Bertagna Burgundy	*Cherry red youthful appearance, reflecting the vibrant cherry fruit flavours on a light, fresh palate.*	**£22.00**	RSS	B
Nuits-St-Georges Premier Cru LesVignes Rondes 1992, Domaine Daniel Rion & Fils Burgundy	*Mature, slightly animal nose. Crisp palate remains herbacious, with developed fruit and oak flavours.*	**£23.80**	M&V CFN DNL SWN	B

Wine	Description	Price	Stockists	Award
Volnay Premier Cru Les Chevrets 1996, Jean-Marc Boillot Burgundy	*Cherry notes singing in concert with sauteed mushrooms. Silky tannin structure and lovely fruit acidity to balance.*	**£23.80**	CAC WTS	S
Pommard Premier Cru Rugiens-Bas Aleth le Royer-Girardin 1996, Aleth le Royer-Girardin Burgundy	*Seductive, just roasted lamb drizzled in juniper berry jus with shitake slipperiness and a spiralling peacock tail. Words fail.*	**£23.90**	L&W	G TROPHY WINE
Nuits-St-Georges Premier Cru Clos des Forets St Georges de Smet 1996, Jean Pierre de Smet Burgundy	*Inviting cherry fruits with a hint of old barnyard and slightly vegetal aromas precede a fine tannin palate.*	**£24.60**	L&W WRC BUP CAC ABY	S
Nuits-St-Georges Premier Cru Clos l'Arlot de Smet 1996, Jean Pierre de Smet Burgundy	*Luscious restrained fruit mingles with a complex array earthy of aromas and velvety persistent structure.*	**£24.90**	L&W CAC ABY	B
Mazis-Chambertin Château les Mazis 1996, Michel Tortochot Burgundy	*Savouries and strawberries with a hint of herbal characters on the nose, intense fruit and a firm tannin palate.*	**£31.10**	ABY	S
Charmes-Chambertin 1987, Vallet Frères Burgundy	*Lovely developed characters of mushrooms and fresh hay lead to a full-bodied cherry pie palate.*	**£39.50**	GSH BPW BOO	B

Pinpoint who sells the wine you wish to buy by turning to the stockist codes. If you know the name of the wine you want to buy, use the alphabetical index. If the price is your motivation, refer to the invaluable price guide index; red and white wines under £5, sparkling wines under £12 and champagne under £16. Happy hunting!

FRANCE • BURGUNDY • ROSÉ

Château de Marsannay Rosé 1998, Noémie Vernaux Burgundy	*An elegant wine showing delicate mineral fruit characters and good balance.*	**£9.20**	NIC SGL NAD	B

FRANCE • BURGUNDY • SPARKLING

Safeway Cremant de Bourgogne Brut NV, Lugny Burgundy	*Cheesy, yeasty aromas on a complex, developed palate with a refreshingly tart finish.*	**£7.00**	SAF	B

FRANCE • BURGUNDY • WHITE

Tesco Mâcon Blanc Villages 1998, Cave de Vire Burgundy	*Lots of ripe tropical fruit with good palate weight and a slightly bitter finish.*	**£5.00**	TOS	B
Tesco White Burgundy Cave de Vire 1998, Cave De Vire Burgundy	*A lovely lemon dominance reigns over an orchestra of light apple and peach scents.*	**£5.00**	TOS	B
Vaucher Mâcon Blanc Villages 1997, Vaucher Pere Et Fils Burgundy	*A delicate nose of stone fruits with a minerally palate and clean fruit acid finish.*	**£6.50**	T&T	B

Wine	Description	Price	Stockists	Award
DOMAINE TOUZOT CHARDONNAY 1997, DOMAINE TOUZOT Burgundy	*Ripe grapefruit with nicely integrated oak and moderate acid make for a well balanced wine.*	**£7.00**	BDR	B
BOURGOGNE BLANC CÔTE CHALONNAISE 1997, LES VIGNERONS DE BUXY Burgundy	*Rich tropical fruits are covered in a veil of mineral and earth characters leading to a fine finish.*	**£7.50**	NAD SGL	B
SOMERFIELD CHABLIS 1997, LA CHABLISIENNE Burgundy	*A clean apple and melon nose gives way to a tight, minerally palate with good mouthfeel and length.*	**£7.50**	SMF	S
BOURGOGNE CHARDONNAY 1996, LOUIS JADOT Burgundy	*Delicate mineral style with mild tropical aromas and a zesty citrus fruit palate with subtle oak characters.*	**£8.40**	WCR WRC BUP MAR THS TSR VWE VWC HMA	B
BERRYS' CHABLIS 1997, WILLIAM FÉVRE Burgundy	*A full fruit nose with a touch of oak and hint of butterscotch with herbs on the palate.*	**£9.30**	BBR	B
CHABLIS PREMIER CRU CÔTE DE JOUAN 1997, JEAN-MARC BROCARD Burgundy	*Firm,clear cut varietal flavours with an interesting marzipan vein. Impressive length.*	**£10.00**	JSM JBF	B
SAINT-VÉRAND 1997, DOMAINE CORSIN Burgundy	*Creamy melon characters with nuances of lemon and lime preceed a crisp, tart apple finish.*	**£10.20**	RBS SGL NAD SCA CTL	B
CHABLIS PREMIER CRU BEAUREGARD JEAN-MARC BROCARD 1997, JEAN-MARC BROCARD Burgundy	*A superbly balanced wine showing a range of fruits including lychee, melon and pineapple.*	**£11.00**	JBF	S

Wine	Description	Price	Stockists	Award
CHABLIS PREMIER CRU 1997, VAUCHER PERE & FILS Burgundy	*A touch of oak on the nose precedes a lime palate with an attractive steely structure.*	**£11.00**	SMF TOS	B
CHABLIS LES VIEILLES VIGNES 1996, LA CHABLISIENNE Burgundy	*Cool climate flavours of apples and stone fruits with notes of creamy citrus characters on a minerally finish.*	**£11.10**	VLW MAR VWE NAD RML SGL	B
CHABLIS PREMIER CRU FOURCHAUME CHATEAU DE MALIGNY 1997, JEAN DURUP Burgundy	*Mealy, leesy, milky aromas introduce a full bodied honey and pear palate.*	**£11.10**	ABY WRC BUP THS	B
CHABLIS DOMAINES 1997, JOSEPH DROUHIN Burgundy	*Restrained, soft apricot and melon nose precede a pleasant palate with some mineral tones.*	**£11.20**	JNW MGN MZC	B
AUXEY-DURESSES 1996, LOUIS JADOT Burgundy	*Subtle lees and yeast notes on the nose. Ripe melon fruits and crisp citrus acidity create lovely balance.*	**£11.30**	WRC BUP MAR THS HMA	S
CHABLIS PREMIER CRU MONTMAINS JEAN-MARC BROCARD 1997, JEAN-MARC BROCARD Burgundy	*A clean wine with nutty, pineapple tones leads to a full bodied, refreshing palate.*	**£11.90**	J&B BWC CAC MVN JBF	B
SAINT-AUBIN 1996, LOUIS JADOT Burgundy	*Aromas of lychees, spice and buttery oak. Full-bodied melon and creamy citrus fruit.*	**£12.50**	HMA UNS	S
CHABLIS PREMIER CRU VAULIGNOT DOMAINE LOUIS MOREAU 1997, DOMAINE LOUIS MOREAU Burgundy	*A light but highly appealing style with mineral and melon forming a complex palate.*	**£12.70**	EUW	B

Wine	Description	Price	Stockists	Award
SANTENAY FRANÇOIS D'ALLAINES 1997, FRANÇOIS D'ALLAINES Burgundy	*Intense dried grass and exotic fruits on the nose with a crisp, clean palate with a mineral bent.*	**£12.70**	M&V BUT	S
CHABLIS PREMIER CRU MONTMAINS DOMAINE GOULLEY 1998, DOMAINE GOULLEY Burgundy	*Some peach and melon on the nose with a light but well structured palate.*	**£13.00**	VRT	B
CHABLIS PREMIER CRU LES VAILLONS 1997, DOMAINE BILLAUD-SIMON Burgundy	*Chalky mineral characters on a crisp and peppery bed of fruit. Interesting wine.*	**£14.30**	NYW ABA	B
ST AUBIN PREMIER CRU EN REMILLY 1996, HUBERT LAMY Burgundy	*A heady nose of intense fruit tones hint at the complexity of the delicious palate that follows.*	**£14.30**	L&W NYW	S
POUILLY FUISSÉ LES BIRBETTES 1997, CHÂTEAU DES RONTETS Burgundy	*Floral and fresh peach aromas with a stony palate well integrated with subtle oak.*	**£15.00**	ENO	B
MARSANNAY LES SAINTS JACQUES 1997, DOMAINE FOUGERAY DE BEAUCLAIR Burgundy	*Inviting cashews and pears flow to the rich palate displaying soft appley acid and chewy texture.*	**£15.00**	HOB CHN	B
CHÂTEAU MEURSAULT 1994, DOMAINE DU CHÂTEAU DE MEURSAULT Burgundy	*Fresh and lively with an intense flavour contributes considerable length of lovely melon and mineral notes.*	**£16.00**	SAF NIC PAT	G
POUILLY-FUISSÉ TÊTE DE CUVÉE 1997, VERGET Burgundy	*Citrus aromas sing in harmony with a cool, oaky nose and cascade onto a long palate .*	**£16.20**	L&W NYW	S

Wine	Tasting note	Price	Stockists	Award
PULIGNY-MONTRACHET LES CHARMES 1997, GERARD CHAVY Burgundy	*Intriguing start of Granny Smith's and vanillan oak flowing to the concentrated, complex , persistent palate.*	**£16.50**	SAF	S
CHABLIS GRAND CRU LES PREUSES DOMAINE SERVIN 1997, DOMAINE SERVIN Burgundy	*Lemon and oak aromas, crisp with a lovely citrus palate of subtle oak and a good lengthy finish.*	**£17.00**	BDR PLB	B
VOUGEOT BLANC CLOS DU PRIEURE 1997, DOMAINE PONNELLE Burgundy	*Cinnamon, toasty oak and cigar box hints on the nose, ripe tropical fruit on palate.*	**£17.50**	BAB HAY	S
CHABLIS GRAND CRU GRENOUILLES 1995, LA CHABLISIENNE Burgundy	*Upfront herb and mineral charcaters cascade onto a luscious fruit palate that is clean and crisp.*	**£18.50**	VLW SAF J&B	S
CHABLIS GRAND CRU VAUDESIRS DOMAINE DES MALANDES 1995, LYNE ET JEAN-BERNARD MARCHIVE Burgundy	*Delicious minerally tones supported by a steely structure and a fine river pebble like texture.*	**£19.00**	ESL HAL CHN	S
CHABLIS GRAND CRU GRENOUILLES 1996, LA CHABLISIENNE Burgundy	*Rich sweet buttery flavours of caramalized bananas meet melon and grapefruit on a long palate.*	**£20.70**	VLW SGL NAD	B
PULIGNY-MONTRACHET 1996, DOMAINE CARILLON Burgundy	*Lovely tropical floral aromas, simple clean slightly aromatic fruit on the palate with moderate acidity.*	**£22.30**	HHF WRC JNW L&W	B
CHABLIS PREMIER CRU FOURCHAUMES 1996, VERGET Burgundy	*Intense mineral and floral nose cascade onto a steely palate supporting restrained, exotic fruits.*	**£22.50**	L&W NYW	G

Wine	Description	Price	Stockists	Award
NUITS-ST-GEORGES PREMIER CRU CLOS DE L'ARLOT 1997, JEAN PIERRE DE SMET Burgundy	*Lovely fruit opening up upon the apple ladened palate with a long and impressive mineral finish.*	**£23.30**	L&W BUP ABY WRC CAC	B
CHABLIS PREMIER CRU LES PREUSES 1996, DOMAINE BILLAUD-SIMON Burgundy	*Creamy with seamless fruit flavours running through the mineral veined palate. Great balance and length.*	**£24.00**	NYW ABA	B
MEURSAULT PREMIER CRU CHÂTEAU DE MEURSAULT 1997, DOMAINE DU CHÂTEAU DE MEURSAULT Burgundy	*Floral, tropical and citrus fruit aromas on a lovely citrus fruit palate with well integrated oak.*	**£25.00**	PAT	B
MEURSAULT-GENEVRIÈRES 1995, JOBARD Burgundy	*Lifted, sweet toasty nose offers some floral and bready characters with gorgeous balancing acidity.*	**£30.50**	HHF J&B	B
MEURSAULT BLAGNY 1996, LOUIS JADOT Burgundy	*Elegant fruit characters on the nose, the well structured palate demonstrates fruit and acid complexity.*	**£35.00**	BUP TSR VWE WRC HMA	G
MEURSAULT PREMIER CRU LES BOUCHÈRES 1996, LOUIS JADOT Burgundy	*Inviting nutty and mealy characters greet the nose and flow on to a well defined palate of considerable length.*	**£39.60**	NIC HMA	G
BÂTARD-MONTRACHET 1994, DOMAINE LEFLAVE Burgundy	*Intensely floral with a superbly fresh veil of mineral nuances and a beautifully textured palate. Divine.*	**£66.90**	L&W J&B QST	G

Pinpoint who sells the wine you wish to buy by turning to the stockist codes. If you know the name of the wine you want to buy, use the alphabetical index. If the price is your motivation, refer to the invaluable price guide index; red and white wines under £5, sparkling wines under £12 and Champagne under £16. Happy hunting!

FRANCE • CHAMPAGNE • WHITE

Wine	Description	Price	Stockists	Award
Alexandre Bonnet Brut NV, A Bonnet Champagne	*Lime and leesy characters on the nose combine with nutty aromas flowing nicely onto a long, moussy palate.*	**£10.00**	WRC BUP MAR THS RSN	S WINE OF THE YEAR
André Simon Champagne Brut NV, Marne et Champagne Champagne	*A bold sparkling that takes charge of your palate adding a splash of citrus and spiced bubbles.*	**£12.50**	WRT	B
Champagne J F Bourgeois Brut, Marne et Champagne Champagne	*Effervescent bubbles and astute citrus fruit swirls with herbal undertones and a long and clean finish.*	**£12.50**	SAF MCD	B
Albert Etienne Brut NV, Lanson Pere & Fils Champagne	*Excellent light mousse with scented fruit and yeast on the nose, finishes fine and crisp.*	**£13.50**	SAF MCD	B
MHV The House Brut Champagne NV, Champagne F Bonnet Champagne	*Firm compact mousse with a gentle aromatic nose and athletic structure housing strong full fruit.*	**£13.80**	MHV	S
Champagne Jean Moutardier Carte d'Or Brut NV, J Moutardier Champagne	*Rustic beaded mousse with lots of fresh bready yeast tones and a full fruit palate.*	**£14.00**	GRT	S
Marne et Champagne Jean de Braieux Brut NV, Marne & Champagne Champagne	*A compact classy sparkling with a delicate flowery bouquet and stylish tangy fruit palate.*	**£14.00**	MCD	B

Wine	Description	Price	Stockists	Award
DRAPPIER CARTE D'0R 1991, MICHEL DRAPPIER Champagne	*Tiny bubbles excite the palate and ignite a sherbet powered mousse that leaves a lasting impression.*	**£14.60**	ABY WRC BUP THS	S
AYALA BRUT NV, AYALA CHATEAU D'AY Champagne	*Freshly picked lemons on the nose with a crisp clean citrus fruit palate and long balanced acidity.*	**£14.80**	FRT GSJ	B
MANSARD BLANC DE BLANCS GRAND CRU 1992, CHAMPAGNE MANSARD Champagne	*Elegant with a seductive bouchier nose and sensual, well defined body. Complex and sophisticated..*	**£15.50**	FTH	B
LE BRUN DE NEUVILLE CUVEE SELECTION BRUT NV, LE BRUN DE NEUVILLE Champagne	*Superb blend of flavours with distinct notes of clotted cream and warm honey oozing from a caramelised almond palate.*	**£15.80**	TRO WAW	G
ALBERT ETIENNE SPECIAL CUVÉE 1993, LANSON PERE & FILS Champagne	*Good mousse consisting of small persistent bubbles, a fairly high level of acid that provides its liveliness.*	**£16.00**	SAF MCD	B
ASDA VINTAGE CHAMPAGNE 1992, NICOLAS FEUILLATTE Champagne	*Attractive cheese on toast character leads to a breezy fresh fruit palate and zippy finish.*	**£16.00**	ASD	B
BARON EDOUARD MASSÉ BRUT NV, LANSON PERE & FILS Champagne	*An elegant style fizz with light yeasty aromas and soft gentle fruit palate with excellent length.*	**£16.50**	MCD	B
LE BRUN DE NEUVILLE CUVEE BLANC DE BLANCS NV, LE BRUN DE NEUVILLE Champagne	*Lively lemon and lime on the nose with good toasty flavours on the palate that has a lenghty finish.*	**£16.50**	WAW TRO DBY	B

Wine	Description	Price	Stockists	Award
LEON LAUNOIS PRESTIGE 1995, CHAMPAGNE LEON LAUNDIS Champagne	*A lemon and cream nose lead to a mid weight palate of fine texture which carries a persistent bead.*	**£16.50**	CHI	B
ANDRÉ SIMON CHAMPAGNE VINTAGE 1990, MARNE ET CHAMPAGNE Champagne	*A dose of vegetal sappy characters, the palate contains citrus fruit and finishes long and dry.*	**£17.00**	WRT	S
PREMIER CRU RÉSERVE PARTICULIÈRE NV, CHAMPAGNE NICOLAS FEUILLATTE Champagne	*Yeasty aromas with a creamy buttery palate with reasonable length and slightly chalky finish.*	**£17.00**	UNS MAR VWE T&T	B
CHAMPAGNE POL D'AMBERT BRUT NV, POL D'AMBERT Champagne	*An inviting nose of grapefruit and strawberry overtures and superb depth of character lead to a lasting impression.*	**£17.00**	BDR	G
CHAMPAGNE DRAPPIER BLANC DE BLANCS 1990, MICHEL DRAPPIER Champagne	*Delicate citrus fruit, a touch of lime and overtones of yeast on an elegant palate.*	**£17.50**	ABY WRC BUP THS	S
CHAMPAGNE NICOLAS FEUILLATTE BLANC DE BLANCS NV, CHAMPAGNE NICOLAS FEUILLATTE Champagne	*Superb nutty aromas on a palate which has a slight caramalised biscuit character surrounding the fruit.*	**£17.50**	SAF ASD T&T	B
CHARLES DE CAZANONE BRUT CLASSIQUE NV, CHAMPAGNE CHARLES DE CAZANONE Champagne	*Rich sweet fruit showing some class on the finish and a freshly baked cream doughnut nose.*	**£17.60**	HWK HWA	B
LOUIS DE BELMANCE VINTAGE CHAMPAGNE 1990, DANIEL THIBAULT Champagne	*Marvellous funky strawberries and cream, frisky finesse witha lemon meringue backlash.*	**£17.80**	MHV	G TROPHY WINE

	WHITE • CHAMPAGNE • FRANCE			
Besserat de Bellefon Cuvée des Moines Brut NV, Besserat de Bellefon Champagne	*Gentle and lasting with good balance between fruit and acidity and lovely fresh strawberry characters.*	**£18.00**	MCD	(B)
Champagne H Blin et Cië 1991, Champagne H Blin Champagne	*Lovely green gold reflections from the glass with a fine mousse and dry full elegant mouthfeel.*	**£18.00**	JBF	(B)
Champagne Joseph Perrier Cuvée Royale NV, Champagne Joseph Perrier Champagne	*Enticing combination of aromas with a full fleshy fruit palate and an elegant lengthy finish.*	**£18.00**	RBS GRT CHN	(B)
Duchatel Brut Vintage 1993, A Thienot Champagne	*A creamy inviting nose of toasty oak embedded in a deep palate of strawberry and cream. Great structure.*	**£18.00**	UNS PNA	(B)
F Duchatel & Cie Brut Vintage 1994, A Thienot Champagne	*The palate shows loads of ripe fruit characters with extremely good integrated acidity.*	**£18.00**	UNS PNA	(S)
Jacquart Brut Tradition NV, Jacquart Champagne	*Honeyed fruit aromas combined with rich ripe fruit palate, with a pleasant finish.*	**£18.00**	PAT	(B)
Marne et Champagne Jean de Bracieux 1990, Marne et Champagne Champagne	*Light and refreshing, with fresh lively citrus characters balanced by developed leesy notes.*	**£18.00**	MCD	(B)
Waitrose Champagne Vintage Brut 1990, F Bonnet Champagne	*Amazing amount of interesting developed characters wrapped together with fabulous acidity and a toasty yeastiness.*	**£18.00**	WTS	(S)

FRANCE • CHAMPAGNE • WHITE

Wine	Description	Price	Stockists	Award
Champagne Drappier Cuvee du Millenaire 1995, Michel Drappier Champagne	*Vibrant aromas and a fine bead showing elegance on the palate and a light yeasty finish.*	£18.80	ABY WRC BUP THS	S
Baron Edouard Massé Brut Millésime 1993, Lanson Pere & Fils Champagne	*Creamy fruit aromas, medium bead with good yeasty character and refreshing acidity.*	£19.00	MCD	B
Bruno Paillard Brut Premiere Cuvée NV, Bruno Paillard Champagne	*Crisp citrus mingled with creamy lanolin aromas and an extremely long palate with zesty acidity.*	£19.00	BDR NIC WIN PHI BEL BWL	S
Piper-Heidsieck Demi-Sec NV, Piper-Heidsieck Champagne	*Clean, attractive pineappley nose with butter and freshly made dough characters. An elegant and attractive wine.*	£19.00	TOS HDB	S
Champagne Drappier Grande Sendree 1989, Michel Drappier Champagne	*A full bodied fine beaded vintage champagne with yeasty aromas and full round fruit, finishing long.*	£19.20	ABY WRC BUP THS ABY	S
Mumm Cordon Rouge NV, GH Mumm & Cie Champagne	*An inviting yet subtle strawberry nose with an intense palate loaded with lively fruit.*	£19.40	Widely Available	B
Lanson Black Label Brut NV, Lanson Pere & Fils Champagne	*Soft bready aromas greet the nose and lead to a sweet fruit and bready-palate of intoxicating style and finesse.*	£19.90	UNS WCR SAF MHV TOS MCD	G
Chanoine Vintage 1989, Chanoine Champagne	*Mineral, light elegant nose with mineral characteristics following through on the palate to a pleasant finish.*	£20.00	LAW	B

Wine	Description	Price	Stockists	Award
FINDLATER MACKIE TODD 21ST CENTURY BRUT NV, DANIEL THIBAULT Champagne	*Lots of sweet biscuit aromas on a full broad fruit driven palate, held together with moderate acidity.*	**£20.00**	WTS	B
LANSON IVORY LABEL NV, LANSON PERE & FILS Champagne	*Doughy, cheesy characters abound in this well balanced wine with concentrated fruit on the palate.*	**£20.00**	SAF MCD	B
LE BRUN DE NEUVILLE CUVÉE DU ROI CLOVIS NV, LE BRUN DE NEUVILLE Champagne	*Charming minerals and a touch of yeast on the nose followed by a full flavoured palate.*	**£20.00**	WAW	B
TESCO PREMIER CRU VINTAGE CHAMPAGNE 1993, CHAMPAGNE NICOLAS FEUILLATTE Champagne	*A pale golden liquid signals the soft yeasty nose and developed fruit characters to come.*	**£20.00**	TOS T&T	S
DEUTZ BRUT CLASSIQUE NV, CHAMPAGNE DEUTZ Champagne	*A bout of yeast and green apples on the nose with a zippy long citrus fruit palate with attractive creamy notes.*	**£20.50**	NIC BWC	G
CANARD-DUCHÊNE VINTAGE 1991, CANARD-DUCHENE Champagne	*A highly developed bread and cream nose leads to a palate of ripe honeyed apricots with a lime streak.*	**£22.00**	BUP MAR ODD MWW EDC PTR NRW PRG	B
R DE RUINART NV, CHAMPAGNE RUINART Champagne	*Breaded aromas with a hint of butter and a fresh appley mineral palate.*	**£23.30**	WCR L&W BUP MAR RUK	B
TAITTINGER BRUT RESERVE NV, CHAMPAGNE TAITTINGER Champagne	*Very restrained on the nose the palate is fresh and youthful with a slight bitter apple finish.*	**£23.40**	Widely Available	B

Wine	Description	Price	Stockists	Award
Charles Heidsieck Brut Réserve Mis en Cave 1995, Charles Heidsieck Champagne	*Toasty and buttery with lovely crisp dry acidity ahead of a fresh fruit palate that offers real length*	**£23.50**	VLW SAF WRC BUP MAR THS TOS HDB	B
Veuve Clicquot White Label Demi Sec NV, Veuve Clicquot Ponsardin Champagne	*Fresh baked biscuits and ripe fruits on the nose herald in a complex fine beaded palate with a sweet fruit crescendo.*	**£23.80**	Widely Available	S
Marne et Champagne Gauthier Millésime 1990, Marne et Champagne Champagne	*Delightful ripe fruit and cheese nose palate with with hints of lanolin and toast on the nose.*	**£24.00**	MCD	B
Charles Heidsieck Brut Réserve Mis en Cave 1993, Charles Heidsieck Champagne	*Clotted cream and citrus rinds are drenched by fruit that slips down the throat like a fresh oyster in lime juice.*	**£24.10**	UNS VLW WRC BUP BDR MAR THS HDB	S
Champagne Gosset Brut Excellence NV, Champagne Gosset Champagne	*Floral aromas mingle with delightful lees notes on a refreshing sherbety palate.*	**£24.20**	BUP BDR MAR NYW MKV	B
Piper-Heidsieck Brut Vintage 1990, Piper-Heidsieck Champagne	*Buttery popcorn and fresh limes on the mose leading to a soft and zesty ruit palate.*	**£24.80**	SAF WRC BUP MAR HDB	B
Champagne Devaux Distinction Brut 1990, Champagne Devaux Champagne	*This wine shows strong yeasty aromas and sumptuous complex fruit on the palate.*	**£25.00**	VEX	B
Champagne Joseph Perrier Cuvée Royale 1990, Champagne Joseph Perrier Champagne	*Extremely elegant symphony of fresh ripe fruit, spiralling acidity and delicate length.*	**£25.00**	CHN	S

WHITE • CHAMPAGNE • FRANCE				
Jacquart Blanc de Blancs 1992, Jacquart Champagne	*Hay,strawberry and vegemite aromas in a creamy textured palate with lots of soft complex fruit.*	£25.00	PAT	B
Jacquart Vintage 1990, Jacquart Champagne	*Full rich yeasty aromas with warm toasty traces on the nose with a long lasting finish.*	£25.00	PAT	S
Mumm Cordon Rouge 1990, GH Mumm & Cie Champagne	*Cream cheese and vanilla aromas with a clean and generous palate of rich bready flavours.*	£25.00	Widely Available	B
Waitrose Cuvée 2000 1990, Daniel Thibault Champagne	*Pronounced fruit driven wine with a slightly oily palate leading to a generous finish. Don't wait for the Millenium*	£25.00	WTS	B
Champagne Drappier Grande Sendree 1990, Michel Drappier Champagne	*Elegant citrus fruit and fantastic perfumed aromas along with lightly cooked appley characters.*	£25.50	QWW ABY OFW	S
Pommery Brut Vintage 1991, Champagne Pommery Champagne	*Crisp clean fruit on the palate with subtle yeasty aromas and a wonderful cleansing acididy.*	£26.00	TOS CAC PFC	B
Pommery Summertime Blanc de Blancs NV, Champagne Pommery Champagne	*This blanc de blanc combines fresh lingering citrus fruit with a lovely touch of lees.*	£26.00	PFC	B
Pommery Wintertime Blanc de Noirs NV, Pommery Champagne	*Bready fresh lactic characters on the nose with crisp lively fruit and slightly crude structure.*	£26.00	PFC	B

FRANCE • CHAMPAGNE • WHITE

Wine	Description	Price	Stockists	Award
MOËT & CHANDON BRUT IMPÉRIAL VINTAGE 1993, MOËT & CHANDON Champagne	*Fresh apples on the nose with yeasty overtones, and lovely fruit complexity and a creamy mousse.*	**£27.50**	Widely Available	B
MUMM DE CREMANT NV, GH MUMM & CIE Champagne	*Subtle, slightly complex nose with a crisp clean fruit palate which has balanced acidity and length.*	**£27.70**	RBS MAR ODD SEA	B
CANARD-DUCHÊNE GRANDE CUVÉE CHARLES VII NV, CANARD-DUCHENE Champagne	*The garden in a glass, fresh floral and earthy aromas with a well balance stylishly dry palate.*	**£30.00**	WRC WSP PRG	B
TAITTINGER VINTAGE 1992, CHAMPAGNE TAITTINGER Champagne	*A remarkable biscuity nose with sweet bread and caramel notes leads to a full bodied, persistent palate.*	**£34.00**	RBS WRC BUP WIM HMA	S
VEUVE CLICQUOT VINTAGE RESERVE 1991, VEUVE CLICQUOT PONSARDIN Champagne	*Grilled almonds and mineral aromas followed by a full and complex , ever expanding palate with a very fine mousse.*	**£34.80**	Widely Available	S
MUMM CUVÉE LIMITÉE 1990, GH MUMM & CIE Champagne	*Creamy mineral aromas with distinctively ripe fruit palate showing complexity and development.*	**£35.00**	TOS ODD VWE WRT EOR SEA	B
VEUVE CLICQUOT RICH RESERVE 1991, VEUVE CLICQUOT PONSARDIN Champagne	*A buttery, creamy rich nose leads to a persistent mousse in this beautifully balanced, luscious wine.*	**£35.20**	Widely Available	B
HEIDSIECK MONOPOLE DIAMANT BLEU 1989, HEIDSIECK & CO Champagne	*A fine beaded palate which is warm, ripe and supple with magnificent integration and balance.*	**£36.00**	TOS ODD CAC SEA	S

WHITE • CHAMPAGNE • FRANCE				
CHAMPAGNE NICOLAS FEUILLATTE PREMIER CRU 1992, CHAMPAGNE NICOLAS FEUILLATTE Champagne	*Subtle fresh citrus nose with crisp lemons on the palate and pleasingly elegant finish.*	**£37.50**	T&T	B
CHARLES HEIDSIECK RÉSERVE CHARLIE BRUT RÉSERVE MIS EN CAVE 1990, CHARLES HEIDSIECK Champagne	*A complex citrus and bready nose leads to smoky, yeasty notes and rich smooth fruit in a full bodied palate.*	**£40.00**	VLW HDB	G
JACQUART CUVÉE NOMINÉE 1988, JACQUART Champagne	*A beady, savoury and buttery character greets the nose and leads to a deep pool of bready and berry notes.*	**£40.00**	PAT	G
BOLLINGER GRANDE ANNÉE 1990, BOLLINGER Champagne	*Enticing lemon meringue and mocha notes greet the nose before a full ripe fruit and malt palate of great length and finesse.*	**£40.90**	Widely Available	S
CHAMPAGNE JOSEPH PERRIER CUVÉE JOSÉPHINE 1989, CHAMPAGNE JOSEPH PERRIER Champagne	*Very honeyed, slightly nutty aromas mingled with an exotic, opulent and endless palate.*	**£50.00**	GNW CHN	B
CHAMPAGNE NICOLAS FEUILLATTE PALMES D'OR 1992, CHAMPAGNE NICOLAS FEUILLATTE Champagne	*A subtle waft of smokiness lifts from the glass followed by a crisp complex savoury palate.*	**£50.00**	MAR T&T	B
MIGNON & PIERREL PREMIER CRU MILLÉSIMÉ 1992, PIERREL Champagne	*The palate is smooth and creamy with a lively crispness and subtle, sophisticated herb bread nuances.*	**£50.00**	FCC	G
MUMM CORDON ROUGE GRAND CORDON 1990, GH MUMM & CIE Champagne	*Fantastic structure with crisp apples, soft apricots, honey and finishes with a touch of breadiness.*	**£50.00**	TOS ODD SEA	G

FRANCE • CHAMPAGNE • WHITE

Wine	Description	Price	Stockists	Award
Champagne Perrier-Jouët Belle Epoque 1990, Champagne Perrier-Jouët Champagne	*Rich ripe complexity on the nose and palate with a soft lingering berry and vanilla wash.*	**£53.20**	Widely Available	B
Pommery Louise Blanc 1990, Champagne Pommery Champagne	*The palate shows maturity whilst still remaining lively with a crisp acidity and long, creamy soft finish.*	**£55.00**	TOS PFC	S
Lanson Noble Cuvée 1988, Lanson Pere & Fils Champagne	*Yeasty, citrus aromas herald in a zippy fresh citrus palate with crusty bread and cream notes.*	**£55.90**	UNS BUP MAR TOS MCD	S
Dom Ruinart Blanc de Blancs 1990, Champagne Ruinart Champagne	*Bready yeasty aromas before oyster characters and a palate with full ripe fruit finishes with grace. Very complex*	**£58.70**	WRC BUP MAR RUK	G
Taittinger Comtes de Champagne Blanc de Blancs 1990, Champagne Taittinger Champagne	*A broad and buxom palate offers rich cake and fruit tart notes ahead of zesty acidity.*	**£63.00**	RBS GRT WIM CAC HMA	S
Cuvée Dom Pérignon 1992, Moët & Chandon Champagne	*Superbly structured wine offering generous fruit and yeasty notes and a steely structure that can only get better.*	**£63.90**	Widely Available	S
Taittinger Comtes de Champagne Blanc de Blancs 1993, Champagne Taittinger Champagne	*Fresh picked fruits and rich yeasty tones are the hallmarks of this still sleeping beauty.*	**£64.00**	RBS WIM CAC HMA	S
Charles Heidsieck Champagne Charlie 1985, Charles Heidsieck Champagne	*Full butter and toffee aromas, with a slighty cheesy and oxidative fruity palate, with a lingering finish.*	**£64.50**	NIC WRC BUP HDB	G

VEUVE CLICQUOT LA GRANDE DAME 1990, VEUVE CLICQUOT PONSARDIN Champagne	*Overt full ripe fruits including papaya and quince immersed in an exquisite creamy buttery texture.*	**£65.90**	Widely Available	S
TAITTINGER COMTES DE CHAMPAGNE BLANC DE BLANCS 1989, CHAMPAGNE TAITTINGER Champagne	*Buttery biscuit aromas and a touch of marmity lees combined with toasty chardonnay fruit and a gorgeous acid tail.*	**£67.30**	Widely Available	S

FRANCE • CHAMPAGNE • ROSÉ

CHAMPAGNE A MARGAINE ROSÉ BRUT NV, ARNUND MARGAINE Champagne	*Almost grey blush colour with a complex, creamy and toasty palate, slippery texture and fine mousse.*	**£14.90**	GGW GGW	S
CHAMPAGNE DRAPPIER ROSE VAL DES DEMOISELLES NV, MICHEL DRAPPIER Champagne	*A lovely yeasty nose with light summer fruit notes preludes a classy palate of strawberries and pears.*	**£15.30**	ABY WRC BUP THS ABY	S
CHAMPAGNE BERNARD BRÉMONT BRUT GRAND CRU ROSÉ NV, BERNARD BRÉMONT Champagne	*Salmon pink with gentle strawberry aromas and a broad, soft, red fruit flavoured palate.*	**£15.50**	FCC	S
CHAMPAGNE DRAPPIER GRANDE SENDREE ROSÉ 1990, MICHEL DRAPPIER Champagne	*Orangey pink with a slightly chalky nose and fruit laden palate. Clean finish.*	**£18.30**	ABY	B
BESSERAT DE BELLEFON CUVÉE DES MOINES ROSÉ NV, BESSERAT DE BELLEFON Champagne	*A faint strawberry and sugarcane nose introduces a finely balanced, enjoyable wine.*	**£19.00**	MCD	B

Wine	Description	Price	Stockists	Award
Piper-Heidsieck Brut Rosé NV, Piper-Heidsieck Champagne	*Attractive doughy nose with a light raspberry and yeast palate followed by a clean, crisp finish.*	**£19.00**	TOS HDB	B
Jacquart Rosé Mosaïque NV, Jacquart Champagne	*Spicey, strawberry ice-cream, lovely balance on the round palate and a nice weighty finish.*	**£21.80**	RBS PAT	B
Bruno Paillard Rose Premiere Cuveé NV, Bruno Paillard Champagne	*Ripe red fruit giving good depth on the palate, leading to a finish showing class.*	**£22.00**	BDR NYW PHI BWL	B
Lanson Brut Rosé NV, Lanson Pere & Fils Champagne	*Lovely berries layered between shortbread, attractive fruit acids sing on the palate, soft, creamy conclusion.*	**£24.00**	UNS WCR MHV WRC BUP MAR THS MCD	B
Moët & Chandon Brut Impérial Rosé NV, Moët & Chandon Champagne	*Lovely fresh strawberries and cream joined by lemon scents, crisp and bready on the palate.*	**£24.20**	WAC VLW FUL SAF MAR CAC MHU	B
Champagne Devaux Distinction Rosé 1990, Champagne Devaux Champagne	*Nice touch of age well balanced by fresh berries and creamy mousse. Persistant beading dances on the tongue.*	**£25.00**	VEX	B
Taittinger Brut Prestige Rosé NV, Champagne Taittinger Champagne	*Soft, ripe and creamy nose, crème brûlée on the palate running through to the finish.*	**£26.00**	WIM ETV HMA	B
R de Ruinart Rosé NV, Champagne Ruinart Champagne	*Rich, jammy berries to the fore with nice biscuit characters on the palate. Finishing long and creamy.*	**£29.50**	WCR NIC WRC BUP RUK	S

ROSE • CHAMPAGNE • FRANCE				
Moët & Chandon Brut Impérial Vintage Rosé 1993, Moët & Chandon Champagne	*Nice fresh raspberries and strawberries, good structure and palate weight, nice length with a full finish."*	**£31.90**	RBS VLW F&M LAY HAR HVN SEL MHU	S
Veuve Clicquot Rosé Reserve 1990, Veuve Clicquot Ponsardin Champagne	*Rich biscuity berries and cream flow to a full bodied palate with finesse, concentration and fulfilling length.*	**£37.00**	Widely Available	G
Champagne Fleury Millenium Brut 1992, Fleury Champagne	*Great Champagne yeast character matched by nutty stonefruit and cherry berries. Old fashioned yet attractive characteristics.*	**£37.50**	VR VRT	S
Bollinger Grande Année Rosé 1990, Bollinger Champagne	*Ripe full blown big fruity style, showing raw apples and strawberries from a rich berry and cream texture.*	**£42.70**	WAC VLW L&W NYW HAR BLS FTH MZC	B
Pommery Louise Rosé 1990, Champagne Pommery Champagne	*Delicate, complex nose, creamy acid structure and emerging aged characters. Charming with a long future.*	**£65.00**	TOS PFC	S
Dom Pérignon Rosé 1988, Moët & Chandon Champagne	*Smoky classic nose some tea leaf, great structure and acidity, long and beautifully balanced. Great wine!*	**£154.30**	UNS RBS VLW HHC HAR FAR BWL MHU	G

Pinpoint who sells the wine you wish to buy by turning to the stockist codes. If you know the name of the wine you want to buy, use the alphabetical index. If the price is your motivation, refer to the invaluable price guide index; red and white wines under £5, sparkling wines under £12 and champagne under £16. Happy hunting!

FRANCE • LANGUEDOC • RED

De Neuville Cabernet Sauvignon 1997, De Neauville Languedoc Roussillon	*Tinned red fruit nose. Soft initial fruit with some herbaceous character. Good acidity and length.*	**£3.80**	TAV	(B)
Foncalieu Syrah Special 1998, Foncalieu Languedoc Roussillon	*Garnet coloured rim confirming some developing characteristics and ripe rounded fruit too, complex and long.*	**£3.80**	PLB	(B)
Bellefontaine Syrah 1998, Paul Boutinot France Languedoc Roussillon	*Ripe fruit with hint of greenness a bit closed still, has tight structure and balanced palate.*	**£4.00**	WCR NYW BPW AMW COK	(B)
Big Franks Red Minervois 1997, Big Frank Languedoc Roussillon	*A purple wine with plumy damson fruit flavours on the palate, smoky on the finish.*	**£4.00**	MAR THR, VWC, BUP, WRC GYW	(B)
Domaine Sainte Bauzille Cabernet Sauvignon Syrah VdP d'Oc 1997, Domaines Virginie Berzieb Languedoc	*Bright plum aromas and onion skins with soft, light ripe berry fruit palate.*	**£4.00**	FRT GSJ	(B)
Foncalieu Syrah Top 1998, Foncalieu Languedoc Roussillon	*Luscious red colour with strong oak astringent character, spicy light fruit and firm tannin finish.*	**£4.00**	WRC BUP MAR THS PLB	(B)
"Top" Cabernet Sauvignon 1998, Foncalieu Languedoc Roussillon	*Ripe plum and blackcurrant nose. Savoury, minty palate with drying tannins and a bold, tannic finish.*	**£4.00**	PLB	(B)

Wine	Description	Price	Stockists	Award
DOMAINE DE MADAME COSTIÈRES DE NÎMES 1997, NICOLE DELON Languedoc Roussillon	*Lovely sweet fruit with herbal edges, leather and spice. Gamey notes and attractive tannins finish well.*	£4.50	DLA	B
TRILOGIE VDP D'OC 1997, MAUREL VEDEAU Languedoc Roussillon	*Full and ripe, a smoky savoury wine with good acidity, balance and finish.*	£4.50	TOS T&T	B
CHÂTEAU SAINT BENOIT MINERVOIS 1997, MAUREL VEDEAU Languedoc Roussillon	*An herbaceousness precedes brambly fruit characters and continues on to a fruit palate offering good length.*	£4.90	HOH SMF T&T	S
BARTON & GUESTIER VIGNE RARE CABERNET SAUVIGNON 1997, BARTON & GUESTIER Languedoc Roussillon	*Good blackberry character with a hint of spirit, nice tannins and lingering acid tail.*	£5.00	SEA	B
CHÂTEAU DE CAMPUGET COSTIÈRES DE NIMES 1998, CHÂTEAU DE CAMPUGET Languedoc Roussillon	*Youthful and chewy with characterful earthy spicy fruit aromas on the nose lead to a classy palate of succulent fruit .*	£5.00	Widely Available	S
CHÂTEAU DE VAUGELAS CORBIÈRES 1997, NICOLAS DASPET Languedoc Roussillon	*A well balanced wine with good wood and fruit character and impressive length.*	£5.00	ASD SKW	S
CHÂTEAU LAMARGUE ROUGE 1997, CHÂTEAU LAMARGUE Languedoc Roussillon	*Fragrant and delicate, a well balanced wine with bright fruit flavours and good acidity.*	£5.00	JNW WCR	B
DOMAINE FORCA REAL CÔTES DU ROUSSILLON VILLAGES 1996, SOCIETE J P HENRIQUES Languedoc Roussillon	*Big chocolatey, tarry spiced fruit. Chunky and leathery, a wine poised for a bright future.*	£5.00	FUL BPW	S

FRANCE • LANGUEDOC • RED

L'IF MERLOT CARIGNAN MONT-TAUCH 1998, MONT TAUCH Languedoc Roussillon	*A herbaceous spicey wine, soft and juicy with attractive ripe blackcurrant fruit flavours.*	**£5.00**	SAF TOS LCC T&T	B
VIENNETS BARRIQUE D'OC 1997, VIENNETS Languedoc Roussillon	*Light and easy but with some complexity, a well balanced clean wine with nice tannins.*	**£5.00**	FUL BGL	B
WILD PIG BARREL RESERVE SHIRAZ VDP D'OC 1998, GABRIEL MEFFRE Languedoc Roussillon	*Vibrant and fruity on the nose, this wine has excellent smoky oak and expansive fruit flavours.*	**£5.00**	WCR FUL WRC GYW	S
CUVÉE DES CHANOINES 1998, CAVE DE VILLENEUVE Languedoc Roussillon	*Rich ripe fruit with cinnamon pepper and spice lead to youthful exuberant tannins, needs time.*	**£5.30**	BDR	B
CUVÉE RÉSERVÉE VDP D'OC 1997, DOMAINE ST MARTIN DE LA GARRIGUE Languedoc Roussillon	*Soft and juicy, a fruit driven style with warm herby southern flavours and a clean tail.*	**£5.30**	CAC WLL	B
VDP D'OC CABERNET SAUVIGNON DOMAINE SAINTE AGATHE 1997, MAUREL VEDEAU Languedoc Roussillon	*With great vegetal characters, full of character, this wine has a good mouthfeel with nice length.*	**£5.30**	SMF T&T	B
ABBOTTS CUMULUS MINERVOIS SHIRAZ MOURVÈDRE 1997, ABBOTTS Languedoc Roussillon	*Soft spicey fruit gives medium weight, a nice style with good acidity and pleasing drying tannins.*	**£5.50**	WRC BUP MAR THS FRT GSJ	B
BERGERIE DE L'ARBOUS COTEAUX DU LANGUEDOC 1996, JEAN JEAN Languedoc Roussillon	*An aromatic wine with an impressive deep colour, excellent with good length.*	**£5.50**	SAF	B

Wine	Description	Price	Stockists	Award
Cuvée l'Arjolle VdP des Côtes de Thongues 1996, Domaine Teisserenc Languedoc Roussillon	*Jammy raspberry fruit on the nose and palate. A clean wine with good tannins and pleasing acidity.*	**£5.50**	J&B	B
Château Mire l'Etang la Clape 1998, Earl CLR Languedoc Roussillon	*A powerful style showing plum and black fruit characters following onto a full bodied, well structured palate.*	**£5.70**	UNS STG	S
Domaine de Granoupiac VdP 1997, C Flavard Languedoc Roussillon	*A concentrated wine of reasonable length with some nice fruit flavours, good complexity.*	**£6.00**	JNW	B
Maurel Vedeau VdP d'Oc Cabernet Franc 1998, Maurel Vedeau Languedoc Roussillon	*Deep, dark berry fruit and leather aromas. Easy, sweet, ripe fruit on palate, with stalky tannins.*	**£6.00**	T&T	B
Caves d'Embres Corbieres 1998, Cave d'Embres Castelmaure Languedoc Roussillon	*Slightly minty nose with stewed fruit. Pleasant supple fruit palate. Shows promise.*	**£6.20**	BDR	B
La Cuvée Mythique VdP d'Oc 1997, Val d'Orbien Languedoc Roussillon	*A deeply coloured, good black fruit on the nose, distinctively packaged, with great concentration.*	**£6.20**	SAF CWS VDO	S
Château de Lastours Corbières Cuvée Simone 1995, Château de Lastours Languedoc Roussillon	*Well balanced, a juicy wine with good herbal fruit flavours and a vibrant youthful appearance.*	**£6.40**	GSH THS BPW	B
Domaine la Tour Boisée Cuvée Marie Claude Minervois 1997, Jean-Louis & Marie Claude Poudou	*A long and peppery wine with good dark cherry fruit and bubblegum aromas.*	**£6.50**	WAW	B

FRANCE • LANGUEDOC • RED

Château de Lastours Corbieres Futs de Chene 1995, Château de Lastours Languedoc Roussillon	*Full rich and complex. A well balanced wine with firm tannins and excellent fruit.*	**£6.80**	THS BPW	(B)
Mont Tauch Prestige Fitou 1997, Mont Tauch Languedoc Roussillon	*A balanced serious wine, with good primary fruit, tannins and a very dry finish.*	**£6.80**	T&T, SMF	(B)
Asda Tramontane Reserve Syrah 1996, Domaine de la Baume/BRL Hardy Languedoc Roussillon	*Great deep colour, offering floral notes with a touch of tar and a complex, well structured palate with good length.*	**£7.00**	ASD	(B)
Chateau de l'Amarine Cuvee des Bernis Rouge 1997, Château de l'Amarine Languedoc Roussillon	*Deep purple in colour, this wine has lovely ripe blackberry fruit on the nose and a firm finish.*	**£7.00**	NYW DBY NRW BPW	(B)
Château Maylandie Villa Ferrae Corbières 1996, Château Maylandie Languedoc Roussillon	*A superbly structured wine, soft sweet and earthy on the nose, it is pleasantly tight in the mouth.*	**£7.00**	WLL	(S)
Ermitage du Pic St Loup Cuvée Sainte Agnes 1997, Ermitage du Pic Languedoc Roussillon	*Suggestive start of cracked pepper and plums, nicely structured palate with green acidity flowing to grippy oak tannins.*	**£7.00**	FUL GYW	(S)
La Baume Tête du Cuvee 1997, BRL Hardy Languedoc Roussillon	*A pleasingly ripe, spicey wine with impressive depth of rich fruit and firm tannins.*	**£7.00**	HBR	(B)
Penval Pazac Costière de Nîmes 1998, Penval Languedoc Roussillon	*Stylishly made, this wine has a deep purple colour and attractive ripe fruit aromas.*	**£7.20**	TOS	(B)

DOMAINE LE BAUME MERLOT 1997, BRL HARDY Languedoc Roussillon	*Up front fruit style with obvious appeal, demonstrating good use of wood.*	**£7.50**	WCR FUL JSM HBR	B
ABBOTTS CUMULO NIMBUS MINERVOIS 1998, ABBOTTS Languedoc Roussillon	*Very deep colours, this wine has a good black fruit nose, with great concentration and structure.*	**£7.70**	SAF WRS, ODD FUL GYW	S
DOMAINE DE VILLEMAJOU 1996, DOMAINE DE VILLEMAJOU Languedoc Roussillon	*A well balanced wine with herby ripe fruit flavours a certain but enjoyable firmness.*	**£8.50**	NIC	B
CHÂTEAU HELENE CUVÉE DE TROIE 1995, MARIE-HELENE GAU Languedoc Roussillon	*Herbal and oaky on the nose offering vibrant spicy fruit flavours on the palate.*	**£8.70**	WAW	S
TERROIR DU TUCHAN FITOU 1995, MONT TAUCH Languedoc Roussillon	*Attractively structured an easy wine for early drinking, good and ripe with a lifted fruit nose.*	**£8.70**	WRC BUP MAR TOS	B
PIC ST LOUP CÔTEOUX DU LONGUEDOC GRANDE CUVÉE 1997, CHÂTEAU DE LANCYRE Languedoc Roussillon	*Lifted perfume mingles with plum pudding, lovely palate of velvety fruit tannins and vibrant acidity.*	**£9.00**	FUL TOS BGL	S
COMTE CATHARE CABERNET SAUVIGNON PRESTIGE VDP D'OC 1996, DOMAINE DE COMBEBELLE Languedoc Roussillon	*Full on the palate, quite a firm wine showing good oak and subtle fruit characters.*	**£9.00**	VRT	B
L'EXCEPTION AOC FITOU 1998, MONT TAUCH Languedoc Roussillon	*Rich, firm concentration,this wine has immense deep of colour and great fruity intensity on the nose.*	**£9.70**	SAF TOS T&T	G

FRANCE • LANGUEDOC • RED

Reserve Fortant de France Cabernet Sauvignon 1996, Skalli Languedoc Roussillon	*Delicate fruit cake nose with some sweet fruit on the palate and complementary drying tannins.*	**£10.00**	PWI PEA CAX	(B)
Daumas Gassac Rouge VdP de l'Herault 1997, Moulin de Gassac Languedoc Roussillon	*Intriguing, an unusual wine with a curious fruit nose and loose tannic structure.*	**£15.40**	RBS NIC JNW TOS HAS	(B)

FRANCE • LANGUEDOC • ROSÉ

Big Franks Deep Pink Rosé 1998, Big Frank Languedoc Roussillon	*A pleasingly clean wine with a lifted fruit nose and relatively deep colour.*	**£4.00**	BUP MAR THS THR, VWC WRC GYW	(B)

FRANCE • LANGUEDOC • WHITE

La Croix Blanc 1998, Foncalieu Languedoc Roussillon	*Refreshing and stylish with lively fruit, with a hint of spice and a crisp clean finish.*	**£3.60**	PHI GGW BOL BWL	(B)
Bellefontaine Terret Sauvignon VdP d'Oc 1998, Paul Boutinot France Languedoc Roussillon	*Herbaceous upfront fruit nose with simple tropical fruit characters and a hint of spice.*	**£4.00**	NYW WNS SAN BPW	(B)
Reserve St Marc Sauvignon Blanc 1998, Foncalieu Languedoc Roussillon	*Lifted passionfruit and gooseberries to start with a fresh palate displaying lovely poise and persistence.*	**£4.30**	JSM	(B)

Wine	Description	Price	Stockists	Award
Fortant de France VdP d'Oc Chardonnay 1998, Skalli Languedoc Roussillon	*Rich buttery fruit aromas with a balanced palate of integrated oak and moderate acidity, good finish.*	£4.50	WCR SAF HOU PWI CAX	B
Les Frères Scaramouche VdP d'Oc Chardonnay 1998, Les Vignobles la Reze Languedoc Roussillon	*Pineapple and lemony aromas with an abundance of ripe fruit and a lovely oak finish.*	£4.50	CRS PEC	B
French Connection Chardonnay Viognier 1998, Viennets Languedoc Roussillon	*Wonderful citrus aromas with a voluptuous palate of apricot kernels and hints of butterscotch.*	£4.90	WRC BUP MAR THS VWE BGL	B
Asda Tramontane Reserve Viognier 1998, Domaine Viennets Languedoc Roussillon	*Crisp spritely lime fruit aromas with a clean pungent palate and crisp dry acidity.*	£5.00	ASD	S
Frederic Roger Barrique Marsanne Roussanne 1998, Frederic Roger Languedoc Roussillon	*Subtle honeysuckle and exotic fruit aromas lead to a well balanced toasty palate, lacks character.*	£5.00	TOS BGL	B
James Herrick VdP d'Oc Chardonnay 1998, James Herrick Languedoc Roussillon	*Lemon and lime on a well structured palate leading to a clean, zippy finish.*	£5.00	Widely Available	B
La Domeque Tête de Cuvée Vielles Vignes Blanc VdP d'Oc 1998, Frederic Roger Languedoc Roussillon	*Fine floral nose with hints of herbaceous characters and hints of spice. Plenty of citrus fruit characters.*	£5.00	ASD BGL	S, WINE OF THE YEAR
Les Fleurs Chardonnay Sauvignon Blanc 1998, Yves Grassa Languedoc Roussillon	*Herbaceous citrus fruit with moderate acidity, good intensity of fruit and a clean, long finish.*	£6.00	WTS	B

FRANCE • LANGUEDOC • WHITE

Wine	Description	Price	Stockists	
La Baume Chardonnay Viognier 1997, BRL Hardy Languedoc Roussillon	*Lovely fig and cream approach, soft, toasty, nutty ripe style with lovely acid structure.*	**£8.00**	VLW SAF HBR	(S)
Daumas Gassac Blanc 1998, Moulin de Gassac Languedoc Roussillon	*Interesting nose of smoked almonds and tropical fruit. Bright grapefruit style interwoven with fresh acidity .*	**£17.30**	RBS JNW TOS HAS	(S)

FRANCE • LOIRE • OTHER

Wine	Description	Price	Stockists	
MHV Rose D'Anjou 1998, Dominique Baud Loire	*A balanced, pale wine with good acidity and a curiously pleasing bubblegum fruit nose.*	**£3.40**	MHV	(B)
Rosé D'Anjou Vitrines du Monde 1998, Vinival Loire	*A lovely wine with ripe fruit characters and great mouthfeel. Enjoy now.*	**£4.00**	T&T	(B)
Sparkling Chenin Brut NV, Ackerman Loire	*Sparkling chenin from with a hip attitude and an abundance of citrus fruit and long enduring acidity.*	**£4.50**	SAF	(S)
Domaine de Cray Rosé 1998, Chapelle de Cray Loire	*A lively wine pale in colour but bright in the mouth. Good fruit and acidity.*	**£5.00**	MHA BPW	(B)

Pinpoint who sells the wine you wish to buy by turning to the stockist codes. If you know the name of the wine you want to buy, use the alphabetical index. If the price is your motivation, refer to the invaluable price guide index; red and white wines under £5, sparkling wines under £12 and Champagne under £16. Happy hunting!

FRANCE • LOIRE • RED

Wine	Description	Price	Stockists	Award
CHINON LES GRAVIERES 1998, COULY DUTHEIL Loire	*Light ruby in colour, a juice yielding wine with leafy fruit characters and dusty tannins.*	**£6.50**	UNS T&T	B
SAUMUR -CHAMPIGNY DOMAINE DE LA CUNE 1997, JEAN-LUC & JEAN-ALBERT MARY Loire	*Fresh and sweet on the nose, a nicely textured wine clean and long.*	**£7.40**	3DW	B
CHINON CHÂTEAU DE LA GRILLE 1995, LAURENT GOSSET Loire	*A light and refreshing wine with curranty fruit flavours, pale ruby colour and complex structure.*	**£7.50**	MKV	B
BOURGUEIL VIEILLES VIGNES DOMAINE DE LA CHEVALERIE 1996, PIERRE CASLOT Loire	*Great texture to this chewy and dense wine, with very good leafy blackcurrant fruit flavours.*	**£8.00**	3DW	B
CHINON CHRISTOPHE CHAUVEAU CUVÉE NATHAN 1996, CHRISTOPHE CHAUVEAU Loire	*Deeply coloured a firm, stylish wine, lean on both the nose and palate.*	**£8.40**	3DW	B
LANGLOIS CHÂTEAU DE VARRAINS SAUMUR CHAMPIGNY 1996, LANGLOIS Loire	*A well balanced wine with good fruit sweetness, firm tannins and delicious mineral qualities.*	**£9.00**	GON MZC	B
CHINON CLOS DE L'ECHO 1996, COULY DUTHEIL Loire	*A stylish minerally wine exhibiting a firm tannic structure, leafy berry fruit and good length.*	**£10.00**	T&T	S

FRANCE • LOIRE • RED

Sancerre Rouge Les Cailleries 1997, Domaine Vacheron Loire	*Soft but full bodied with pronounced berry fruit and a good finish.*	**£10.70**	UNS NAD CKB RBS DBY SGL	B
Sancerre Rouge Belle Dame 1996, Domaine Vacheron Loire	*Elegant, aromatic and well balanced, a deeply coloured wine exhibiting classy flavours and acidity.*	**£17.90**	UNS NAD SGL	B
Generation XIX Sancerre Rouge 1997, Alphonse Mellot Loire	*Showing early maturity of stewed red fruits, vegetal and farmyardy aromas.*	**£23.50**	AVB HOH	B

FRANCE • LOIRE • WHITE

Château du Coing de St Fiacre 1997, Chéreau Carré Loire	*Peachstones and pears stimulate the nose followed by a delicate, light weight mouthwatering palate.*	**£5.00**	DLA	B
Domaine de Cray Sauvignon 1998, Chapelle de Cray Loire	*Lovely perfumed passionfruit and leafiness, the gooseberry palate contains long acidity and a slippery finish.*	**£5.00**	WCR NYW BPW P&R	B
Domaine de Cray VdP du Jardin de la France Chardonnay 1997, Chapelle de Cray Loire	*Buttery oak and tropical fruit nose, lemon acidity combined with soft creamy flavours, well balanced.*	**£5.00**	WCR BPW WSO NRW	S
Quincy le Rimonet 1997, Joseph Mellot Loire	*Warm and aromatic with hints of grass and legumes. Nice minerally palate with zesty acid.*	**£6.00**	GRA	B

Wine	Tasting note	Price	Stockists	Award
Reuilly Blanc 1998, Henri Beurdin & Fils Loire	*Lifted gooseberry, grapefruit and sherbet dip, lovely, lively palate held together by fresh spicy acid.*	**£6.00**	SGL NAD EBA PTR SGL	S
Domaine de la Motte Coteaux du Layon Rochefort 1997, Gilles Sorin Loire	*Pale lemon with delicate floral aromas and smooth spicey, strongly perfumed fruit.*	**£6.50**	3DW	B
Clos de Cray Chardonnay 1997, Chapelle de Cray Loire	*Leesy, buttery tones interspersed with stone fruit characters give way to a perfectly weighted palate.*	**£6.90**	NYW BPW WES SAN BW BPW	S
Château du Coing Comte de St Hubert 1997, Chéreau Carré Loire	*Dry concentrated fruit character on the nose and palate with mineral steeliness in the background.*	**£7.00**	DLA	B
Somerfield Sancerre Fouassier 1998, Fouassier Pere & Fils Loire	*Inviting chalky fruit on the nose, in the mouth herbs mix with racy acidity.*	**£7.50**	SMF	B
Muscadet de Sevre et Maine sur Lie Château de la Ragotiere 1997, Couillaud Loire	*A light style Muscadet with zesty citrus fruit characters slightly waxy texture and good length.*	**£7.80**	VIW HWL	B
Sancerre Domaine Raimbault 1998, Domaines Saget Loire	*Intense and focussed, green beans and gooseberry aromas leading to classic spicey notes with lifted asparagus.*	**£8.20**	CWS CAC	S
Michel Bailly Pouilly Fumé Les Griottines 1998, Michel Bailly Loire	*An inviting nose of almonds, apple blossom and spice introduce a warm but crisp palate.*	**£8.50**	SMF UNS T&T	B

WHITE • LOIRE • FRANCE

Wine	Tasting note	Price	Stockists	Award
Henri Bourgeois Les Bonnes Bonches Sancerre 1998, Henri Bourgeois Loire	*Nice fresh apples and cut grass to the fore, good complex palate showing pebbly, zippy acid.*	**£9.00**	SAF SAF	S
Pouilly-Fumé 1998, Domaine Masson Blondelet Loire	*Grass and green beans to the fore, good depth and juiciness leading to a firm finish.*	**£9.50**	GSH WTS	B
J Verdier Sancerre 1998, Joseph Verdier Loire	*Grassy, peppers and tomato leaf aromas, nice minerally palate showing hints of flint, lean and green.*	**£9.60**	MAK	B
Marc Bredif Vouvray 1997, Marc Bredif Loire	*Slightly dusty aromatic aromas on a greenish fruit palate which has clearly defined acidity.*	**£9.80**	MWW BBR YWL PLA THP PRG	B
Domaine du Carrou Sancerre 1998, Dominique Roger Loire	*Nice subtle, zippy fruit with a pinch of herbs flows to a minerally palate, dry, stony finish.*	**£10.00**	Eno ENO	B
Domaine Vacheron les Roches Sancerre Blanc 1998, Domaine Vacheron Loire	*Classical Sancerre nose, slightly oily on the palate with flinty acid and crisp, clean conclusion.*	**£11.10**	UNS RBS NAD GNW ROD BEN SGL	B
Pascal Jolivet Sancerre Blanc Le Chéne Marchand 1997, Pascal Jolivet Loire	*Tight herbal peachy nose with wafts of struck flint. Lovely structure at the finish.*	**£14.70**	MMD	S
De Ladoucette Sancerre Comte Lafond Blanc 1997, De Ladoucette Loire	*Soft lemons and herbs on the nose flowing to an honest palate with racey, chalky acidity.*	**£15.00**	MWW THP PLA SCA PRG	S

Wine	Tasting note	Price	Stockists	Award
De LadoucettePouilly Fume 1997, De Ladoucette Loire	*Slightly cheesy on the nose, nice tangy, herbal palate. Good lemony acid cleaning up the finish.*	**£16.90**	UNS RBS MWW HAR COE HVN SCA PRG	B
Domaine Vacheron Sancerre Blanc les Romains 1997, Domaine Vacheron Loire	*Delicate grassy nose betraying the intense citrus on the palate, nice creamy alcoholic texture. Finishes well.*	**£17.90**	SGL NAD SGL	B
Sancerre Comte Lafond Grande Cuvée Blanc 1995, De Ladoucette Loire	*Deep, honeyed vegetal nose to start, the palate shows prickly lemony fruit and offer a fresh conclusion.*	**£21.50**	F&M NIC FWC PRG	B
Champalou Tries de Vendange Vouvray Cuvée 1997, Didier Champalou Loire	*Blooms almost at once to reveal a delightful multi-layered palate, with enthusiastic acid and good length.*	**£22.00**	Eno ENO	S

FRANCE • PROVENCE • OTHER

Wine	Tasting note	Price	Stockists	Award
Château Miraval Côtes de Provence Rosé 1998, Château Miraval Provence	*Very lightly coloured this is an extremely well balanced, firm, dry and clean wine.*	**£5.70**	MKV	B
Les Grandes Pallieres Vermentino 1998, Les Vins Breban Provence	*Clean fresh herbaceous nose with pronounced asparagus and zesty fruit palate, long dry finish.*	**£6.00**	BDR	B
Château de Pibarnon 1998, Château de Pibarnon Provence	*This wine is subtle with apple fruit characters and a gentle mix of spices.*	**£11.00**	ABY	B

Wine	Tasting note	Price	Stockists	Award
Rouge Aquarelle Côtes du Luberon Vieilles Vignes 1990, Château de l'Isolette Provence	*Restrained fruit on the nose with a touch of herb and apple blossom. Superb tannin structure and length.*	**£11.00**	BPW HOL COK	S
Château de Pibarnon 1996, Château de Pibarnon Provence	*Exceptionally fine with superb fruit and herb flavours and balancing tannins.*	**£12.60**	ABY	B
Château de Pibarnon Bandol 1997, Château de Pibarnon Provence	*Complex and rich on the nose, a firm wine both well balanced and intriguing.*	**£13.80**	ABY	B

FRANCE • RHÔNE • RED

Wine	Tasting note	Price	Stockists	Award
Clairette de Die NV, Comtesse de Die Rhône	*Appley, toasty nose with a fruity palate of subtle, dry flavours of toast and yeast.*	**£3.50**	WTS	B
Joanis 1998, Château Val Joanis Rhône	*Lovely lifted nose of rose petal and pot-pourri, structural acidity tightens the earthy fruit palate.*	**£4.00**	ABY	S
Joanis VdP de Vaucluse 1997, Château Val Joanis Rhône	*An elegant wine, a delicious fragrant nose and wonderful peppery fruit characters.*	**£3.80**	ABY	S
La Tour du Prévot 1998, Domaines Perrin Rhône	*Leathery fruit sprinkled with spice, warm palate with soft structure, very honest.*	**£4.00**	M&S	B

Wine	Tasting note	Price	Stockists	Award
Côtes du Rhône Rouge Cuvée Speciale 1998, Les Vignerons des Beaumes de Venise Rhone	*A dense gamey and chocolate plums nose supported by good acid structure and appetising tannins.*	**£4.90**	T&T	B
Côtes du Rhône la Vielle Ferme 1997, Domaines Perrin Rhône	*Intense spice and rich fruit nose, the palate is clean with nice subtle oak and reasonable length.*	**£5.00**	JNW TOS CAC MIS	B
Château Val Joanis 1998, Château Val Joanis Rhône	*A full flavoured wine with fresh acidity and peppery fruit is well balanced and finishes clean.*	**£5.10**	ABY	B
Dardaillon Merlot 1998, Cave de Valvigneres Rhône	*An attractive reddish, purple with good tannins and fruit finish. Should open up in the short term.*	**£5.20**	BDR	B
Château Saint Maurice Côtes du Rhône 1997, Christophe Valat Rhône	*Subtle and interesting nose of wood shavings and seaweed. Has loads of intense sweet fruit.*	**£5.50**	NIC WTS MIS	B
La Tour du Prévot Reserve Côtes du Rhône 1997, Paul Sapin Rhône	*A firm fruity wine with an inviting dusty nose. Robustly structured with meaty, cooked fruit characters.*	**£5.50**	M&S	S
Côtes du Rhône Cuvée de la Haie aux Grives 1996, Jean-Claude et Béatrice Bouche Rhône	*Sprinkling of white pepper on stylish fruit, delicate layered flavours, elegant oak. Classy, complex stuff!*	**£5.80**	J&B	G
Côtes du Rhône Belleruche 1998, Chapoutier Rhône	*Juicy, spicy fruit showing character, a bit young? A generous palate shows firm tannins.*	**£6.00**	PSC EOO MZC	B

RED • RHÔNE • FRANCE

Wine	Tasting note	Price	Stockists	Award
Crozes-Hermitage 1998, Louis Mousset Rhône	*Complex , toasty, tarry aroma, juicy fruit, pepper, licorice notes and a balanced, long grippy finish.*	**£6.00**	UNS CWS VAU STG	S
Crozes-Hermitage Domaine du Murinais 1998, Louis Mousset Rhône	*Sweet restrained oak with rich damson and blackcurrant pastille aromas, spicey flavours and decent length.*	**£6.00**	STG	B
Domaine de la Soleïade Vacqueyras 1998, Soleïade Vacqueyras Rhône	*Classy cherries with nice earthiness leads to gamey sweetness and a long peppery finish.*	**£6.00**	UNS SMF	S
Côtes du Rhône Terroir du Trias 1998, Les Vignerons des Beaumes de Venise Rhône	*A minerals and fruit nose signal the shot of gunpowder to come on the palate.*	**£6.20**	SMF TOS T&T	B
Côtes du Rhône Villages Valreas Domaine de la Grande Bellane 1998, Earl Gaia Rhône	*Deep, dark, ground coffee and spicey fruit lead to tight tannins that will come around.*	**£6.20**	CWS MAR JSM VER VWE TOS BGL	B
Côtes du Rhône 1998, Cave de Chusclan Rhône	*Smoky spicy blackcurrants and cigar box lead to a deep palate. Subtle tannins lead to tremendous length.*	**£6.50**	BDR	B
La Barque Vieille 1998, Cave de Chusclan Rhône	*A perfumed fleshy, cherry nose shows rich ripe fruit, tannins are pleasant and drying.*	**£6.50**	BDR	B
Crozes-Hermitage 1998, Cave de Tain l'Hermitage Rhône	*Lovely raspberry fruit dusted with black pepper and spice, restrained oak helps the nice finish.*	**£6.70**	NIC TOS TRO CGW BPW	B

Wine	Description	Price	Stockists	Award
Crozes-Hermitage 1997, Cave de Tain l'Hermitage Rhône	*Ripe fruit flavours here. Spice and tar tones combine on the palate leading to a long drying finish.*	**£6.80**	NIC BDR TOS HOU P&R BPW	S
Crozes-Hermitage 1997, Cave des Clairmonts Rhône	*Lovely strong fruit with grippy drying tannins on a layered mineral and herb palate with an elegant finish.*	**£7.00**	WTS	B
La Tour du Prévôt Cuvée Speciale Syrah 1997, Mistral Wines Rhône	*Luscious plump fruit characters. Deep with good lengh and mysteriously complex fruit and wood flavours.*	**£7.00**	M&S	S
Jean Luc Colombo la Serine Pointue 1997, Jean Luc Colombo Rhône	*Bright cherry colour with loads of fine berry fruit and juicy tannins and spice on the long finish.*	**£8.30**	L&W	B
Alain Paret Côtes du Rhône Innocent VI 1997, Alain Paret Rhône	*A spicey, rich wine with an intense berry fruit nose and a dark, rich colour.*	**£8.50**	PHI WSG	B
Gigondas Domaine Saint Francois Xavier 1997, Cave Saint Peirre Rhône	*Nice light plums with subtle nutmeg and cinnamon, builds nicely to round fruit tannins with good length.*	**£8.50**	FRT GSJ	B
Cave de St Desirat St Joseph Cuvée Medaille d'Or 1996, Cave de St Desirat Rhône	*Spicey berries with pleasant earthiness and mushrooms. A complex palate just starting to hit the mark.*	**£9.00**	WTS	S
Côtes du Rhône Villages Cairanne 1998, Domaine Richaud Rhône	*Pepper and spice on the nose with elements of mint on the sweet, jammy palate.*	**£9.00**	LIB	S

Wine	Description	Price	Stockists	Award
GIGONDAS LA RAMILLADE CHÂTEAU DE TRIGNON 1997, CHÂTEAU DE TRIGNON Rhone	*Rustic cherry, earthy, leathery nose with nicely balanced spicey oak finish, pleasant traditional style.*	**£9.00**	CDB WRC	B
ANDRÉ SIMON CHÂTEAUNEUF-DU-PAPE LES RONDELIERES 1998, JEAN BEAUQUIN Rhône	*Intense, ripe smoky, brambly ripe plums with floral lift. A gorgeously layered palate shows persistence.*	**£10.00**	WRT	G
CHÂTEAUNEUF-DU-PAPE 1998, PARC DES PAPES Rhône	*Lovely old fashioned plummy nose, good concentration with fresh acidity finishing with balanced tannins.*	**£10.00**	TOS MIS	B
CÔTES DU RHÔNE LES GARRIGUES 1997, DOMAINE DE LA JANASSE Rhône	*Tight, complex wild fruit and earthiness to start. Well structured, finishing with a nice tannic tail.*	**£10.00**	NYW ENO	S
CROZES-HERMITAGE CHÂTEAU CURSON 1996, DOMAINE ETIENNE POCHON Rhône	*Movie theatre popcorn and burnt toffee notes are the hallmarks of this densely flavoured, complex wine with good structure.*	**£10.20**	NYW J&B	B
CROZES-HERMITAGE 1998, DOMAINE COMBIER Rhône	*A rich, nutty and smokey bacon nose with strong tannins and acid supporting subtle fruits.*	**£10.50**	ENO	B
CÔTES DU RHÔNE CAIRANNE VENDENGE CHABRILLE 1997, DOMAINE BRUSSET Rhône	*Approachable soft plums and liquorice on the nose, a dusting of soft tannins providing nice structure.*	**£10.70**	NYW ENO	G
GIGONDAS 1997, CHÂTEAU DU TRIGNON Rhône	*Ripe, complex, tarry fruit and a hint of earthiness lead to a palate showing charm and length.*	**£10.80**	VLW BDR	S

Wine	Description	Price	Stockists	Award
CHÂTEAUNEUF-DU-PAPE 1997, DOMAINE DE GRAND TINEL Rhône	*Nice, direct light red fruit. Displaying lovely big wood tannins adding to the tight acid structure.*	**£11.20**	AVB HOH	B
CORNAS 1995, CAVE DE TAIN L'HERMITAGE Rhône	*Big, herbal style, chocabloc of ripe smoky fruit. A very fine tannin structure and lovely fruit acid balance with good length.*	**£11.90**	NIC MAR VWE TOS BPW	S
GIGONDAS LE GRAND MONTMIRAIL 1997, DOMAINE BRUSSET Rhône	*Bright, shiny, fragrant, wild black fruits with lifted violets and carbonic bounce on the palate.*	**£13.70**	NYW ENO	S
CHÂTEAUNEUF-DU-PAPE DOMAINE LA ROQUETTE 1995, BRUNIER ET FILS Rhône	*Great fruit with lovely herbal essences, excellent levels of tannin and fruit acidity and a super finish.*	**£13.90**	JLW	S
GIGONDAS MONTIRIUS 1998, CHRISTINE & ERIC SAUREL Rhône	*A savoury nose with a hint of mocha leads to a fleshy, cherry dominated palate with excellent acidity.*	**£15.00**	TOS BGL	S
CHÂTEAUNEUF-DU-PAPE DOMAINE FONT DE MICHELLE 1997, LES FILS D'ETIENNE GONNET Rhône	*A very characterful nose of rose petals, moss and plum fruits. Well-rounded with a full, peppercorn and mint palate.*	**£16.00**	WRC BUP THS AMW WWI WSG	B
JEAN LUC COLOMBO CORNAS LES MEJEANS 1996, JEAN LUC COLOMBO Rhône	*Violets and raspberries precede a dense palate laden with fruits of the forest coated in cream.*	**£16.70**	L&W JLW	S
CHÂTEAUNEUF-DU-PAPE CHAUPIN 1997, DOMAINE DE LA JANASSE Rhône	*Great wafts of oak, herb and plum fruits introduce a well integrated fruit palate with nice length.*	**£17.00**	NYW ENO	B

RED • RHÔNE • FRANCE

Wine	Description	Price	Stockists	Award
Gigondas Les Hauts de Montmirail 1997, Domaine Brusset Rhône	*Fruit driven style with notes of herb and mineral. Great tannin structure and nice length.*	**£17.00**	NYW ENO	G
Gambert de Loche 1995, Cave de Tain l'Hermitage Rhône	*Stewed fruit and a little jammy, fresh acidity and pleasant, peppery finish.*	**£20.00**	WER P&R BPW	B
Côte Rotie Les Rochains 1997, PC Bonnefond Rhône	*Dry and lean with spicey plum fruit in a wine of good length and weight.*	**£23.00**	WIN	B

FRANCE • RHÔNE • WHITE

Wine	Description	Price	Stockists	Award
Costieres de Nimes 1998, Château l'Hermitage Rhône	*Very pleasant big ripe perfumed aromas with a ripe fruit palate and moderate acidity.*	**£7.50**	WCR PEC	B
Côtes du Rhône Les Figuières Blanc 1997, Jean Luc Colombo Rhône	*Herbaceous summer fruit aromas with floral fruit on the palate and a spicey dry finish.*	**£9.40**	L&W	B
Domaine de Monteillet Condrieu 1997, Domaine de Monteillet Rhône	*A youthful punchy wine with intense rich ripe fruit characters, oily in texture and complexity.*	**£18.40**	BDR GRT	G
Condrieu les Ceps du Nebadon 1997, Alain Paret Rhône	*Mineral notes and a touch of freshly picked herbs. Superb palate weight with impressive length.*	**£119.00**	NYW ADN PLA ACH WSG	S

FRANCE • SOUTH WEST • RED

Andre Daguin Côtes de St Mont 1997, Plaimont Producteurs South West France	*Soft and easy, a savoury wine that expands to offer ripe black fruit characters.*	**£3.80**	ABY	S
Alain Brumont Tannat VdP des Côtes de Gascogne 1998, Alain Brumont South West France	*Soft and light with animal and spicey fruit aromas. Well balanced with a finely tuned structure.*	**£3.90**	ABY	B
Foncalieu Ceps du Sud Old Vine Grenache 1997, Foncalieu Southern France	*A spicey array of forest fruits match some rich gaminess, interesting character and balanced grip.*	**£4.90**	GGW BOL BWL	B
Abbotts Cirrus Cabardès 1998, Abbotts South West France	*Sweetly scented, a deeply coloured wine that is firm and juicy but should develop.*	**£5.00**	GYW	B
Bergerac Rouge Château des Eyssards 1997, Château des Eyssards South West France	*Calm, soft tones on a nicely balanced nose. Gentle red fruit character on palate and a clean finish.*	**£5.50**	L&T	B
Château Croix du Mayne Cahors 1997, CVGSO South West France	*Well balanced, a firmly structured wine with good jammy, baked fruit aromas.*	**£6.00**	VER BGL	B
Folie de Roi Madiran 1996, Cave de Crouseilles South West France	*Appealingly rustic, a firm tough wine with good animal and farmyard characters.*	**£6.00**	T&T	B

RED • SOUTHWEST • FRANCE

Wine	Description	Price	Stockists	Award
Noblesse de Serenac 1997, Cave de Labastide de Levis South West France	*A very easy to drink style offering ripe berry fruit flavours well integrated with subtle oak.*	**£6.00**	BDR	S
Château le Raz Côtes de Bergerac Cuvée Grande Chêne 1996, Château le Raz South West France	*Green, crunchy fruit character with red berry fruit palate. Medium length with dry tannins.*	**£6.10**	NIC UNS T&T	B
Le Madiran d'André Daguin Cuvée Prestige 1996, Plaimont Producteurs South West France	*Well balanced and weighty, a clean grippy wine pleasingly dry on the finish.*	**£6.40**	ABY	B
Buzet Château Baleste 1998 Vignerons de Buzet South West France	*Juicy blackcurrant fruit nose. Chunky, vibrant, ripe fruit palate with young, furry tannins.*	**£7.00**	T&T	B
Château Laulerie Bergerac 1996, Château Laulerie South West France	*Bramble fruit and pepper aromas. Some fruit complexity on palate and integrated with drying tannins.*	**£7.30**	NIC	B
Prieure de Cenac Cahors 1996, F&J Rigal South West France	*A spicey, fruity medium weight wine that offers subtle tannins and a cleansing acid tail.*	**£7.30**	ENO	S
Château de Sabazan 1995, Producteurs Plaimont South West France	*A nice minty fragrance here with a lively fresh palate with savoury notes and spice. Good length.*	**£8.60**	ALZ NIC	B

Pinpoint who sells the wine you wish to buy by turning to the stockist codes. If you know the name of the wine you want to buy, use the alphabetical index. If the price is your motivation, refer to the invaluable price guide index; red and white wines under £5, sparkling wines under £12 and champagne under £16. Happy hunting!

FRANCE • SOUTH WEST • SWEET

Wine	Description	Price	Stockist	Award
Domaine du Haut Rauly Monbazillac 1997, Pierre Alard South West France	*Peachy grapefruit and honeyed aromas smoky well textured fruit on the palate and concentrated fruit.*	**£4.50**	CWS	B
Expert Club Monbazillac 1997, Fiée des Lois South West	*Caramel aromas with honey and citrus fruit elegance, clean style medium weight and a string of acidity.*	**£6.10**	WEX	B
Château des Eyssards Saussignac 1996, Château des Eyssards South West France	*Honeycombe and candied orangepeel aromas to the fore while rich marmelade and tangello fruits trumpet in cleasing tail.*	**£6.40**	L&T	S
Château le Payral Cuvée Marie Jean Saussignac 1996, Château le Payral South West France	*Syrupy and smoky aromas. Fresh grapefruit acidity, dense glazed fruit and orange jam, with a soft mellow finish.*	**£12.50**	ENO	B
Château Richard Coup de Coeur Saussignac 1996, Château Richard Bordeaux	*Intense tropical fruit with good viscosity and obvious botrytis infection. showing balanced ripe tropical fruit, hints of floralness.*	**£12.70**	VRT	S
Domaine Castera Jurancon Cuvée Privilége 1996, Domaine Castera South West France	*Biscuit and yeasty aromas signal a fresh citrus style fruit palate of good length and weight.*	**£13.00**	GRT	S
Domaine Léonce Cuisset Saussignac 1996,Domaine Léonce Cuisset South West France	*Clean citrus, orange peel and grassy aromas crisp acidity with caremelised mandarin palate intensity.*	**£17.00**	T&T	B

FRANCE • SOUTH WEST • WHITE

Wine	Description	Price	Stockists	Award
VdP du Jardin de la France Sauvignon Blanc NV, Lacheteau South West France	*Warm floral approach followed by a palate full of tight, austere grassiness with good length.*	**£3.30**	ODD WST	B
Vivian Ducorneau VdP Côtes de Gascogne 1997, Plaimont Co-op - Vivian Duccurneau South West France	*Subtle lemon fruit on the nose and palate with a slightly waxy texture and crisp clean acidity.*	**£4.00**	MWW	B
Domaine du Tariquet 1998, Grassa Fille et Fils South West France	*Asparagus, gooseberry and herbaceous characters on the nose, palate with soft fruit and apple acidity.*	**£4.40**	Widely Available	B
Foncalieu Ceps du Sud Old Vine Vermentino 1998, Foncalieu Southern France	*Fresh gooseberry and pear aromas with plenty of lively yet elegant fruit and a clean dry finish.*	**£4.40**	GGW NYW JOV BWL	B
Foncalieu Ceps du Sud Muscat Sec 1998, Foncalieu Southern France	*An intriguing nose of vinous purity with a rich, viscous mouthfeel and a sweet fruit finish.*	**£4.50**	GGW BOL BWL	B
Domaine de Tariquet 1997, Y Grassa South West France	*Nice ripe nose with green pea, aparagus and tropical fruit, lots of personality in the mouth.*	**£5.20**	VLW WRC BUP MAR THS WCR	S
Domaine de Maubet Gros Manseng 1998, Domaine de Maubet South West France	*Baked apples on a string of lovely long acidity with a ripe fruit palate and slightly bitter finish.*	**£5.50**	COK BPW	B

GERMANY

The UK is continuing to consume increasing amounts of German wine from rich sweeties to tongue tingling dry Rieslings. Producers battle steep slopes and a climate that often does not permit full ripeness of their grapes. Despite the over bureaucratic nature of their labels, these wines are well worth seeking out. Labelling is starting to move towards the New World manner easing the duress previously encountered by those experimenting with some of the value offered by this country.

GERMANY • SWEET

Wine	Description	Price	Stockists	Award
SERRIGER VOGELSUNG RIESLING AUSLESE 1989, PETER KIESGEN WEINKOMMISSION Mosel-Saar-Ruwer	*Serious octane aromas mingled with mineral and honeyed fruit; the palate is incredibly long with excellent structure.*	**£6.00**	MWW	G TROPHY WINE
HEYMANN LOWENSTEIN WINNINGER ROTTGEN RIESLING AUSLESE 1997, WEINGUT HEYMANN LOWENSTEIN Mosel	*Fresh green apples pack this crisp, rich wine leading to a very cleansing finish.*	**£16.80**	M&V NYW PTR	B
SCHLOSS JOHANNISBERG AUSLESE RIESLING 1997, WEINGUT SCHLOSS JOHANNISBERG Rheingau	*A rich botrytis nose precedes a long lingering palate integrated with course orange marmalade.*	**£21.00**	BPW	B
BERNKASTELER LAY RIESLING EISWEIN 1998, DR LOOSEN Mosel-Saar-Ruwer	*Delicate grapey aromas are followed by a spritz on the tongue and tangy lime and honey flavours. Sublime.*	**£42.50**	NYW WSG	S

Pinpoint who sells the wine you wish to buy by turning to the stockist codes. If you know the name of the wine you want to buy, use the alphabetical index. If the price is your motivation, refer to the invaluable price guide index; red and white wines under £5, sparkling wines under £12 and Champagne under £16. Happy hunting!

GERMANY • WHITE

Reh Kendermann Bend In The River 1998, Reh Kendermann GmbH Pfalz	*Very pale lemon in colour with a light zesty fruit palate with hints of minerals and melon.*	**£3.50**	TOS	B
Kiedricher Grafenberg Riesling Spätlese 1989, Gehrt Gebhart Rheingau	*A rich aromatic nose palate exudes elegance with balanced acidity long lushes ripe fruit and fine integration .*	**£5.00**	WTS	G
Josef Leitz Rudesheimer Klosterlay 1997, Josef Leitz Rheingau	*Mineral and vegetal characters on the nose with ripe fruit and a barley sugar finish.*	**£6.00**	RML CHF CPW WSG	B
Ockfener Bockstein Riesling 1996, Von Kesselstatt Mosel-Saar-Ruwer	*This deceivingly light style offers nutty, mineral aromas with a delicate fruit driven palate and clean finish.*	**£6.00**	CWS	S
Wehlener Sonnenuhr Riesling Käbinett 1997, Dr Pauly-Bergweiler Mosel	*Intense floral and gooseberry aromas. Slightly confected and grapey on the palate with a well textured finish.*	**£9.00**	FWM BBR	S
Riesling Käbinett 1997, Weingut Schloss Johannisberg Rheingau	*honey and lemon on the nose with a firm palate of textured tropical fruit and mineral characters, quite a finish.*	**£9.50**	BPW	B
Ruppertsberger Reiterpfad Riesling Auslese Trocken 1996, Winzerrerein Ruppertsberg Pfalz	*Herbaceous nose with a fruit laden complex palate supported by a crisp backbone of acidity and a pleasing dry finish.*	**£10.00**	RSN	G TROPHY WINE

Wine	Description	Price	Stockists	Award
WEHLENER SONNENUHR RIESLING SPATLESE 1997, WEINGUT SELBACH OSTER Mosel-Saar-Ruwer	*Citrus fruit mingled with hints of petrol slightly oily texture and a firm acid structure.*	**£10.50**	BUT M&V	B
FRITZ HAAG RIESLING 1996, FRITZ HAAG Mosel	*Pale and young. clean stone fruit, loads of mineral complexity and a savoury and very long ripe fruit finish.*	**£12.20**	J&B L&W	G
PRUM GRAACHER HIMMELREICH SPATLESE 1994, JOH JOS PRUM Mosel-Saar-Ruwer	*Intriguing aromas of floral rose petals and kerosene, the palate opens up with full fruit and firm acidity.*	**£12.20**	J&B WTS	S
BERNKASTELER DOCTOR RIESLING SPATLESE 1997, DR THANISCH Mosel-Saar-Ruwer	*Lighter style with lychee fruit characters a touch of pepper and floral honeysuckle aromas.*	**£14.90**	WTS CAC D&D	B

GREECE

We welcome Greece for the first time to the main body of the book. This country of truly ancient vinous tradition is now producing wines from indigenous and the well known noble varieties. Modern techniques are used in subtle compliment to traditional methods, producing wines not only of quality but definate typicity. Forget the retsina and delve into the world of Muscat of Sámos or a delightful Cabernet from Zitsa the delights of Greece are available to all.

GREECE • FORTIFIED

SÁMOS MUSCAT NV, UCV SÁMOS Sámos	*Smoky honeyed aromas on a slightly heavy but incredibly juicy marmalade palate.*	**£5.00**	UNS ADE	B

GREECE • RED

KOUROS NEMEA 1996, D KOURTAKIS Nemea	*Up front peppers and spice on the nose with a rambling fruit palate and perfumed finish.*	**£4.80**	UNS ADE	B
STROFILIA RED 1995, STROFILIA Attica	*A sweet fruit nose with a hint of mustard, good fruit flavours in the mouth completed by a neat finish.*	**£6.00**	ODD	B
SEMELI NEMEA 1997, SEMELI Nemea	*A clean nose showing fruit smoothie characteristics that cascade onto a firm tannin palate with a lingering aftertaste.*	**£7.50**	HWL	B

KAPNIAS CABERNET SAUVIGNON 1996, HATZIMICHALIS Central Greece	*Warm, spicy fruit nose. Balanced and structured with summer fruit, dense and developed.*	**£11.30**	WCR GWC	(S)
HATZIMICHALIS MERLOT 1997, HATZIMICHALIS Central Greece	*Ripe fruit with a hint of posh spice on the nose, fine tannins and well-balanced finish.*	**£13.50**	GWC	(S)
CHÂTEAU SEMELI 1996, SEMELI Nemea	*Gently perfumed with a touch of spice and quite minerally on the palate.*	**£15.00**	HWL HWL	(B)

GREECE • WHITE

SAMOS VIN DOUX GREEK MUSCAT NV, UNION DES CO-OP VINICOLES DE SAMOS Samos	*Barley sugar, rich raisins and vinous aromas, a sweet palate matched by fresh acid, nice finish.*	**£3.00**	SMF	(B)
SPIROPOULOS DOMAINE 1998, SPIRIPOULOS Mantinia	*A facinating wine with hints of herb, lemon and lime and a touch of fig.*	**£6.00**	GWC	(B)
HATZIMICHALIS DOMAINE WHITE 1998, HATZIMICHALIS Central Greece	*Fresh and lively with crisp apple characters, hints of lime, asparagus and herbaceousness, good acidity.*	**£7.00**	GWC	(B)
HATZIMICHALIS BARRIQUESAUVIGNON BLANC 1998, HATZIMICHALIS Central Greece	*Good clean passionfruit with evidence of lees work, a delicate citrus driven palate with a firm finish.*	**£8.50**	GWC	(B)

Wine	Tasting note	Price	Stockist	
Spiropoulos Reserve 1996, Spiripoulos Mantinia	*Nice clean citrus and oak entry, nice buttery vanilla on the balanced palate, zingy finish.*	**£8.50**	GWC	B
Hatzimichalis Laas 1997, Hatzimichalis Central Greece	*Light citrus fruit characters on the nose, with crisp lemon characters and balanced acidity on the palate.*	**£9.00**	GWC	B

Pinpoint who sells the wine you wish to buy by turning to the stockist codes. If you know the name of the wine you want to buy, use the alphabetical index. If the price is your motivation, refer to the invaluable price guide index; red and white wines under £5, sparkling wines under £12 and champagne under £16. Happy hunting!

ITALY

Beaming with a string of recent successful vintages Italy is reinforcing its position as a passionate, wine and food nation. Renowned for its bouncing Barolos and curvaceous Chiantis, Italy has this year excelled itself by taking away the prestigeous White Wine Trophy. While wines from Sicily, Marches and Campania have all stayed staunchly parochial. We have seen them, this year deliver impressive quality and character when pitched against their illustrious cousins from the north.

ITALY • FORTIFIED

Wine	Description	Price	Stockists	Award
BARONA ROSSO VERMOUTH NV, BARONA Piedmont	*Showing sweet cloves and cinnamon, good vivacious acidity providing a cleansing finish.*	**£3.10**	MHV	B
MARSALA GARIBALDI DOLCE NV, CARLO PELLEGRINO Sicily	*Warm treacle,brown sugar and scorched almonds, palate is unctuous but not cloying, persistent finish.*	**£6.00**	Widely Available	B
RALLO MARSALA VERGINE 12 YEAR OLD, RALLO Sicily	*A gorgeous nose of deep, cooked fruit and coffee leading to a sweet, subtle cleansing conclusion.*	**£6.00**	TOS SAF WTS MRN KWI GRA	S

ITALY • PIEDMONT

Wine	Description	Price	Stockists	Award
BARBERA D'ASTI SUPERIORE LE CROCI 1996, TENUTE NEIRANO Piedmont	*Mature cherries and plums greet the nose and follow through to good acidity and lovely balance.*	**£4.50**	CTL	B

Wine	Description	Price	Stockists	Award
Barbera d'Asti Callissano 1997, GIV Piedmont	*Oak blended with concentrated fruit leads to sweet and sour cherries on the palate, culminating in a lingering, creamy finish.*	**£5.00**	TOS	S
Barbera d'Asti 1997, Firesteed Piedmont	*A big fruit nose with a mineral vein leads to a cherry palate wih a distinct chalky tone.*	**£5.50**	JNW LIB	S
Dolcetto di Dogliani 1997, Manfredi Piedmont	*A deep, modern, well-made wine displaying ripe morello cherries and a soft, gentle tannin finish.*	**£6.00**	BPW	B
Dolcetto d'Alba 1998, Villadoria Piedmont	*Lush mocha and cherry aromas. Full bodied, the palate reflect these flavours and finishes with finesse.*	**£6.10**	AFI	B
Barbera d'asti 1997, Ca Bianca Piedmont	*Seductive nose of dried fruits and almonds before a palate of grippy tannins leading to a bitter chocolate tail.*	**£7.30**	BWL	B
Barbera d'Alba Sucule 1997, Villa Lanata Piedmont	*Sweet candied fruits abound in this well-structured wine with firm tannins and lovely length.*	**£9.00**	GRA FRT	B
Dolcetto d'Alba Coste e Fossati 1997, Aldo Vajra Piedmont	*Full of sharp summer fruits blended with spice and oak, this wine shows good development and balance.*	**£10.00**	LIB	S
Barbera d'Alba Vignota 1997, Conterno Fantino Piedmont	*Youthful black fruit blends harmoniously with pepper in this balanced, well-structured wine.*	**£10.50**	ENO	B

Wine	Description	Price	Stockists	Award
Viberti Barbera d'Alba 1996, Viberti Piedmont	*Leather and plums are dominant in the massive palate of this wonderfully complex, gamey wine.*	**£12.20**	RBS GGW VRT	S
Barbera d'Alba 1997, Aldo Vajra Piedmont	*A lively blend of bitter cherries and crisp acidity with a long, soft and colourful finish.*	**£13.00**	LIB	B
Barbaresco Campo Quadro 1995, Punset Piedmont	*A lovely mixture of boiled ripe fruit in this smooth tannin medium-weight wine with crisp acidity.*	**£14.00**	WAW	B
Barbera d'Alba 1997, Grimaldi Piedmont	*Classic black bitter cherries predominate a whole host of complex aromas and flavours.*	**£15.00**	WIN	S
Langhe DOC Freisa Kye 1997, Aldo Vajra Piedmont	*Minty flavours combine with herbal fruit and firm tannins in a lingering finish.*	**£20.00**	LIB	B
Roberto Voerzio Vignaserra 1996, Roberto Voerzio Piedmont	*Fresh blackberries are knitted with oak flavours in this superbly complex wine with good acidity and strong tannins.*	**£20.00**	ENO	S
Podere di Montalupa Syrah 1997, Giacomo Ascheri Piedmont	*A green pepper nose and vibrant raspberry palate with gentle tannins and a smooth finish.*	**£24.50**	ENO	B
Monfalletto Barolo 1995, Cordero di Montezemolo Piedmont	*A complex wine of mature cherries and oaky characters, firm tannins with fine acid structure.*	**£28.00**	EUW	S

BAROLO SORI GINESTRA 1995, CONTERNO FANTINO Piedmont	*A wonderful balance between cherry and cigar box aromas in this mature wine with a drying finish.*	**£29.00**	ENO	B
CORDERO DI MONTEZEMOLO ENRICO VI BAROLO 1995, CORDERO DI MONTEZEMOLO Piedmont	*Mature cherries blended with oakey characteristics in a well structured wine, strong acid levels with a firm tannin finish.*	**£31.90**	EUW	S

ITALY • RED • OTHER

CANTINE & PALME ROSSO DI PUGLIA NV, CANTINE & PALME Puglia	*Sharp, green fruits combine with violets in this well-structured wine with good length.*	**£3.50**	CTL	B
CO-OP VENETO MERLOT NV, GIRELLI Veneto	*A flowery nose with sweet fruit on the palate. An easy drinking style with good weight.*	**£3.50**	VEX CWS	B
CASA GIRELLI CANALETTO MERLOT DEL VENETO 1998, CASA GIRELLI Veneto	*Nice blackcurrant fruits and tobacco on the nose with a nice level of tannin and good length.*	**£3.80**	VLW VEX CGI	B
BRICCOLO 1997, VINI SNC BIDOLI Friuli	*Smooth and mature with chocolate and creamy cherry fruit and coffee and toffee flavours waiting to emerge.*	**£4.40**	FUL WST	S
VILLA ICONA SANGIOVESE 1998, MONCARO TERRE CORTESI Marches	*A ripe fruit nose is accompanied by green, slightly bitter tannins and welcome racey acidity.*	**£4.40**	BDR EUW	B

Merum Primitivo 1998, Mondo del Vino Umbria	*Floral aromas are in perfect harmony with warm ripe black cherry flavours. Greenish tannins suggest ageing potential.*	**£4.50**	WST	(S)
Chiaro di Luna Montepulciano d'Abruzzo Oak Aged 1998, Madonna dei Miracoli Abruzzo	*A nose of fresh berries with superbly infused oak follows on to a superb tannin structure.*	**£4.80**	SAF WST	(S)
Basilicata Rosso 1998, Basilium Basilicata	*Baked black cherry and blueberry fruit with herbal tones, approachable tannins and a clean finish.*	**£4.90**	HOH BDR	(B)
Chiaro di Luna Montepulciano d'Abruzzo Oak Aged 1997, Madonna dei Miracoli Abruzzo	*Rich, dense, sweet nose with sour cherry and plummy ripe fruit leads to balancing tannins and a long berry finish.*	**£5.00**	SAF	(B)
Connubio Nero d'Avola 1998, Cantina Delibori Sicily	*Well-balanced wine crammed with cherry fruit, oak flavours, powerful tannins and a drying finish.*	**£5.00**	SBS ENO	(B)
L'Arco Cabernet Franc 1997, Cabert Friuli	*Subtle fine tannins delicious fruit flavours, and a wonderful mysterious complexity, combine to set this wine apart.*	**£5.00**	TOS SMF JSM EHL	(S)
Montepulciano d'Abruzzo 1997, Barone Cornacchia Abruzzo	*Attractive wine packed with red fruit and gentle new oak, soft tannins and a long, fruity finish.*	**£5.00**	MWW	(B)
Tre Uve 1997, Mondo del Vino Abruzzo	*Pronounced nose of vanilla oak and spice with hints of herbaceousness around good prune and cherry fruit.*	**£5.00**	SAF ODD WST	(B)

Wine	Description	Price	Stockists	Medal
Le Franzine Rosso Terre di Franciacorta 1997, Barone Pizzini Veneto	*A clean sweet oak nose and a savoury, chewy palate meet a sweet berry and tannin finish.*	**£5.20**	FRT GSJ	S
Vallone Salice Salentino 1996, Agricola Vallone Puglia	*A leathery nose with plum fruit tones and sweet, ripe fruit finishing clean and dry.*	**£5.20**	Widely Available	S
Trulli Primitivo IGT 1997, Azienda Vinicola Cantele Puglia	*A lovely big wine with plenty of rich cherries balanced with pleasing tannins and acidity.*	**£5.40**	Widely Available	B
Bright Brothers Barrel Aged Nero d'Avola 1998, Bright Brothers Sicily	*Packed with vibrant strawberry and raspberry aromas, the judicial use of oak makes for a well balanced wine.*	**£5.50**	EHL	S
Donnafugata Tancredi Contessa Entellina 1996, Donnafugata Sicily	*A mature, vegetal, tarry wine with smoky overtones and dried fruit on the palate.*	**£5.50**	VIN	B
Duca di Castelmonte Centare Rosso Nero d'Avola 1997, Duca di Castelmonte Sicily	*Perfumed cherry spice aromas lead into a nice wine with good fresh fruit and good length.*	**£5.50**	TRO ODD WCR WTS WIN AVB HOH	B
Basilium Cabernet Merlot 1998, Basilium Basilicata	*Nice ripe black fruit and mint tones here with a gamey edge. Firm tannins and length.*	**£5.60**	HOH V&V WTS AVB	S
Donnafugata Mille Un Notte 1995, Donnafugata Sicily	*Black cherry fruits accompanied by a spicy, charred meat character and notable tannins.*	**£5.60**	VIN	B

Wine	Description	Price	Stockists	Award
Settesoli Nero d'Avola Cabernet Sauvignon 1998, Settesoli Sicily	*A well-made example of a modern style wine with creamy soft fruit and good wood with ripe tannins.*	**£5.60**	EHL	B
Aglianico del Vulture 1997, Basilium Basilicata	*Berry fruits play to an orchestra of plum and damson in a full tannin palate.*	**£5.70**	V&V AVB HOH	S
Riparosso 1997, Dino Illuminati Abruzza	*Lots of primary fruit aromas of blackcurrant and cherries lead to a full bodied palate.*	**£5.70**	SMF BLN EHL	S
Cantele Caramia Negroamaro 1997, Azienda Vinicola Cantele Puglia	*Blueberries on the nose are followed by strong tannins and creamy raspberries with an attractive finish.*	**£6.00**	WRC BUP MAR TOS THS IWS	B
Cantele Caramia Primitivo 1997, Azienda Vinicola Cantele Puglia	*Poached berry fruit blended with subtle oak in this complex wine with firm tannins.*	**£6.00**	WRC BUP MAR THS SMF IWS	B
Ciro Rosso Classico 1997,Librandi Calabria	*Maturing leather and tobacco aromas, a dry style with cherry and cedarwood, well balanced tannin behind fruit.*	**£6.00**	V&V ENO	S
Emporio Nero d'Avola Syrah 1998, Firriato	*Complex ripe fruit on the palate, perfectly balanced by firm tannins and moderate acidity.*	**£6.00**	WRC BUP TOS THS IWS	S
Sangiovese di Romagna Superiore Riserva 1995, Gruppo Coltiva Emilia Romagna	*A ripe fruit nose, a touch confected with good flavours and structure on the finish.*	**£6.00**	BPW CER	B

Wine	Description	Price	Stockists	Award
Villa Pigna Cabernasco 1997, Villa Pigna Marches	*A complex nose of plums, spice and blackcurrant herald a ripe palate of full blown tannins. Great length.*	£6.00	TOS	B
Notarpanaro 1994, Agricola Taurino Puglia	*Medium brick red in colour with maturing meaty and somewhat toasty aromas. Well intergrated tannin.*	£6.10	V&V MWW ODD AVB HOH	S
Salice Salentino Riserva 1996, Agricola Taurino Puglia	*Rich red brick colour with inviting mature farm yard aromas and fresh and dried red berry fruits with spicey tones.*	£6.10	SAF V&V THS ODD MWW AVB HOH	B
Vallone Brindisi Rosso 1995, Agricola Vallone Puglia	*A big, vegetal nose is followed by intense juicy fruit and cream in this well-balanced wine.*	£6.10	TRO BPW	S
I Portali Aglianico del Vulture 1997, Basilium Basilicata	*Youthful upfront ripe plummy fruit, concentrated blackcurrent with underlying tones of vanilla and caramel.*	£6.20	MWW AVB HOH	B
Rosso Conero 1996, Moncaro Terre Cortesi Marches	*A rich truffle nose, creamy and sweet gathers pace on a superbly textured palate.*	£6.20	EUW	B
Bonera 1995, Sicily	*A brooding wine packed with rich chocolate,old oak and wild cherries and a long-lasting finish.*	£6.30	EHL	B
Valpolicella Classico Superiore 1997, Cantina Sociale Valpolicella Negrar Domini Veneti Veneto	*A full weighty palate laden with forest fruits and almonds before a sweet baked fruit tart finish.*	£6.40	GRA	B

Wine	Description	Price	Stockist	Award
Montepulciano d'Abruzzo 1996, Barone Cornacchia Abruzzo	*Subtle and maturing nose with hints of game and spice. Soft and round, dark current fruit finishing with a savory tang.*	£6.50	VIN	B
Colli del Trasimeno Rosso 1998, Pieve Del Vescovo Umbria	*Rich with black cherry, burnt almond and mint flavours with fine grained tannins and a cleansing finish.*	£6.70	NYW LIB	B
Duca di Castelmonte Ulysse Etna Rosso 1996, Duca di Castelmonte Sicily	*A compact wine with leather and spice on the nose, ripe fruit flavours and a warm finish.*	£6.70	HOH AVB	B
Le Bine Valpolicella 1997,Campagnola Veneto	*Zappy and youthful, with crisp minty aromas. Fresh plummy fruit with balaned tannins and acidity.*	£6.90	EUW	B
Stephano Antonucci Rosso 1995, Santa Barbara Marches	*Ripe black cherries and dark chocolate balance perfectly on the palate with firm, grainy tannins.*	£6.90	VIN	S
d'Istinto Magnifico 1997, BRL Hardy Sicily	*Olive and bramble aromas combine in a rich palate crammed with ripe fruit and hints of toffee and tobacco.*	£7.00	HBR	S
Laruso Ripassato 1997, Arcadia Veneto	*Raspberries and runner beans make for an interesting contrast in this well balanced and vibrant wine.*	£7.00	TOS	B
Tre Uve Ultima 1997, Mondo del Vino Abruzzo	*Spicey cream and vanillan oak showing black cherries through well intergrated tannins.*	£7.00	SMF WST	G

Wine	Description	Price	Stockists	Award
Cappello di Prete 1995, Francesco Candido Puglia	*A nicely-balanced wine with fragrant fruit, hints of bitter herbs and an excellent structure.*	**£7.20**	NYW ENO	B
Montepulciano d'Abruzzo Jorio 1997, Umani Ronchi Abruzzo	*Shining cherries and black fruits with a hint of basil, sing from this well structured, long finisher.*	**£7.30**	RBS VLW WCR ENO	B
Rosso Conero Riserva 1996, Moncaro Terre Cortesi Marches	*A lively Italian showing sexy blueberries set against a landscape of oregano and fresh ciabatta.*	**£7.40**	EUW	B
Ripasso Valpolicella Classico 1995, Tommasi Viticoltori Veneto	*An inviting fruit entry to this ripe wine showing mulberry flavours that will gain more depth with time.*	**£7.80**	L&T	S
RipassaValpolicella Classico Superiore 1996, Zenato Veneto	*Black fruits with hints of candied limes and incredible, dense fruits of the forest palate with superb tannin structure.*	**£7.90**	WRC BUP MAR THS EUW	G
Cannonau di Sardegna Riserva 1995, Sella & Mosca Sardinia	*A mineral and fruit nose leads to a medium bodied wine with fine tannins and a tidy tail.*	**£8.20**	GSH V&V HVN LUD ALI	B
Zenato Merlot delle Venezie 1996, Zenato Venato	*Cedarwood and black fruit nose. Good fruit character with hints of licorice. Lovely structure, with soft tannins.*	**£8.20**	EUW	B
D'Angelo Aglianico del Vulture 1996, D'Angelo Basilicata	*Subtle nose with warm ripe sweet dark fruit, firm tannin balance with a full fruit finish.*	**£8.40**	RBS LUD SEL WIM V&C ALI	B

Wine	Description	Price	Stockists	Award
AGLIANICO RISERVA 1992, CANTINA DEL TABURNO Campania	*Super complexity to be found on the nose and palate of this perfectly mature stylish wine.*	**£8.50**	CTH	B
REFOSCO 1997, LIVON Friuli	*Maraschino cherries and currants lead to a palate of fine grained tannins with great finesse.*	**£8.70**	EUW	B
AGONTANO ROSSO CONERO RISERVA 1995, CASA VINICOLA GIOACCHINO GAROFOLI Marches	*Gentle good-for-you nose, with redcurrants and oak flavours. Tannins are softening so drink now.*	**£9.00**	IWS	B
FALERNO DEL MASSICO ROSSO 1997, FATTORIA VILLA MATILDE Campania	*Herby black cherry aromas come to the fore, with just a sprinkling of black pepper.*	**£9.30**	LIB	B
DOLCETTO D'ALBA 1997, MAURO VEGLIO Piedmont	*Deep purple colour. Succulent with lots of sweet berry fruit, balanced acidity and good length.*	**£9.50**	WIN	B
CIRO CLASSICO RISERVA DUCA SAN FELICE 1995, LIBRANDI Calabria	*Some maturing earthy plummy aromas leading to a rich spicey, vegetal, long and complex palate structure.*	**£10.00**	ENO	B
VALLE DEL TRONO AGLIANICO DEL VULTURE 1996, BASILIUM Basilicata	*Stewed spicey prunes and vanilla toasted bread showing good length and tight finish.*	**£10.00**	MWW AVB HOH	B
SELLA & MOSCA TANCA FARRA' ALGHERO 1994, SELLA & MOSCA Sardinia	*Wonderful blackcurrant and fig nose leads to a powerful and well structured with smoky redberry fruit.*	**£10.40**	GSH V&V SEL WIM ALI	S

Wine	Tasting note	Price	Stockists	Award
Rocca Rubia Carignano del Sulcis Riserva 1995, Santadi Sardinia	*Attractive morello cherry and plums trumpet in a warm palate of fine tannins which point to a clean fruit acid finish.*	**£10.50**	RBS VLW NYW ENO	S
La Prendina Cabernet Sauvignon Il Falcone 1996, La Prendina Veneto	*Firm tannins with licorice, good acid and some neat oak before a tidy fruit acid tail.*	**£11.50**	VIN	B
Umani Ronchi Cumaro Rosso Conero 1995, Umani Ronchi Marches	*Superb fruit concentration and lovely vanillin oak nuances lead to a well balanced palate with firm tannins.*	**£11.70**	RBS VLW JNW NYW ENO	S
Amarone Della Valpolicella Classico 1994, Rocca Sveva Veneto	*Berry red youthful appearance, reflecting vibrant cherry fruit flavours on a light, fresh palate.*	**£12.00**	UNS	B
Duca di Aragona 1993, Francesco Candido Puglia	*A mature wine with rich dried fruit flavours, an immense structure and lovely complexity.*	**£12.00**	ENO	S
Liano Sangiovese Cabernet 1996, Umberto Cesari Emilia Romagna	*Attractive floral nose and a rich, full palate laden with ripe fruit and clean tannins.*	**£12.00**	LUD ALI	B
Montepulciano d'Abruzzo Zanna 1995, Dino Illuminati Controguerra Abruzzo	*Pronounced mixed fruit, blackcurrent, rhubarb and delicate spice prelude a well rounded palate.*	**£12.00**	BLN EHL	B
Vigneti di Torbe Valpolicella Classico Superiore 1996, Cantina Sociale Valpolicella Negrar Veneto	*Perfumed with violets, plums and dark chocolate hint at the luscious fruit laden palate to come.*	**£12.00**	GRA FRT	B

Il Vessillo Rosso Dell'Umbria 1995, Lungarotti Umbria	*Aromatic cedary nose, dry fruits on the palate with a great tannin structure and a clean fruit finish.*	**£12.50**	LUD V&C ALI	B
Amarone Classico 1995,Filli Tedeschi Veneto	*Game and fruit play cat and mouse in this superbly crafted wine with great length.*	**£13.60**	WCR SAF V&V MWW WIN SEL HOH	B
Amarone Della Valpolicella Classico Marano 1994, Boscaini Veneto	*A light fragrant style offering some soft cherry and gentle herbal notes. Nice inky consistency on the palate.*	**£14.00**	SMF BLN EHL	B
Brigaldara Amarone della Valpolicella Classico 1994, Brigaldara Veneto	*Appealing concentration of fruit and tannin and delightful developed gamey notes make for superb drinking now.*	**£14.00**	VIN	B
Amarone Della Valpolicella Classico 1995, Campagnola Veneto	*Closed nose, but showing potential for the future. Fresh blackcurrant flavours with good oak balance.*	**£15.00**	EUW	B
Le Vigne Amarone Della Valpolicella Valpantena 1995, Arcadia Vini Veneto	*Showcasing stewed red fruits, vegetal and farm-yardy aromas before a palate studded with perky tannins and cherry fruit.*	**£15.00**	ENO	B
Salice Salentino Reserva "Donna Lisa" 1995, Leone de Castris Pulgia	*A lean wine with aromas of poached red fruits, cinammon and hints of vanilla.*	**£15.00**	MON	B
Gravello 1993, Librandi Calabria	*Rich intense upfront aromas of dark fruit and dense, toasty oak with rich dark, chocolatey and plummy fruit.*	**£15.20**	V&V ENO	S

Wine	Tasting note	Price	Stockists	Award
CESARI AMARONE CLASSICO DELLA VALPOLICELLA VIGNETO IL BOSCO 1993, CESARI Veneto	*Complex offering of spice and liquorice on the nose as well as a touch of fruitcake and marzipan.*	**£15.50**	AFI	G
PLANETA CABERNET SAUVIGNON 1997, PLANETA Sicily	*Light, fragrant berry nose ahead of a raspberry flavoured tannin extravaganza.*	**£15.50**	VLW NYW ENO	B
VALPOLICELLA CLASSICO SUPERIORE MARANO 1997, BOSCAINI Veneto	*Light, florally perfumed fruit on the nose. Well reflected in a well structured, rounded palate.*	**£15.50**	EHL	B
AMARONE DELLA VALPOLICELLA CLASSICO VIGNETO "MONTE MASUA" 1995, IL SESTANTE Veneto	*Full and concentrated licorice and aniseed notes and great strucure. Will benefit from further rest, but why wait.*	**£15.60**	BWC	B
AMARONE CLASSICO 1995, TOMMASI VITICOLTORI Veneto	*A rich nose showing good complexity. Liquorice, rosehip and stewed red fruit flavours predominating.*	**£16.00**	L&T	B
DOMINI VENETI VIGNETI DI JAGO AMARONE CLASSICO 1995, CANTINA SOCIALE VALPOLICELLA NEGRAR Veneto	*Intense small berried fruit notes meld with fresh cut herbs and just a hint of cedar.*	**£16.00**	GRA	G
CAMPOLONGO DI TORBE AMARONE CLASSICO 1993, MASI Veneto	*Ripe fruit with a nudge of Toblerone before a creamy tannin palate and a firm finish.*	**£16.50**	EHL	B
CAPITEL RECIOTO CLASSICO MONTE FONTANA 1995, F.ILLI TEDESCHI Veneto	*Displays great finesse on the nose and palate. Ripe fruit is masked by still youthful tannins. An absolute gun.*	**£16.60**	V&V NYW AVB HOH	S

Wine	Description	Price	Stockists	Award
Lucciaio Colli del Trasimeno 1997, Pieve del Vescovo Umbria	*Big wafts of ginger and cinnamon matched beautifully with black-currant and cigar box flavours.*	£17.00	LIB	S
Planeta Merlot 1997, Planeta Sicily	*Pronounced blackberry and mint notes immersed in fine dusty tannins and with great fruit acidity.*	£17.00	VLW NYW ENO	S
Vigna Camarato 1995, Fattoria Villa Matilde Campania	*This developing marzi-pan and pommygranite flavoured wine will leave you with a healthy glow.*	£17.00	LIB	B
Dino Illuminati Nico 1995, Azienda Agricola Abruzzo	*Maturing red cherry spice and sour cherry aromas with hints of green leaf leading to an explosion of juicy fruit.*	£17.50	BLN EHL	B
Palazzo Della Torre 1995, Allegrini Veneto	*A lovely satisfying mouth feel of morello cherries leads to a sophisticated tannin tail.*	£17.50	BDR ENO	B
Planeta Santa Cecilia Nero d'Avola 1997, Planeta Sicily	*A well-balanced, youth-ful wine with minty tones and green, stalky fruit and a reasonable finish.*	£17.50	NYW ENO	B
Amorone Classico 1993, Zenato Venato	*A remarkable wine of great character offfering lifted red berry fruit and maraschino cherry notes and a luscious palate.*	£18.00	WRC MAR EUW	G
Terre Brune Carignano del Sulcis 1995, Santadi Sardinia	*A rich purple verging on inky black with delight-ful cherry and bitter almond notes to the fore of a full bodied palate.*	£18.30	RBS NYW ENO	G

ITALY • RED • OTHER

Wine	Description	Price	Stockists	Award
Osar 1995, Masi Veneto	*Cherry wood fire embers with a screen of black fruit notes. The palate of burnt toffee peaks with a clean, tannin tail.*	**£18.50**	NYW BLN EHL	G
Tiareblu Livon 1995, Livon Collio	*Light, straightforward easy-drinking style with hints of blackcurrant and some minerally characters and a pleasant finish.*	**£18.50**	EUW	B
Lumen Montepulciano d'Abruzzo 1994, Dino Illuminati Controguerra Abruzzo	*Earthy vegetal and tarry fruit aromas lead to leathery spicey rich red fruit complexities on the palate.*	**£20.00**	BLN EHL	S
Umani Ronchi Pelago 1996, Umani Ronchi Marches	*Rich cigar box and tobacco characters add complexity to this soft, mellow wine with understated power and elegance.*	**£20.40**	RBS VLW JNW NYW ENO	G
Capitel Monti Olmi Amarone Classico 1995, Filli Tedeschi Veneto	*Aniseed rings and marzipan signal a wine of great complexity and depth.*	**£20.70**	HOH V&V MWW V&C AVB	B
Loredan Gasparini Capo di Stato 1996, Venegazzu Veneto	*Lovely mature wine showing ripe blackberry and blueberry fruits open into a full bodied palate.*	**£20.70**	V&V AVB HOH	S
Fobiano 1997, La Carraia Umbria	*A herb and cherry tomato nose leads to a fruit basket of wildberries with nutty notes.*	**£21.00**	NYW LIB	S
Amarone Della Valpolicella 1993, Allegrini Veneto	*A rich nose of plums, damson and cherries with just a hint of well measured oak before a perfectly weighted palate.*	**£21.60**	RBS V&V NYW ENO	G

Wine	Description	Price	Stockists	Medal
Il Patriglione 1993, Taurino Puglia	*Multitudes of sultana, raisin and dried fig fruit with good depth and length.*	**£22.00**	V&V AVB HOH	G
Cabernet Sanct Valentin 1995, St Michael Eppan Alto Adige	*Attractive colour with clean fruit and bell pepper characters and a nice acid finish.*	**£22.90**	EUW	B
Ca de Loi Amarone Della Valpolicella Classico 1993, Boscaini Veneto	*Characteristic almond and bitter cherry nose.Light body showing great finesse with an elegant long finish.*	**£25.00**	BLN EHL	S
La Grola 1995, Allegrini Veneto	*An inviting nose of sweet bramble fruit leads to a well defined palate of kind tannins.*	**£25.00**	ENO	B
Amarone Della Valpolicella 1995, Allegrini Veneto	*Intense, slightly confected fruity nose on a fairy floss textured palate before a sweet, acid finish.*	**£27.00**	ENO	G
La Poja 1995, Allegrini Veneto	*Fruit to the fore in this jam packed red. Thick with plums, strawberries and cherries.*	**£28.00**	ENO	S
Amarone Classico Reserva 1990, Sergio Zenato Veneto	*Rich velvety fruit to the fore on the bitter sweet palate promises greater things to come.*	**£32.00**	WTS	S
Sergio Zenato Amarone Riserva 1990, Zenato Venato	*Big,bold and adventurous, offering a plethora of figs, dates, prunes and marzipan notes. Superb finish.*	**£40.80**	EUW	G

ITALY • ROSÉ

Wine	Description	Price	Stockists	Award
Bardolino Chiaretto 1998, Cavalchina Azienda Agricola Veneto	*A well structured wine with good weight, colour and fruit on both the nose and palate.*	**£5.00**	VIN	B

ITALY • SPARKLING

Wine	Description	Price	Stockists	Award
Safeway Asti Spumante NV, Perlino Piedmont	*Very fresh with a lemony nose and a good dose of sweetness and very glug-gable.*	**£4.80**	SAF	B
Somerfield Asti Spumante NV, Dolce Perlino Piedmont	*A yeasty, grapey nose with a good level of sweetness balanced by crisp, apple acidity.*	**£4.80**	SMF	S
Rialto Asti Spumante 1998, Capetta I Vip Piedmont	*A fresh and forward grapey, muscat nose with good mousse, sweetness and balancing acidity.*	**£5.00**	CTL	B
Martini d'Asti Spumante NV, Martini & Rossi Piedmont	*A subtle nose offering complex flavours in the mouth and crisp acidity to finish.*	**£5.80**	UNS SAF TOS ASD SMF	B
Bellavista Gran Cuvée Brut 1994, Bellavista Lombardia	*Toasty buttery aromas linger in the glass and soft rounded fruit treat the palate.*	**£19.80**	V&C LUD ALI	B

ITALY • TUSCANY

Wine	Description	Price	Stockists	Award
Barrelaia 1997, Piccini Tuscany	*Dry, fresh lively and peppery with bountiful, herbacious fruit, well-balanced tannins and fresh acidity.*	**£4.00**	CWS	S
Sangiovese di Toscana 1997, Cecchi Tuscany	*Impressive nose of soft ripe cherries, leading to a supple palate of taught acidity and upfront tannin.*	**£4.00**	WRC BUP MAR THS TOS WTS	S
Mimosa Sangiovese di Maremma 1997, Luigi Cecchi & Figli Tuscany	*Soft and full spicy nose, showing hints of basil and oregano. Nice fruit balance with firm tannins and acidity.*	**£5.00**	SAF JSM IWS	B
Morellino di Scansano 1997, Azienda Agraria Val Delle Rose Tuscany	*Subtle leathery oak with masses of spicy fruit aromas. Soft and spicy blackcurrant flavours.*	**£6.00**	TOS WRC BUP IWS	B
Chianti Classico 1997, Geografico Tuscany	*A creamy nutty nose, raspberry and cherry fruit character intergrated tannin and good length.*	**£6.20**	AFI	B
Paolo Masi Chianti Riserva 1996, Renzo Masi Tuscany	*A bold and striking black olive flirts with a pretty blueberry on a bed of warm tannins.*	**£6.80**	BDR	B
Messer Pietro di Teuzzo Chianti Classico Cecchi Classico 1997, Casa Vinicola Luigi Cecchi & Figli Tuscany	*Pitted black olives and herbed tomatoes kick off the nose. Rich tobacco and bitter liquorice finish.*	**£7.00**	JSM IWS	S

Wine	Description	Price	Stockists	Medal
Brusco dei Barbi 1997, Fattoria dei Barbi Tuscany	*A mad nutty nose, with lots of pepper and spice wakes from the luxury of a smooth tannin bed.*	£7.30	ENO	B
Villa Vistarenni Chianti Classico 1997, Vistarenni Tuscany	*Glorious in style, intense red cherry fruit is supported by upright tannins and firm acidity.*	£7.60	ALI	B
Carpineto Dogajolo 1997, Casa Vinicola Carpineto Tuscany	*Soft appealing fruit aromas firm, well balanced spicey red cherries with a long tannic, lingering finish.*	£7.70	HOH V&V MWW AVB	B
Cetamura Chianti 1997, Badia A Coltibuono Tuscany	*Lovely leather and tarry cherry aromas, stand up tannins and tight acidity offer structure, crisp finish.*	£7.70	GSH V&V AVB HOH	S
Barco Reale di Carmignano 1998, Tenuta di Capezzana Tuscany	*Subtle aromas of flowers and bubblegum, with raspberries on the palate balanced with good tannins and acidity.*	£8.20	JNW GGW LIB	B
Montegiachi Chianti Classico Riserva 1995, Geografico Montegiachi Tuscany	*Hints of tea leaves and red fruits, followed by a green wine with good acidity and firm tannins.*	£8.60	AFI	B
Villa Vistarenni Chianti Classico Vigneto Assolo 1996, Vistarenni Tuscany	*Driven by rich red fruits on the nose, this wine has silky smooth tannins and firm acidity.*	£8.90	ALI	B
Castello di Nipozzano Riserva Chianti Rufina 1996, Marchesi de' Frescobaldi Tuscany	*Well developed with an open fruit and herbal nose leaching into a rich fruit palate.*	£9.00	FRT ODD MWW GRA	B

Wine	Description	Price	Stockists	Award
Morellino di Scansano 1998, Le Pupille Tuscany	*Elegant summer fruit aromas lead to a rich palate blending fruit and oak with good length.*	**£9.00**	VLW NYW LIB	B
Chianti Rufina 1997, Fattoria Selvapiana Tuscany	*Chocolate and cocoa beans with a hint of herb lead to soft fruit and mineral flavours and a cleansing finish.*	**£9.10**	RBS GGW NYW LIB	S
Lamole di Lamole Chianti Classico 1996, Pile e Lamole Tuscany	*Cigar box aromas blended with ripe cherries produce a ripe, elegant structure on this strapping wine.*	**£9.70**	V&V ALI	S
Carpineto Chianti Classico 1997,Casa Vinicola Carpineto Tuscany	*Complex ripe black cherry fruit with spicey tones swoon into well structured smooth tannins.*	**£9.90**	HOH V&V DLS AVB	B
Cerraia Vino Nobile di Montepulciano 1996, Federico Carletti Tuscany	*Sweet ripe fruit with hints of tobacco leaf on the nose joined by crisp acidity on the palate.*	**£10.00**	AFI	B
Renzo Masi I Pini Fattoria di Basciano 1997, Renzo Masi Tuscany	*HIgh spirited fruit engages the senses and prepares for a fruit and spice extravaganza.*	**£10.00**	BDR QST	B
Rocca Guicciarda Chianti Classico Riserva 1996, Barone Ricasoli Tuscany	*Complex earth and licorice play second fiddle to prickly pears and buxom cherries. Great finish.*	**£10.00**	ENO	B
Rosso di Montalcino 1996, Castello Banfi Tuscany	*A sweet, big-structured chewy wine with high acidity, toasty notes and a drying finish.*	**£10.00**	VIN	B

ITALY • TUSCANY

Wine	Description	Price	Stockists	Award
CHIANTI CLASSICO 1997, CASTELLO DI FONTERUTOLI Tuscany	*Heady Belgian chocolate truffle aromas splash onto the palate with seemingly infinite concentrated fruit.*	**£10.10**	VLW JNW NYW ENO	S
CARMIGNANO 1997, TENUTA DI CAPEZZANA Tuscany	*Youthful and well-structured, this wine blends fresh cherries and oak, balanced with high acidity and tannins.*	**£10.30**	JNW GGW CAC LIB	S
CHIANTI CLASSICO ROBERTO STUCCHI 1996, BADIA A COLTIBUONO Tuscany	*Herbaceous nose of prostrate rosemary and sage heralds in a full fruit, finely tuned palate.*	**£10.50**	V&V AVB HOH	B
PARRINA RISERVA 1997, LA PARRINA Tuscany	*Matured in oak, this typical Italian wine is packed with blackcurrants which fill the lingering palate.*	**£10.50**	VLW LIB	B
CHIANTI CLASSICO RISERVA CAPRAIA 1995, ROCCA DI CASTAGNOLI Tuscany	*Immerse yourself in a sea of blueberries and float among spice and chocolate flavours. Awesome finish.*	**£10.60**	MAR VWE EUW	S
LE MASSE DI GREVE CHIANTI CLASSICO RISERVA 1995, CARLA GUARNIERI Tuscany	*With a subtle blend of oak and red cherries, this wine displays an elegant fruit character and exceptional length.*	**£10.90**	WAW	B
CHIANTI RUFINA RISERVA 1995, FATTORIA SELVAPIANA Tuscany	*An elegant wine with leathery notes on the nose and citrus fruits on the palate.*	**£11.50**	GGW LIB	B
CHIANTI CLASSICO 1997, FELSINA BERARDENGA Tuscany	*A rich, smoky wine with notes of meat and tar and a gripping finish.*	**£11.90**	RBS GGW NYW LIB	B

CHIANTI CLASSICO 1997, TENUTA FONTODI Tuscany	*Aromas of spice and leather, this wine is full-bodied with a long length. Very pleasant!*	**£12.10**	VLW NYW LIB	B
BRUNELLO DI MONTALCINO VIGNA SPUNTALI 1993, TENIMENTI ANGELINI Tuscany	*Terrific brambly fruit on the nose with hint of marzipan and great follow through to a fine tannin palate.*	**£12.30**	EHL	B
CHIANTI SAN ZIO 1997, CANTINE LEONARDO Tuscany	*A soft, approachable wine with good fruit lingering on the palate, along with drying tannins.*	**£12.90**	GGW LIB	B
LE CASALTE VINO NOBILE DE MONTEPULCIANO 1996, LE CASALTE Tuscany	*Powerful complex forrest floor and dark fruit aromas. Licorice and dried fruit flavours excellent length.*	**£13.00**	NYW GNW BPW	S
BRIGANTE DEI BARBI 1995, FATTORIA DEI BARBI Tuscany	*Concentration of ripe, raisiny fruit is given layers of complexity by liquorice, spice and dark chocolate flavours.*	**£13.70**	V&V ENO	S
CASAVECCHIA CHIANTI CLASSICO 1996, GIOVANNI PUIATTI Tuscany	*A cabaret of black fruits and raisins set against a backdrop of marzipan and wedding cake.*	**£14.00**	ENO	B
FARNITO CARPINETO CABERNET SAUVIGNON 1995, CASA VINICOLA CARPINETO Tuscany	*Hints of farmyard on nose. Restrained style with red summer fruits and cedar on palate . Classy.*	**£14.50**	BDR V&V NYW RBS AVB HOH	G
VINO NOBILE DI MONTEPULCIANO 1996, AVIGNONESI Tuscany	*Cherries and maturing tar characters on the nose of this well structured wine of fine length.*	**£14.50**	RBS EUW	B

Wine	Description	Price	Stockists	Award
CARMIGNANO RISERVA 1996, TENUTA DI CAPEZZANA Tuscany	*A classy wine with subtle fruit aromas and a good balance of ripe fruit, tannins and acidity.*	**£14.90**	JNW GGW LIB	S
TAVERNELLE CABERNET SAUVIGNON 1995, CASTELLO BANFI Tuscany	*A well-made, balanced wine with rich, creamy chocolate and black cherry characteristics and an everlasting finish.*	**£15.00**	VIN	B
LAMOLE DI LAMOLE CHIANTI CLASSICO RISERVA 1994, PILE E LAMOLE Tuscany	*A delicious combination of creamy, strong, concentrated fruit and chocolate balanced with lovely tannins and acidity.*	**£15.40**	ALI	S
LE CASALTE VINO NOBILE DE MONTEPULCIANO RISERVA 1995, LE CASALTE Tuscany	*Wonderfully elegant, full of dried fruit and cherries, this wine has lovely tannins, acidity and a well-rounded palate.*	**£15.50**	NYW GNW BPW	S
IL MARZOCCO VDT 1997,AVIGNONESI Tuscany	*Licorice and mushrooms meix with the crisp cherries and bitter chocolate, tight tannins and brisk acidity finishes well.*	**£16.00**	EUW	G
POGGIO ANTICO BRUNELLO DI MONTALCINO RISERVA 1993, POGGIO ANTICO Tuscany	*Well measured oak adds richness and finesse to an already full, fruity palate.*	**£16.00**	EHL	B
BUCERCHIALE CHIANTI RUFINA RISERVA 1995, FATTORIA SELVAPIANA Tuscany	*A well-integrated wine with balanced fruit and acidity and a memorable finish.*	**£16.80**	LIB	B
CHIANTI CLASSICO RISERVA 1996, CASTELLO DI FONTERUTOLI Tuscany	*A super concentrated fruit driven style offering spicy and leathery notes well integrated oak.*	**£16.90**	VLW JNW NYW ENO	G

Wine	Description	Price	Stockists	Award
CASTEL GIOCONDO BRUNELLO DI MONTALCINO 1994, MARCHESI DE' FRESCOBALDI Tuscany	*A tongue tingling front palate gives way to rich orange peel and concentrated dark cherries nuances.*	**£17.00**	GRA FRT AFI	B
CHIANTI CLASSICO RISERVA 1996, TENUTA FONTODI Tuscany	*A heady aroma of spice and black fruits lead into a well-bodied wine packed with fruit.*	**£17.50**	LIB	B
SAN IPPOLITO 1997, CANTINE LEONARDO Tuscany	*Deeply coloured, this wine is packed full of elegant red fruits, fine tannins and balanced acidity.*	**£17.60**	GGW LIB	S
RUFFINO RISERVA DUCALE GOLD 1993, RUFFINO Tuscany	*Well-balanced and sweet, the palate is full of classy fruit and tannins with earthy hints.*	**£17.80**	V&V ALI LLY	S
BRANCAIA 1996, CASTELLO DI FONTERUTOLI Tuscany	*Black fruit jams and freshly ground herbs with superb balancing fruit tannins all peak in a magnificent long tail.*	**£18.00**	VLW JNW NYW ENO	G
CAPARZO CA' DEL PAZZO 1993, TENUTA CAPARZO Tuscany	*A classy wine with truffle and black fruit aromas following onto the palate with true depth and length.*	**£18.00**	V&V	S
CARPINETO CHIANTI CLASSICO RISERVA 1990, CASA VINICOLA CARPINETO Tuscany	*Full of summer fruits with just a tinge of violets. Rounded by well structured tannins.*	**£18.40**	V&V MWW AVB HOH	B
COL D'ORCIA BRUNELLO DI MONTALCINO 1994, COL D'ORCIA Tuscany	*A superb wine with red cherries on the nose and balancing tannins. Elegant and light.*	**£19.20**	GSH LUD V&C HVN ALI	B

Wine	Description	Price	Stockists	Award
Vigneto Rancia Chianti Classico Riserva 1995, Felsina Berardenga Tuscany	*In typical Italian style, this wine has a ripe, roasted nose followed by cherries and oak.*	£19.30	LIB	B
Frescobaldi Lamaione Merlot di Castelgiocondo 1995, Marchesi de' Frescobaldi Tuscany	*Very deep ageing colour, hints of cassis and berries and velvety mouth feel, let it breathe.*	£19.60	V&V NYW GRA FRT ODD	S
I Grifi 1996, Avignonesi Tuscany	*Refined fruit and toasty oak are the hallmarks of this still young wine. Get it while you can.*	£19.90	WRC BUP MAR THS EUW	B
Brunello di Montalcino 1994, Castello Banfi Tuscany	*A maturing wine with leathery overtones and lovely, soft raisin and fig flavours lasting through.*	£20.00	VIN	B
Brunello di Montalcino 1994, Il Poggione Tuscany	*Showing development on the toasty oak nose leading to a palate packed with plums and damsons.*	£20.00	ENO	B
Poggio Antico Brunello di Montalcino 1991, Poggio Antico Tuscany	*Tomato and basil sit happily on top of this generously flavoured, black fruit mountain.*	£20.00	WTS	B
Chianti Classico Riserva 1996, Castello della Paneretta Tuscany	*Aromas of herbs and tobacco blend with the spicy black fruit in this voluptuous wine crammed with succulent fruit.*	£20.10	VIN	G
Vino Nobile di Montepulciano Vigna Asinone 1995, Poliziano Tuscany	*With an massive oaked nose and packed-down complex fruit and tobacco on the palate,this is a true 'big boy'.*	£20.80	V&V NYW ENO	G

Wine	Description	Price	Stockists	Award
Casalferro 1996, Castello di Brolio Tuscany	*Subdued chocolatey nose it still needs time. The rich, complex palate shows how good it could be.*	**£21.50**	JNW V&V NYW ENO	S
Ruffino Cabreo Il Borgo 1995, Ruffino Tuscany	*A wild, rustic wine with ripe sweet cherry fruit, firm tannins and long finish.*	**£21.80**	V&V ALI LLY	B
Fornace Chianti Rufina Riserva 1995, Fattoria Selvapiana Tuscany	*A well-structured full-bodied wine packed with cherries, with a long, drying finish.*	**£22.00**	TOS LIB	B
Montesodi Chianti Rufina 1996, Marchesi de' Frescobaldi Tuscany	*Lovely smokey cherries are joined by truffles and herbs, lithe palate of tight tannins, finishing well.*	**£22.70**	V&V GRA FRT	S
Montevertine Riserva 1995, Montevertine Tuscany	*Soft leathery nose belies a fairly robust palate of firm plum and cherry fruit.*	**£22.90**	EUW	S
Le Stanze Cabernet Sauvignon 1996, Poliziano Tuscany	*Showing waxy fruit on the nose with tints of herbaceuosness, this wine has great depth and structure.*	**£24.50**	V&V ENO	S
Mormoreto 1996, Marchesi de' Frescobaldi Tuscany	*A raw, greenish edge. It has plenty of juicy extract, which bodes well for the future.*	**£24.50**	V&V GRA FRT	S
Cignale 1994, Castello di Querceto Tuscany	*A perplexing wine showing herbal characters followed by fine grained tannins and good length.*	**£24.70**	J&B	S

Wine	Description	Price	Stockist	Award
Brunello di Montalcino Prime Donne 1993, Donatella Cinelli Colombini Tuscany	*Full bitter chocolate and morello cherries filter through a fine almond flavoured tannin structure.*	**£24.80**	ENO	B
Brunello di Montalcino Tenuta Nouva 1994, Casa Nova di Neri Tuscany	*Bright summer fruit pudding nose. Rich fruit flavours integrating beautifully with dusty youthful tannins.*	**£25.50**	EUW	S
Flaccianello Della Pieve 1996, Tenuta Fontodi Tuscany	*Rich spicy aromas are followed by a palate of great elegance, depth and ripeness of fruit.*	**£25.80**	LIB	S
Caparzo Brunello di Montalcino 1993, Tenuta Caparzo Tuscany	*An amazing bouquet of tea leaves and currants, followed by burnt cherry flavours, masked by high tannins.*	**£27.00**	V&V	B
Summus 1995, Castello Banfi Tuscany	*An extremely big wine with a complex palate of high tannins, cherries and bitter chocolate.*	**£30.00**	VIN	B
Siepi 1996, Castello di Fonterutoli Tuscany	*Sensual fruits of the forest and dried figs and herb lead to a grippy palate of plum fruit and ripe tannins.*	**£30.70**	VLW NYW ENO	G
Brunello Vigna del Fiore 1993, Fattoria dei Barbi Tuscany	*Vibrant fruit, well balanced oak and green spices with well matched tannins.*	**£32.70**	ENO	B
Poggio All'Oro Brunello di Montalcino Riserva 1993, Castello Banfi Tuscany	*A complex maturing wine with tobacco and fig aromas, followed by a massive mouthful of rich ripe fruit.*	**£39.00**	V&V VIN	S

ITALY • WHITE

Wine	Description	Price	Stockists	Award
VERDICCHIO CLASSICO INANFORA 1998, PIERSANTI Marches	*Fruit and floral notes develop nicely on the palate with long balancing acidity providing crispness.*	**£3.90**	AFI	B
GIOACCHINO GAROFOLI VERDICCHIO CLASSICO CLASSICO 1998, CASA VINICOLA GIOACCHINO GAROFOLI Marches	*Fresh fragrant and flowery with nuts on the nose and palate with a delicate structure.*	**£4.00**	TOS IWS	B
VERDICCHIO DEI CASTELLI DI JESI CLASSICO 1998, MONCARO Marches	*Complex and earthy with apricots and blossom aromas and a simply soft peach fruit palate.*	**£4.00**	SAF	B
FRASCATI SUPERIORE SELEZIONE SATINATA 1997, SAN MARCO Veneto	*Mized nuts on the nose with an inviting fruit palate of good acidity and length.*	**£4.10**	FRT	B
MHV FRASCATI SUPERIORE 1998, CANTINE SAN MARCO Veneto	*Forest mushrooms with soft dusty fruit on the nose and a delicate fruit palate with good balance.*	**£4.20**	MHV	B
CANALETTO GARSANESA DEL VENETO PINOT GRIGIO 1998, CASA SIRELLI SPA Trentino	*Fresh tropical fruit aromas spring from a juicy palate with a bitter twist of acid on the finish.*	**£4.30**	CGI VEX	B
FALERIO DEI COLLI ASCOLANI SALADINI PILASTRI 1998, SALADINI PILASTRI Marches	*Bitter almond aromas on a well balanced, fresh fruit palate with a lovely zesty lemon finish.*	**£4.60**	WRC BUP MAR THS GGW LIB	B

Wine	Description	Price	Stockists	Award
I Portali Greco 1998, Basilium Srl Basilicata	*Fragrant intense fruit aromas with a mineral and herby fruit palate with some complexity.*	£5.00	HOH AVB	B
Villa del Borgo Pinot Grigio 1997, Puiatti Friuli-Venezia-Giulia	*Floral fresh fruit with grassy, herbaceous overtones, good balanced acidity, and a zippy tail.*	£5.00	TOS	B
Soave Vigneto Colombare 1998, Zenato Veneto	*Clean, crisp and herbaceous with soft acidity and a refreshing light lingering fruit palate.*	£5.10	WRC BUP MAR THS EUW	B
Caramia Chardonnay 1998, Azienda Vini Cola Cantele Puglia	*Some toasty oak with a vanillin, nutty character on a rich, full fruit palate of apples and pears.*	£5.20	Widely Available	B
Santagostino Catarrato Chardonnay 1997, Firriato Sicily	*An unusual wine releasing honeyed aromas on a long subtle fruit palate with vegetal tones.*	£5.50	IWS	B
Soave Classico 1998, F.lli Tedeschi Veneto	*Reticent, fragrant, mineral nose with a delicate juicy ripe structured fruit palate.*	£5.50	V&V MWW WIN A&N V&C AVB HOH	S
Gravina Bianco 1998, Botromagno Puglia	*A wonderfully sweet fruit palate, with crisp notes of nectarine, cumquat and minerals.*	£5.90	ENO	B
Podium Verdicchio Classico Superiore 1997, Casa Vinicola Gioacchino Garofoli Marches	*Warm mineral fruit on the nose with a light floral fruit palate.*	£6.00	IWS	B

Wine	Description	Price	Stockists	Award
Il Prospetto Verdicchio de Castelli di Jesi Classico 1998, Moncaro Terre Cortesi Marches	*Austere yet intriguing offering of fig, lime, lemon peel and mineral, with a river pebble texture in the mouth.*	**£6.10**	BDR EUW	S
Frascati Superiore 'Selezione' 1998, Cantine San Marco Frascati	*An inviting melon and fig nose precedes a crisp palate, with a clean, acid finish.*	**£6.20**	UNS BLN EHL	B
Pinot Grigio Grave del Friuli 1998, Pighin Friuli-Venezia-Giulia	*Full, floral characters on the nose with a soft round fruit palate and crisp, dry tail.*	**£6.70**	MON	B
Poggio Calvelli Orvieto Classico, La Carraia 1998, La Carraia Umbria	*Full bodied fruit on the nose with mineral overtones, a rich round body with moderate acidity.*	**£7.00**	LIB	B
Stephano Antonucci Bianco Verdicchio dei Cast di Jesi 1997, Santa Barbara Marches	*Succulently sweet peaches and passionfruit on the nose leads to a palate with nice length and poise.*	**£7.00**	VIN	B
Marca Trevigiana La Gioiosa Pinot Grigio 1998, La Gioiosa Spa Veneto	*Beautiful floral perfume on the nose with a slightly oily palate which exudes nuts, spices and peppery flavours.*	**£7.20**	TOS D&D	B
Ciafraie 1998, Azienda Agricola Dino Illuminati Controguerra	*An intriguing wine with notes of melon and underripe pears flowing onto a well defined palate.*	**£7.50**	BLN EHL	B
Prato Ca' Dei Frati 1997, Ca' Dei Frati Lombardy	*Vibrant yellow colour, very ripe fruit flavours on the palate, beautifully made with refreshing length.*	**£7.50**	LIB	S

Wine	Description	Price	Stockists	Award
Soave Classico Superiore Pieropan 1998, Pieropan Veneto	*A true to style wine with notes of stone fruit and fig leaves before a clean acid palate.*	£7.70	VLW GGW NYW LIB	B
Soave Classico Superiore Montegrande 1998, Azienda Agricola Pra Veneto	*A steely nose with hints of fig and olive follow through nicely onto a well structured palate.*	£8.00	BPW COK HOL	B
Gavi di Gavi Raccolto Tardivo 1998, Villa Lanata Piedmont	*Very perfumed bouquet on a slightly austere palate with a pleasant sweetness and strong finish.*	£8.50	GRA MWW	B
Lugana Ca' Dei Frati 1998, Ca' Dei Frati Lombardy	*Complex, earthy, peach and nut aromas with a fresh and lively delicate structured palate.*	£8.50	RBS VLW LIB	S
Pinot Grigio Isonzo 1998, Giovanni Puiatti Friuli-Venezia-Giulia	*Fresh lime fruit on the nose, subtle herbal undertones on the palate with good acidity and a successful finish.*	£8.50	ENO	B
Bosco del Merlo Prime Organic Chardonnay 1998, Paladin Veneto	*Upfront tropical fruit leads to a well rounded palate of good fruit and clean acid finishing with a mineral blast.*	£8.80	AFI	B
Beni di Batasiolo Langhe Cru Vigneto Morino Chardonnnay 1996, Beni di Batasiolo Piedmont	*Fruit and mineral aromas with sweet round fruit on the palate, well balanced with integrated oak.*	£9.00	MON	B
Plenio Verdicchio Classico Reserva 1996, Umani Ronchi Umbria	*Floral fruit nose with a touch of honey and spice on a well rounded fruit palate.*	£9.00	ENO	B

Fiorese Verdicchio Classico CLASSICO 1996, CASA VINICO-LA Gioacchino Garofoli Marches	*Honey, creamed vanilla and apricots, with a creamy fruit palate, good acidity and moderate length.*	**£10.00**	IWS	S
Verdicchio di Castelli di Jesi Il Coroncino 1997, Fattoria Coroncino Central Italy	*Restrained on the nose with warm rounded front palate travelling through a floral grappey middle, finishing long and dry .*	**£10.00**	L&W	S
Vigneti Lugarara Gavi di Gavi La Giustiniana 1998, La Giustiniana Piedmont	*Floral aromas with a clean fruit palate which is a little austere but with depth and length.*	**£10.00**	LIB	B
Vigneti Vigneta Gavi di Gavi La Giustiniana 1998, La Giustiniana Piedmont	*A thoroughly enjoyable wine with light fresh balanced fruit and integrated acidity.*	**£10.00**	LIB	B
Vittorio Puietti Pinot Grigio 1997, Puiatti Friuli-Venezia-Giulia	*Vanilla and goat cheese intrigue the nose, the palate is light and delicate with a bit of abite.*	**£10.00**	TOS	B
Vernaccia di San Gimignano 1998, Panizzi Tuscany	*A touch of spritz with sweet almonds initially followed by a clean, long, balanced fruit palate.*	**£10.30**	ENO	B
Villa Bucci Reserva 1995, Bucci Marches	*Spiced on the nose with intense apricot characters, the palate is powerful with firm acidity.*	**£10.40**	AFI	B
Pinot Grigio Collio 1998, Vittorio Puiatti Friuli-Venezia-Giulia	*Lightly perfumed and subtle on the nose, a crisp zesty fruit palate with a metallic edge.*	**£10.50**	TOS ENO	B

ITALY • WHITE

Wine	Description	Price	Stockists	Award
Le Busche 1997, Umani Ronchi Umbria	*Incredibly lively lemon grass and pineapple fruit which is long, well balanced and very classy.*	**£11.00**	EMO	S
Passito di Pantelleria Mare d'Ambra NV, Rallo Sicily	*Heady toffee and lemon aromas are a prelude to the rich, caramel palate which follows. Excellent length.*	**£11.00**	GRA FRT	B
Montezemolo Elioro Chardonnay 1997, Cordero di Montezemolo Piedmont	*Lovely floral fruit with toasty oak aromas with sweet slightly nutty characters on the palate.*	**£11.20**	EUW	B
Alteserre 1997, Bava Piedmont	*Creamy, buttery fruit characters on the nose with a well rounded and generous palate.*	**£11.30**	V&V VIN	B
Verdicchio Dei Castelli di Jesi Classico Superiore Balciana Sartarelli 1997, Sartarelli Marches	*Punchy asparagus full fruit nose, the palate is round with mouth watering acidity and fantastic length.*	**£12.50**	V&V	G TROPHY WINE
Planeta Chardonnay 1997, Planeta Sicily	*Fresh from the herb garden this soft and fluffy wine is certain to calm you.*	**£13.90**	VLW NYW ENO	B
Zenato Chardonnay del Veneto 1996, Zenato Veneto	*A peachy, herbaceous and fine oak nose flows to a finely textured palate with finesse and grace.*	**£14.80**	EUW	S
Sanct Valentin Chardonnay 1998, St Michael Eppan Alto Adige	*Warm nutty new oak integrated with soft well-balanced fruit are the hallmarks of this well made wine.*	**£17.00**	EUW	B

Vernaccia di San Gimignano Riserva 1997, Panizzi Tuscany	*A simple lively wine with fresh citrus fruit on the nose and palate, finished long and lemony.*	**£17.70**	ENO	B
Giacomo Ascheri Podere di Montalupa Viognier 1998, Giacomo Ascheri Piedmont	*Intense perfumed nose consisting of floral apricot characters. An off-dry style, balanced acidity and attractive aromatics.*	**£23.70**	NYW ENO	G
Ben Rye Passito di Panteleria 1998, Donnafugata Sicily	*Mature and complex, this full-bodied wine is packed with orange and tangerine flavours. Delicious.*	**£24.00**	V&V VIN	B
Lugana Villa Flora Zenato 1998, Sergio Zenato Veneto	*A delicately citrus nose gaining strength on the palate with full bodied fruit and a savouriness.*	**£25.00**	WTS	S

Pinpoint who sells the wine you wish to buy by turning to the stockist codes. If you know the name of the wine you want to buy, use the alphabetical index. If the price is your motivation, refer to the invaluable price guide index; red and white wines under £5, sparkling wines under £12 and champagne under £16. Happy hunting!

NORTH AMERICA

North America once again flexes its muscles winning not only the Chardonnay Trophy but also the Red Wine Trophy. The Californians are moving from the "big is best" attitude and following the lead of their neighbours to produce wines of more elegance and finesse. The smaller regions are shining with Virginia picking up her first Gold and Canada is continuing her run of medals. These pages reflect the diversity, consistent quality and increasing finesse that Nort America has to offer.

N. AMERICA • CALIFORNIA • CABERNET

Wine	Tasting note	Price	Stockists	Award
MYSTIC CLIFFS CABERNET SAUVIGNON 1995, CANANDAIGUA WINE CO California	*Attractive cooked fruits with herby and leafy notes. Warm palate of grainy tannins and impressive length.*	**£5.00**	CAN	B
NATHANSON CREEK CABERNET SAUVIGNON 1996, SEBASTINI California	*Lovely ripe cassis fruit with leafy undertones, a soft texture and decent follow through.*	**£5.00**	MRN EWD PLB	B
SUTTER HOME CABERNET SAUVIGNON 1996, SUTTER HOME California	*Nice blend of fruit and oak on the nose with some spicey tannins, high acidity and good length.*	**£5.10**	Widely Available	B
SAFEWAY CALIFORNIAN OAK AGED CABERNET SAUVIGNON 1997, FETZER VINYARDS California	*Perfumed, almost syrupy nose with lovely fruit backed up with spicey tannins.*	**£5.50**	SAF	B
STONYBROOK CABERNET SAUVIGNON 1997, STONYBROOK VINEYARDS California	*Leafy, green peppery nose. Sweet, rich long palate with assertive fruit, high acids and good length.*	**£5.50**	JSM BRF	B

Wine	Description	Price	Stockists	Award
CANYON ROAD CABERNET SAUVIGNON 1997, CANYON ROAD WINERY California	*Lovely, cherry-type fruit nose. Juicy fruit palate, soft with long finish and moderate tannins.*	**£6.00**	HBJ	B
SYCAMORE CANYON CABERNET SAUVIGNON 1995, ERNEST & JULIO GALLO California	*Subtle red fruits and ripe cassis on the nose. Soft and round in the mouth with great depth.*	**£6.50**	WTS E&J	S
FETZER VALLEY OAKS CABERNET SAUVIGNON 1996, FETZER VINEYARDS California	*Plenty of fruit here with attractive runner bean and asparagus undertones. Fine grained tannins run to a tail of refreshing acidity.*	**£6.70**	UNS WCR CWS WTS	S
MONTERRA CABERNET SAUVIGNON 1995, MONTERRA WINES California	*Predominant berry fruits on the nose introdcue a warm palate of grainy tannins and nice length.*	**£8.00**	TOS DWL	B
VILLA MOUNT EDEN CABERNET SAUVIGNON 1995, VILLA MOUNT EDEN California	*Lively nose of cinnamon and spice, red fruits and plums. Lovely rounded tannins with great balancing acidity.*	**£8.30**	WCR LIB	S
BERINGER VINEYARDS CABERNET SAUVIGNON 1996, BERINGER VINEYARDS California	*An appealing wine with dark fruit and licorice nose and a clean finish.*	**£8.60**	BWC	S
BONTERRA VINEYARDS CABERNET SAUVIGNON 1997, BONTERRA VINEYARDS California	*Spicey plum fruit nose, velvety fruit with ripe, minty flavours. Balanced with light, easy tannins."*	**£9.00**	Widely Available	S
VILLA MOUNT EDEN CABERNET SAUVIGNON 1996, VILLA MOUNT EDEN California	*Spicy cassis nose with well-balanced tannins and juicy cherry fruit. Grippy finish and still youthful character.*	**£9.00**	NYW LIB	S

N. AMERICA • CALIFORNIA • CABERNET

Wine	Description	Price	Stockists	Award
Bonterra Cabernet Sauvignon 1996, Borderra Vineyards California	*Berry and spice nose with big up-front palate. Red berries and tobacco, with minty fruit notes, soft but firm tannins..*	**£9.20**	QWW WRC BUP MAR TOS WTS	S
St Francis Cabernet Sauvignon 1996, St Francis California	*Loads of fruit here with a spicey, cedary vein running through the warm and seductive nose. Great mouthfeel and grippy tannins.*	**£9.20**	QWW HMA	G
Cypress Cabernet Sauvignon 1996, Cypress California	*A fruity nose of pastilles and currants introduces a palate of good balance and soft, gentle tannins.*	**£9.50**	ENO	S
BV Napa Cabernet Sauvignon 1995, Beaulieu Vineyards California	*Showing some age this oaky style offers cigar box and cedar characters to showcase an array of fruits.*	**£10.00**	PFC	S
Sebastiani Sonoma County Cabernet Sauvignon 1996, Sebastiani California	*The nose shows ripe cassis, mint and sweet smelling sandelwood and the palate swims in oak drenched fruit tannins.*	**£10.00**	PLB	S
Robert Mondavi Coastal Cabernet Sauvignon 1996, Robert Mondavi California	*Fruit and earth with a hint of mint meet herbal tones and ever so grainy tannins.*	**£10.70**	QWW JNW TOS WCR MZC	S
Renaissance Cabernet Sauvignon 1994, Renaissance California	*Bright, clean blackcurrant nose leading to a medium-bodied with nice tannin and length.*	**£10.80**	THW	S
Dry Creek Valley Cabernet Sauvignon 1996, Ernest & Julio Gallo California	*Young, jammy fruit nose with spicy oak. Intense fruit, oak and mint with lovely, balanced mid-palate.*	**£12.00**	PAT	B

Wine	Description	Price	Stockists	Award
Barrelli Creek Cabernet Sauvignon 1995, Ernest & Julio Gallo California	*Minty, herbaceous cassis aromas. Fine ripe tannins, balanced by cassis and spicey cedar. Impressive.*	£12.70	WCR HAR E&J	S
Frei Ranch Cabernet Sauvignon 1994, Ernest & Julio Gallo California	*Closed, gamey nose. Slightly green cassis and spiced fruit palate and good firm tannins.*	£13.00	HAR E&J	B
Frei Ranch Cabernet Sauvignon 1995, Ernest & Julio Gallo California	*Pungent nose with orange peel aromas, dense and tannic with some elegance, particularly on back palate.*	£13.00	ODF E&J	B
Stefani Vineyard Cabernet Sauvignon 1994, Ernest & Julio Gallo California	*Tarry nose with cassis aromas, summer fruits and oak on palate with a long finish of gently drying tannins.*	£13.00	HAR E&J	S
St Francis Reserve Cabernet Sauvignon 1995, St Francis California	*Rasiny rich concentration, good length with firm tannins and a concise dry finish.*	£15.00	HMA	B
Cecchetti Sebastiani Cabernet Sauvignon 1994, Cecchetti Sebastiani Cellar California	*Yummy rhubarb pie here interspersed with a careful measure of spice and cedar rolls to a palate of chalky tannins.*	£15.90	VNO	G
Renaissance Cabernet Sauvignon Reserve 1993, Renaissance California	*Bright fruit and a green edge served up on a creamy palate of ripe tannins of good length.*	£16.00	THW	S
Hilltop Paso Robles Cabernet Sauvignon 1995, J Lohr California	*Deep colour with cassis, coffee and leathery characters. Classy style with great length.*	£17.00	VLW ENO	G

Wine	Tasting note	Price	Stockists	Award
Dry Creek Valley Cabernet Sauvignon 1994, Ernest & Julio Gallo California	*Deep brooding wine holding up well with nice fruit cake aromas and a full palate with pleasing length.*	**£17.50**	HAR E&J	B
Clos du Val Cabernet Sauvignon 1996, Clos du Val California	*Lose yourself in the colour before discovering a black fruit laden nose with fresh cut herb notes.*	**£18.20**	HOH AVB	S
Sutter Home M Trinchero Founders Estate Cabernet Sauvignon 1995, Sutter Home California	*Ripe, full bodied new world style offering chunky minty fruit with great concentration of flavour.*	**£20.00**	PRG	S
Geyser Peak Reserve Alexander Valley Cabernet Sauvignon 1995, Geyser Peak Winery California	*Lovely ripe fruit here with cassis galore and lashings of mocha and minty topping. And, the flavour goes on.*	**£21.00**	HBJ	G
Geyser Peak Reserve Alexandre 1996, Geyser Peak Winery California	*A spicey fruit nose with a mint hint and a mid weight palate of good firm structure with nice fruit follow through.*	**£23.00**	HBJ	S
Northern Sonoma Estate Bottled Cabernet Sauvignon 1994, Ernest & Julio Gallo California	*This beautiful wine has richness, complexity and tannins melding with fruit structure, elegant finish.*	**£30.00**	WCR HAR SEL SOB E&J	S
Northern Sonoma Estate Bottled Cabernet Sauvignon 1995, Ernest & Julio Gallo California	*Spice and gentle fruit characters while a tight tannin structure and nice texture add balance and poise.*	**£30.00**	WCR HAR SEL SOB E&J	S
Clos du Val Reserve Cabernet Sauvignon 1995, Clos du Val California	*Cassis, cigar box and stewed fruit characters rise from a palate of powdered tannins and good length.*	**£38.00**	AVB HOH	S

Wine	Description	Price	Stockists	Award
BV Georges de Latour Cabernet Sauvignon 1995, Beaulieu Vineyards California	*Rich, chocolately sweet fruit here served up on a bed of solid tannins with exceptional balance and a silky texture.*	**£40.00**	PFC	G
Ridge Monte Bello 1994, Ridge Vineyards California	*Luscious fruits of the forest are enhanced by licorice and anise characters. A well balanced, mature and elegant wine.*	**£59.20**	Widely Available	S
Opus One 1995, Baron Philippe de Rothschild & Mondavi California	*Ripe cassis and fruitcake aromas sing with cedar and herbal tones. An extraordinarily complex and elegant wine.*	**£71.10**	Widely Available	G

N. AMERICA • CALIFORNIA • CHARDONNAY

Wine	Description	Price	Stockists	Award
California Mountain Vineyards Chardonnay 1997, Les Grand Chais de France California	*Toasted oak flavours in a mango terrrine with a cleansing, long finish.*	**£4.00**	ALD GCF	B
Arius Reserve Chardonnay 1997, California Direct California	*Ripe tropical fruit with citrus, french oak on the nose, harmonised fruit palate, good length.*	**£5.00**	ASD CDL	G
Mystic Cliffs Chardonnay 1997, Canandaigua Wine Co California	*Big oaky toast aromas. Ripe lemon and peach fruit, high acidity and big buttery oak.*	**£5.00**	CAN	B
Stonybrook Chardonnay 1998, Stonybrook Vineyards California	*Clean, white fruits on the nose with a hint of tropical leads to a well balanced and defined palate.*	**£5.00**	JSM BRF	B

Wine	Description	Price	Stockists	Award
SEBASTIANI SONOMA COUNTY CHARDONNAY 1996, SEBASTIANI California	*Awesome citrus aromas with buttery ripe fruit and fresh acidity, finishing toasty and dry.*	**£5.50**	EOR PLB	B
WENTE ESTATE CHARDONNAY 1997, WENTE California	*Clean stone fruit and citrus aromas before a powerful, rich palate.*	**£6.60**	UNS FRT GRA	B
VILLA MOUNT EDEN CHARDONNAY 1997, VILLA MOUNT EDEN California	*Biscuity and toasty aromas with ripe fruit characters integrated with lovely oak and offering good length.*	**£7.80**	UNS WCR LIB	B
BONTERRA CHARDONNAY 1996, BONTERRA VINEYARDS California	*Fresh apples with lime zest and peach flavours throughout and a good dose of sweet oak on the palate.*	**£8.00**	Widely Available	S
FETZER BARREL SELECT CHARDONNAY 1997, FETZER VINEYARDS California	*Elegant fruit combined with subtle oak on nose, delicate mango flavours with zappy citrus finish.*	**£8.00**	TOS MWW FRT BRF	G
STERLING VINEYARDS CHARDONNAY 1997, SEAGRAM California	*Caramel, lychees and toasty oak followed by a palate consisting of zesty lemons and ripe melons.*	**£8.00**	ODD SEA	S
SAINT FRANCIS CHARDONNAY 1997, ST FRANCIS California	*Delicate floral characters with subtle toasty oak aromas cascade to a full blown palate of lychees and cream.*	**£8.50**	HMA	B
WENTE RIVA RANCH RESERVE CHARDONNAY 1997, WENTE California	*Rich buttery oak combines with ripe fruit in a frontal assault with a clean acid finish.*	**£9.00**	WRC FRT THS GRA	S

Wine	Tasting note	Price	Stockists	Medal
Edna Valley Chardonnay 1996, Edna Valley California	*Mandarins and lemons with lively zesty acid and a wonderful fruit structure gives way to a generous sweet oak wash.*	£9.30	WDM BWL WTS	S
Echelon Edna Valley Vineyard Chardonnay 1997, Echelon Wine Group California	*Grapefruit and aromatic aromas, loads of fruit with creamy integrated oak and a crisp finish.*	£9.90	WDM BWL NYW CWG	S
Dunnewood Dry Silk Chardonnay 1996, Canandaigua Wine Co California	*Lemon curd, tropical fruit and honey, integrated oak and balanced acidity with long toasty finish.*	£10.00	CAN	S
Firestone Chardonnay 1997, Firestone California	*Quite subtle fruit mixes well with creamy oak, on the palate pears and tropical fruit emerge.*	£10.00	FRT GRA	S
Robert Mondavi Coastal Chardonnay 1997, Robert Mondavi California	*Peaches and blossoms on the nose trumpet a citrus fruit and honeyed texture.*	£10.50	WCR MGN DVY MZC	B
Buena Vista Carneros Chardonnay 1995, Buena Vista California	*Appealing biscuity vegetal nose with lovely ripe fruit hazelnuts and butter with firm balanced acidity.*	£10.90	CAC CCW	B
J Lohr Riverstone Chardonnay 1997, J Lohr California	*Creamy oak with full fruit flavours and fresh cut grass lead to a soft smooth palate.*	£11.50	VLW ENO	B
Au Bon Climat Wild Boy Chardonnay 1997, Au Bon Climat California	*Funky lemon and citrus aromas, fresh tropical fruit palate and a touch of oak.*	£11.60	TRO HVN DBY HOU M&V	B

Wine	Description	Price	Stockists	Award
Stefani Ranch Chardonnay 1996, Ernest & Julio Gallo California	*Restrained, elegant nose with resinous oak then ripe stone fruit and bananas with grapefruit hints.*	**£11.80**	WCR MWW SEL E&J	G
Gallo Laguna Ranch Chardonnay 1996, Ernest & Julio Gallo California	*Rich flavours of toasted oak, ripe tropical fruits and limey, kiwi fruit highlights on the palate.*	**£12.00**	HAR SOB ADN E&J	G
Renaissance Chardonnay 1996, Renaissance California	*Ripe aromas of tropical fruits with hints of coconut cream are reflected on the rich palate.*	**£13.00**	THW	B
Clos du Val Carneros Chardonnay 1997, Clos du Val California	*Ripe tropical fruit with toasty buttery oak, good body with a hint of bitter almond on the finish.*	**£13.30**	AVB HOH	B
Seven Peaks Reserve Chardonnay 1997, Seven Peaks California	*Caramel, toffee toasty oak and melon on the nose, pineapple and caramel toffee characters on the palate.*	**£13.70**	ABA	S
Crichton Hall Chardonnay 1996, Crichton Hall California	*Lush toffee and banana aromas from a full bodied palate with sweet oak and fine acidity.*	**£13.80**	CAC PAT	B
Robert Mondavi Napa Valley Chardonnay 1997, Robert Mondavi California	*Lemon curd, peach characters combine with a slightly oily texture and almond shavings.*	**£14.00**	WAC MWW THR MGN MZC	B
Au Bon Climat Chardonnay 1997, Au Bon Climat California	*Butter and lemon on the nose with a hint of oak served on a buttery smooth palate.*	**£14.70**	Widely Available	B

Wine	Description	Price	Stockists	Award
Durney Vineyards Estate Bottled Chardonnay 1993, Durney Vineyards Estate California	*Lemons and tangerine with waxy oak. Attractive florals, well balanced fruit and integrated oak palate.*	**£15.00**	KDA	B
Villa Mount Eden Bien Nacido Grand Reserve Chardonnay 1997, Villa Mount Eden California	*Peaches and spice with lots of toasty oak and a big splash of spice.*	**£15.00**	LIB	B
BV Carneros Chardonnay Reserve 1995, Beaulieu Vineyards California	*Subtle fruit characters mingled with sweet vanilla oak on the nose. Lively acidity, finishes long and toasty.*	**£16.00**	PFC	S
Geyser Peak Reserve Chardonnay 1996, Geyser Peak Winery California	*Deep golden colour with grapefruit and tropical fruit aromas. Complex fruit palate with integrated oak finish.*	**£16.00**	HBJ	S
Marimar Torres Chardonnay 1996, Marimar Torres Estate California	*Sensational up front fruit preludes well integrated oak on a tangy crisp peach palate.*	**£16.30**	POR GRO SCA GGW LUC	G
J Lohr Arroyo Seco Vista Chardonnay 1996, J Lohr California	*Pears, melon and gauvas dripping with cream flow to charry oak and a tight acid finish.*	**£20.00**	ENO	S
Northern Sonoma Estate Bottled Chardonnay 1992, Ernest & Julio Gallo California	*Quite a big wine here with all pervading melon and peach flavours and well integrated sweet vanilla oak.*	**£20.00**	WCR SOB A&N HAR SEL E&J	S
Northern Sonoma Estate Bottled Chardonnay 1994, Ernest & Julio Gallo California	*A complex wine of fresh citrus and some leathery tones intertwine in a mouthfilling swirl.*	**£20.00**	HAR SEL SOB A&N E&J	S

N. AMERICA • CALIFORNIA • CHARDONNAY

NORTHERN SONOMA ESTATE BOTTLED CHARDONNAY 1996, ERNEST & JULIO GALLO California	*Ripe melon, fig, peach, lemon and candy characters vaporise from a great wash of sweet oak and fruit on the palate.*	£20.00	WCR SEL HAR A&N E&J	G TROPHY WINE
SUTTER HOME M TRINCHERO FOUNDERS ESTATE CHARDONNAY 1997, SUTTER HOME California	*Rich peachy, tropical fruit characters, toasty oak and nutty hints on the nose and palate.*	£20.00	PRG	G

N. AMERICA • CALIFORNIA • FORTIFIED

STARBOARD BATCH 88 NV, QUADY WINERY California	*Rich ripe raisins with burnt butter and spirit on the nose the palate is sweet and supple.*	£7.70	WCR HOH JNW ADN AVB	B
QUADY'S STARBOARD VINTAGE 1990, QUADY WINERY California	*A Californian starboard which possesses a spiced fruit palate with good balance and length.*	£11.50	JNW AVB HOH	B
VYA EXTRA DRY VERMOUTH NV, QUADY WINERY California	*Nice herbal nose showing arrowroot and cinnamon with a pleasant aldehydic sherry palate and long finish*	£12.50	JNW AVB HOH	B
VYA SWEET VERMOUTH NV, QUADY WINERY California	*Extraordinory nose with fresh ginger, cinnamon and caramelised figs showing textural depth and spicy length.*	£12.50	JNW AVB HOH	G

Pinpoint who sells the wine you wish to buy by turning to the stockist codes. If you know the name of the wine you want to buy, use the alphabetical index. If the price is your motivation, refer to the invaluable price guide index; red and white wines under £5, sparkling wines under £12 and Champagne under £16. Happy hunting!

N. AMERICA • CALIFORNIA • PINOT NOIR

FETZER PINOT NOIR 1997, FETZER VINEYARDS California	*Ripe savoury fruit on the nose with a palate of ripe raspberries and supple tannins.*	**£7.00**	WCR TOS SAF ODD MWW FRT WFL BRF	B
SONOMA COUNTY PINOT NOIR 1995, ERNEST & JULIO GALLO California	*Powerful fruit intensity with a subtle backbone of oak and a good acidic drive lingers for some time.*	**£8.00**	WCR ODF E&J	B
GLEN ELLEN PINOT NOIR 1997, GLENELLEN California	*Deep colour with developed raspberry fruit. quite dry with sweet spicey fruit on the palate.*	**£8.00**	VNO PFC	B
QUATRO PINOT NOIR 1995, CECCHETTI SEBASTIANI CELLAR California	*Nice balance of fruit, acidity and tannin rounded off with subtle use of oak.*	**£10.00**	VNO	B
CARNEROS CREEK ESTATE GROWN PINOT NOIR 1997, CARNEROS CREEK WINERY California	*Fruits of the forest on the palate with velvety mouth feel and good palate weight, lovely finish.*	**£10.50**	JNW HAL HAE	S
BUENA VISTA CARNEROS PINOT NOIR 1996, BUENA VISTA California	*Lovely berry fruit with caramel overtones and vegetal characters on the nose. Fruit palate with moderate acidity.*	**£11.00**	CAC CCW	S
ROBERT MONDAVI COASTAL PINOT NOIR 1997, ROBERT MONDAVI California	*Up front cherry and hints of cashew on the nose precede a fine silky palate.*	**£13.00**	WCR TOS JSM BKT MZC	B

Wine	Description	Price	Stockists	Award
Seven Peaks Pinot Noir 1997, Seven Peaks California	*Gentle raspberry and strawberry notes greet the nose before a soft tannin palate with a clean finish.*	**£13.70**	ABA	B
Au Bon Climat Pinot Noir 1997, Au Bon Climat California	*Up-for-it summer fruit characters with great balance on the palate and a long nutty finish.*	**£14.90**	RBS M&V HOU UNC HAR AUB	B
Crichton Hall Pinot Noir 1996, Crichton Hall California	*Fresh black cherry fruit introduces a richly textured palate with a clean acid tail.*	**£15.00**	PAT	B
Villa Mount Eden Bien Nacido Grand Reserve Pinot Noir 1996, Villa Mount Eden California	*A violet red colour offers crunchy plum fruit along with hints of leafy brambles.*	**£15.00**	LIB	B
Robert Sinskey Los Carneros Pinot Noir 1996, Sinskey California	*Mature in appearance, showing good complexity. Liquorice, rosehip and stewed red fruit flavours predominating.*	**£19.00**	WIN	B
Buena Vista Grand Reserve Pinot Noir 1995, Buena Vista California	*Bright ripe cherry characters on the nose, intense berry fruit on the palate. Fine tannin structure.*	**£20.00**	CAC CCW	S
Famous Gate Carneros Pinot Noir 1995, Domaine Carneros California	*Farmer Joe's barnyard and leathery characters on the nose with integrated firm tannins and balanced acidity.*	**£22.50**	VLW WIM HMA	S
Famous Gate Carneros Pinot Noir 1996, Domaine Carneros California	*Meaty fruit with gamey characters and a touch of mint, youthful cherry fruit on the palate with liquorice notes.*	**£22.50**	VLW WIM HMA	G

N. AMERICA • CALIFORNIA • RED • OTHER

Wine	Description	Price	Stockists	Award
California Mountain Genache Cabernet 1997, California Mountain Vineyards California	*Blueberry and plum notes, well-balanced and complex with savoury characters in a bed of fine grained tannins.*	**£3.70**	ALD CDL	S
Vendange Red 1997, Sebastini California	*Fresh, fragrant berries with soft, sweet perfumed sandelwood scents in a full bodied style.*	**£4.30**	QWW WRC BUP MAR THS PLB	S
Black Ridge Carignan Grenache 1997, California Direct California	*Very soft on the palate with mint, liquorice and lifted raspberries. A big, smoky vanilla finish mops up nicely.*	**£4.50**	JSM CDL	B
Delicato Syrah 1997, Delicato Family Vineyard California	*Rich, plump fruit with dry wood textures complex fresh and crisp style and reasonable length.*	**£5.00**	DWL	B
Collins Ranch Old Vine Grenache 1997, Associated Vintage Group California	*Soft jammy fruit showing slightly burnt characters, good depth and a long well balanced finish.*	**£5.50**	BWL	B
Lee Jones Ranches Merlot 1997, Associated Vintage Group California	*Chocolate mint and spiced fruits in this well made wine that is drinking beautifully now.*	**£5.90**	BWL PHI NYW	S
Beringer Vineyards Zinfandel Blush 1998, Beringer Vineyards California	*Very pale in colour a soft easy style of wine, well balanced clean and floral.*	**£6.00**	BWC	B

Wine	Description	Price	Stockists	Award
California Old Vine Estates Carignan 1996, Black Ridge Vineyards California	*Lovely fruit upfront, flows onto a well-rounded palate of smooth tannins with a clean finish.*	**£6.00**	FUL TOS CDL	B
Pepperwood Grove Cabernet Franc 1996, Cecchetti Sebastiani Cellar California	*A labrynth of herbal and small berried fruit tones co-exist in ecstacy in a silky tannin bed draped in a velvet texture.*	**£6.20**	QWW VNO	S
Fetzer Vineyards Eagle Peak Merlot 1997, Fetzer Vineyards California	*Complexities of cedar and nutmeg with a lifted floral tone prelude a lively and long palate structure.*	**£6.50**	Widely Available	B
McDowell Valley Grenache Rosé 1997, McDowell Valley Vineyards California	*Pleasantly fruity on the nose and in the mouth this wine has an appealing sweetness.*	**£6.90**	SPR BKI	B
Canyon Road Merlot 1997, Canyon Road Winery California	*Soft fruity blackcurrant and hay nose with a light fruit palate and silky tannins.*	**£7.00**	HBJ	B
Parducci Charbono Old Vines 1995, Parducci California	*Exotic fruits on the nose with port like aromas and plenty of spice. A party for the palate.*	**£7.00**	PAT	B
Comcannon Petit Sirah 1996, Cowcannon California	*Sweet, fragrant aromas of brambly cassis, a little obvious on the palate, rustic and characterful.*	**£8.00**	AWS	B
Delicato Monterra Syrah 1995, Delicato Family Vineyard California	*Deep red with spicey smoky nose, showing lovely intense berry fruits and tight grippy finish.*	**£8.00**	DWL	B

OTHER • RED • CALIFORNIA • N. AMERICA				
Fetzer Vineyards Syrah 1997, Fetzer Vineyards California	*Very smooth with spice and cinnamon on a generous palate of grippy tannins and a pleasant finish.*	**£8.00**	TOS ODD FUL UNS FRT BRF	B
Fog Mountain Merlot 1997, Fog Mountain Vineyard California	*Mineral and leafy fruit nose, subtle oak on the fruit driven palate, nice fresh finish.*	**£8.00**	BLN EHL	B
McDowell Valley Syrah 1997, McDowell Valley Vineyards California	*Loads of fruits and a touch of herb precede a rounded spicey wine with smooth, soft tannins.*	**£8.00**	JSM BKI	B
Monterra Merlot 1995, Delicato Family Vineyard California	*Balanced, light fresh fruit nose, black cherries on the palate with high acidity, good persistance.*	**£8.00**	DWL	B
Montevina Barbera 1996, Montevina Winery California	*Fresh sappy berry fruit aromas with plummy fruit, soft tannin and fresh acidity coming through on the finish.*	**£8.00**	PRG	B
Meridian Vineyards Merlot 1996, Meridian Vineyards California	*Slightly smoky, intense fruit nose, rich curranty fruit with balanced finish. Velvety and elegant with firm finish.*	**£8.50**	BWC	B
Beringer Vineyards Merlot 1996, Beringer Vineyards California	*Rich ripe plum pudding and capsicum aromas, full palate with nice fleshiness, crisp finish.*	**£9.00**	BWC	B
Fetzer Vineyards Barrel Select Merlot 1997, Fetzer Vineyards California	*Clean, fresh, fruit nose with earthy notes, light and green palate, pleasant conclusion.*	**£9.00**	MWW FRT BRF	B

Wine	Tasting note	Price	Stockists	Medal
HIDDEN CELLARS HILLSIDE RED 1995, HIDDEN CELLARS OF MENDOCINO California	*A very attractive fruit nose with nice tannins and blancing fruit acidity and good length.*	**£9.00**	SPR BKI	B
PARDUCCI PETITE SIRAH 1996, PARDUCCI California	*Sweet vanilla aromas accompanied by ripe brambly fruit, nice cinnamon on the palate. Easy going.*	**£9.00**	PAT	B
BENZIGER MERLOT 1995, BENZIGER California	*Menthol and crushed berry fruits on nose with coconut oakiness. Opulent, mouthfilling fruit which lasts well.*	**£9.50**	CDT WAV	B
CRANE RIDGE RESERVE MERLOT 1997, WENTE California	*Spicey cherry fruit on nose, soft black cherry fruit on balanced palate. Good finish.*	**£9.50**	FRT GRA	B
SEVEN PEAKS MERLOT 1997, SEVEN PEAKS California	*Intense cassis nose with spicey oak, juicy red fruit with elegant cherry finish and tannic grip.*	**£9.70**	NYW ABA	S
CURTIS SYRAH 1996, CURTIS California	*A rich spicey, ripe cherry nose with good follow through and a wonderful tannin tail.*	**£10.00**	GRA	B
EHLERS GROVE DOLCETTO 1997, EHLERS GROVE WINERY California	*Deep red, ripe cherry and cassis aromas, upfront fresh vibrant fruit palate*	**£10.00**	TOS T&T	B
FIRESTONE MERLOT 1996, FIRESTONE California	*Developed spice and cedar bouquet, firm palate with soft, developed fruit, drying out towards finish.*	**£11.00**	GRA	S

HIDDEN CELLARS SYRAH 1996, HIDDEN CELLARS OF MENDOCINO California	*Ripe and fresh berry notes, well-balanced with good fruit and spice flavours.*	**£11.00**	SPR BKI	B
VINO NOCETO SANGIOVESE 1996, VINO NOCETO California	*Maturing cherry smoky aromas with rich sweet morello cherry fruit, soft oak and balanced tannin.*	**£11.50**	RBS NYW ENO	S
BARRELLI CREEK VALDIGUIE 1995, ERNEST & JULIO GALLO California	*A complex nose of vanilla, blackcurrants and green peppers marry on the palate with bursts of juicy fruit.*	**£12.00**	ODF E&J	S
BONTERRA VINEYARDS SYRAH 1997, FETZER VINEYARDS California	*Rich fruit cake spice, big earthy tannins and nice acidity wrapped up in vanillan wood notes.*	**£12.00**	FUL ODD BRF	B
BARRELLI CREEK MERLOT 1995, ERNEST & JULIO GALLO California	*Ripe plums on nose with hint of spice, well balanced palate, fine tannins and good structure.*	**£13.00**	HAR E&J	B
SUTTER HOME TERRA D'ORO BARBERA 1995, SUTTER HOME California	*Deep and intense, plummy jammy chocolatey and minty aromas, excellent balance, long finish.*	**£13.00**	PRG	S
CLOS DU BOIS MERLOT 1997, CLOS DU BOIS California	*Intense red berry nose, ripe but slightly green palate with dry, peppery fruit character.*	**£13.40**	YWL	B
CLOS DU BOIS MERLOT 1996, CLOS DU BOIS California	*Ripe, almost porty nose, fruity on the palate with great structure. Sweet tannins to finish.*	**£14.00**	YWL WRC	B

Wine	Description	Price	Stockists	Award
Fetzer Vineyards Private Collection Petite Sirah 1996, Fetzer Vineyards California	*Lifted minty, black cherries, sweet and juicy on the palate with subdued tannins, nice balance and length.*	**£14.00**	ODD BRF	B
Jade Mountain Syrah 1995, Jade Mountain California	*Offering great plum fruit with kaffir lime leaf notes this full bodied wine has great mouthfeel and length.*	**£14.60**	JNW F&M WIM LVN BOL M&V	B
St Francis Reserve Merlot 1995, St Francis California	*Complex vanilla, currant aromas. Rich fruit with firm, powdery tannins. Soft and velvety, long raisiny finish.*	**£15.00**	HMA	B
Villa Mount Eden India Springs Grand Reserve Syrah 1996, Villa Mount Eden California	*Vanilla, plum jam and white pepper notes. A lovely mouthful of fruit with a firm tannic finish.*	**£15.00**	LIB	B
Les Jumeaux 1995, Jade Mountain California	*Rich fruit with plenty of wood on the nose but in balance with nice structure.*	**£15.30**	JNW NYW SAN DBY TAN M&V	B
Renaissance Merlot Unfiltered 1996, Renaissance California	*Broad, sweet, porty nose. Enveloping tannins but lots of ripe, sunny fruit and hefty finish.*	**£16.00**	THW	B
Le Cigare Volant 1996, Bonny Doon Vineyards California	*Like a great mystery novel, you have to swallow each chapter of flavour before being astonished by the fantastic finish.*	**£16.10**	Widely Available	S
Qupe Bien Nacido Syrah 1996, Qupe Winery California	*Quite austere on the nose but offering generous fruit on a peppered, tar palate.*	**£17.00**	M&V AUB WIM NYW M&V	B

Wine	Description	Price	Stockists	Award
Chrichton Hall Merlot 1996, Chrichton Hall California	*Attractive violet and stewed plum nose with a touch of vanilla and spice. Great length and finesse.*	**£18.00**	CAC PAT	S
Qupe Hillside Select Syrah 1996, Qupe Winery California	*Menthol and oak notes on the nose run into a deeply textured palate of fruit and spice with great length.*	**£20.00**	NYW DBY UNC WIM MRF M&V	S
Geyser Peak Reserve Merlot 1996, Geyser Peak Winery California	*Attractive deep purple colour with rich, fresh fruit aromas and offers well integrated oak and soft chewy tannins.*	**£23.00**	HBJ	S
Geyser Peak Reserve Shiraz 1996, Geyser Peak Winery California	*Nose has spice, black fruits, cherries and crispy bacon. Lots of fruit on the palate.*	**£23.00**	HBJ	S

N. AMERICA • CALIFORNIA • SPARKLING

Wine	Description	Price	Stockists	Award
Cuvée Napa by Mumm Rose NV, Mumm California	*Clean inviting nose showing up front fruit and a well balanced palate with a clean fruit finish.*	**£10.90**	Widely Available	B
Louis Roederer Quartet Anderson Valley NV, Louis Roederer California	*Bready aromas and a zap of freshness from the citrus fruit characteristic which softly bubbles on the palate to end on a soft note.*	**£14.40**	JNW BUP MWW WTS MMD	G WINE OF THE YEAR
Domaine Carneros NV, Domaine Carneros California	*Yeasty dry nose with relatively full front palate and long clean fresh herbal finish.*	**£16.00**	WIM HMA	B

N. AMERICA • CALIFORNIA • WHITE • OTHER

Wine	Description	Price	Stockists	Award
Stratford Chenin Barrel Fermented 1998, Ehlers Grove Winery California	*A sweet start gives way to sherbet nose with primary fruit lift. Nice vanillin conclusion.*	**£5.00**	TOS T&T	B
Geyser Peak Sauvignon Blanc 1998, Geyser Peak Winery California	*Attractive fresh, ripe tropical fruit and lemons balanced by bracing acidity, lovely zingy persistance.*	**£6.00**	HBJ	S
Jekel Vineyards Riesling 1998, Jekel Vineyards California	*Citrus notes of lemon and zesty lime laid on tropical currants to carry through the palate.*	**£6.00**	BRF	B
Beringer Vineyards Sauvignon Blanc 1997, Beringer Vineyards California	*Citrus and toasty oak on the nose, creamy malolactic palate showing pleasant balance and good persistence.*	**£6.50**	UNS BWC	B
Fetzer Vineyards Barrel Select Viognier 1997, Fetzer Vineyards California	*Lots of sweet vanilla fruit with toasty oak aromas and a fabulously creamy texture.*	**£8.00**	TOS BRF	G
Fetzer Vineyards Viognier 1998, Fetzer Vineyards California	*Tropical fruit mingled with citrus aromas, the palate is reminiscent of your childhood candy shops.*	**£8.00**	Widely Available	B
Bonny Doon Malvasia 1997, Bonny Doon Vineyards California	*A nose of baked lemon tart and honeyed fig characters sing from a minerally, viscousy palate of smooth, river pebble texture.*	**£8.10**	Widely Available	G

Wine	Description	Price	Stockists	Award
SAINT SUPERY SAUVIGNON BLANC 1997, SAINT SUPERY California	*Tropical fruit and apples, palate featuring crisp linear acid and richness on the finish.*	**£8.30**	WRC BUP MAR THS LIB	S
BONTERRA VINEYARDS VIOGNIER 1998, BONTERRA VINEYARDS California	*Warm tropical fruit combined with dried apricots and overtones of nuts on a powerful palate.*	**£10.00**	FUL VRT VER ORG ODD BRF	S
CURTIS VIOGNIER 1997, CURTIS California	*Great interpretation of the variety with notes of honey, lemon and fig before an impressive, luscious palate.*	**£11.00**	GRA	B
BARRELLI CREEK SAUVIGNON BLANC 1995, ERNEST & JULIO GALLO California	*Floral herbs and vegetal notes spring from the glass and soft sweet fruit drips upon the tongue.*	**£12.00**	HAR E&J	B
MCDOWELL VALLEY VIOGNIER 1997, MCDOWELL VALLEY VINEYARDS California	*Upfront rich fruit, honeyed characters and underlying toasty oak. Excellent structure, balanced and long.*	**£13.00**	SPR BKI	S
RENAISSANCE VIOGNIER 1997, RENAISSANCE California	*A rich style laden with luscious complexity and great texture explodes in the mouth with fruit fireworks.*	**£14.70**	THW	S

N. AMERICA • CALIFORNIA • ZINFANDEL

Wine	Description	Price	Stockists	Award
BLOSSOM HILL WINERY CALIFORNIA WHITE ZINFANDEL 1997, BLOSSOM HILL WINERY California	*Nice salmon, fresh berry nose, a little sweet but balanced by nice tannins and acid. Fresh and easy.*	**£4.50**	MHV PFC	B

Wine	Tasting note	Price	Stockists	Award
California Old Vine Estates Zinfandel 1996, California Direct California	*Maturing vegetal and spicey nose, concentrated strawberry and plum jams in a clean oaky structure.*	**£6.00**	JSM FUL TOS CDL	B
Lee Jones Ranch Old Vine Zinfandel 1997, Associated Vintage Group California	*Soft leather and a bitter cherry nose lead to a spicey and vegetal palate with good length.*	**£6.00**	BWL PHI	B
Pepperwood Grove Zinfandel 1997, Cecchetti Sebastiani Cellar California	*Jammy plum fruits with wonderful chewy texture and spicey characters backed up by firm tannins.*	**£6.00**	QWW VNO	G WINE OF THE YEAR
Beringer Vineyards Zinfandel 1996, Beringer Vineyards California	*Upfront spicey oaky aromas with a sweet plum vein and soft intergrated tannins and a long, cleansing firm finish.*	**£6.50**	UNS BWC	B
Fetzer Barrel Select Zinfandel 1997, Fetzer Vineyards California	*Restrained black berry fruit nose ripe and well-balanced spicey cherry palate with a gamey, sappy finish.*	**£9.00**	TOS ODD FRT BRF	B
Bonterra Zinfandel 1997, Bonterra Vineyards California	*Rich cherry, plummy fruit and vanilla oak marry well on a firm, jammy fruit palate.*	**£9.20**	QWW ODD FRT ORG VRT BRF	S
Sutter Home Amador County Reserve Zinfandel 1992, Sutter Home California	*Pleasing upfront brambly fruit and loganberries. Nice earthy, maturity shows on the chewy, long palate.*	**£10.00**	WAC C&H VHW P&R SPG PRG	B
Geyser Peak Zinfandel 1996, Geyser Peak Winery California	*Solid 'toothy' fruit very savoury with a long and deliciously dry finish with plenty of power.*	**£12.00**	HBJ	B

Wine	Description	Price	Stockists	Award
Renaissance Zinfandel 1996, Renaissance California	*Sweet, solid and peppery fruit, a mature style still showing youthful aromas with a robust finish, quite powerful.*	**£12.70**	THW	B
Chiotti Zinfandel 1997, Ernest & Julio Gallo California	*Fists of berry fruit and smoky aromas lead to a fine structure of toasty oak and extracted fruit.*	**£13.00**	HAR E&J	S
Dry Creek Old Vines Zinfandel 1997, Dry Creek Vineyard California	*A complex nose of damson and dark cherry fruit herlalds in a smoke and vanilla spice palate.*	**£13.00**	PAT	S
Montevina Terra d'Oro Zinfandel 1995, Sutter Home California	*Powerful aromas of toffee and ripe berry fruit precede a firm, tannin palate. Drinking well now.*	**£13.00**	PRG	B
Robert Mondavi Napa Valley Zinfandel 1997, Robert Mondavi California	*Restrained herb and mint nose leading to a generous palate of spicey brambly fruit.*	**£13.50**	MWW FUL FTH MZC	S
Saint Francis Old Vines Zinfandel 1996, St Francis California	*A mint and oak entry to a creamy, fresh berry palate with cigar, hay and barnyard notes.*	**£14.10**	QWW HMA	G
Chiles Mill Zinfandel 1996, Green & Red Vineyards California	*Attractive perfumed blackberry fruit and spice aromas with layers of deep jammy fruit.*	**£16.00**	WIN	S
Hidden Cellars Mendocino Heritage Sorcery 1996, Hidden Cellars Of Mendocino California	*Very tight structure giving rise to a massive spicey, full bodied palate with superb length.*	**£16.00**	UNS SPR BKI	G

N. AMERICA • CALIFORNIA • ZINFANDEL

Wine	Description	Price	Stockists	Award
Clos du Val Zinfandel 1997, Clos du Val California	*Primary berry fruit and ground black pepper notes precede a tight tannic structure. Will grow.*	**£16.70**	HOH AVB	B
Ridge Geyserville Zinfandel 1997, Ridge Vineyards California	*Red berry and brambly fruit lead to tarry, spicey, smokey oak complexities ahead of a clove and coffee finish.*	**£17.60**	Widely Available	G
Ridge Lytton Springs Zinfandel 1996, Ridge Vineyards California	*Superb complexities of sweet brambly fruit coming to a chocolate and coconut crescendo. Totally luxurious.*	**£17.80**	RBS L&W HHF M&V BDR NYW JNW	G

N. AMERICA • CANADA • WHITE

Wine	Description	Price	Stockists	Award
Southbrook Chardonnay 1997, Southbrook Winery Ontario	*A ripe fruit basket balanced with good acidity and a touch of warmth on a clean finish.*	**£7.50**	EHL	S

N. AMERICA • OREGON • RED

Wine	Description	Price	Stockists	Award
Willamette Valley Vineyards Pinot Noir 1996, Willamette Valley Vineyards Oregon	*Well extracted red berry notes complemented by subtle oak on a fine, silky palate.*	**£13.00**	WLI	B
King Estate Pinot Noir 1995, King Estate Oregon	*Ripe fruit with some attractive pepper characters before a full bodied palate hiding mushrooms and gamey flavours.*	**£14.00**	THW	S

Wine	Description	Price	Stockists	Award
Henry Estate Barrel Select Pinot Noir 1995, Henry Estate Winery Oregon	*Black fruit and cherry characters with some savoury notes on the palate, lovely tannins well-balanced with fruit acidity.*	**£14.70**	SPR BKI	S
Rex Hill Willamette Valley Pinot Noir 1996, Rex Hill Oregon	*Waxy cherry and red berry on the nose leading to a medium bodied palate of pleasing length.*	**£17.00**	HAY HVN MOR	B
Domaine Drouhin Pinot Noir 1996, Joseph Drouhin Oregon	*Vibrant fruit, well balanced oak and green spices with well matched tannins.*	**£21.00**	JNW HWB BWL MZC	B

N. AMERICA • OREGON • WHITE

Wine	Description	Price	Stockists	Award
Henry Estate Oregon Pinot Gris 1997, Henry Estate Winery Oregon	*Nutty almond aromas with a full bodied palate, fine acidity and soft spicey overtones.*	**£8.90**	SPR BKI	B
King Estate Pinot Gris 1996, King Estate Oregon	*High toned stewed fruit aromas, intensity of fruit combined with earthy overtones and moderate acidity.*	**£12.00**	THW	B
King Estate Chardonnay 1995, King Estate Oregon	*Tropical fruits and nuts on the nose lead to a well balanced palate with a clean fruit finish.*	**£13.00**	THW	B

Pinpoint who sells the wine you wish to buy by turning to the stockist codes. If you know the name of the wine you want to buy, use the alphabetical index. If the price is your motivation, refer to the invaluable price guide index; red and white wines under £5, sparkling wines under £12 and Champagne under £16. Happy hunting!

N. AMERICA • WASHINGTON STATE • RED

Wine	Description	Price	Stockists	Award
HOGUE BARREL SELECT CABERNET SAUVIGNON 1996, HOGUE CELLARS Washington State	*Interesting fruits including gooseberry notes introduce a rounded and smooth palate. Nice length.*	**£10.30**	THW	B
HOGUE BARREL SELECT MERLOT 1996, HOGUE CELLARS Washington State	*A lighter style showing pastilles and currants with moderate oak treatment and pleasant mouthfeel.*	**£10.30**	THW	B
CHÂTEAU STE MICHELLE CABERNET SAUVIGNON 1995, CHÂTEAU STE MICHELLE Washington State	*A herbaceous nose with currant notes follows on to a dusty, nicely balanced palate with plenty of fruit flavour.*	**£10.50**	LIB	S
COLUMBIA CREST MERLOT 1995, COLUMBIA CREST Washington State	*Blackberry nose with herbal notes and a subtle oak palate with complex cassis, cigar box and licorice flavours.*	**£12.00**	UNS RBS WCR LIB	S
CHÂTEAU STE MICHELLE CANOE RIDGE MERLOT 1996, CHÂTEAU STE MICHELLE Washington State	*Ripe dark fruit and new oak in excellent balance. Firm tannins lead to vanilla tones on the finish.*	**£30.00**	LIB NFF	S

N. AMERICA • WASHINGTON STATE • WHITE

Wine	Description	Price	Stockists	Award
COLUMBIA CREST CHARDONNAY 1997, COLUMBIA CREST Washington State	*Yellow with green tinges, rich toasty oak and ripe pineapple and mango on the nose.*	**£6.50**	WRC BUP MAR THS TOS LIB	S

Wine	Description	Price	Stockists	Award
HOGUE FRUIT FORWARD CHENIN BLANC 1997, HOGUE CELLARS Washington State	*Pleasant grapey and banana skin characters with ripe fruit on the palate and a clean acid finish.*	**£6.50**	THW	B
COLUMBIA CREST CHARDONNAY 1996, COLUMBIA CREST Washington State	*Lean citrus fruit and apply notes are well matched with a good measure of sweet oak.*	**£7.30**	WCR WRC BUP MAR THS TOS LIB	S
COLUMBIA WYCKOFF CHARDONNAY 1996, COLUMBIA WINERY Washington State	*Full oaky vanilla aromas with rich full bodied tropical fruit, lovely lemon acidity on finish.*	**£8.60**	FTH	B
CHÂTEAU STE MICHELLE CHARDONNAY 1996, CHÂTEAU STE MICHELLE Washington State	*Subtle buttery mango and spicy lemon aromas with mild oak influence and a clean finish.*	**£9.00**	WCR LIB	B

Pinpoint who sells the wine you wish to buy by turning to the stockist codes. If you know the name of the wine you want to buy, use the alphabetical index. If the price is your motivation, refer to the invaluable price guide index; red and white wines under £5, sparkling wines under £12 and champagne under £16. Happy hunting!

NEW ZEALAND

New Zealand continues to shine as a producer of top class wines. Marlborough once again held the Sauvignon Blanc Trophy against fierce competition from the Loire even with a 'hot' vintage. A surprise was the success of the red wines picking up more Gold medals than the whites. The Bordelais styles excelled, strengthening New Zealand's formidable armoury. So, be it zippy Rieslings, fantastic fizz, up front Sauvignon or intense Merlot there is no shortage from this little wonder.

NEW ZEALAND • CABERNET/MERLOT

Wine	Description	Price	Stockists	Award
TERRACE VIEW CABERNET SAUVIGNON MERLOT 1997, JOHN KEMBLE Hawke's Bay	*Rich currant nose. Brambles and good fruit on the palate with firm, grippy tannins and elegant structure.*	**£5.50**	CWS HAL FSW CHN	B
M&S KAITUNA HILLS CABERNET MERLOT 1998, MONTANA WINES Hawke's Bay	*An intriguing nose introduces ripe fruit laying back on some nice oak supported by a fine tannin backbone.*	**£6.00**	MTW M&S	B
VIDAL CABERNET SAUVIGNON MERLOT 1997, VIDAL ESTATE Hawke's Bay	*Some evolution evident as juicy fruit melds into pudding and farmy characters. Nice structure and a pleasant acid tail.*	**£8.00**	GRA FRT	B
VIDAL THE BAYS MERLOT CABERNET SAUVIGNON 1995, VIDAL ESTATE Hawke's Bay	*Blackcurrant and cigar box characters seep from this nicely structured wine with good persistance of flavour.*	**£8.50**	GRA	B
DELEGAT'S HAWKE'S BAY RESERVE CABERNET SAUVIGNON 1997, DELEGAT'S Hawke's Bay	*Remarkable complexities of asparagus, beans, redcurrents, raisins and spice before a superb fruits of the forest tannin structure.*	**£8.70**	MCT SAF BKT FRT GSJ	G

Wine	Description	Price	Stockists	Award
CHURCH ROAD CABERNET SAUVIGNON MERLOT 1997, MONTANA WINES Hawke's Bay	*Bright plum red with a light oaky nose with fresh fruit tannins and a gentle finish.*	**£9.00**	Widely Available	B
ESK VALLEY MERLOT CABERNET SAUVIGNON 1997, ESK VALLEY ESTATES Hawke's Bay	*Cherry jam on the nose with some mint. Fresh fruit, cleansing tannins with blackcurrant finish.*	**£9.00**	WCR WRC HMA	B
VILLA MARIA CELLAR SELECTION CABERNET MERLOT 1996, VILLA MARIA ESTATES Hawke's Bay	*Cedar and blackcurrant with a tad of cassis cruise on to a silky palate offering good length.*	**£9.30**	QWW WCR HMA WTS	S
VILLA MARIA CELLAR SELECTION CABERNET SAUVIGNON MERLOT 1996, VILLA MARIA ESTATES Hawke's Bay	*Toasty oak and fruit on the nose introduce a dense palate of concentrated fruit with generous length.*	**£10.30**	QWW HMA	S
VILLA MARIA CELLAR SELECTION CABERNET SAUVIGNON MERLOT 1997, VILLA MARIA ESTATES Hawke's Bay	*Juicy, jammy fruit with pronouced red berries and a hint of herb make for a well balanced wine.*	**£10.30**	QWW HMA	S
BASKET PRESS SACRED HILL CABERNET SAUVIGNON 1997, SACRED HILL Auckland	*Nice cedary, blackcurrant and wiffs of crushed tomato leaf. Good integration, balance and persistence.*	**£10.50**	UNS FUL- WLI	B
CHURCH ROAD RESERVE CABERNET MERLOT 1995, MONTANA WINES Hawke's Bay	*Ripe cedar nose with luxurious cigar box characters lead to a well defined palate of fine grained fruit tannins.*	**£10.50**	WRC BUP MAR SEA MTW	S
ELSPETH CABERNET MERLOT 1997, MILLS REEF Hawkes Bay	*Cherries and plums, soaked in a potion of mint and herbs, infused with a touch of delicate oak.*	**£11.40**	FTH	S

NEW ZEALAND • CABERNET/MERLOT

Dartmoor Smith Cabernet Sauvignon 1997, Matua Valley Hawkes Bay	*Herbaceous bouquet with spicy cedar. Crisp, fine tannins with plummy, ripe fruit and a rich, spicy finish.*	**£11.50**	QWW UNS RML MZC	S
Sacred Hill Basket Press Merlot Cabernet Sauvignon 1995, Sacred Hill Hawke's Bay	*Mint and eucalypt seep from this elegant wine. A fair dose of oak marries with neat fruit engages the palate.*	**£11.90**	UNS FUL-WLI	B
Alpha Domus The Navigator 1997, Alpha Domus Hawke's Bay	*Lovely perfumed fuits on the nose with a soft and creamy tannin tail.*	**£13.00**	MKV	B
Villa Maria Reserve Merlot Cabernet Sauvignon 1995, Villa Maria Estates Hawke's Bay	*A classic restrained fruit style showing lovely herbaceous characters singing harmoniously with subtle vanilla and toasted oak notes.*	**£13.00**	WCR HMA	G
Vidal Reserve Cabernet Sauvignon 1995, Vidal Estate Hawke's Bay	*Earthy, ripe cherry fruit nose, with some vanilla oak. Flavoursome palate with chunky tannins.*	**£15.00**	GRA FRT	B
Villa Maria Reserve Merlot Cabernet Sauvignon 1996, Villa Maria Estates Hawke's Bay	*Cigar box, mint on nose, balanced fruit and oak palate. Good acidity, firm tannins. Long elegant structure.*	**£15.00**	HMA	B
Vidal Reserve Cabernet Merlot 1996, Vidal Estate Hawke's Bay	*Fruit-driven complex wine with firm tannins. Solid, rich flavours will reward even more in time.*	**£15.20**	GRA NYW	S
Esk Valley Reserve Merlot Malbec Cabernet Sauvignon 1995, Esk Valley Estates Hawke's Bay	*Very dark concentrated purple hints at the brooding blackberries, anise and plum pudding characters to come.*	**£17.00**	WIM HMA	S

CABERNET/MERLOT • NEW ZEALAND

Esk Valley Reserve Merlot Malbec Cabernet Sauvignon 1996, Esk Valley Estates Hawke's Bay	*Concentrated plum fruits and blackcurrant before a palate of fine supple tannins integrated with the perfect measure of oak.*	**£17.00**	WIM HMA	S
Te Motu 1996, Waiheke Vineyards Waiheke Island	*Opulent fruit as well as gamey, earthy characters make this a truly complex wine. Perfectly harmonious.*	**£24.00**	FNZ	G
Goldwater Cabernet Merlot 1996, Goldwater Estate Waiheke Island	*Plum and fruits in nectar on the nose lead to a full bodied palate of generous length.*	**£26.40**	NYW AVB HOH	S

NEW ZEALAND • CHARDONNAY

Lawson's Dry Hills Chardonnay 1997, Lawson's Dry Hills Marlborough	*Creamy oak and melon flavours combine with refreshing lime and lemon on a zippy palate.*	**£4.90**	BWL	B
Sanctuary Chardonnay 1997, Grove Mill Marlborough	*Peachy, creamy fruit leads to a powerful, oily full body with honey and lemon notes.*	**£6.00**	LAW	B
Sanctuary Chardonnay 1998, Grove Mill Marlborough	*Exotic fruits greet the nose and appear again on a well structured palate.*	**£6.00**	LAW	B
Babich Mara Estate Chardonnay 1995, Babich Wines Hawke's Bay	*Bright gold with a green hue, pronounced citrus characters on the nose. Full palate with banana and melon flavors.*	**£7.50**	PFC	S

NEW ZEALAND • CHARDONNAY

Wine	Description	Price	Stockists	Award
Villa Maria Cellar Selection Chardonnay 1997, Villa Maria Estates Hawke's Bay	*Creamy nuances of toasty oak dominate a palate full of ripe tropical mangos.*	£7.50	WCR ODD HMA	S
Kim Crawford Unoaked Chardonnay 1998, Kim Crawford Marlborough	*A mild citrus nose leads to a complex palate of tropical fruits and crisp clean acid.*	£7.90	WCR NYW LIB	B
Giesen Estate Chardonnay 1998, Giesen Wine Estate Canterbury/ Marlborough	*A clean, fresh and very appealing fruit driven nose of tropical and ripe banana fruits.*	£8.00	THW	S
M&S Kaituna Hills Reserve Chardonnay 1998, Montana Wines Gisborne	*Gorgeous honey and coconut on the nose with plenty of rich ripe fruit, medium length.*	£8.00	MTW M&S	B
Montana Reserve Gisborne Chardonnay 1998, Montana Wines Gisborne	*Limes, tropical fruit and vanilla oak nose, lively citrus fruit on palate with integrated oak.*	£8.00	VLW MTW	S WINE OF THE YEAR
Montana Reserve Chardonnay 1998, Montana Wines Marlborough	*Tropical fruit with buttery charred oak aromas, elegant lemon and pineapple fruit characters on palate.*	£8.20	Widely Available	S
Mudhouse Chardonnay 1998, Mudhouse Wine Marlborough	*Well layered with sweet and sour characters a hint of lemon honey providing interest.*	£8.20	GRT ABA	B
Esk Valley Chardonnay 1997, Esk Valley Estates Hawke's Bay	*Lean zingy citrus fruit characters lead to a buxom palate of cream tinctured with tangerine.*	£8.50	QWW WCR HMA	B

Wine	Description	Price	Stockists	Award
Nobilo Poverty Bay Chardonnay 1998, Nobilo Vintners Poverty Bay	*A closed nose at this stage but a promising palate of ripe fruit with lovely acidity.*	£8.50	HBR	B
Delegat's Hawke's Bay Reserve Chardonnay 1997, Delegat's Hawke's Bay	*Florals and fresh lemons combine with aromatic grapefruit before a balanced palate of tropical fruit.*	£8.60	MCT SAF BKT WCR FRT GSJ	S
Delegat's Hawke's Bay Reserve Chardonnay 1998, Delegat's Hawke's Bay	*Subtle vanilla oak on the nose leading to a palate offering a full spectrum of stone fruits.*	£8.60	MCT BKT WCR SAF FRT GSJ	S
Esk Valley Chardonnay 1998, Esk Valley Estates Hawke's Bay	*A remarkable wine showcasing nutty barrel ferment and stone fruit characters shining from a clove and pepper palate.*	£8.60	QWW WCR HMA	G
Saint Clair Omaka Chardonnay 1998, Saint Clair Marlborough	*Toasty buttery apricots on the palate with sweet medium-body fruit and spirally, acid finish.*	£8.70	QWW AVB HOH	B
Church Road Chardonnay 1998, Montana Wines Hawke's Bay	*Citrus fruit and buttery oak on the nose, palate has toasty characters and crisp apple acidity.*	£8.90	VLW ABY WRC BUP MAR MTW SEA	S
Morton Estate Riverview Chardonnay 1997, Morton Estate Hawke's Bay	*Lovely spicey fruit and toasty oak on the nose with a palate of soft clean acidity.*	£9.20	RBS BWC	B
Morton Estate White Label Hawke's Bay Chardonnay 1997, Morton Estate Hawke's Bay	*Quince combined with complex buttery oak on the nose, upfront fruit and a clean acid finish.*	£9.20	RBS NYW BWC	B

NEW ZEALAND • CHARDONNAY

Wine	Description	Price	Stockists	Award
Sacred Hill Barrel Fermented Chardonnay 1997, Sacred Hill Hawke's Bay	*A buttery, toasty nose belies the zesty stone fruit and minerally palate that follow.*	**£9.20**	UNS MHV WLI	S
Villa Maria Reserve Chardonnay 1998, Villa Maria Estates Hawke's Bay	*Toasted oak overtones to a richly flavoured palate of hot pineapple chunks and crisp mouthwatering starfruit.*	**£9.50**	UNS HMA	S
Alpha Domus Chardonnay 1998, Alpha Domus Hawke's Bay	*Nutty oak and delicate fruit with malo creaminess and elegant clean citrus fruit. Delicate finish.*	**£10.00**	MKV	S
Forrest Estate Chardonnay 1997, Forrest Estate Marlborough	*Lovely new oak and citrus aromas, rich round fruit with slight sweetness and balanced oak.*	**£10.00**	ADN HAS	B
Giesen Estate Marlborough Chardonnay Reserve 1997, Giesen Wine Estate Marlborough	*Rich aromas of melons and oak spill into a pool of cool pineapples and vanilla.*	**£10.00**	THW	B
Isabel Estate Chardonnay 1997, Isabel Estate Marlborough	*A restrained fruit and mineral nose signal an elegant wine with a myriad of complex elements.*	**£10.00**	M&V GGW JUS DBY	S
Vidal Reserve Chardonnay 1995, Vidal Estate Hawke's Bay	*Lime apples and spiced palate with integrated toasty oak lead to a clean finish.*	**£10.00**	GRA FRT	B
Vidal Reserve Chardonnay 1996, Vidal Estate Hawke's Bay	*Light lime characters with a touch of creamy vanilla oak and refreshing acidity with good length.*	**£10.00**	GRA FRT	B

Wine	Description	Price	Stockists	Award
Waipara West Chardonnay 1996, Tutton Sienko & Hill Waipara	*Floral and lime aromas with balanced, rich, slightly waxy fruit and gentle acidity.*	£10.00	HOL P&R DVY WAW	B
Goldwater Roseland Chardonnay 1997, Goldwater Marlborough	*Attractive aroma of green fruits with a subtle oak influence introduce a well-rounded juicy palate.*	£10.20	ETV SEL WIM MWW AVB HOH	S
Palliser Estate Chardonnay 1997, Palliser Estate Martinborough	*Concentrated nose with light apple and citrus fruit combined with fine oak and elegant acidity.*	£10.40	ABY WRC BUP MAR THS	B
Vavasour Chardonnay 1998, Vavasour Wines Marlborough	*Nose has hints of asparagus and vegetal characters. Ripe full-bodied fruit with vanilla flavours. Well balanced.*	£10.50	JNW ORB	S
Montana Ormond Estate Chardonnay 1998, Montana Wines Gisborne	*Lovely approach with a fragrant elegant fruit palate and herbal characters on the nose.*	£11.00	WRC BUP MAR THS SEA MTW	B
Montana Renwick Estate Chardonnay 1997, Montana Wines Marlborough	*Peaches, cashews and toasty aromas with lovely citrus fruit with good weight and a long finish.*	£11.00	SEA MTW	B
Villa Maria Reserve Marlborough Chardonnay 1997, Villa Maria Estates Hawke's Bay	*Ripe flavours of mangos, melons and pineapples abound on a palate displaying creamy, vanilla oak characters.*	£11.00	HMA	S
Church Road Reserve Chardonnay 1996, Montana Wines Hawke's Bay	*Rich fruit and vanilla oak on nose, lemon and lime flavours, excellent structure and length.*	£11.10	VLW ABY WRC BUP MAR MTW SEA	G

NEW ZEALAND • CHARDONNAY				
CHURCH ROAD CUVÉE SERIES CHARDONNAY 1995, MONTANA WINES Hawke's Bay	*A classy wine bursting with tangerines and tropical medium dry fruit with toasty kernel oak.*	£12.00	MTW WTS	S
JACKSON ESTATE RESERVE CHARDONNAY 1997, JACKSON ESTATE Marlborough	*Stylish on the nose with marmalade fruit characters, then clean acid with subtle integrated oak.*	£12.00	HWL SVT	B
COTTAGE BLOCK CHARDONNAY 1997, CORBANS WINES Marlborough	*Tropical fruit mingles with subtle oak aromas, some complexity with balanced acidity and good length.*	£13.00	SLM SOH PEA CAX	B
ESK VALLEY RESERVE CHARDONNAY 1996, ESK VALLEY ESTATES Hawke's Bay	*Soothing, tropical fruit aromas with a full body and a cleansing I-want-more finish.*	£13.00	WIM HMA	B
MATUA VALLEY JUDD ESTATE CHARDONNAY 1998, MATUA VALLEY Poverty Bay	*Smoky vanilla oak aromas with delicate fruit mineral characters and clean crisp acidity.*	£13.00	HAR SEN MZC	B
SEIFRIED NELSON BARRIQUE FERMENTED WINEMAKERS COLLECTION CHARDONNAY 1997, SEIFRIED ESTATE Nelson	*Honeyed slightly minty nose with subtle oak and full-bodied tropical fruit flavours with good acid balance.*	£13.00	CWA	B
OKAHU ESTATE CLIFTON PROPRIETOR'S RESERVE CHARDONNAY 1997, OKAHU ESTATE North Island	*Pale gold with green highlights. Opulent fruit with integrated new oak moderate acidity and elegant finish.*	£14.40	GGW	S
LA STRADA MARLBOROUGH CHARDONNAY 1997, FROMM WINERY Marlborough	*A very serious style with vanilla oak, soft melon fruit, peach and apple notes.Fantastic structural finish.*	£14.90	NYW L&W	S

Kim Crawford Tietjen Gisborne Chardonnay 1998, Kim Crawford Gisborne	*Hot ripe buttery aromas with lovely balanced fruit, moderate acidity and subtle integrated oak characters.*	**£15.00**	NYW LIB	

NEW ZEALAND • PINOT NOIR

Montana Reserve Pinot Noir 1997, Montana Wines Marlborough	*Berry fruit characters on the nose followed by a palate that is soft and round with well integrated tannins.*	**£10.20**	UNS VLW HHF WRC BUP MAR MTW	S
Palliser Estate Pinot Noir 1997, Palliser Estate Martinborough	*Sweet licorice confection heads off huge mouthfulls of plums and dense red fruit. Slippery-dip finish.*	**£10.80**	NYW WRC BUP DBY C&B ABY	S
Waipara West Pinot Noir 1998, Tutton Sienko & Hill Waipara	*Earthy tones and oak on the nose, raspberry fruit palate, meaty complex characters and firm tannins.*	**£11.20**	WAW P&R	S
Isabel Estate Pinot Noir 1997, Isabel Estate Marlborough	*Mushrooms and compost with underlying cherry and some lollipop flavours on a silky, long palate.*	**£12.10**	GGW NYW UNC WIL MRF M&V	S
Giesen Canterbury Pinot Noir Reserve 1997, Giesen Wine Estate Canterbury	*A dusty nose with heady mint and cherry notes, well developed and mature with a healthy tannin finish.*	**£13.00**	THW	B
La Strada Pinot Noir 1997, Fromm Winery Marlborough	*Well developed with an open toasty oak and butterscotch nose. Firm but approachable now.*	**£14.90**	L&W NYW	B

NEW ZEALAND • PINOT NOIR

Wine	Description	Price	Stockists	Award
Felton Road Pinot Noir 1997, Felton Road Wines Central Otago	*Full and concentrated red cherry and black fruit notes lead to a well proportioned oak palate with a clean acid finish.*	£15.00	WRC WSC	B
Dry River Pinot Noir 1997, Neil McCullum Martinborough	*Cherries with mint on the nose and a well balanced palate of fine grained tannins and fruit acidity.*	£20.50	NYW J&B	S
Martinborough Vineyard Reserve Pinot Noir 1996, Martinborough Vineyard Martinborough	*Hints of coffee, spice and oak on the nose, fantastically defined fruit on the palate with body and weight.*	£26.40	ADN	G

NEW ZEALAND • RED • OTHER

Wine	Description	Price	Stockists	Award
MHV New Zealand Red NV, Sacred Hill Hawke's Bay	*Fruit, cherry and honeysuckle abound before a rounded palate of firm tannins and good length.*	£5.00	MHV WLI	B
Kemblefield Merlot 1997, Kemblefield Estate North Island	*Herbaceousness with a nice touch of fruit are the offerings from this wine of ripe tannins and good length.*	£7.80	UNS CHN	B
Delegat's Hawke's Bay Reserve Merlot 1997, Delegat's Hawke's Bay	*Plum and prune nose and a touch of fresh herbs. Medium bodied with good length and balance.*	£8.00	FRT GSJ	S
Montana Reserve Merlot 1997, Montana Wines Marlborough	*Youthful, with good mint flavours and palate weight will improve further with time.*	£9.00	WRC BUP MAR TOS SEA MTW	B

Wine	Description	Price	Stockists	Award
Whitecliff New Zealand Merlot 1998, Sacred Hill Hawke's Bay	*Meaty lift on the nose with minty tones, swirling black fruits on the back palate with a bitter twist.*	£9.30	MHV WLI	S
Broken Stone Sacred Hill Merlot 1997, Sacred Hill Auckland	*Intriguing,with a touch of tobacco and cedar on the nose and spiciness on the palate. Nice texture.*	£11.00	FUL WLI	S
CJ Pask Merlot Reserve 1997, CJ Pask Winery North Island	*New oak on nose, with butterscotch and toffee. Well-balanced fruit and great length. Savoury and stylish.*	£11.90	L&W JLW CAC	G
Unison Hawke's Bay Selection Reserve 1997, Unison Vineyard Hawke's Bay	*Generous oaky nose with bright, loud fruit characters, a green edge and a long finish.*	£16.00	WTS	S
Kaz Shiraz 1997, Okahu Estate North Island	*Ripe and complex with a long finish. Well balanced with ideal balance of fruit acid and tannin.*	£20.60	GGW	S

NEW ZEALAND • SAUVIGNON BLANC

Wine	Description	Price	Stockists	Award
Kohi Point Sauvignon Blanc Semillon 1998, Montana Wines Marlborough	*Flinty dusty characters on the nose, the palate is full bodied with lots of citrus fruit.*	£4.00	MTW SAF	B
Azure Bay Sauvignon Blanc Semillon 1998, Montana Wines Gisborne	*Zingy citrus fruit combined with tropical richness and moderate acidity producing a refreshing drop.*	£5.00	WRC BUP MAR THS MTW	B

Wine	Description	Price	Stockists	Award
Timara Sauvignon Blanc Semillon 1998, Montana Wines Marlborough	*Delicate citrus fruit on the nose and palate with moderate acidity and a clean long finish.*	£5.00	MTW SEA	B
Giesen Estate Sauvignon Blanc 1998, Giesen Wine Estate Marlborough	*Pronounced passionfruit and freshly cut grass, a palate with nice oily viscosity and cutting acidity.*	£7.00	THW	S
Saint Clair Marlborough Sauvignon Blanc 1996, Saint Clair Marlborough	*Big, fat asparagus nose, quite well defined, a light oaking adds to the structure, quite persistent.*	£7.00	QWW HOH SPR	B
Seifried Nelson Sauvignon Blanc 1998, Seifried Estate Nelson	*Very fresh, zesty limes, delicate floral palate showing good depth and structural acidity, nice length.*	£7.00	CWA	S
Villa Maria Private Bin East Coast Chardonnay 1998, Villa Maria Estates East Coast	*Melon and buttery oak aromas, summer tropical fruit on an oak infused palate.*	£7.00	ODD WCR UNS VWE WTS HMA	B
Villa Maria Private Bin Sauvignon Blanc 1998, Villa Maria Estates Marlborough	*Soft, lightly peachy nose leading to a balanced palate with a nicely defined citric finish.*	£7.00	Widely Available	B
Nobilo Marlborough Sauvignon Blanc 1998, Nobilo Vintners Marlborough	*Crisp and fresh with pungent gooseberries and freshly cut grass. Elegant balance of fruit and acid.*	£7.10	BDR HBR	S
Aotea Sauvignon Blanc 1998, Aotea Vineyards Nelson	*Crisp, open nose displaying fat gooseberries and tomato leaf. Lovely full mouthfeel showing concentration and depth.*	£7.20	RBS CAC FNZ	S

SAUVIGNON BLANC • NEW ZEALAND

MORTON ESTATE COLEFIELD SAUVIGNON BLANC 1997, MORTON ESTATE Hawke's Bay	*Masses of gooseberries, asparagus and herbs, a nutty palate well supported by zesty acid., and great length.*	**£7.20**	BWC	S
DASHWOOD SAUVIGNON BLANC 1998, VAVASOUR WINES Marlborough	*Delicate, light fruit and tinned peas on the nose flow to a flinty, minerally palate.*	**£7.30**	WRC BUP JNW MAR THS ORB	B
GROVE MILL SAUVIGNON BLANC 1998, GROVE MILL Marlborough	*Intense sweet goosberries and green beans and the palate features zingy pineapple fruit and grippy acid.*	**£7.30**	NYW LAW JSM	S
BABICH MARA ESTATE SAUVIGNON BLANC 1998, BABICH WINES Hawkes Bay	*A promise of class here, lifted perfumed fruit to start, frisky acid structure, crisp fruity finish.*	**£7.50**	PFC	S
CHANCELLOR SAUVIGNON BLANC 1997, CHANCELLOR WINES Waipara	*Pungent asparagus with nettly accompianments and smoky overhang. Gooseberry palate and appealing, long crisp finish.*	**£7.50**	GRT	S
CHANCELLOR SAUVIGNON BLANC 1998, CHANCELLOR WINES Waipara	*Restrained peaches and peas to start followed by a well balanced sweet fruit palate.*	**£7.50**	GRT	B
RED BIRCH SAUVIGNON BLANC 1998, RED BIRCH WINERY Marlborough	*Ripe watermelon and stewed apples, quite full in the mouth with just enough acid.*	**£7.50**	SPR BKI	B
BABICH FAMILY RESERVE SAUVIGNON BLANC 1998, BABICH WINES Marlborough	*A clean fresh nose of gooseberries and nettles, round, ripe and full with flashy lean acidity.*	**£7.70**	BDR	B

NEW ZEALAND • SAUVIGNON BLANC				
KIM CRAWFORD MARLBOROUGH SAUVIGNON BLANC 1998, KIM CRAWFORD Marlborough	*Powerful nettles and sweet honeyed fruit, cleansing acid on the full palate, persistent finish.*	**£7.80**	WCR NYW TOS LIB	B
CHURCH ROAD SAUVIGNON BLANC 1997, MONTANA WINES Hawke's Bay/Marlborough	*Vegetal, grassy nose, rich goosberies on the palate showing balance and poise. Good zesty finish.*	**£8.00**	VLW SEA MTW	B
CLIFFORD BAY SAUVIGNON BLANC 1998, CLIFFORD BAY North Island	*The nose is showing cut limes and floral notes. Dry and concentrated with zippy acid.*	**£8.00**	FRI	S
DE GYFFARDE SAUVIGNON BLANC 1998, DE GYFFARDE WINES South Island	*Grassy with a hint of aniseed, good fruit palate, nice zesty acid and a refreshing conclusion.*	**£8.00**	GNW	B
FORREST ESTATE SAUVIGNON BLANC 1998, FORREST ESTATE Marlborough	*Tight fruit with a whack of asparagus, nice acid a little simple but very slurpable.*	**£8.00**	NYW ADN BEN HAS	B
LAWSON'S DRY HILLS SAUVIGNON BLANC 1998, LAWSON'S DRY HILLS Marlborough	*Nice spicey pineapples and grassiness, lean acidity on the fresh and citrussy palate.Good length.*	**£8.00**	BWL WTS	B
WHITECLIFFE SACRED HILL SAUVIGNON BLANC 1997, SACRED HILL Auckland	*Lovely, clean grassy, gooseberry and gauva aromas, palate showing mouthwatering acidity, balanced and elegant.*	**£8.00**	MHV WLI	S
ALLAN SCOTT SAUVIGNON BLANC 1998, ALLAN SCOTT WINERY Marlborough	*Classic grassy, straw and sweet tropical fruit, nice depth of flavour, well balanced finish.*	**£8.20**	L&W NYW JLW	S

Wine	Description	Price	Stockists	Award
MUDHOUSE SINGLE VINEYARD SAUVIGNON BLANC 1998, MUDHOUSE WINE Marlborough	*Pronounced minerally, gooseberry approach, clean crisp palate containing juicy fruit. Good length and fresh finish.*	**£8.60**	NYW ABA	B
PALLISER ESTATE SAUVIGNON BLANC 1998, PALLISER ESTATE Martinborough	*Creamy, soft fruit and melon aromas, a little warm on the palate but the acid manages well.*	**£9.00**	Widely Available	B
JACKSON ESTATE SAUVIGNON BLANC 1998, JACKSON ESTATE Marlborough	*Good concentrated fruit on the nose flowing to supporting acidity on the palate, finishes well.*	**£9.20**	Widely Available	B
ISABEL ESTATE SAUVIGNON BLANC 1998, ISABEL ESTATE Marlborough	*Wonderful cats pee, gooseberry and tomato leaf aromas on the complex nose. Delivers crunchy acidity and persistance.*	**£9.30**	RBS TRO GGW NYW UNC HAR PHI M&V	G TROPHY WINE
VILLA MARIA RESERVE WAIRAU VALLEY SAUVIGNON BLANC 1998, VILLA MARIA ESTATES Marlborough	*Fair, clean nose if a little closed, palate opens to nice intense qauvas and gooseberries.*	**£9.60**	Widely Available	B
VILLA MARIA RESERVE CLIFFORD BAY SAUVIGNON BLANC 1998, VILLA MARIA ESTATES Marlborough	*Fresh passionfruit and banana aromas, nice palate weight with crisp fruit and grassiness, finishes well.*	**£10.00**	ODD HMA	B
VAVASOUR SAUVIGNON BLANC 1998, VAVASOUR WINES Marlborough	*Full, ripe peaches and passionfruit with a powdering of tomato leaf flows into a zesty palate.*	**£10.50**	JNW ORB	S
HUNTER'S SAUVIGNON BLANC 1998, HUNTER'S WINES Marlborough	*Lovely tropical fruit and asparagus are apparent, nice crunchy acidity on the full palate. Extremely well made.*	**£11.50**	Widely Available	B

NEW ZEALAND • SAUVIGNON BLANC

Wine	Description	Price	Stockists	Award
Corbans Cottage Block Sauvignon Blanc 1998, Corbans Wines Marlborough	*Slightly smoky approach with nice asparagus and grassy aromas, racy acidity balances well, crisp finish.*	£12.00	WTS CAX	B
Delegat's Hawke's Bay Sauvignon Blanc 1998, Delegat's Hawke's Bay	*Quite delicate and floral over a fresh grass character. Nicely balanced with a smoky finish.*	£13.00	FRT GSJ	B

NEW ZEALAND • SPARKLING

Wine	Description	Price	Stockists	Award
Deutz Marlborough Cuvée NV, Montana Wines Marlborough	*Green apples and citrus fruit characters on the nose with a full complex crisply balanced palate.*	£11.10	VLW WRC BUP MAR THS TOS MTW SEA	B
Deutz Blanc de Blancs 1994, Montana Wines Marlborough	*Very dry style cool climate Sparkling from New Zealand with searing acidity and very lively fruit palate.*	£12.00	SEA MTW	S
Hunter's Miru Miru Marlborough Brut 1996, Hunter's Wines Marlborough	*Light with a touch of herbaceous grassy aromas and a palate which is dry and zesty.*	£12.10	BDR NYW CAC MWW FNZ J&B MJW	B
Daniel le Brun Brut Tache NV, Daniel le Brun Marlborough	*Starting with castor sugar sprinkled berries, followed by a lighter palate, finishing off crisply.*	£13.00	RBS HWL	B
Daniel le Brun NV, Daniel le Brun Marlborough	*Intense perfumed lychee aromas, full bodied slightly chalky fruit palate before a clean close.*	£13.00	F&M HAR RBS HWL	B

Pelorus 1994, Cloudy Bay Marlborough	*Golden in colour with bubbles rupturing from the glass, great balance and lovely nutty flavours.*	**£14.20**	Widely Available	S
Elstree Brut 1995, Highfield Marlborough	*Exciting citrus with herbaceous overtones and lots of creamy fruit on the palate.*	**£15.00**	WST	S

NEW ZEALAND • WHITE • OTHER

Lawson's Dry Hills Gewürztraminer 1998, Lawson's Dry Hills Marlborough	*A complex nose with plenty of spice and citrus characteristics and a well structured, medium weight palate.*	**£4.70**	TOS BWL	S
Stoneleigh Riesling 1998, Corbans Wines Marlborough	*Cool climate soft, citrus fruit with balanced acidity, zippy, kerosene character and full finish.*	**£5.00**	WRC BUP MAR THS CAX	B
Villa Maria Private Bin Riesling 1998, Villa Maria Estates Marlborough	*Melodic aroma on a forward nose, the palate offers honeysuckle and spice with a long finish.*	**£5.50**	WRC BUP MAR THS TSR WTS HMA	B
Babich Gisborne Semillon Chardonnay 1998, Babich Wines Gisborne	*Delicate minerally nose showing some crisp stone fruit, nice citric palate showing balance, finishes well.*	**£6.00**	PFC	B
Whitehaven Marlborough Riesling 1996, Whitehaven Winery Marlborough	*Bright lemon and creamy lime notes on a lively fresh palate with soft citric notes.*	**£6.30**	WAC	B

NEW ZEALAND • WHITE • OTHER

Wine	Tasting note	Price	Stockists	Award
Lawson's Dry Hills Riesling 1998, Lawson's Dry Hills Marlborough	*Kiwi fruit and gooseberry on the nose lead to a kaleidoscope of fruit flavours on the palate. Excellent acid finish.*	**£6.90**	BWL	S
Giesen Estate Riesling 1998, Giesen Wine Estate Canterbury	*Crisp nose with a palate to match, ripe peachy citrus fruit and a long finish.*	**£7.00**	THW	B
Villa Maria Private Bin Gewürztraminer 1998, Villa Maria Estates Marlborough	*An intriguing nose of nutty aromas with buttery peachy flavours and some leafy overtones.*	**£7.20**	QWW HMA	S
Grove Mill Riesling 1998, Grove Mill Malborough	*Subtle lemon and lime nose, upifting acidity and ripe melon fruit on a balanced palate.*	**£7.50**	NYW LAW WTS	B
Jackson Estate Riesling 1998, Jackson Estate Marlborough	*Inviting fragrant nose leads to a crisp lemon mouthfeel and a long finish.*	**£7.50**	NYW MWW TAN GRO HWL	B
Esk Valley Riesling 1998, Esk Valley Estates Hawke's Bay	*Exotic fruit nose with a nice acidic backbone and a unique fruit texture on a broad palate.*	**£8.00**	WIM HMA	B
Montana Reserve Awatere Riesling 1998, Montana Wines Marlborough	*Well balanced fresh fruit nose with a tight citrus backbone and a well textured palate.*	**£8.00**	MTW SEA	B
Montana Reserve Gewürztraminer 1998, Montana Wines Gisborne	*Amazing lime and lemon flavours with a well balanced, viscous palate and a spicey finish.*	**£8.00**	WRC BUP MAR THS SEA MTW	B

Wine	Tasting note	Price	Stockists	Award
FRAMINGHAM DRY RIESLING 1998, FRAMINGHAM Marlborough	*Bright and clean with tropical and grapey aromas lead to a crisp grapefruit palate and full finish.*	**£8.20**	CTH YWL	S
MARTINBOROUGH VINEYARD RIESLING 1998, MARTINBOROUGH VINEYARDS Martinborough	*Crispy lime and citrus nose, showing evolution of riesling characters. Resinous with a full, long and attractive finish.*	**£8.50**	HAR ADN HAS	S
KIM CRAWFORD MARLBOROUGH DRY RIESLING 1998, KIM CRAWFORD Marlborough	*Apple and gooseberry nose leading to a lively palate and a clean fruit finish.*	**£8.60**	RBS NYW LIB	S
WAIPARA WEST RIESLING 1998, TUTTON SIENKO & HILL South Island	*Young and fresh with tropical fruit on the palate with a clean, acid finish.*	**£8.70**	WAW FNZ DIR P&R WAW	B
MILLTON BARREL FERMENTED CHENIN BLANC 1997, MILLTON VINYARDS Gisborne	*Syrupy nose with dry grapefruit and pineapple, mouth coating acidity and a persistent finish.*	**£9.00**	RBS TOS BGL	B
ESK VALLEY RESERVE CHENIN BLANC 1996, ESK VALLEY ESTATES Hawke's Bay	*This gorgeous sweet ripe wine has a touch of stalkiness, fresh acidity and excellent length.*	**£10.00**	WIM HMA	S
MONTANA PATUTAHI ESTATE GEWÜRZTRAMINER 1996, MONTANA WINES Gisborne	*Mineral and subtle kerosene notes with well placed layers of rich honeyed flavours and fresh acidity.*	**£10.70**	VLW SEA MTW	S
VILLA MARIA RESERVE RIESLING 1998, VILLA MARIA ESTATES Marlborough	*Tight nose giving way to a mild, mineral palate with a high acid backbone and a fine close.*	**£11.00**	WRC BUP MAR THS HMA	S

OTHER COUNTRIES

We warmly welcome Mexico back to this section and with over 450 years of winemaking history is showing consistent quality with its burly, characterful red wines. England continues to extract pleasant whites and very good sweet wines from her vinously undesirable summers. It is also warming to see Israel continue quality winemaking in the face of adversity. May this section continue to grow and change as it offers bibers the chance to sample from all corners of the globe.

OTHER COUNTRIES • ENGLAND

Wine	Description	Price	Stockists	Award
CHAPEL DOWN SUMMERHILL OAKED NV, CHAPEL DOWN Surrey	*Unusual but good fruit with charry oak on the nose, quite full on the palate.*	**£4.30**	TOS CDO	B
CHAPEL DOWN EPOCH V 1996, CHAPEL DOWN Surrey	*Juicy tropical fruit and fragrant aromas, the palate shows glycerol richness and sweet oak.*	**£5.50**	QWW SAF TOS CDO	B
CHAPEL DOWN BACCHUS 1997, CHAPEL DOWN Surrey	*Perfumed musky, herbaceous nose, palate offers nice full tropical fruit and a creamy finish.*	**£6.40**	QWW TOS CAC CDO	B
HIDDEN SPRING SUSSEX SUNSET 1998, HIDDEN SPRING Southern Counties	*Clean and approachable, fresh strawberries flow to the well structured palate, aromatic finish.*	**£6.50**	HSV	B
CHAPEL DOWN ORTEGA 1997, CHAPEL DOWN Surrey	*A soft wine holding intense ripe fruit with citrus and lychee nuances on a rich palate.*	**£7.20**	FRT GSJ	B

Astley Madeleine Angevine 1997, Astley Vineyards Worcestshire	*Elderflowers and rose petals are the predominant character with a soft balanced acidity to clean tail.*	**£8.00**	AST	B
Denbies Special Late Harvest Dessert 1997, Denbies Wine Estate Surrey	*Rich and floral on the nose, this honeyed wine is well-balanced with a lingering finish.*	**£14.00**	DBS	S

OTHER COUNTRIES • ISRAEL

Gamla Cabernet Sauvignon 1996, Golan Heights Winery Galilee	*Tarry dark berries to start leading to roast capsicums on the palate, lovely grip.*	**£8.10**	RBS NIC SEL AVB HOH	B

OTHER COUNTRIES • MEXICO

LA Cetto Nebbiolo 1995, LA Cetto Baja California	*Deep maturing plum characters on the nose with ripe soft chewy fruit and balanced tannin and acidity.*	**£4.50**	AWS	B
LA Cetto Zinfandel 1998, LA Cetto Baja California	*Plums, game and salami nose, very aromatic with sweet jammy fruit and good finish.*	**£4.50**	UNS AWS	B
Doña Elena Cabernet Sauvignon Malbec 1997, Overseas Wine Company Baja California	*This light, elegant style offers redcurrant and toasted cedar characters and has a neat tail.*	**£5.10**	MRN CRS PEC PEC	B

Wine	Description	Price	Stockists	Award
Cetto Petite Sirah 1997, Cetto Baja California	*Serious peppery, plummy characters, palate shows nice weight with spicy oak and lovely balance.*	**£5.20**	UNS RBS GSH CTH CWS AWS	S
Casa Madero Cabernet Sauvignon 1998, Casa Madero Parras Valley	*Mint and cedar nose, cassis palate, quite firm with smooth tannins on the long finish.*	**£6.00**	VWE BLN EHL	B
Santo Tomas Cabernet Sauvignon 1995, Bodegas Santo Tomas Baja California	*Vegetal overtones with good fruit on the palate, nice balancing tannins and length.*	**£6.50**	BWL GGW	B
Casa Madero Casa Grande 1997, Casa Madero Parras Valley	*Ripe berry fruit and apple nose, aniseed and plum palate, fruity and complex, well-defined tannins.*	**£8.00**	EHL	S
Vino de Pièdra 1997, Casa de Pièdra Baja California	*This dramatically big wine offers minty fruits and pronounced plummy characters which flow onto the palate with grace.*	**£21.00**	BWL	S

Pinpoint who sells the wine you wish to buy by turning to the stockist codes. If you know the name of the wine you want to buy, use the alphabetical index. If the price is your motivation, refer to the invaluable price guide index; red and white wines under £5, sparkling wines under £12 and champagne under £16. Happy hunting!

PORTUGAL

Too often thought of as a nation producing dry, astringent reds and watery whites, this year's Challenge showed the true potential of this country and its diverse grape varieties. Continued investment from the EC and input from various wine-makers have helped raise the standard of the wines further. DFJ Vinhos Ramada 1998 is proof, winning Wine of the Year. The exceptional standard of Ports again shone through, with Warre's Quinta da Cavadinha 1987 receiving the Port Trophy of the Year.

PORTUGAL • MADIERA

Wine	Description	Price	Stockists	Award
Blandy's Duke Of Clarence NV, Blandy's Madeira	*Nice wine with rich oranges and spicey nuts delicately displayed upon a creamy, rich fresh palate.*	**£9.40**	Widely Available	B
Malmsey 5 Year Old NV, HM Borges Madeira	*Lovely nose displaying burnt toffee, caramel and dried currants, the palate is refreshingly light, smooth and long.*	**£12.00**	REY	S
Cossart Gordon 5 Year Old Malmsey NV, Cossart Gordon & Co Madeira	*Aromatic honey and butter shine on the nose flowing to a rather opulent palate with medium sweetness.*	**£12.70**	GGW ODD MWW FRT JEF	B
Blandy's Five Year Old Malmsey NV, Blandy's Madeira	*Freshly baked, warm spicy fruit dripping in Golden Syrup. Rich, fragant, mouthfeel with impeccable balance.*	**£12.80**	GSH GGW NYW ODD MWW FRT JEF	G
Cossart Gordon Five Year Old Bual NV, Cossart Gordon & Co Madeira	*Attractive spicey and smoky candied orange peel aromas lead to a palate showing marvellous fresh, fiery structure.*	**£12.90**	GGW ODD MWW FRT JEF	S

PORTUGAL • MADEIRA

Wine	Tasting note	Price	Stockists	Award
Blandy's Ten Year Old Malmsey NV, Blandy's Madeira	*Attractive coffee and marmalade lift, followed by treacle covered raisin cake rounding out with a luxurious finish.*	**£16.20**	WAW ODD WTS VWE MCO JEF	S
Henriques & Henriques 10 Year Old Sercial, Henriques & Henriques Madeira	*Stylish, scorched almonds, green walnuts and warmed honey. Gorgeous balance with great length.*	**£16.30**	Widely Available	G
Cossart Gordon 10 Year Old Bual NV, Cossart Gordon & Co Madeira	*Lovely dark, sweet, nutty fullness with firm tannins concluding with nice acidity.*	**£16.70**	TRO GGW JEF ODD WTS VWE MCO	B
Malmsey 10 Year Old Reserve NV, HM Borges Madeira	*Heady atmosphere of nuts and fruit, treacley sweetness and balancing acid culminate in a luscious finish.*	**£20.00**	REY	S
Henriques & Henriques 15 Year Old Malmsey, Henriques & Henriques Madeira	*An amazing nose, 'your Grandmother's best matured fruitcake - from Christmas 1943' absolutely mindblowing!*	**£20.50**	QWW SEL F&M NYW MFS HWL	G TROPHY WINE
Henriques & Henriques 15 Year Old Verdelho, Henriques & Henriques Madeira	*Complex nose of nuttiness, sweet vanilla bean, smokiness and honeycomb. Showing elegance and brilliant acidity.*	**£21.30**	QWW NYW HWL	G
Blandy's Fifteen Year Old Malmsey NV, Blandy's Madeira	*Brimming with rich, fragrant coffee and treacley nuttiness. The palate is unbelieviably creamy with balancing tang.*	**£24.90**	BDR GGW NYW DIR JEF	G

Pinpoint who sells the wine you wish to buy by turning to the stockist codes. If you know the name of the wine you want to buy, use the alphabetical index. If the price is your motivation, refer to the invaluable price guide index; red and white wines under £5, sparkling wines under £12 and Champagne under £16. Happy hunting!

PORTUGAL • OTHER

Wine	Description	Price	Stockists	Medal
Moscatel de Setubal 1990, JPF Vinhos Setubal	*Big, rich, spirity style with marmalade, rancio and spice aromas and a fairly warm, complex palate.*	**£18.00**	MAJ BLN EHL	 S

PORTUGAL • PORT

Wine	Description	Price	Stockists	Medal
Co-op Fine Ruby Port NV, Smith Woodhouse Douro	*A superbly structured port with fine integrated tannins on a very fruit driven palate.*	**£5.00**	CWS	B
Somerfield Navigators Ruby Port Real Companhia Velha NV, Real Companhia Velha Douro	*Soft and supple with lots of rich, luscious and delightfully rounded fruit on the palate.*	**£5.00**	SMF	S
Somerfield Navigators Vintage Character Port Real Companhia Velha VCP, Real Companhia Velha Douro	*Intense and ripe slightly spirited, brambley fruit aromas with a touch of spice and sweet ripe fruit.*	**£6.50**	SMF	S
Safeway Vintage Character Port NV, Lauriston Wines Douro	*Rich and textural, this port has lush Christmas pudding characters with a fine dusting of espresso.*	**£6.60**	SAF	S
Co-op Vintage Character Port NV, Smith Woodhouse Douro	*Fruit cake, cherries and citrus blossom on the nose and palate.*	**£6.90**	CWS	B

Wine	Description	Price	Stockists	Medal
Cooperative Vintage Character Port No.1 NV, Smith Woodhouse Douro	*Complex coffee aromas combined with warm red berries and spice set the stage for this port.*	**£7.00**	JEF CRS	S
MHV Regimental Special Reserve NV, Silva & Cosens Douro	*An understated figgy nose with a powerful palate and integrated tannins with a persistent finish.*	**£7.20**	MHV	B
Safeway Late Bottled Vintage 1994, Smith Woodhouse Douro	*Slightly closed on the nose with a lovely stewed fruit palate and good clean finish.*	**£7.60**	SAF	B
Taylors First Estate NV, Taylors Douro	*Superbly made with young characters of raspberries, blackcurrants and liquorice, very long on the finish.*	**£8.10**	UNS MHV NYW TOS JSM MWN MZC	B
Royal Oporto LBV Porto 1994, Real Companhia Velha Douro	*Raisins and black berry aromas combined with a concentrated fruit mouthful which finishes neatly.*	**£8.30**	PLB	B
Warre's Warrior Reserve NV, Warre & Ca Douro	*Heady spice combined with dark cherry and a hint of chocolate richness, with a firm tannin structure.*	**£8.40**	Widely Available	B
Fonseca Bin 27 NV, Fonseca Douro	*Smokey blue berry and spiced aroma, with a lovely fat attack of fruit on the palate.*	**£9.00**	Widely Available	G
Krohn Vintage Character, Wiese & Krohn Douro	*A dense smoky nose with a rich pitted prune palate, exceptional balance and high acidity.*	**£9.00**	BPW	B

Wine	Description	Price	Stockists	Award
Quinta do Sagrado 10 Year Old Tawny Port, Quinta do Sagrado Duoro	*Rich nutty aromas with a luscious fruit palate with some pepper and a high spirited finish.*	**£9.00**	LAU	B
Quinta do Noval Colheita 1982, Quinta do Noval Douro	*Showing development with delicate rancio and cherry a sweet zing of acid and lively fruit.*	**£9.30**	WRC BUP F&M SPG VLW TAN HAC PRG	S
Chuchill's Finest Vintage Character NV, Churchill Graham Douro	*Delicate fruit aromas with strong fruit on an elegantly structured palate.*	**£9.40**	WAC QWW NYW BTH DBY HWL	B
Dow's Trademark Reserve NV, Silva & Cosens Douro	*A strong wine with lots of red berry fruit and cassis on the nose, also in the mouth.*	**£9.60**	RBS FRT DIR ROD POP JEF	B
Dow's Late Bottled Vintage 1994, Silva & Cosens Douro	*The palate offers baked plums and chocolate concentration with a smooth soft textural finish.*	**£9.80**	SMF CWS JEF TOS JSM VWE WTS	S
Churchill's White NV, Churchill Graham Douro	*Bread and butter pudding on the nose with a slightly hot, concentrated fruit driven palate.*	**£10.00**	QWW WTS TAN IRV CPW BTH HWL	B
Fonseca Traditional LBV 1983, Fonseca Guimeraens Douro	*This oxidative style port has complex dried fruit characters with sinewy length and excellent balance.*	**£10.00**	VLW WTS	S
Sandeman LBV 1994, House Of Sandeman Douro	*Stewed plums and toffee on a beefy concentrated fruit palate, with nice definition.*	**£10.00**	SEA ODD	B

Wine	Description	Price	Stockists	Award
Dow's Christmas Reserve Port NV, Silva & Cosens Duoro	*Juicy simple and delicious with burnt herbal characters on the palate and sound structure.*	**£10.30**	CWS JEF TOS JSM THS ODD ASD	B
Noval LBV 1994, Quinta do Noval Douro	*Slightly oxidative nose with a complex fruit palate, firm tannins and balanced acidity.*	**£10.30**	WAC QWW PRG	S
Graham's LBV 1994, W&J Graham & Co Douro	*Softening spiced pepper, bitter chocolate and liquorice aromas, fresh blackberry palate and a lovely tannic tail.*	**£10.50**	Widely Available	G
Noval Traditional LBV 1991, Quinta do Noval Douro	*A deep colour with spicey, luscious fruit on the nose and quite dry fruit palate.*	**£10.70**	UNS NYW JSM CRH SOH PRG	B
Quinta de La Rosa LBV 1994, Quinta de La Rosa Douro	*Meaty, baked cherries and hints of marmite on the nose, with good extraction of fruit on the palate.*	**£10.80**	JNW NYW HVN M&V	S
Quinta do Noval Colheita 1981, Quinta do Noval Douro	*Dark color with a slightly shy nose the palate contains lovely rich dark berry fruit.*	**£11.00**	EPO PRG	B
Graham's Six Grapes Reserve, W&J Graham & Co Duoro	*Jammy black berries on a slightly sticky cloying fruit palate with a clean finish.*	**£11.70**	Widely Available	B
Burmester LBV 1995, JW Burmester Douro	*Palate is long and smooth with lots of ripe fruit and has a lovely lingering after taste.*	**£12.00**	HBJ	S

Wine	Description	Price	Stockists	Award
Cockburn's 10 Year Old Tawny NV, Cockburn Smithes Duoro	*Nutty characters and good intensity of fruit on the nose, the palate is long and persistent.*	£12.30	JSM ASD SAF ADD	S
Barros Colheita 1987, Barros Almeida Douro	*The palate has some tarry, leather and fig characters with a soft spiced finish.*	£12.50	WCR AVB SIJ HOH	S
Quinta de La Rosa Vintage Port 1995, Quinta de La Rosa Douro	*An amazing palate with rich concentrated fruit which is complex and has a classic structure.*	£12.90	M&V JNW NYW SAN RAV	G
Delaforce His Eminence's Choice 10 Year Old Tawny Port NV, Delaforce Douro	*A lovely spiced, fruit cake aromatised port with a soft smooth mouthfeel and good balance.*	£13.00	J&B PFC	S
Pocas Colheita 1983, Manoel Domingues Pocas Junior Duoro	*Lovely sweet fruit with integrated oak and rancio characters on the palate, good balance.*	£13.10	CAC CCW	B
Graham's Ten Year Old, W&J Graham & Co Douro	*Nice lighter port with integrated wood, cherries and raisins on a lovely sweet caramel palate.*	£13.50	JNW ODD FRT JEF	B
Quinta do Noval Colheita 1976, Quinta do Noval Douro	*Palate is extremley delicate and in its prime, sweet, complex fruit and drying finish.*	£13.50	HVN SEL HOL EPO PRG	S
Royal Oporto Special Reserve NV, Real Companhia Velha Douro	*Sippin' style with good intensity on the palate, hints of spice and a lovely long finish.*	£13.80	WRT PLB	B

PORTUGAL • PORT

Wine	Description	Price	Stockists	Award
Gilberts 10Year Old Tawny Port NV, Gilberts & Ca Duoro	*Clean, fresh mint mingles with baked plums and soft nuttiness on a long spicey, sinewy palate.*	£14.00	VSC	S
Smith Woodhouse LBV 1990, Smith Woodhouse & Co Douro	*Hugely extracted fruit aromas with a soft juicy palate that has racy acidity and moderate length.*	£14.00	C&B SMF SVT AVB JEF	B
Warre's Traditional LBV 1984, Warre & Ca Douro	*Rich berry aromas and softened chocòlate palate with intense integrated fruit, finishes well. Delicious.*	£14.50	WTS	B
Cockburn's Quinta dos Canais 1995, Cockburn Smithes Duoro	*Harmonious dark chocolate lightly spiced nose with full ripe fruit on a softly developed tannin structure.*	£14.70	ODD WRC ADD	B
Noval 10 Year Old Tawny Port, Quinta do Noval Douro	*Young, lively and robust with rich chocolate characters, hints of cinnamon and growing midpalate.*	£14.70	UNS WTS RNS JUS PRG	B
Churchill's 10 Year Old Tawny NV, Churchill Graham Douro	*This aged tawny has a pale amber colour with a dryer style palate and a kind, lively structure.*	£15.00	QWW GRO TAN IRV DBY HWL	B
Gilberts LBV 1990, Gilberts & Ca Douro	*Stewed fruit and oxidative aromas on a sweet ripe fruit palate with a warming finish.*	£15.00	VSC	B
Warre's Bottle Matured LBV 1990, Warre & Ca Douro	*Excellent colour with a terrific complex lift, this port has rich, juicy mouth filling fruit.*	£15.00	NYW TOS SAF WTS JSM JEF	G

Wine	Description	Price	Stockists	Award
WARRE'S SIR WILLIAM TEN YEAR OLD NV, WARRE & CA Douro	*Orange zest with heady volatile acidity and a bitter chocolate edge with great body and harmony.*	£15.00	JEF HHC LOH	B
WARRE'S TWENTY YEAR OLD NV, WARRE & CA Douro	*Fresh nuttiness on a soft balanced rich ripe fruit palate with a long gently drying tannin finish.*	£15.00	JEF	S
DOW'S TEN YEAR OLD NV, SILVA & COSENS Douro	*Excellent rancio and fruit integration with a rich palate of citrus and nuttiness and a tight tail.*	£15.20	Widely Available	S
TAYLORS10 YR OLD TAWNY NV, TAYLORS Douro	*Very ripe fruit with hints of bacon the palate offers fruit of elegance and length.*	£15.60	UNS MHV JSM MWW CAC MZC	B
QUINTA DE LA ROSA VINTAGE PORT 1997, QUINTA DE LA ROSA Douro	*Beautifully soft fruit splashes across the palate being pulled into line with firm tannins and incredible complexity.*	£17.00	RAV SAN SEL M&V	G
POCAS COLHEITA 1975, MANOEL DOMINGUES POCAS JUNIOR Duoro	*Exotic fruit on the palate with excellent aged characters result in a pleasing drink-me-now drop.*	£17.20	CAC CCW	S
QUINTA DO COTTO VINTAGE PORT 1995, MONTEZ CHAMPALIMAUD Douro	*Soft appealing nose with full fruit, chocolate and a touch of spice on the palate.*	£17.30	L&S	S
BURMESTER COLHEITA 1991, JW BURMESTER Douro	*Rich toffeed, caramelised aromas with youthful cherries and rancio characters on a balanced palate.*	£17.50	HBJ	B

PORTUGAL • PORT

Wine	Description	Price	Stockists	Award
QUINTO DO CASTRO VINTAGE PORT 1987, SOCIEDODE AGRICOLA DA QUINTA DO CASTRO Douro	*Inviting rich ripe full fruit aromas lead to prune fruit characters, candied dried stone fruit with a coffee and spice infusion.*	**£18.20**	NYW ENO	G
QUINTA DO SAGRADO VINTAGE 1994, CALLEM Douro	*Raisins, tobacco and candied lemon provide plenty of flavour to mull over, finishes very well.*	**£19.00**	LAU	B
TAYLORS QUINTA DE TERRA FEITA 1986, TAYLORS Douro	*Developing complexity with smooth weighty fruit palate and softening yet firm tannin structure.*	**£19.00**	MWW WCR VWC MZC	B
BARROS 20 YEAR OLD PORT NV, BARROS ALMEIDA Douro	*Extraordinarily complex, this port has a slightly hot and spicy palate with a prickly finish. Wow.*	**£20.00**	AVB HOH	B
DOW'S 20 YEAR OLD NV, SILVA & COSENS Douro	*Subtle, elegant wine with good acidity and lovely nutty complexity on the palate.*	**£20.00**	CWS JEF SAF VWE	B
GILBERTS VINTAGE PORT 1994, GILBERTS & CA Douro	*Herby, spiced aromas and fruit lead to a smooth palate which is , rounded and very satisfying.*	**£20.00**	VSC	B
JW BURMESTER VINTAGE 1996, J W BURMESTER Duoro	*Palate is tight but has big balanced fruit with a refined structure and long finish. Let it sleep.*	**£20.00**	HBJ	S

Pinpoint who sells the wine you wish to buy by turning to the stockist codes. If you know the name of the wine you want to buy, use the alphabetical index. If the price is your motivation, refer to the invaluable price guide index; red and white wines under £5, sparkling wines under £12 and champagne under £16. Happy hunting!

Wine	Description	Price	Stockists	Award
Symington's Quinta do Vesuvio 1997, Da Quinta Douro	*A huge concentrated fruit palate with a massive dose of spice and a long clinging finish, a sleeping beauty.*	**£20.00**	RBS JEF	G
Graham's Malvedos 1988, W&J Graham & Co Douro	*The palate is developing with liquorice, milk chocolate and savouriness, the finish is long and peppery.*	**£20.40**	CWS JNW JEF ODD JSM TOS	G
Fonseca Guimaraens 1984, Fonseca Douro	*Developing cedar nose, the palate is soft and smooth with cherry fruit in a full body. Ready soon.*	**£20.70**	UNS VLW L&W JSM THS SAF MZC	G
Warre's Quinta Da Cavadinha 1987, Warre & Ca Douro	*Lovely ripe characters on the nose with lots of raspberry, chocolate flavours and balanced tannins.*	**£20.70**	RBS SMF NYW ODD SAF WTS JEF	S TROPHY WINE
Dow's Quinta do Bomfim 1986, Silva & Cosens Douro	*This is a fantastically intriguing wine with a nut and herb nose and a huge concentrated fruit palate.*	**£21.10**	RBS L&W NYW JSM ODD SKW JEF	G
Dow's Quinta do Bomfim 1987, Silva & Cosens Douro	*Tight chocolate and spiced aromas with a ripe rich full palate of great depth.*	**£21.50**	RBS JSM ODD SKW JEF	G
Graham's Malvedos 1987, W&J Graham & Co Douro	*Earthy meaty aroma combined with chocolate and warm spirit, drinking well now with its softened palate.*	**£21.50**	ODD JSM TOS JEF	S
Taylors Quinta de Vargellas 1986, Taylors Douro	*Lots of chocolate and warm spirit on the nose, a sweet cherry fruit palate.*	**£21.50**	UNS L&W TOS MHV MAK MZC	S

WARRE'S QUINTA DA CAVADINHA 1987, WARRE & CA Douro	*A still youthful port with massive palate, length and power, needing more time.*	**£21.50**	RBS L&W WRC BUP MAR THS NYW WTS	S
QUINTA DE LA ROSA VINTAGE PORT 1996, QUINTA DE LA ROSA Douro	*A curranty, rich, spiced licorice nose and intensely rich palate with weighty spiced fruit.*	**£21.70**	M&V NYW	S
QUINTA DO NOVAL COLHEITA 1971, QUINTA DO NOVAL Douro	*The palate has mince pie and rancio on a fine tannin structure with a soft finish.*	**£21.70**	WON PRG	S
DOW'S QUINTA DO BONFIM 1984, SILVA & COSENS Douro	*The palate demonstrates superb balance with subtle fruit, integrated tannins and persisting length.*	**£22.00**	RBS WTS	S
GILBERTS PORT COLHEITA TAWNY SWEET 1955, GILBERTS & CA Douro	*Lots of walnuts and rancio characters on the palate and a clean fruit finish.*	**£22.00**	VSC	S
QUINTA DO CRASTO VINTAGE PORT 1997, QUINTA DO CRASTO Douro	*Huge, extracted rich aromas with pepperiness and an abundance of ripe, dense, full berry fruit.*	**£22.00**	ENO	S
BARROS COLHEITA 1975, BARROS ALMEIDA Douro	*Gentle fruit start leaves toffeed cherries and caramel characters on a creamy palate with a liquorice finish.*	**£22.30**	HOH AVB SIJ	S
DELAFORCE CURIOUS & ANCIENT 20 YEAR OLD TAWNY PORT NV, DELAFORCE Douro	*Sweet, soft and long on the palate with a nice backbone, a super silky sipper.*	**£22.50**	PFC	S

Wine	Description	Price	Stockists	Award
Graham's Twenty Year Old, W&J Graham & Co Douro	*Slightly burnt bacon aromas with an enjoyable sweetness and persistence with a long clean, fine tannin tail.*	£23.20	JNW TOS JSM JEF	S
Chuchill's Vintage 1991, Churchill Graham Douro	*Power and concentration on the nose, the palate is full of inky black fruit with firm tannins.*	£24.50	J&B BTH DBY HWL	S
Calem Quinta da Foz Vintage 1996, Calem & Filho Douro	*A youthful closed nose giving off some liquorice aromas and palate with huge intense, chocolatey fruit.*	£25.00	UNS PNA	S
Chuchill's Vintage 1997, Churchill Graham Douro	*Very intense, rich and slightly stalky aromas combined with a youthful palate. Just put to bed.*	£25.00	BTH DBY HWL	B
Niepoort Colheita 1985, Niepoort Vinhos Douro	*Lots of youthful cherry fruit and rich caramel aromas on a complex fruit and nut palate.*	£25.00	REY BWL	S
Sandeman 20 Year Old Tawny Port, House Of Sandeman Douro	*Dried fruit mingled with chocolate and spice on the nose flowing to a viscous toffee apple palate.*	£25.00	ODD LEA SEA	B
Sandeman Vau Vintage 1997, House Of Sandeman Douro	*Vanilla and spice aromas with smooth, rich luscious fruit with a soft tannin structure and a flowing long finish.*	£25.00	SEA	G
Taylors 20 Year Old Tawny Port NV, Taylors Douro	*Creamy, vanilla aromas on a mellow palate which gradually expands in the mouth.*	£26.90	UNS RBS WAC L&W MHV MAR FTH MZC	B

Quinta da Eira Velha 1992, Martinez Douro	*Some delightfully delicate fruit characters on the nose, the palate is dark and brooding with sweet fruit.*	**£27.00**	WSG	(B)
Quinta do Crasto LBV 1995, Quinta do Crasto Douro	*A Christmas pudding nose leads to a wonderfully fresh palate of fine complexity with concentration and length.*	**£28.30**	JNW MAR THS NYW ENO	(G)
Croft Vintage Port 1985, Croft Douro	*A green stalky aroma, light in style with spicey palate, integrated acidity and good length.*	**£29.50**	UNS PFC	(B)
Burmester Vintage 1997, JW Burmester Douro	*Herbs and crisp brambly fruit on the nose with a young harmonious, vibrant fruit palate.*	**£30.00**	HBJ	(B)
Quinta do Noval Colheita 1995, Quinta do Noval Douro	*Traditional, cigar box, plum, spicey and fresh pine aromas with full fruit on a youthful palate.*	**£30.00**	UNS STE F&M HAC HSL PRG	(S)
Ramos Pinto Vintage 1982, Adriano Ramos Pinto Douro	*Developed dark chocolate aromas with a full rich chocolate fruit palate and supple tannins.*	**£32.10**	VLW MMD	(B)
Dow's 30 Year Old NV, Silva & Cosens Douro	*Vanilla and toffee mingled with almond coffee aromas and a spirity sweet fruit palate.*	**£35.00**	BBR JEF	(B)
Quinta do Noval Colheita 1967, Quinta do Noval Douro	*Baked fruit characters on the nose followed by an intense dried fruit palate with a touch of cinnamon.*	**£40.00**	WON PRG	(S)

TAYLORS VINTAGE PORT 1985, TAYLORS Douro	*Brambly fruit aromas and creamy oak on a youthful cherry fruit palate with a slight oxidation.*	**£43.00**	UNS L&W SAF TOS WTS MZC	B
KROHN COLHEITA 1963, WIESE & KROHN Duoro	*Wonderful grandfather figure feeling from this intense, old dark chocolate and sun-dried fig wine.*	**£45.00**	BPW	B
CROFT VINTAGE PORT 1977, CROFT Douro	*A soft milk chocolate and plum flavour titillates the taste buds and finishes with lingering length.*	**£46.30**	WRC BUP J&B PFC	G
GRAHAM'S THIRTY YEAR OLD, W&J GRAHAM & CO Douro	*Toffee nut and orange spice on the nose with a Christmas pudding, nutty fresh finish.*	**£49.60**	RBS JEF VHW	G
QUINTA DO NOVAL COLHEITA 1964, QUINTA DO NOVAL Douro	*Bronze in colour with chocolate and fig characters on the nose, the palate offers layers of historical complexity.*	**£55.00**	WON PRG	G
NOVAL OVER 40 YEARS OLD, QUINTA DO NOVAL Douro	*Toffee, cherry and caramel aromas before a myriad of developed fruit notes make for a remarkable experience.*	**£67.50**	F&M PRG	S
GRAHAM'S FORTY YEAR OLD, W&J GRAHAM & CO Douro	*Rustic rich caramel characters, fine spirit and nutty rancio sit on a creamy full palate.*	**£69.00**	RBS JEF	S
CALEM COLHEITA 1961, CALEN & FILHO Douro	*A lovely aged Port showing Great Gatsbian maturity, it shows complex toffee apples and candied fruits.*	**£75.00**	UNS WIM JEH PNA	B

Wine	Description	Price	Stockists	Award
Burmester Colheita 1963, JW Burmester Douro	*A rich creamy texture with lots of fruitcake, ripe plums and spice and notes of dried figs.*	£80.00	HBJ	B
Tordiz 40 Year Old Tawny NV, JW Burmester Douro	*Stunning fruit complexities of orange, spice nuts and exotic fruits. Incredible length.*	£100.00	HBJ	S

PORTUGAL • RED

Wine	Description	Price	Stockists	Award
Ramada 1998, DFJ Vinhos Estremadura	*Smoky, preserved fruits waft from a full-on blueberry, tarry cigar-box palate with a smooth finish.*	£3.50	SMF CWS WRC BUP MAR THS WTS D&F	S WINE OF THE YEAR
Foral Douro Reserva Red 1997, Caves Alianca Douro	*An interesting, gamey nose signals a fresh and fruity red wine with a touch of green tannins.*	£4.00	ODD BPW	B
Portada 1997, DFJ Vinhos Estremadura	*Spice and banana-skin nose, followed by a dry, savoury palate with a subtle sweet, woody edge.*	£4.10	UNS SMF GRT CWS ODD WCR BTH D&F	B
Segada Baga-Trincadeira 1997, DFJ Vinhos Ribatejo	*Nose of depth and complexity, this is doubled on the palate with cassis and pepper as flavour.*	£4.30	WAW UNS BUD ODD VEC WRC D&F	B
Pedras do Monte 1998, DFJ Vinhos Terras do Sado	*A perfumed, spicey aroma introduces ripe, baked-fruit flavours with herbal notes well supported by a firm tannin structure.*	£4.40	UNS WCR MWW BKC D&F	S

Wine	Description	Price	Stockists	Award
Bright Brothers Atlantic Vines Baga 1998, Bright Brothers Bairrada	*A powerful, brambley, plummy nose follows onto a smoky, tarry palate with a pleasant rustic structure.*	**£4.70**	SMF JSM TOS EHL	B
Alianca Dão Reserva Red 1997, Caves Alianca Dão	*Warm jammy fruit on the nose the palate has moderate weight with some richness and fine tannins.*	**£4.80**	BPW	B
Herdade do Esporao Monte Velho 1997, Herdade do Esporao Alentejo	*Rich red berries on the nose with a touch of chocolate and supple fresh fruit.*	**£4.80**	WRC BUP THS D&F	B
Palmela Castelao 1997, DFJ Vinhos Palmela	*Rich polish, fig and raisin aromas with elegantly structured ripe fruit and acidity for freshness.*	**£4.80**	D&F	B
Bairrada Dom Ferraz 1997, DFJ Vinhos Bairrado	*Attractive earth tones with stewed fruit on the palate which has a balanced structure.*	**£5.00**	TOS D&F	B
Belafonte Baga 1998, DFJ Vinhos Beiras	*Excellent fragrant characters on the nose with juicy fruit and drying chalky tannins.*	**£5.00**	NYW ODD TOS UNS SAF D&F	B
Bright Brothers Douro 1997, Bright Brothers Douro	*A restrained nose of blueberry and spice with a smoothly intense and harmoniously balance palate.*	**£5.00**	Widely Available	B
Bright Brothers Douro 1998, Bright Brothers Douro	*A herby, aromatic quality is found on the nose with a touch of spice and sweet ripe fruit.*	**£5.00**	WRC BUP MAR THS TOS JSM EHL	B

PORTUGAL • RED				
Dão Dom Ferraz 1997, DFJ Vinhos Dão	*Slightly green fruit on the nose with a palate of rich chocolate characters which provide depth and character.*	£5.00	UNS WRC BUP MAR THS TOS D&F	S
Quinta das Setencostas 1998, Quinta da Boavista Alenquer	*Sweet ripe raisin, loganberries and springtime flower characters with body and slightly drying tannins.*	£5.00	UNS ODD BTH RBS AVB D&F	B
Sinfonia 1998, Joao Portugal Ramos Alentejo	*Chocolate and spices mingled with concentrated fruit twined around an interesting structure.*	£5.00	WTS	B
Fiuza Bright Classic Cabernet Sauvignon 1996, Fiuza Bright Ribatejo	*Soft ripe berries of depth and complexity are balanced with tannins and good oak use.*	£5.30	EHL	S
Quinta da Cortezia Touriga Nacional 1997, Caves Alianca Alentejo	*Slightly oxidative nose with lots of juicy ripe blackberries, some complexity and slightly drying tannins.*	£5.50	BPW	B
JP Vinhos Tinto da Anfora 1995, JP Vinhos Alentejo	*Lots of creamy oak on the nose with a punchy middle palate and polished finish.*	£5.60	SAF BLN EHL	B
Bright Brothers Palmela 1998, Bright Brothers Douro	*Intense jammy blackcurrant aromas and carries through onto the palate with good zesty acidity.*	£5.80	EHL	B
Convento da Vila Colheita Seleccionada Reserva 1996, Borba Co-op Alentejo	*The palate shows signs of maturity with softened cherries, warm spice and astute tannins .*	£6.00	D&F	S

Wine	Description	Price	Stockists	Award
Quinta da Lagoalva 1995, Quinta da Lagoalva Ribatejo	*Matured soft cherry aromas with a stylish soft, sweet palate and good grip of tannin.*	**£6.00**	ODD WCR BKC RBS ADW D&F	B
Quinta das Caldas 1996, Domingos Alves de Sousa Douro	*Very ripe porty style with rich dark chocolately aromas on a strong, balanced tannic palate.*	**£6.00**	D&F	B
Touriz Regional Estremadura 1998, Quinta da Boavista Estremadura	*The palate is structured with ripe berry fruit, dark chocolate and chewy tannins, needs time.*	**£6.00**	D&F D&F	S
Palha Canas 1998, Quinta da Boavista Estremadura	*Black-purple in colour with very full ripe berry fruit and real thickness to the palate.*	**£6.20**	UNS PFT BEL D&F	B
Quinta de la Rosa Douro Tinto 1997, Quinta de la Rosa Douro	*Ripe raspberries and blackberries with a grassy edge and exotic fruit palate, with fantastic tannins.*	**£6.30**	Widely Available	S
Quinta do Crasto Douro 1998, Quinta do Crasto Douro	*A zippy, raspberry nose and balanced tannins mingle with blackberry ripple and hickory wood in the mouth.*	**£6.50**	JNW NYW ENO	S
Quinta do Crasto Touriga Nacional 1996, Quinta do Crasto Douro	*Big rustic old style wine with lots of earthy, black plum aromas and full fleshy fruit.*	**£6.50**	NYW ENO	B
Chamine 1998, Cortes de Cima Alentejo	*Peppery spice and concentrated dusty fruit is held snuggly by a firm tannin structure with length.*	**£6.70**	QWW MWW ADN HWL	B

Wine	Tasting note	Price	Stockists	Award
Quinta da Abrigada Allenquer 1996, Quinta da Abrigada Alenquer	*Ripe, jammy redcurrent fruits lay back on a palate of firm tannins. Good length.*	**£6.80**	REY HHF	B
Velhas Almeirim Garrafeira 1995, Caves Velhas Almeirim	*To drink now, this wine has lifted sweet character on a sweet ripe berry palate with light tannins.*	**£6.90**	PGA	B
Aliança Particular Palmela Red 1995, Caves Aliança Palmela	*Spicy, cherry and oak nose develops in the mouth with lush, dark cherry flavours and a dusting of pepper.*	**£7.00**	TOS BPW	B
Casa Santos Lima Touriga Nacional 1998, Quinta da Boavista Estremadura	*Extracted berry fruit on the nose with a juicy fruit palate, tailored tannins and extraordinary length.*	**£7.00**	D&F	S
Herdade do Esporao Cabernet Sauvignon 1997, Herdade do Esporao Alentejo	*Dark brooding fruit with dry tannins showing delicious underlying fruit and chewy richness.*	**£7.00**	WCS D&F	B
Herdade do Esporao Esporao Reserva 1995, Herdade do Esporao Reguengos	*A delicate berryfruit nose leads to a rustic palate with a staggering array of succulent flavours.*	**£7.00**	ODD WRC BUP TOS RBS D&F	S
Herdade do Esporao Touriga Nacional 1997, Herdade do Esporao Alentejo	*Singing with notes of black fruit and spice offering calm and mild tannins and balancing acidity.*	**£7.00**	D&F	S
Horta da Nazare 1995, Quinta da Santo Andre Ribatejo	*Peppery, fruit aromas precede a body rich in firm tannins but with solid ripe fruit flavours.*	**£7.00**	REY	B

Wine	Description	Price	Stockists	Medal
Manuel Pinto Hespanhol Calços do Tanha 1996, Manuel Pinto Hespanhol Douro	*A restrained nose in contrast to the full-bodied, blackfruit palate and well-balanced tannins.*	**£7.00**	REY	B
Quinta do Vale da Raposa 1997, Domingos Alves de Sousa Douro	*Gentle herbaceous nose and a rich mixture of flavours backed up by fresh tannins.*	**£7.00**	WCR BKC ADW BBB SHJ D&F	B
Herdade do Esporao Aragones 1997, Herdade do Esporao Alentejo	*Slightly tarry nose with rich burnt cherry fruit notes and complexitising flavours of black fruits and damsons.*	**£7.50**	UNS TOS WCS FUL D&F	S
Herdade do Esporao Trincadeira Preta 1997, Herdade do Esporao Alentejo	*An intriguing cedar and prune nose, almost overwhelms an old-style, oaky palate with delicate fruit flavours.*	**£7.50**	UNS ODD WCS ADW D&F	G
Vila Santa 1997, Joao Portugal Ramos Alentejo	*Classy oak and fruit combination on the nose and palate with a great backbone.*	**£7.50**	CWS WTS	B
Quinta do Crasto Tinta Roriz 1997, Quinta do Crasto Douro	*Lots of full fruit and pepper on the nose with soft ripe fruit and ripe tannins on the palate.*	**£7.80**	ENO	B
Cortes de Cima 1998, Cortes de Cima Alentejo	*A palate with lots of body and firm streamlined tannins resulting in a fantastically textured wine.*	**£7.90**	NYW SVT CFP HWL	S
Meia Pipa 1994, JP Vinhos Terras do Sado	*Showing oxidation but retains its fruit intensity and displays a leathery, soft ripe palate.*	**£7.90**	EHL	B

Wine	Tasting note	Price	Stockists	Award
JP VINHOS HEREDADE DE SANTA MARTA 1995, JP VINHOS Alentejo	*Light berry characters mingle with tar on the nose, a balanced fruit palate and big tannins.*	**£8.10**	EHL	B
QUINTA DO CRASTO DOURO RESERVA 1997, QUINTA DO CRASTO Douro	*A fairly rigid palate with firm tannins and a mineral edge, given time it will soften.*	**£8.50**	JNW NYW ENO	S
QUINTA DO RIBEIRINHO PRIMEIRA ESCOLHA 1997, LUIS PATO Bairrada	*Big, mouth filling fruit with sweet cabbage and berry flavours on a firm tannin palate.*	**£8.50**	WFD	B
QUINTA DE SAES TOURIGO NACIONAL RORIZ 1997, QUINTA DE SAES Dão	*Complex spice and jam amalgam with some earthiness. A chewy palate of ripe fruit tannins.*	**£9.50**	VLW L&S	B
QUINTA DO COTTO 1997, MONTEZ CHAMPALIMAUD Douro	*Traditional barnyard and berry aromas and a palate which is rich with lots of supple tannin.*	**£9.60**	VLW L&S	S
QUINTA DE PELLADA TINTA RORIZ 1996, QUINTA DE SAES Dão	*Dark dried fruit with peppered spice and a big dose of hearty oak on a rich, ripe fruit palate.*	**£9.90**	VLW L&S	B
MANUEL PINTO HESPANHOL CALÇOS DO TANHA RESERVA 1996, MANUEL PINTO HESPANHOL Douro	*Soft and slightly restrained cassis with mineral notes, on the structured palate, woody finish.*	**£10.50**	REY	B
CARTUXA 1995, FUNDACAO EUGENIO DE ALMEDIA Evora	*Tobacco and earthy fruit aromas, the palate is serious with blackberries and supple tannins.*	**£10.90**	NYW REY	S

Quinta do Grotto 1996, Sociede Agricola Gabbanaz Palmela	*Upfront charm and sophistication gives way to a feral palate with old spice notes, up-for-it wood and a characterful tail.*	**£11.00**	Widely Available	B
Quinta do Carmo 1995, Domaines Barons de Rothschild (Lafite) Alentejo	*Tar, licorice and plums stimulate the nasal passages whilst ripe plummy fruit visits the tongue.*	**£11.90**	WDM NET CLA MZC	B
Boas Quintas Touriga Nacional 1997, Sociedade Agricola Boas Quintas Dão	*A finely sculptured wine with fine tannins, powers along the palate with great strength.*	**£14.00**	REY	G

PORTUGAL • WHITE

Cortes de Cima Reserva 1997, Cortes de Cima Alentejo	*Spiced blackberries and a generous dose of sweet oak. Huge tannin structure, a powerful wine.*	**£14.20**	NYW HWL	S
Herdade do Esporao Monte Velho 1998, Herdade do Esporao Alentejo	*Ripe fruit combined with herbaceous characters on the nose, palate is long with a soft finish*	**£4.80**	BBB D&F	B
JP Blanco NV, JP Vinhos Terras do Sado	*A slightly siced nose with floral tones precedes a lemony palate with well measured acidity.*	**£4.90**	THS EHL	B
Esporao Reserva 1997, Herdade do Esporao Reguengos	*Lovely sweet tropical fruit on the nose, ripe gauvas and pears on the palate adding chewy texture in cohorts with the oak.*	**£7.00**	ODD WRC BUP RBS D&F	S

South America

Funk and passion were words oft used by judges at this years WINE Challenge to describe many of the South American entries. Argentinian and Chilean winemakers are beginning to break free of the 'traditionalè' methods and are opting instead to make wines that reflect the character of their diverse lands and climate conditions. Up front fruit and laid back oak are the hallmarks of wines that offer an exciting range of fresh styles and real character. Use these pages to find yours.

SOUTH AMERICA • ARGENTINA • RED

Wine	Description	Price	Stockists	Award
Vista Andes Cabernet Sauvignon Reserva 1997, Viña Morandé Mendoza	*A big style brimming with fruits and fresh herbs. The medium firm palate displays a clean finish.*	**£2.70**	ENO	B
Etchart Rio de Plata Malbec 1996, Etchart Mendoza	*A herbal, minerally nose with a light palate structure, and good length.*	**£3.20**	WCR AMA CRS ASD CAX	B
Co-op Los Pampas Cabernet Malbec 1998, Peñaflor Mendoza	*An herbaceous nose, with green pepper and strawberry, cassis and sandalwood fruit and spice. Good acidity.*	**£4.00**	CWS	B
Marcus James Cabernet Sauvignon 1996, Marcus James Vineyards Mendoza	*Hot, jammy nose with pleasant warm stewed fruits, hints of soft strawberry and light tannins.*	**£4.00**	CAN	B
Rio de Plata Tempranillo Malbec 1998, Etchart Mendoza	*Some subtle strawberry and cherry fruits with a soft and creamy palate.*	**£4.00**	AMA SLM PEA CAX	B

Wine	Tasting note	Price	Stockists	Award
Trivento Syrah 1998, Vina Patagonia Mendoza	*Lovely up front fruit that rises from a well defined palate of good structure and impressive length.*	£4.20	SMF WST	B
Balbi Vineyard Malbec 1998, Bodegas Balbi Mendoza	*Very clear and delicate nose of violets and red fruits, that carries into the mouth nicely with chalky tannins.*	£4.50	SAF CWS ODD WRC GYW	B
Santiago Graffigna Cabernet Sauvignon Syrah 1998, Santiago Graffigna San Juan	*A toasty, oaky nose with plenty of spice and cedar and a firm fruit tannin palate.*	£4.90	CWS BDR	S
Bright Brothers Reserve Cabernet Sauvignon 1998, Bright Brothers San Juan	*A pepper nose with red fruit underneath, followed by a full bodied powerful palate and a neat tail.*	£5.00	SMF SOM EHL	B
Fantelli Barbera Cabernet 1998, Fantelli Wines Mendoza	*Tangy, with sweet and sour raisiny fruit, developing tea and caramel coffee complexity on the persistent palate.*	£5.00	SAF PLE	S
Inti Valley Cabernet Fer 1998, Jean Rivier Mendoza	*Spicey and fragrant with an added touch of spice on the nose that continues through the medium weight flowery palate.*	£5.00	COK WSG	B
Martins Malbec 1997, Arco Bodegas Unidas Mendoza	*A tight palate structure with some developed fruit characters and a pleasant cleansing finish.*	£5.00	D&D	B
Santa Aña Cabernet Sauvignon 1997, Santa Aña Mendoza	*Cherries and ribena spring from this well crafted mid weight style with a crisp finish.*	£5.00	CDT WAV	B

Wine	Description	Price	Stockists	Award
Finca Flichman Cabernet Sauvignon 1997, Finca Flichman Mendoza	*Cassis, spicey, oak aromas. Soft and fleshy, good fruit with soft tannins. Well-structured and harmonious.*	£5.30	GSH NYW FRT GRA	S
Nieto & Senetiner Valle de Vistalba Cabernet Sauvignon 1996, Nieto & Senetiner Mendoza	*Big jammy fruit and strawberries on the nose leads to a fruit laden soft palate with a fine tannin structure.*	£5.30	WCR BPW	B
Etchart Cabernet Sauvignon 1996, Bodegas Etchart Cafayate	*Ripe black fruits on the nose and soft on the palate with nice length. A pleasure to drink now.*	£5.60	WCR TOS PEA SLM CWS ASD CAX	B
Condor Peak Cabernet Sauvignon Reserve 1997, Peñaflor San Juan	*Strong redcurrants and plums on the nose, fresh fruit palate with leather and spice, creating wonderful balance.*	£5.80	NYW BLN EHL	B
Finca el Retiro Tempranillo 1998, Finca el Retiro Mendoza	*A beady porty nose of jelly fruits leads to a full bodied palate of well integrated tannins and fruits.*	£5.80	GGW RBS NYW LIB	S
Finca el Retiro Cabernet Sauvignon 1998, Finca el Retiro Mendoza	*Herbal characters interspersed with tobacco and cassis rise from a fine grained palate with good length.*	£5.90	GGW LIB	B
Finca el Retiro Malbec 1998, Finca el Retiro Mendoza	*A pleasing wine offering intense red fruits and a well balanced palate with good length.*	£5.90	GGW NYW LIB	B
Balbi Vineyard Malbec Barrel Reserve 1998, Bodegas Balbi Mendoza	*Nice depth of character on the nose showing licorice, annise, mushroom and spiced up fruits, with a clean acid finish.*	£6.00	GYW	S

Wine	Tasting note	Price	Stockists	Award
Balbi Vineyard Shiraz Barrel Reserve 1998, Bodegas Balbi Mendoza	*Clean, elegant nose, a well-balanced fruity structure with slight grainy tannins showing elegance and length.*	£6.00	GYW	B
Bodega Norton Malbec Salmon Label 1996, Bodega Norton Mendoza	*Nice, fragrant Pinot like characters. Well balanced and grippy tannins with good length.*	£6.00	JNW BWC	B
La Agricola Santa Julia Bonarda Sangiovese Reserve 1998, La Agricola Mendoza	*A blend of black cherries and stewing prunes wrapped in new Milanese leather, vibrant acid with poise and persistance.*	£6.00	UNS SMF TOS T&T	G
Marquès de Griñon Domino de Agrelo 1997, Arco Bodegas Unidas Mendoza	*An attractive full bodied wine with laid back fruit and a touch of spirit.*	£6.00	CWS D&D	B
Santa Julia Malbec Oak Reserve 1996, La Agricola Mendoza	*Raspberry fizz on a simple but lively palate of spicey fruit grains.*	£6.00	UNS TOS T&T	B
Finca Flichman Reserva Cabernet Sauvignon 1996, Finca Flichman Mendoza	*Attractive medium weight wine showing notes of plum jam and a hint of mint, that carries through to a lengthy finish.*	£6.50	FRT GRA	B
Humberto Canale Merlot 1998, Humberto Canale Rio Negro	*Young, ripe plummy nose of cherry fruit and chocolate, green tannins relaxing with time will become a sumptuous wine.*	£6.50	SVT CFP JOV HWL	S
Finca Flichman Reserva Malbec 1997, Finca Flichman Mendoza	*Soft, rich, and oaky black fruit signal the fleshy, tannin mouthfeel that follows.*	£6.70	NYW FRT GRA	B

Wine	Description	Price	Stockists	Award
Bright Brothers Reserve San Juan Cabernet Sauvignon 1998, Bright Brothers San Juan	*Light with a brick edge and plum heat. Stewed fruits nicely developed with good mouthfeel.*	**£7.00**	SOM EHL	B
Humberto Canale Pinot Noir 1998, Humberto Canale Rio Negro	*Raspberry and mulberry nose, with an attractive perfume of nuts and flowers softly palated in the finish.*	**£7.00**	SVT HWL	B
Rafael Estate Malbec 1997, Finca Flichmann Mendoza	*A luscious deep colour, with lively fruit on the nose and a velvety mouthfeel with a clean finish.*	**£7.00**	SAF	B
Bodega Norton Cabernet Sauvignon Reserva 1997, Bodega Norton Mendoza	*Fun, warm sandalwood nose of spice, cedar and blackberries with just a hint of mint.*	**£7.30**	JNW BWC	B
Bodega Norton Malbec Reserva 1997, Bodega Norton Mendoza	*A happy combination of wood and fruit on the nose that introduces a well balanced, if slightly warm palate.*	**£7.30**	NYW JNW BWC	B
Luigi Bosca Malbec 1996, Leoncio Arizu Mendoza	*Subtle confected fruits on the nose with a pleasant mouthfeel and clean finish.*	**£7.40**	WAW ADN HAS	B
Familia Zuccardi Q Cabernet Sauvignon 1998, La Agricola Mendoza	*Sweet, ripe fruit on nose and gentle spice, well crafted wine of fleshy, jammy fruit character settling on well-balanced tannins*	**£8.00**	T&T	S
Familia Zuccardi Q Malbec 1998, La Agricola Mendoza	*Lovely oak and vanilla chocolate on the nose coupled with a warm mouthfeel and minty finish.*	**£8.00**	T&T	B

Wine	Description	Price	Stockists	Award
Familia Zuccardi Q Merlot 1998, La Agricola Mendoza	*Elegant meaty, spicey structure, sweet ripe fruit with good tannin structure and length.*	**£8.00**	T&T	B
Familia Zuccardi Q Tempranillo 1997, La Agricola Mendoza	*A nose of elegant vanilla hints at the fruit driven oaky tannin palate to come. Great length and finesse .*	**£8.00**	TOS T&T	S
Weinert Malbec 1994, Bodegas y Cavas de Weinert Mendoza	*An intriguing mature nose offering savoury and fruitcake notes with a dash of roast peppers.*	**£8.90**	RBS VLW CWS NAD SGL	B
Simonassi Cabernet Sauvignon Gran Reserva 1998, Simonassi Wines Mendoza	*Big, cherry nose with savoury oak. Rubbery, vegetal palate. Moderately tannic, with good acidity.*	**£9.00**	PLE	S
Catena Cabernet Sauvignon 1995, Catena Mendoza	*Spicey nose with hints of cinnamon and tar, a rich and concentrated palate with good structure, and heavy tannins.*	**£9.20**	GGW NYW SAF	B
Balbi Barbaro 1997, Bodegas Balbi Mendoza	*A warm, oaky nose with lots of blackcurrant and plum, a well composed wine with a fresh minty finish.*	**£10.00**	MRN, SAF GYW	B
Finca Flichman Dedicado 1996, Finca Flichman Mendoza	*Minty nose with big, ripe juicy fruit, loaded with blackcurrants and tannins finishing well.*	**£10.00**	FRT GRA	B
Weinert Cabernet Sauvignon 1995, Bodegas y Cavas de Weinert Mendoza	*Raisin fruitcake aromas with a hint of weathered wood on the nose, great power and richness in the mouth.*	**£10.20**	RBS VLW NAD SGL	S

SOUTH AMERICA • ARGENTIANA • RED

Wine	Description	Price	Stockists	Award
Cavas de Weinert 1994, Bodegas y Cavas de Weinert Mendoza	*Lifted, intense cassis aromas, a rich, dark fruit under strong tannic grip with a wonderful fruit finish.*	**£10.60**	GSH VLW SGL NAD	B
Peñaflor Cabernet Barrica 1998, Peñaflor San Juan	*Perfumed mint and plum with a cassis and licorice edge before a palate of fruity tannins.*	**£12.00**	EHL CWS	S
Peñaflor Cabernet Syrah Barrica 1998, Peñaflor Mendoza	*An attractive colour with a jammy, spirity nose leading to soft, well integrated and rounded tannins.*	**£12.00**	EHL CWS	S
Peñaflor Malbec Barricas 1998, Peñaflor Mendoza	*Rich, curranty nose with lovely oak characters and plum fruit. Great structure and poise.*	**£12.00**	CWS	S
Medalla Cabernet Sauvignon 1996, Trapiche Mendoza	*Smoky, biscuity nose with classy cedar and fruit on the palate, an oakey lengthy wine.*	**£13.00**	BLN EHL	B
Nieto & Senetiner Cadus Malbec 1997, Nieto & Senetiner Mendoza	*Hay and meadows on the nose with a good dose of fruit on the palate, a complementary wine.*	**£17.70**	NYW BPW	B
Clocher 1995,	*Ripe fruit characters interwoven with minerally flavours and a touch of honey leads to a generous finish.*	**£23.00**	EHL	S

Pinpoint who sells the wine you wish to buy by turning to the stockist codes. If you know the name of the wine you want to buy, use the alphabetical index. If the price is your motivation, refer to the invaluable price guide index; red and white wines under £5, sparkling wines under £12 and Champagne under £16. Happy hunting!

SOUTH AMERICA • ARGENTINA • WHITE

Wine	Description	Price	Stockists	Award
ARGENTA CHENIN BLANC CHARDONNAY 1998, FINCA FLICHMAN Mendoza	*Chunky ripe citrus fruit with herbal overtones and a touch of perfume on the nose and palate.*	**£4.00**	GRA	B
BRIGHT BROTHERS RESERVE CHARDONNAY 1998, BRIGHT BROTHERS San Juan	*Clean, nice and easygoing with well balanced ripe fruit and subtle oak to finish.*	**£5.00**	SMF CWS SOM EHL	B
PICAJUAN PEAK VIOGNIER NV, LA AGRICOLA Mendoza	*Floral and citrus characters on the nose with a soft, delicate palate and pleasant perfumed finish.*	**£6.20**	TOS	B
FINCA FLICHMAN RESERVA CHARDONNAY 1998, FINCA FLICHMAN Mendoza	*Deep and golden, ripe peaches and cream. Zesty acid leads into the mouth followed by creamy tropical fruit.*	**£6.70**	NYW FRT GRA	S
BRIGHT BROTHERS BARRICA CHARDONNAY 1998, BRIGHT BROTHERS San Juan	*Rich, fresh and hot. This is a wonderful example of a crisp, bright Chardonnay.*	**£7.00**	TOS EHL	B
ETCHART CAFAYATE BARREL FERMENTED CHARDONNAY 1998, BODEGAS ETCHART Cafayate	*Slightly restrained nose with ripe tropical fruit palate, moderate acidity and a clean finish.*	**£8.50**	CEN CAP SLM CAX	B
CATENA CHARDONNAY 1996, CATENA Mendoza	*Creamy scents of mangos, pineapples and melons mingle with fresh oak. Nice work and finishes well.*	**£9.20**	GGW NYW SAF	S

SOUTH AMERICA • CHILE • CABERNET

Wine	Description	Price	Stockists	Award
CALITERRA CABERNET SAUVIGNON 1998, CALITERRA Central Valley	*Ripe and plummy with sweet jams and pleasant herbaceous tones. Well balanced with a neat finish.*	£5.00	WRC MAR THS TSR VWE BUP SBS WIM HMA	B
ISLA NEGRA CABERNET SAUVIGNON 1998, VIÑA CONO SUR Rapel Valley	*Concentrated spicey, fruit nose. Intense fruit on palate, good depth of flavour and length.*	£5.00	Widely Available	S
TERRAMATER CABERNET SAUVIGNON 1997, TERRAMATER Central Valley	*Intense red berry fruit and spice on nose, soft and balanced chocolate, vanilla and bramble palate.*	£5.00	SWS TOS SAF	B
VIÑA PORTA CABERNET SAUVIGNON 1998, VIÑA PORTA Cachapoal Valley	*Vegetal nose with clean fruit and some savoury notes with good length and a tidy tail.*	£5.00	ODD SEA	B
VIÑA PORTA LIMITED EDITION CABERNET SAUVIGNON 1996, VIÑA PORTA Cachapoal Valley	*Earthy, berry nose. Good, ripe red fruits on the palate, with balanced tannins, a pleasant finish.*	£5.00	SEA	B
TESCO CHILEAN CABERNET SAUVIGNON RESERVE NV, TERRA MASTER Chile	*Perfumed flowers and mints with a basket of baked fruits and warming finish.*	£5.10	TOS	B
CARTA VIEJA ANTIGUA SELECCION CABERNET SAUVIGNON 1995, CARTA VIEJA Maule	*Jammy, plum and cedar nose introduce a palate of grainy tannins with good use of oak. Well balanced with lovely fruit concentration*	£5.20	MHV WBU	S

Wine	Tasting note	Price	Stockists	Award
Errazuriz Estates Cabernet Sauvignon 1997, Errazuriz Estates Aconcagua Valley	*Intense ripe fruity nose. with good fruit concentration on the palate. Some spice towards the finish.*	**£5.50**	Widely Available	B
Errazuriz Estates Cabernet Sauvignon 1998, Errazuriz Estates Aconcagua Valley	*Generous blackcurrant and herbal nose with good fruit tannins and a pleasant finish.*	**£5.50**	Widely Available	B
Luis Felipe Edwards Cabernet Sauvignon 1997, Luis Edwards Colchagua Valley	*Good fruit weight with pleasant dusty tannins and a well structured and generous palate.*	**£5.50**	VLW QWW D&D	B
M De Gras Cabernet Sauvignon 1998, M De Gras Colchagua Valley	*A floral nose with berry notes. A silky mouthfeel is well balanced with a clean acid tail.*	**£5.70**	NYW ENO	S
Casa La Joya Selection Cabernet Sauvignon 1997, Vina Bisquertt Colchagua Valley	*A bouquet garnee of spearmint, peppermint and sage are complemented by fresh fruits cascading onto a bed of fine grained tannins.*	**£5.80**	FRT GRA	S
Trio Cabernet Sauvignon 1997, Concha y Toro Maipo Valley	*Herbaceous nose with hints of runner bean carrying over onto the soft, black fruit driven palate.*	**£5.90**	VLW WRC BUP MAR THS CWA	B
Carmen Cabernet Sauvignon Reserve 1996, Carmen Vineyards Maipo Valley	*Rich blackcurrant nose with complexities of cassis and tobacco lead on to a gentle palate of some length.*	**£6.00**	UNS SGL NAD ODD WSO	B
Cono Sur Cabernet Sauvignon Reserve 1997, Viña Cono Sur Rapel Valley	*An archetyple nose with welcoming plum brandy, brambles and vanilla notes supported on a bed of powdered tannins.*	**£6.00**	FUL MWW ODD ASD WST	G

Wine	Description	Price	Stockists	Award
Cono Sur Reserve Syrah Cabernet 1998, Viña Cono Sur Rapel Valley	*A splash of blackcurrent and complementary plum fruits with some savoury characters and creamy, vanillin oak.*	**£6.00**	ASD WST	S
Domaine Oriental Clos Centenaire Cabernet Sauvignon Reserva 1997, Agricola Salve Central Valley	*Light, soft red fruit aromas, pleasant rounded palate with supple tannins, well-structured.*	**£6.00**	UNS WIM JEH P&R PNA	B
Luis Felipe Edwards Cabernet Sauvignon Reserve 1997, Luis Edwards Colchagua Valley	*Nice up front fruit with firm tannins giving a soft and round mouthfeel.*	**£6.00**	VLW QWW TOS D&D	B
Montes Reserve Cabernet Sauvignon 1997, Montes Curicó	*Well made and balanced wine with good use of oak, fine tannins and lifted fruit on the palate.*	**£6.00**	WON TAN L&W HWL	B
Santa Digna Cabernet Sauvignon 1997, Miguel Torres Curicó	*Big blockbusting red full of chocolate and cassis, lively palate with good wood and structure.*	**£6.00**	FEN POR ROD GRO B&B HAR SHJ	B
Terranoble Cabernet Sauvignon 1997, Vinedos Terranoble Central Valley	*Black cherries, plums and toasty vanilla notes with a velvety palate of cedar and talcum powder. Generous finish.*	**£6.00**	GRA	S
Casa la Joya Cabernet Sauvignon 1997, Viña Bisquertt Colchagua Valley	*Ripe red berry fruit and coconut, toasty vanillan oak adds structure, ripe and easy going.*	**£6.20**	FRT GRA	B
Santa Ines Reserve Cabernet Sauvignon Reserva 1997, Santa Ines Vineyard Maipo Valley	*Great blackcurrant nose with hints of oak, leather and spice, tight palate of juicy fruit and leather.*	**£6.30**	MAR BUP WRC TOS IWS	B

Wine	Description	Price	Stockists	Award
SOMERFIELD CHILEAN CABERNET SAUVIGNON 1998, VINA LA ROSA Rapel	*Rich fruits meet with a hint on herb on a palate of supple tannins and come to a spicy finish.*	**£6.40**	SMF	S
PORTAL DEL ALTO CABERNET SAUVIGNON RESERVA 1997, ALEJANDRO HERNANDEZ Maipo	*Gamey nose with touch of banana, beautifully balanced soft palate with plummy currant fruits.*	**£6.50**	CAC CCW	B
TORREON DE PAREDES RESERVE CABERNET SAUVIGNON 1995, TORREON DE PAREDES Rapel Valley	*Powerful blackcurrant aromas with oak, sweet and ripe fruit on palate and good tannin structure.*	**£6.50**	FTH	S
VIÑA GRACIA CABERNET SAUVIGNON RESERVA 1998, VIÑA GRACIA DE CHILE Cachapoal	*Vegetal, blackcurrant nose, sweet plummy fruit on palate with good tannins. Creamy conclusion.*	**£6.50**	UNS CWS PAT	B
ECHEVERRIA CABERNET SAUVIGNON RESERVA 1997, VIÑA ECHEVERRIA Molina	*Chocolate with subtle tobacco and olive notes and a well structured palate of fine grained tannins with good length.*	**£6.80**	NYW HSL AVB MFS A&N HOH	S
CALITERRA CABERNET SAUVIGNON RESERVA 1996, CALITERRA Maipo Valley	*Lifted violets and blackfruits with a tad of mint, lovely tight palate showing class without being overbearing.*	**£7.00**	WRC BUP MAR THS TSR VWE HMA	S
CALITERRA CABERNET SAUVIGNON RESERVA 1997, ROBERT MONDAVI & EDUARDO CHADWICK Maipo Valley	*Ripe fruit nose with violets. Upfront bramble flavours, good balance and structure with prevalent tannins.*	**£7.00**	WRC MAR THS TSR VWE BUP VWC HMA	B
VERAMONTE CABERNET SAUVIGNON 1997, VERAMONTE VINEYARDS Central Valley	*Blackcurrant and crushed mint lead to firm tannins and lingering crisp finish.*	**£7.00**	WRC BUP MAR THS GGW SKW	B

MontGras Cabernet Sauvignon Reserva 1997, MontGras Colchagua Valley	*A subtle, elegant nose introduces an array of rose petals, black fruits, sandalwood and herby characters with a hint of mint and mocha..*	**£7.10**	WCR JNW NYW ENO	G
Santa Helena Seleccion del Directorio Cabernet Sauvignon 1997, Viños de Chile Molina	*Nice combination of loganberry and fruits of the forest with a licorice spike and persistence of flavour.*	**£7.10**	CTH ABY YWL	S
M De Gras Cabernet Sauvignon Reserva 1998, M De Gras Colchagua Valley	*Nice deep purple colour with stewed fruits and mint evident before a textured palate of good weight.*	**£7.20**	NYW ENO	S
Casa la Joya Gran Reserva Cabernet Sauvignon 1997, Vina Bisquertt Colchagua Valley	*Ripe berry and minty fruit nose, firm well-structured palate with good fruit and oak integration.*	**£7.50**	FRT GRA	B
Santa Ines Cabernet Sauvignon Reserva 1996, Santa Ines Vineyard Maipo Valley	*Rich ripe blackcurrants and tomato leaf with toasty aromas tickle the nose. Deep, elegant and distinctive.*	**£7.50**	WCR WRC BUP MAR THS IWS	S
Los Vascos Grande Reserve 1996, Domaines Barons de Rothschild (Lafite) Colchagua	*Mashed fruits, gently stewed make for an easy drinking style with a neat acid tail.*	**£7.70**	GSH HAL SHJ MZC	B
Errazuriz Estates Cabernet Sauvignon Reserva 1996, Errazuriz Estates Aconcagua Valley	*Mint, cassis and pepper aromas, cool, tarry fruit. Complex on the long finish.*	**£8.00**	Widely Available	B
Las Lomas Cabernet Sauvignon Reserve 1998, Cav Cauquenes Maule Valley	*High pitched fruits sing from a palate of luxurious length with a rounded soft finish.*	**£8.00**	G2W	B

Santa Carolina Cabernet Gran Reserva 1996, Santa Carolina Maipo Valley	*Great up front berry fruits with a touch of the herbaceous trumpets a well structured full bodied palate.*	**£8.00**	THW	G
Errazuriz Estates Cabernet Sauvignon Reserva 1997, Errazuriz Estates Aconcagua Valley	*Jammy, earthy aromas, full ripe fruits on thepalate, pleasant depth of flavour. Good persistance.*	**£8.10**	Widely Available	S
Don Amado Cabernet Sauvignon Reserve 1991, Torreonde Paredes Rengo	*Minty chocolate nose, slightly green with new oak. Good fruit, soft and mature.*	**£8.40**	FTH	B
Casablanca el Bosque Cabernet 1997, Viña Casablanca Casablanca Valley	*Subtle, elegant, perfumed nose. Soft, plummy, round sexy style with smooth balance. Complex and long.*	**£8.60**	JNW NYW ODD WSO MOR	S
Viña Alamosa Cabernet Sauvignon Reserve Prestige 1997, Viña de Larose Cachapoal Valley	*Spicey, fruity nose, chunky oaky fruit with notes of leather. Lingering grip.*	**£8.70**	GRT	B
Viña Alamosa Cabernet Sauvignon Reserve 1997, Viña de Larose Cachapoal Valley	*Ripe blackcurrant nose, an abundance of ripe fruit, soft tannins and good acidity.*	**£8.80**	GRT	B
Casablanca Santa Isabel Cabernet 1997, Viña Casablanca Casablanca Valley	*Intense blackcurrant nose, rich plummy cassis fruit, with big tannins. Pleasantly balanced.*	**£9.00**	JNW ALE HVN ODD WSO WWT	B
Valdivieso Cabernet Franc Reserve 1996, Valdivieso Lontue	*Rich, black berry fruits with a touch of spice introduce a fine bed of tannins and balancing acidity.*	**£9.00**	SAF WRC BUP NYW TOS	B

Wine	Tasting note	Price	Stockists	Award
Valdivieso Cabernet Franc Reserve 1997, Valdivieso Central Valley	*Clean coffee and blackcurrant aromas, ripe and savoury with opulent fruit. Well-balanced, fresh with a fine grained finish.*	£9.10	Widely Available	S
Cono Sur 20 Barrels Cabernet Sauvignon 1997, Viña Cono Sur Rapel Valley	*Rich full fruit with smoky notes lead to a soft palate of spice and soft tanins and a luxuriouse mouth feel.*	£10.00	WST	B
Cuvée Alexandre Cabernet Sauvignon 1997, Casa Lapostolle Rapel Valley	*Ripe flower and satsuma flesh with a hint of cigar. Nice plums in the mouth with chalky tannins.*	£10.00	WRC BUP MAR MMD	B
Montes Alpha Cabernet Sauvignon 1997, Montes Curicó	*Mushrooms and mulberries on the nose introduces a long tail with a neat finish.*	£10.00	ODD HVN HAR WFL ADN HWL	B
Santa Carolina Cabernet Sauvignon Reserva de Familia 1996, Santa Carolina Maipo Valley	*Warm leather on a fruit laden nose and a soft and round palate with lively tannins.*	£10.00	THW	S
Caballo Loco No 2 NV, Valdivieso Lontue	*Ripe nose with an intense palate of rich, black fruits and beautifully integrated oak. A delight to drink.*	£12.10	WRC BUP GGW NYW TOS SAF	S
Caballo Loco No 3 NV, Valdivieso Central Valley	*A smoky, tarry nose with hints of cassis followed by mixed fruits and nicely integrated oak.*	£12.40	Widely Available	S
Magnificum Cabernet Sauvignon 1995, Viña Canepa Curico	*Lifted spice and pepper on the nose and a ripe palate with reasonable weight and length.*	£20.00	SCA CFN T&T	B

Almaviva 1996, Baron Philippe de Rothschild Maipo Valley	*Opulent and inky with ripe berrries and fruit-cake aromas. The palate offers fine tannins and great length.*	£37.50	BDR NYW PRG	G

SOUTH AMERICA • CHILE • MERLOT

Castillo de Molina Reserva Merlot 1997, Viña San Pedro Lontué Valley	*Ripe plums with hints of tobacco and and toasty oak, good mouthfeel and length.*	£3.40	RBS BUC	B
Santa Amalia Merlot 1998, Santa Amalia Rapel Valley	*Nice lively berry fruits with good lift and nutty notes leading to a pleasant well weighted palate.*	£5.00	ADE	S
Valdivieso Merlot 1998, Valdivieso Central Valley	*Toasted oak and coffee nose, jammy fruit and licorice palate, balanced lingering finish.*	£5.00	Widely Available	B
Isla Negra Merlot 1998, Viña Cono Sur Rapel Valley	*Blackcurrant and plum jam, excellent palate structure, slippery tannins support a basket of summer fruits.*	£5.20	SMF TOS SAF WST	G
Casa Leona Reserve Merlot 1998, Viña la Rosa Rapel Valley	*Balanced and rich with good plum fruit and soft tannins matched by clever fruit acidity.*	£5.50	M&S HWL	B
Casillero del Diablo Rapel Merlot 1998, Concha y Toro Rapel Valley	*Rich fruit greets the nose and flows on to the palate with well integrated oak.*	£5.50	VLW CWA	S

Wine	Description	Price	Stockists	Award
TERRA ANDINA MERLOT 1997, TERRA ANDINA Central Valley	*Cassis, raspberry and stewed fruit nose with smoky oak providing agreeable soft tannins.*	**£5.50**	EUR LAW CAX	B
TERRANOBLE MERLOT 1998, VINEDOS TERRANOBLE Maule Valley	*Youthful blackberry fruit on nose and palate, good fruit extraction and tannins.*	**£5.50**	FRT GRA	B
MONTGRAS MERLOT 1997, MONTGRAS Colchagua Valley	*A dark fruit nose with tobacco, fleshy palate offering powdery tannins balanced by crisp acidity.*	**£5.60**	JNW NYW TOS ENO	S
CANEPA PRIVATE RESERVE MERLOT 1996, VIÑA CANEPA San Fernando	*Seasoned and soft with nice looking fruit, elegant with good balance and length.*	**£5.80**	SCA CFN MGM SMF T&T	B
CASILLERO DEL DIABLO MAIPO MERLOT 1998, CONCHA Y TORO Maipo Valley	*Toasty oak and blackcurrant with plentiful ripe fruit and subtle but firm tannins.*	**£6.00**	VLW CWA	S
ERRAZURIZ ESTATES MERLOT 1998, ERRAZURIZ ESTATES Curicó	*Cheesy nose with stylish powerful, sweet fruit, spicey with good oak integration and strong tannins.*	**£6.00**	WCR FUL ODD THS VWE TOS HMA	S
LA PALMERIA RESERVE MERLOT 1998, VIÑA LA ROSA Rapel Valley	*Blackcurrant and cedar aromas, rounded fruit with good body and tannins. Some acidity with good length.*	**£6.00**	UNS CWS WTS HWL	S
M DE GRAS MERLOT 1998, M DE GRAS Colchagua Valley	*A basket of fruit woven with classy oak supported by good fruit tannins and a memeorable finish.*	**£6.00**	ENO	B

Wine	Description	Price	Stockists	Award
MONTES RESERVE MERLOT 1998, MONTES Curicó	*Rich flavours of berries and currants with new oak and a hint of menthol and figgy spice.*	**£6.00**	WON WFL GRO HWL	B
MONTGRAS MERLOT 1998, MONTGRAS Colchagua Valley	*Leafy, jammy fruit on the nose, soft ripe, sweet palate with sturdy tannins and good acidity.*	**£6.00**	TOS ENO	B
TERRANOBLE MERLOT OAK AGED 1998, VINEDOS TERRANOBLE San Clemente	*A heady blackcurrant aroma and big basket of fruit. Complex and with a flavour that lingers.*	**£6.00**	GRA	S
TORREALBA MERLOT 1998, TORREALBA Curicó	*Tobacco and reticent vanilla on nose pleasing fruit on palate, oaky and rich.*	**£6.00**	EHL	B
TRIO MERLOT 1997, CONCHA Y TORO Puemo Valley	*Good minty nose, creamy nutmeg spice and herbs. Rich succulent palate displaying good length.*	**£6.00**	VLW WRC BUP MAR THS CWA	B
TRIO MERLOT 1998, CONCHA Y TORO Rapel Valley	*Ripe berries, minty, chocolate fruit with some tobacco. Soft and round on the palate.*	**£6.00**	VLW WRC BUP MAR THS CWA	S
VITISTERRA MERLOT 1998, VIÑA MORANDÉ Central Valley	*Dusty, smoky nose, complex black cherry fruit on the palate. Delicious and lingering.*	**£6.00**	UNS T&T	S
CASABLANCA MERLOT 1998, VIÑA CASABLANCA Casablanca Valley	*Cream and cassis engage with an intense cedar palate of fine tannins.*	**£6.10**	JNW ODD MOR	B

Wine	Description	Price	Stockists	Award
Cono Sur Reserve Merlot 1998, Viña Cono Sur Rapel Valley	*Full earthy, fruity nose with good balance and structure. Long firm finish.*	**£6.20**	SAF WST	B
Casablanca White Label Merlot 1997, Viña Casablanca Casablanca Valley	*Round rich cassis and spicey plum pudding aromas, succulent oozing palate displaying lingering suppleness.*	**£6.30**	Widely Available	S
Tesco Chilean Merlot Reserve NV, Terra Master Chile	*Rich fruit and sweet oak on the nose, concentrated palate of ripe currants and good oak complexity.*	**£6.50**	TOS	B
Viña Gracia Merlot Reserva 1998, Vina Gracia de Chile Maipo	*Violets and black fruits lead on to a palate of fine tannins balanced with just the right dose of acidity. Great length.*	**£6.70**	UNS PAT	S
MontGras Merlot Reserva 1997, MontGras Colchagua Valley	*Rich and ripe black fruits on a bed of powdery tannins. Full bodied with generous length.*	**£6.80**	RBS NYW ENO	S
Caliterra Merlot Reserva 1998, Caliterra Maipo Valley	*Rich plum jam and leathery aromas, soft fruit on the palate with full tannins and good structure.*	**£7.00**	WIM HMA	B
Carmen Merlot Reserve 1997, Carmen Vineyards Maipo Valley	*Deep plum heat with rich extracted chewy fruit. Balanced with very good length.*	**£7.00**	NAD ODD WSO SGL	B
Casa Lapostolle Merlot 1998, Casa Lapostolle Rapel Valley	*Aromatic berries and spicey aromas, rich and elegant palate with a clean finish.*	**£7.00**	WRC BUP MAR MMD	B

Wine	Description	Price	Stockists	Award
Mapocho Reserva Merlot 1995, BRL Hardy Central Valley	*Mulberry and mint are the perfect partners in this mallow easy style with relaxed tannins and infinite length.*	**£7.00**	HBR	B
M De Gras Merlot Reserva 1998, M De Gras Colchagua Valley	*Berry fruits and mint on the nose introduce a powerful wine with great poise.*	**£7.20**	NYW ENO	S
Valdivieso Merlot Reserve 1997, Valdivieso Central Valley	*Fresh cherry fruit nose and nutty oak, ripe dark palate with licorice nuances and firm tannins.*	**£7.20**	SAF GGW NYW BWL	B
Casa la Joya Gran Reserva Merlot 1997, Vina Bisquertt Colchagua Valley	*Hefty plum nose with savoury notes flow on to a palate of finesse and intensity with well integrated oak.*	**£7.50**	FRT GRA	S
La Palmeria Gran Reserva Merlot 1998, Viña la Rosa Rapel Valley	*Smoky currant nose, rich fruit palate with velvety and minty flavours. Good acidity and length.*	**£7.50**	CWS ODD JSM FUL HWL	B
J Bouchon Gran Reserva Merlot 1998, J Bouchon Central Valley	*Rich berry fruits with a touch of spice, this soft and rich wine is well balanced and a fine finish.*	**£8.00**	FNS	B
Santa Carolina Merlot Gran Reserva 1996, Santa Carolina San Fernando	*Mint leaf and fruits of the forest characters drift elegantly on to a palate of generous length.*	**£8.20**	THW	S
Torreon de Paredes Reserve Merlot 1997, Torreon de Paredes Rapel Valley	*A green pepper, aromatic nose leads to a blackcurrant leaf palate with a solid backbone.*	**£8.20**	FTH	S

SOUTH AMERICA • CHILE• MERLOT				
CASABLANCA SANTA ISABEL MERLOT 1997, VIÑA CASABLANCA Casablanca Valley	*Brambly, green mint nose, blackcurrant palate, dense with sweet oak and tannic grip.*	**£9.00**	JNW ODD HNW MOR	S
CASABLANCA SANTA ISABEL MERLOT 1998, VIÑA CASABLANCA Casablanca Valley	*Thick, dark nose with mint and blackcurrant, spicey palate with concentrated blockbuster fruit. Large and chewy.*	**£9.00**	ODD JNW HVN MOR	S
SOMERFIELD CHILEAN MERLOT 1998, VIÑA MORANDÉ Central Valley	*Zesty orange citrus fruit on the nose; fresh fruit driven palate with balanced acidity.*	**£9.20**	WFD ALE HAF VRS SMF	B
CONO SUR 20 BARRELS MERLOT 1998, VIÑA CONO SUR Rapel Valley	*Complex nose of red berry and spice, balanced palate of raspberry and vanilla. Worth waitng for.*	**£10.00**	WST	S
ERRAZURIZ ESTATES MERLOT RESERVA 1997, ERRAZURIZ ESTATES Concagua Valley	*Nice spice and cedar nose with blackcurrant undertones. Minerally characters on the palate, good length.*	**£10.00**	SAF WIM DBY HMA	B
ERRAZURIZ ESTATES MERLOT RESERVA 1998, ERRAZURIZ ESTATES Concagua Valley	*Concentrated raspberry fruit nose with tar and licorice, full and rounded with impressive length.*	**£10.00**	SAF WIM HMA	S
MONTES ALPHA MERLOT 1997, MONTES Curicó	*Cigar box, cedar wood and sherbet fruits followed by big ripe tannins and a crisp clean finish.*	**£10.00**	MWW MRN ADN WFL HWL	G

Pinpoint who sells the wine you wish to buy by turning to the stockist codes. If you know the name of the wine you want to buy, use the alphabetical index. If the price is your motivation, refer to the invaluable price guide index; red and white wines under £5, sparkling wines under £12 and Champagne under £16. Happy hunting!

SOUTH AMERICA • CHILE • OTHER

Wine	Description	Price	Stockists	Award
Castillo de Molina Reserva Pinot Noir 1998, Viña San Pedro Lontué Valley	*Sweet red fruit with savoury complexity, a firm palate showing good balance, superb length and broadness.*	**£3.00**	RBS BUC	B
MontGras Carmenere Reserva 1998, MontGras Colchagua Valley	*A deep plum colour with a minty menthol nose, fine grained tannins and a generous finish.*	**£3.50**	NYW ENO	S
Co-op Chilean Old Vines Carignan 1998, Vina Segu-Olle Maule	*Lovely black fruit nose leads to an impressive palate of berry fruit flavours and freshly cracked peppercorns.*	**£4.00**	CWS	B
Canepa Private Reserve Cabernet Sauvignon Merlot 1995, Viña Canepa Central Valley	*Funky and vibrant, the nose shows sweet fruits with a hint of menthol and mint.*	**£4.80**	ASD T&T	B
La Palmeria Cabernet Merlot Reserve 1998, Viña la Rosa Rapel Valley	*Burnt cherry and black fruits on the nose, a palate of ripe fruit with chunky tannins, with great length.*	**£5.30**	UNS CWS ODD FUL JSM SMF HWL	S
Terra Mater Alma Malbec 1997, Terramater Curicó	*A shiny, floral scented style with good depth of fruit and herb flavours.*	**£5.50**	CWS GNW TPE RAE SWS	B
Valdivieso Cabernet Merlot Reserve 1997, Valdivieso Central Valley	*Strawberry and ripe berry fruit nose, balanced palate of ripe concentrated fruit, with gripping tannins.*	**£5.50**	TOS WTS BWL	S

Wine	Description	Price	Stockists	Award
Alma Terramater Zinfandel Shiraz 1998, Terramater Maipo Valley	*Oaky rubbery aromas with sour plum flavours, juicy acidity, firm tannins under a finish of spicey fruit.*	**£5.70**	CWS NYW GRT WOI SWS	B
Luis Felide Edwards Carmenere 1997, Luis Edwards Colchagua Valley	*Blueberries have taken some myrrh to bed and are laying back in the luxury of a silky tannin blanket.*	**£6.00**	VLW D2D QWW	S
Luis Felipe Edwards Carmenere 1998, Luis Edwards Colchagua Valley	*Concentrated chewy berry fruits and chocolate, with chalky tannins and a touch of sweet spice.*	**£6.00**	VLW D&D	S
Montes Reserve Malbec 1998, Montes Curico	*Attractive nose of cinnamon and spice leads to a medium bodied, fruit driven mouthfeel.*	**£6.00**	HDL IRV HWL	B
Santa Ines Carmenere Reserva Reserva 1997, Santa Ines Vineyard Maipo Valley	*Peppery toasty nose with fruit aromatics following onto the palate with fine tannins, a generous finish.*	**£6.00**	MAR BUP WRC TOS IWS	B
Santa Ines Malbec Reserve Reserva 1997, Santa Ines Vineyard Maipo Valley	*Youthful, sappiness on the nose with a cooked palate of dried fruit and nut flavours.*	**£6.00**	WRC BUP MAR TOS IWS	B
Terranoble Carmenere Reserva 1998, Vinedos Terranoble Maule	*Cedar nose, with rich fruit dominated by strong tannins and oak on the finish.*	**£6.00**	GRA	B
M De Gras Carmenere Reserva 1998, M De Gras Colchagua Valley	*Violets, currants and mint on the nose herald in a palate brimming with flavour and finesse.*	**£6.40**	JNW NYW ENO	G

Wine	Description	Price	Stockists	Award
Carmen Syrah Reserve 1997, Carmen Vineyards Maipo Valley	*A well-balanced, minty soft wine with huge fruit flavours, ripe tannins and inky finish.*	£7.00	NAD ODD SGL	S
Carmen Vineyards Petite Sirah 1997, Carmen Vineyards Maipo Valley	*Intriguing, rustic nuances and conventional sweet plums and bramble berries. Pleasing conclusion of grip and complexity.*	£7.00	NAD SHJ SGL	S
Las Mercedes Malbec 1997, J Bouchon Central Valley	*Glimpses of herb and developing fruit cake aromas leads to a deeply viscous and concentrated black fruit palate.*	£7.00	FNS	S
San Carlos Merlot Malbec 1988, Viña San Carlos Colchagua Valley	*A menthol and savoury nose leads to a broad blackberry flavoured palate with good length.*	£7.00	BDR	B
Undurraga Carmenere Reserva 1998, Undurraga Colchagua Valley	*Deep purple, plum heat with herbaceous and green bean nose supported by a layer of berry fruits.*	£7.00	TOS PLB	B
La Palmeria Gran Reserva Merlot Cabernet 1998, Viña la Rosa Rapel Valley	*Jammy fruit with a touch of cheesiness on the nose and a palate of fine grained tannins and clean acidity.*	£8.00	HWL	G
Alto de Terra Andina 1997, Vinos Terra Andina Curico Central Valley	*Spicey mulberry on the nose, a palate of soft vanilla flavours and a pleasant fruit finish.*	£8.50	PEA CAP CDE CAX	S
Valdivieso Malbec Reserve 1997, Valdivieso Central Valley	*Loads of fruit and oak are matched by clean tannins and fine fruit acidity.*	£9.50	GGW NYW SAF BWL	S

Wine	Description	Price	Stockists	Medal
ERRAZURIZ ESTATES SYRAH RESERVA 1997, ERRAZURIZ ESTATES Acongcagua Valley	*Aromas of spice, white pepper and minty elements. The full palate displays great length and complexity.*	**£9.80**	Widely Available	S
ERRAZURIZ ESTATES SANGIOVESE 1998, ERRAZURIZ ESTATES Concagua Valley	*Deep ruby red upfront toasty aromas leading to sweet forrest fruits, a long dry finish of herbs and spice.*	**£10.00**	WIM HMA	B
VALDIVIESO MALBEC RESERVE 1996, VALDIVIESO Lontué Valley	*A spiced jam nose with a hint of truffle and a well rounded and well-balanced palate.*	**£10.50**	GGW TOS SAF	S
VALDIVIESO RESERVA PREMIUM PINOT NOIR 1997, VALDIVIESO Central Valley	*Good nutty nose, with lots of pepper and spice on the well structured finish.*	**£15.00**	BWL	B
MANSO DE VELASCO 1996, MIGUEL TORRES Curicó	*Cherries and spice lead onto a well structured palate, with big tannins and a long-lasting finish.*	**£15.50**	POR SCA	S
ERRAZURIZ ESTATES DON MAXIMIANO FOUNDER'S RESERVA 1996, ERRAZURIZ ESTATES Concagua Valley	*Strong blackcurrant nose, rich bramble fruit. Firm slightly unripe tannins with balancing acidity to a long finish.*	**£16.20**	QWW WIN WRC MAR FUL TSR VWE BUP HMA	B
ERRAZURIZ ESTATES DON MAXIMIANO FOUNDER'S RESERVA 1997, ERRAZURIZ ESTATES Concagua Valley	*An amalgam of menthol, fruit and burnt coffee characters leading to a memorable finish.*	**£16.70**	QWW WRC BUP FUL TSR VWE HMA	S
CASA LAPOSTOLLE CLOS APALTA 1997, CASA LAPOSTOLLE Rapel Valley	*A big rich wine with no shortage of berry fruit, spice and herb characters, delightful to drink.*	**£25.00**	MMD	G

SOUTH AMERICA • CHILE • SWEET

Errazuriz Estates Late Harvest Sauvignon Blanc 1998, Errazuriz Estates Casablanca Valley	*Bursting with intense citrus flavours, this rich, well-rounded wine, with a seemingly everlasting finish, is truly exceptional!*	**£10.00**	HMA	G

SOUTH AMERICA • CHILE • WHITE

Castillo de Molina Reserva Chardonnay 1997, Viña San Pedro Lontué Valley	*Pale yellow with ripe citrus characters and toasty crispy oak aromas, full body with ripe fruit.*	**£2.80**	MRN RBS BUC	S
Safeway Chilean Semillon Chardonnay 1998, Viña Morandé Central Valley	*Clean cantelope and citrus offering fresh, fruity aromas wrapped up by toasty oak, nice finish.*	**£4.00**	SAF	B
Casa Leona Chardonnay 1998, Viña la Rosa Rapel Valley	*A pear-drop nose introduces a boiled sweet palate with refreshing fruit acidity.*	**£4.20**	M&S	B
Soleca Semillon Chardonnay 1997, Viña Bisquertt Colchagua	*Generous fruity, waxy sémillon nose displaying good mouthfeel and weight and nice length.*	**£4.50**	SAF	B

Pinpoint who sells the wine you wish to buy by turning to the stockist codes. If you know the name of the wine you want to buy, use the alphabetical index. If the price is your motivation, refer to the invaluable price guide index; red and white wines under £5, sparkling wines under £12 and champagne under £16. Happy hunting!

SOUTH AMERICA • CHILE • WHITE

Wine	Description	Price	Stockists	Award
35 Sur Chardonnay 1998, Viña San Pedro Lontué Valley	*Pleasantly tropical with a good dose of acidity and a crisp, clean finish.*	**£4.70**	SAF MRN BUC	B
Santa Amalia Sauvignon Blanc 1998, Santa Amalia Rapel Valley	*Fresh ripe herbal fruit leads to the palate showing good depth and a little creaminess.*	**£4.70**	ADE	B
Valdivieso Chardonnay 1998, Valdivieso Central Valley	*Rich and nutty aromas combined with full bodied tropical fruit and high balanced acidity.*	**£4.70**	GGW WTS BWL	B
Viña Alamosa Semillon 1998, Viña de Larose Cachapoal Valley	*Perfumed gooseberry aromas, this off dry wine has zingy acidity and a clean long finish.*	**£4.80**	GRT	B
35 Sur Sauvignon Blanc 1999, Viña San Pedro Lontué Valley	*Wonderfully intense grassiness and rich, soft tropical fruit. Lovely and ripe with lithe acidity.*	**£5.00**	ASD SAF JSM MRN BUC	G
Millaman Chardonnay 1998, Hacienda el Condor Curicó	*A minerally style offering a fruity palate of melon and peach flavours before a clean finish.*	**£5.00**	CNL SOH WTS HOU ECA	B
Nova Terrarum Sauvignon Blanc 1998, Viña Morandé Central Valley	*Fresh gooseberries and hints of cheese, rich ripe fruit on the palate with seductive acid.*	**£5.00**	T&T	B
Safeway Cordillera Estate Oak Aged Chardonnay 1997, Santa Emiliana Casablanca	*Fragrant blossom meld with the melon, peach and smoky bacon. Nicely balanced and made.*	**£5.00**	SAF	S

SIERRA LOS ANDES CHARDONNAY 1998, CARMEN WINERY Casablanca /Maipo	*Lovely zesty, fruit characters on the nose precede a lush, mouthfilling palate of lees and stonefruit.*	£5.00	M&S M&S	S
VIÑA PORTA CHARDONNAY 1998, VIÑA PORTA Cachapoal Valley	*Rich, tropical fruit with a dusty oak hint and plenty of crisp acid on the palate.*	£5.00	SEA ODD	B
CARTA VIEJA ANTIGUA SELECCION CHARDONNAY 1996, CARTA VIEJA Maule	*Good clean young fruit with a creamy palate and moderate oak influence.*	£5.20	MHV WBU	B
CASILLERO DEL DIABLO CHARDONNAY 1997, CONCHA Y TORO Casablanca Valley	*Marmalade and honey on toast with crisp dry fruit singing with malt and yeast characters.*	£5.20	VLW WRC BUP MAR THS CWA	B
SANTA EMILIANA PALMERAS ESTATE CHARDONNAY 1997, SANTA EMILIANA Casablanca	*Ripe peach and subtle oak rolled together in a slightly oily texture with moderate acidity.*	£5.30	TRO SAF WCR BPW	B
CASABLANCA WHITE LABEL SAUVIGNON 1998, VIÑA CASABLANCA Casablanca Valley	*Lovely, ripe tropical smells, the palate is soft and open flowing to the zippy conclusion.*	£5.40	WAW NYW ODD MWW WSO JNW ALE MOR	B
ECHEVERRIA UNWOODED CHARDONNAY 1998, VINA ECHEVERRIA Molina	*Clean, aromatic wine with a creamy mousse in the mouth and a clean, balancing acid finish.*	£5.50	HOH HSL LUC AVB	B
ERRAZURIZ ESTATES SAUVIGNON BLANC 1998, ERRAZURIZ ESTATES Casablanca Valley	*Pungent gunsmoke and flint on the nose. Palate is well balanced with ripe fruit underneath.*	£5.50	Widely Available	B

La Fortuna Chardonnay 1998, Viña la Fortuna Lontué Valley	*Rounded apple and pear flavours with a buttery palate and crisp finish.*	**£5.50**	PFC	B
Palo Alto Reserva Chardonnay 1998, Francisco de Aguirre Coquimbo Valley	*Pungent oak with hints of honeyed lemon on the nose and a peachy apricot palate.*	**£5.50**	AVB HOH	B
Casablanca White Label Chardonnay 1998, Viña Casablanca Casablanca Valley	*Intense aromas of tropical fruits abound in a rounded, nicely textured wine.*	**£5.60**	Widely Available	B
Errazuriz Chardonnay 1997, Errazuriz Estates Casablanca Valley	*A delicious, leesy nose with ripe fruit notes and a clean, well balanced, fruit palate.*	**£5.70**	Widely Available	S
Errazuriz Estates Chardonnay 1998, Errazuriz Estates Casablanca Valley	*Lemon meringue pie with pineapple toppings in this delightful, rich, full bodied style.*	**£5.70**	Widely Available	S
Explorer Sauvignon Blanc 1998, Concha y Toro Casablanca Valley	*Creamy, ripe nose of peaches, pears and herbs. Very fresh in the mouth with lively acidity.*	**£5.70**	VLW CWA	B
Montes Barrel Fermented Fumé Blanc 1998, Montes Curicó	*Grapefruit and nice herbaceousness aromas, crisp acidity with nice integration leading to a pleasing conclusion.*	**£5.70**	CLA WNC HDL HWL	B
Torreon de Paredes Reserve Chardonnay 1997, Torreon de Paredes Rapel Valley	*Upfront fruit mingled with controlled oak on the nose, zingy citric acid with full-bodied fruit.*	**£5.80**	FTH	B

Wine	Description	Price	Stockists	Award
TRIO CHARDONNAY 1998, CONCHA Y TORO Casablanca Valley	*Chalky lemon nose with a full flavoured steely palate and crisp finish.*	**£5.80**	VLW WRC BUP MAR THS CWA	B
VILLARD ESTATE CHARDONNAY 1997, VILLARD ESTATE Casablanca Valley	*Fresh lemon on the nose, lime and grapefruit palate weight, crisp acidity and subtle complexity.*	**£6.00**	WCR BPW	S
VIÑA GRACIA CHARDONNAY RESERVA SELECT 1998, VIÑA GRACIA DE CHILE Central Valley	*Pear and apple aromas with fresh pleasant fruit characters well-balanced with subtle integrated oak.*	**£6.00**	PAT	B
VIÑA TARAPACA CHARDONNAY RESERVA 1997, VIÑA TARAPACA Maipo Valley	*Delicate nose with soft round citrus fruit and fine length with a tidy acid tail.*	**£6.00**	CDT WAV	B
VITISTERRA CHARDONNAY 1998, VIÑA MORANDÉ Concagua	*Exotic fruits bathe in warm oak in this carefully constructed, stylish wine.*	**£6.00**	T&T	B
ECHEVERRIA CHARDONNAY RESERVA 1997, VIÑA ECHEVERRIA Molina	*Plenty of toasty oak on the nose grapefruit and ripe fruit palate with high acidity.*	**£6.30**	HHF A&N HAR HSL AVB HOH	B
CASA LAPOSTOLLE CHARDONNAY 1998, CASA LAPOSTOLLE Casablanca Valley	*Rich warm tropical fruit on the nose. Plenty of citrus fruit and integrated buttery vanilla oak.*	**£6.50**	MMD	S
VIÑA GRACIA CHARDONNAY RESERVA 1998, VIÑA GRACIA DE CHILE Central Valley	*A nice, creamy style with banana and apple blossom notes. Nicely balanced.*	**£6.90**	UNS CWS PAT	B

Wine	Description	Price	Stockists	Award
CALITERRA CHARDONNAY RESERVA 1997, CALITERRA Casablanca Valley	*Mineral aromas of slatey chalk with nuances of lean melon fruit dominate the nose and palate.*	£7.00	Widely Available	S
CARMEN CHARDONNAY RESERVE 1997, CARMEN VINEYARD Maipo Valley	*Melon, pineapple and kiwi fruit flavours loll about on a creamy, soft bed.*	£7.00	VLW NAD ODD SGL	B
CASABLANCA SANTA ISABEL SAUVIGNON BLANC 1998, VIÑA CASABLANCA Casablanca Valley	*Smoky asparagus and tropical fruit salad to start. Ripe, expansive palate balancing acidity, finishes well.*	£7.00	TOS ODD WSO JNW MOR	B
RESERVE SIERRA LOS ANDES CHARDONNAY 1998, CARMEN WINERY Casablanca	*Tropical fruit driven nose with traces of oak, the palate is full bodied with crisp acidity.*	£7.00	M&S	G
UNDURRAGA CHARDONNAY RESERVA 1998, UNDURRAGA Maipo Valley	*Lovely oak aromas with a buttery almost creamy palate lively fresh acid and good clean finish.*	£7.00	PLB	B
VERAMONTE CHARDONNAY 1998, VERAMONTE VINEYARDS Casablanca Valley	*Fresh coconut aromas, apple and peach fruit flavours and powerful oak balanced with good weighty fruit.*	£7.00	WRC BUP MAR THS GGW SKW	B
VIÑA PORTA RESERVE CHARDONNAY 1997, VIÑA PORTA Cachapoal valley	*A nice hint of toasty oak hides behind a veil of pineapple and grapefruit.*	£7.00	SEA	S
SELECCION DEL DIRECTORIO CHARDONNAY 1997, VINOS DE CHILE Molina	*Fresh citrus and tropical characters on the nose. Zesty lemons and pineapple on the palate.*	£7.30	YWL	S

Wine	Description	Price	Stockists	Award
MontGras Chardonnay Reserva 1998, MontGras Colchagua Valley	*Melon, capsicum and hazelnut aromas with honeyed tropical fruit palate and subtle integrated oak characters.*	**£7.50**	ENO	B
Viña Gracia Chardonnay Reserva 1997, Vina Gracia de Chile Central Valley	*Buttery lemon on the nose with ripe fruit some complexity and fantastic lemon, biscuity finish.*	**£7.50**	UNS PAT	B
Casablanca Santa Isabel Chardonnay 1998, Viña Casablanca Casablanca Valley	*Aromatic citrus peel characters with well-integrated sweet vanilla oak make this a class act.*	**£8.00**	JNW NYW ODD WWT MOR	S
La Palmeria Gran Reserva Chardonnay 1998, Viña la Rosa Rapel Valley	*Creamy melon, mango and pineapple flavours with nuances of vanilla pod dominate this attractive wine.*	**£8.00**	ODD JSM FUL HWL	S
Santa Carolina Chardonnay Gran Reserva 1997, Santa Carolina Maipo Valley	*Richly textured palate with creamy, yeasty notes and a clean fruit finish.*	**£8.00**	THW	B
Terramater Altum Chardonnay 1997, Terramater Maipo Valley	*Perfumed hints of freshly cut herbs on the nose followed by a fruity, subtle oak palate.*	**£8.50**	SWS	B
Villard Estate Reserve Chardonnay 1997, Villard Estate Casablanca Valley	*Floral and fresh lemon characters on the nose with harmonised fruit and lively balanced acidity.*	**£8.50**	BPW	S
Caliterra Tribute Chardonnay 1996, Caliterra Casablanca Valley	*Light citrus fruit and creamy buttery oak notes introduce a richly textured palate of cream and peaches.*	**£9.00**	WTS	G

SOUTH AMERICA • CHILE • WHITE

Wine	Description	Price	Stockists	Award
Cuvée Alexandre Casa Lapostolle Chardonnay 1997, Casa Lapostolle Casablanca Valley	*Full fruit aromas, abundant tropical fruits on the palate with backbone acidity and good balance.*	**£9.20**	SAF MMD	S
Casablanca Barrel Fermented Chardonnay 1997, Viña Casablanca Casablanca Valley	*Honeyed subtle fruit aromas with delicate fruit and oak on the palate with fine balancing acidity.*	**£9.30**	JNW ODD GRO WSO-MOR	B
Casablanca Barrel Fermented Chardonnay 1998, Viña Casablanca Casablanca Valley	*Toasty oak and yeasty aromas seep from a fresh lemon palate with great length.*	**£10.00**	WSO JNW ODD MOR	B
Montes Alpha Chardonnay 1998, Montes Curicó	*Lots of new vanilla oak combined with rich ripe tropical fruit and good persistent length.*	**£10.00**	MWW MRN HVN HAR WON HWL	B
Santa Carolina Reserva de Familia Chardonnay 1997, Santa Carolina Maipo Valley	*Robust smooth fruit with sleek mouthfeel, hints of mineral characters and a clean finish.*	**£10.00**	THW	B

SOUTH AMERICA • URUGUAY • RED

Wine	Description	Price	Stockists	Award
Pisano RPF Tannat 1997, Pisano Progreso	*Round and mellow with good fruit depth and fine grained tannins. Drinking well now.*	**£8.90**	SVT HWL	B
Pisano RPF Pinot Noir 1996, Pisano Progreso	*WIth sweet dark fruit and farmyard aromas this wine has pleasing fruit concentration and balance.*	**£9.00**	SVT HWL	B

South Africa

The awarding of a Pinotage Trophy this year is a sure sign that South Africa is a force to be reckoned with on the world stage. Winemakers are forging ahead making their own individual styles that seek not to emulate those of Australia or France but rather respond to, and capture, the essence of this most natural and spectacular country. These pages offer a journey into a range of proven conisistent performers as well as new and exciting styles that offer sensory stimulation, satisfaction and superb value.

SOUTH AFRICA • FORTIFIED

Wine	Description	Price	Stockists	Award
Graham Beck Rhona Muscadel 1996, Graham Beck Wines Robertson	*Barley sugar and candied peel with excellent floral fruit characters and a good delicate finish.*	£6.00	L&T	S

SOUTH AFRICA • RED

Wine	Description	Price	Stockists	Award
Diemersdal Shiraz 1998, Diemerdal Estate Coastal Region	*Sweet ripe blackberries, cherries and spice lead to a rounded smoky mid palate and long conclusion.*	£3.80	TOS	B
Cape Piper Cinsault Pinotage 1998, Cape Vinex Western Cape	*Atrractive nose with hints of cherry and plum leading to a well-balanced palate, a clean finish.*	£4.00	ORB	B
Two Tribes Red NV, Western Wines Southern Hemisphere	*Lighter style with good strawberry fruits and smooth tannins coming to a clean, fresh finish.*	£4.00	TOS SMF BKT CRS CWS WST	B

Wine	Description	Price	Stockists	Award
Two Oceans Cabernet Merlot 1998, Bergkelder Western Cape	*Vibrant youthful colour showing attractive berry and subtle cedary characters, with a comfortable easy finish.*	£4.70	PFC	S
Plantation Ruby Cabernet 1998, Vinfruco Robertson	*Nearly black in colour with huge dark cherry and blackberry aromas and a luscious middle palate.*	£4.80	SAF IWS	B
Oak Village Cabernet Sauvignon 1996, Vinfruco Coastal Region	*Classic mint and oaky nose leads to a deep, complex palate, with a smooth and lingering flavour.*	£4.90	CWS WRC BUP MAR THS VNF	B
Fairview Malbec 1998, Charles Back Paarl	*Inviting spicey berry fruits that introduce a crushed fruit palate of impressive length.*	£5.00	WTS CHN	B
Fairview Zinfandel Carignan 1998, Charles Back Paarl	*Rich jammy plum nose, generous length of palate with licorice and smokey bacon balanced perfectly.*	£5.00	ODD CHN	B
Graham Beck Railroad Red 1998, Graham Beck Wines Robertson	*Young ruby colour, a light, easy style wine that offers complexity through several layers of fruit.*	£5.00	L&T	B
Kleinbosch Young Vatted Pinotage 1998, Wine Cellars & International Wine Services Winemakers Paarl	*A pleasingly ripe nose with good wood and damson and a pleasant smoky finish.*	£5.00	SAF	B
Long Mountain Merlot Syrah 1998, Long Mountain Wine Co Stellenbosch	*Malty, loganberry up front fruit with a lively palate holding a neat acid tail.*	£5.00	WTS CAX	B

Wine	Description	Price	Stockists	Award
Mount Disa Cape Salut 1997, Coppoolse & Finlayson Western Cape	*Notes of jammy fruit and barnyard aromas open onto a round, soft, full bodied palate, with good balance.*	**£5.00**	SEA	B
Simonsvlei Shiraz 1998, Simonsvlei Co-op Winery Coastal Region	*Plum and damson notes loaded with spice and leather, a warm spirity licorice palate, leads to an herbaceous finish.*	**£5.00**	SAF THP WST	S
Spruitdrift Pinotage 1998, Spruitdrift Cellars Western Cape	*Smoky nose of currants and spice, with a big tannin palate and well constructed finish.*	**£5.00**	SPR BKI	B
Tesco Beyers Truter Pinotage 1998, Beyerskloof Winery Stellenbosch	*A leathered, peppery nose that is followed by a course textured, fruit palate.*	**£5.00**	TOS	B
Kleine Zalze Cabernet Sauvignon 1997, Kleine Zalze Coastal Region	*Spicey, light nose, black-currant and vanilla on the palate with subtle tannins, elegantly balanced finishing long.*	**£5.20**	GRA	S
Château Libertas 1996, SFW Stellenbosch	*Intense nose of fruitcake with subtle barnyard characters herald in a well structured, lengthy palate.*	**£5.30**	SOA CDE CEN EPO CAX	B
Kleine Zalze Shiraz Vineyard Selection 1997, Kleine Zalze Coastal Region	*Rich nose with gentle fruit and a touch of oak, finishing with great balance and length.*	**£5.50**	GRA	B
Sainsbury Reserve Selection South African Pinotage 1998, Kanon Kop Stellenbosch	*Intense, spicey and smoky fruit nose with a commendable level of fruit weight on the palate.*	**£5.50**	JSM	B

SOUTH AFRICA • RED

Wine	Description	Price	Stockists	Award
Andrew Baine Cabernet Sauvignon Merlot 1998, Cape Vineyards Worcester	*Rich dark chocolate on the nose, a well structured palate of fine grained tannins and nice balanced acidity.*	**£6.00**	WST	B
Clos Malverne Cabernet Sauvignon Shiraz 1998, Clos Malverne Stellenbosch	*Spicey, ripe nose with good fruit concentration, some firm tannins and new oak, with considerable length.*	**£6.00**	WCR UNS BPW	B
Fairview Cabernet Franc Merlot 1997, Charles Back Paarl	*Complex earthy and red fruits flavours greet the nose while palate weight and good length complement this introduction.*	**£6.00**	GRT FUL CHN	B
Hercules Paragon Shiraz 1998, Simonsvlei Co-op Winery Coastal Region	*Lovely nose of black fruit and spicey white pepper, lively complex and chewy with austere tannins.*	**£6.00**	SMF WST	S
Kanonkop Kadette 1995, Kanonkop Estate Stellenbosch	*Developed farmyard characters, with touches of smoke and spice. A big wine ready to drink.*	**£6.00**	RSS	B
Longridge Bay View Pinotage 1998, Longridge Winery Western Cape	*Loads of fruit beautifully integrated with fine tannins, this wine is complex and structurally sound.*	**£6.00**	ODD NEG	B
Mount Disa Pinotage 1997, Coppoolse & Finlayson Western Cape	*Coffee, licorice and malasses make for an interesting style with lovely structure and good length.*	**£6.00**	SEA	B
Pinnacle Merlot 1998, Stellenbosch Vineyards Stellenbosch	*Ripe yet leafy nose, creamy, sweet, ripe fruit on palate with a long licorice finish.*	**£6.00**	TOS IWS	B

Wine	Description	Price	Stockists	Award
Savanha Pinotage 1998, Savanha Wines Western Cape	*Spicey notes sing from a fruit basket and cascade onto a sunny palate of dried fruits.*	**£6.00**	DEL	S
Clos Malverne Cabernet Sauvignon Shiraz 1997, Clos Malverne Stellenbosch	*Rich cassis and oak aromas with soft fruit flavour, well structured with crisp acidity.and considerable length.*	**£6.20**	UNS NYW BPW	S
Lievland Estate Wine Lievlander 1996, Lielvand Estate Stellenbosch	*Pleasant fruit and spice characters, well balanced with gentle use of oak, and having good length.*	**£6.20**	BWC	B
Marthinus Cabernet Sauvignon Merlot 1998, Bovlei Winery Paarl	*Deep purply black in colour, plum jam greets the nose before a creamy palate of graceful complexity.*	**£6.20**	BDR	B
The Pinotage Company Bush Vine Pinotage 1998, Claridge Estate Coastal Region	*Very attractive clean lifted fruits with a soft and generous palate. Finishes well.*	**£6.30**	L&W SAF MAR VWE NYW JLW	B
Altus Reserve Merlot 1997, Boland Vineyards Paarl	*Spice and bacon fat aromas, sweet vanilla and cassis fruit with tobacco with great balance and structure.*	**£6.40**	TRO BPW	B
Klein Constantia Shiraz 1997, Klien Constantia Constantia	*Plums and blackcurrants inter mingle with spicey oak, well structured to last, finishing long and strong.*	**£6.50**	BBR MGN MZC	G
Ruitersberg Reserve Cabernet Sauvignon 1997, Ruitersvlei Wine Estate Paarl	*Rich, red berry fruit and mint lead to a palate full of ripe, cleansing tannins.*	**£6.50**	BWC	S

SOUTH AFRICA • RED

Wine	Description	Price	Stockists	Award
Marthinus Cinsault Pinotage 1998, Bovlei Winery Paarl	*Ginger and spice on the nose, blend with fine fruity flavours perch on a finely grained tannin palate.*	**£6.70**	BDR	B
Clos Malverne Pinotage Basket Pressed 1998, Clos Malverne Stellenbosch	*Aromatic soft fruits on the nose lead to cherries, almonds and cedar with a dash of spice.*	**£6.90**	UNS WCR NYW WTS FUL TOS BPW	S
Cardouw Pinotage 1998, Goue Vallei Winery Western Cape	*A rounded fruit nose with a hint of oak leads to a savoury palate and neat finish.*	**£7.00**	CDT WAV	B
Graham Beck Shiraz 1997, Graham Beck Wines Robertson	*Black fruit and white pepper on the nose, this is a spicey, complex wine with firm tannins.*	**£7.00**	L&T	S
La Bri Cabernet Merlot Reserve 1996, La Bri Vineyards Franschoek	*A neat cedary style with nice fruit on the palate and good length of flavour.*	**£7.00**	LAU	B
Mount Disa Shiraz 1998, Coppoolse & Finlayson Western Cape	*Spicey aromas of white pepper carry over onto a smooth palate of creamy oak with smoky, meaty elements.*	**£7.00**	FUL SEA	S
Sommerbosch Cabernet Sauvignon Merlot Reserve 1997, Sommerbosch Wines Stellenbosch	*Mid plum colour with nice vanilla oak, a soft inititial palate with spice indicating further development .*	**£7.00**	SPR BKI	B
Paradyskloof Pinotage 1996, Vriesenhiof Estate Stellenbosch	*A smattering of ginger spice characters and ripe fruits taper into a fine, fruit finish.*	**£7.10**	CTH FTH	S

Wine	Description	Price	Stockists	Award
Springfield Estate Cabernet Sauvignon 1995, Springfield Estate Robertson	*Stewed and candied fruits are the offerings of this cheeky down to earth number. Enjoy.*	**£7.30**	BWL ODF	B
Fleur du Cap Merlot 1996, Bergkelder Stellenbosch	*Meaty nose with fruity tones and a fleshy textured palate an enjoyable mellow drink.*	**£7.50**	PFC	B
Villiera Estate Cru Monro 1997, Villiera Wine Estate Paarl	*Sweet lifted raspberry and coconut aromas, with a concentrated and balanced palate that will gain complexity with age.*	**£7.50**	WRC BUP THS WST	B
Koopmanskloof Cabernet Sauvignon 1997, Koopmanskloof Estate Western Cape	*Nice tones of mint coming through some jammy fruit characters with attractive balancing tannins.*	**£7.60**	SPR BKI	B
Clos Malverne Pinotage Reserve Basket Pressed 1997, Clos Malverne Stellenbosch	*A powerful nose of smoky fruits shine onto a full flavoured palate with a chocolatey finish.*	**£7.80**	WCR NYW FUL BPW	B
Fairview Cyril Back Zinfandel 1997, Fairview Paarl	*Vanilla and coconut nose, blueberries, cedar, plummy flavours and creamy oak shine on a balanced palate.*	**£7.80**	CHN	S
Dieu Donné Cabernet Sauvignon Merlot 1997, Dieu Donné Paarl	*Plums and rounded fruit flavours on the palate integrate with cedary oak and balancing crisp minty acidity.*	**£8.00**	PAT	G
Yonder Hill Merlot 1997, Yonder Hill Stellenbosch	*Ripe mulberries and caffe latte aromas escape from a palate of nice fruit structure and length.*	**£8.00**	RSS	B

SOUTH AFRICA • RED

Wine	Tasting note	Price	Stockists	Award
Villiera Estate Wine Shiraz 1997, Villiera Wine Estate Paarl	*Ground white pepper and rich fruit on a smooth creamy palate of vanilla fruit.*	**£8.30**	WST	B
Villiera Merlot 1997, Villiera Wine Estate Paarl	*Ripe plums and blackcurrants lead to a well balanced palate with a cleansing tannin tail.*	**£8.30**	WRC BUP THS WST	G
Jordan Merlot 1996, Jordan Winery Stellenbosch	*Aged savoury characters intertwined with fruit jams and spice follow through nicely onto smooth velvety palate.*	**£8.40**	GGW AUS	S
Kumala Reserve Cabernet Sauvignon 1998, Sonop Stellenbosch	*Earthy blackcurrant nose with smoke and tar. Rich, ripe fruit, full tannins with a warm finish.*	**£8.70**	VLW SMF ODD TOS WST	G
Cathedral Cellar Pinotage 1996, KWV Paarl	*Intense currant and cherries with a sprinkling of cinnamon, showing depth, poise and astonishing length.*	**£8.90**	NYW BPW ODD TOS WTS	G, TROPHY WINE
La Motte Millennium 1994, Bergkelder Franschhoek Valley	*Hints of licorice and a touch of spirit, a powerful wine full of tannin and oak.*	**£9.00**	JNW PFC	B
Rustenberg Stellenbosch Cabernet Merlot 1998, Rustenberg Cape Town	*Meaty blackcurrant nose with forward fruit, a light, initial fruit palate, but rich and earthy with good length.*	**£9.00**	MZC	G
Kumala Reserve Merlot 1998, Sonop Stellenbosch	*Green peppery nose, ripe, jammy palate with blackcurrants, ending with good acid balance and supple tannins.*	**£9.20**	VLW ODD WST	S

Wine	Tasting note	Price	Stockists	Award
Simonsig Tiara 1996, Simonsig Estate Stellenbosch	*Vegetal, earthy aromas with soft berry fruits, a minty, vegetal palate with good oak towards a lingering finish.*	**£9.50**	SOA CAP PAR SEL LAW	B
RheboksklOof Estate Cabernet Sauvignon 1996, Rheboksklоof Estate Paarl	*Smoky, chocolatey nose, sweet and rich palate. Delicate fruit with soft tannins, very velvety and harmonious.*	**£9.60**	CAC CCW	S
Allesverloren Shiraz 1995, Allesverloren Estate Stellenbosch	*Deep inky red with intense spicey leather and soft ripe fruit notes. Firm tannins and bramble fruit finish.*	**£9.70**	MMD	S
Constantia Uitsig Merlot 1996, Constantia Uitsig Constantia	*Green and stalky on nose with some chocolate. Green palate with prune flavours, well structured.*	**£9.80**	WRC MAR VWE NYW BPW	B
Boschendal Merlot 1996, Boschendal Paarl	*Some ageing apparent as earthy, fruitcake flavours come to the fore. Austere palate but good to drink now.*	**£10.00**	ADN F&M EDC TPE PHI PRG	B
Boschendal Shiraz 1996, Boschendal Paarl	*A rich palate of sweet plummy fruit with lots of tarry spice notes. A hint of mint and eucalyptus.*	**£10.00**	QWW ETV NYW WON SAN F&M PRG	S
Longridge Merlot 1997, Longridge Winery Stellenbosch	*Deep purple with crimson rings small berried fruits ring the bells of a palate that grips and goes on.*	**£10.00**	ODD NEG	B
Uiterwyk Pinotage 1996, Uiterwyk Estate Coastal Region	*A rich and complex wine with herby and gamey notes. Nice drying fruit tannins play a lovely role.*	**£10.40**	RBS L&W NYW JLW	B

Wine	Description	Price	Stockists	Award
BELLINGHAM CABERNET SAUVIGNON 1997, DGB Western Cape	*Toasty oak nose and chocolate precede concentrated tannin and gutsy fruit before a firm finish.*	**£11.00**	EHL	B
BELLINGHAM PREMIUM PINOTAGE 1997, DGB Western Cape	*A flattering nose of fruit pastilles and vanilla introduces a smoky, juicy fruit palate with a tobacco finish.*	**£11.00**	EHL	B
BELLINGHAM PREMIUM SHIRAZ 1996, DGB Stellenbosch	*An inviting, peppery nose, with blackberries and jammy fruit flavours on the palate and a fine conclusion.*	**£11.00**	EHL	S
LE RICHE RESERVE CABERNET SAUVIGNON 1997, ETIENNE LE RICHE Stellenbosch	*Dense fruit on nose, smoky aromas. Rich, dark cherry and chocolate palate. Good balance.*	**£11.70**	GSH BPW	S
BEYERSKLOOF CABERNET 1996, BEYERSKLOOF Stellenbosch	*Oak and spice aromas on the nose blossom in the mouth with sweet vanilla and rich fruit.*	**£12.00**	VLW RSS	S
GALPIN PEAK PINOT NOIR 1997, BOUCHARD FINLAYSON Walkers Bay	*Reasonably concentrated, with a full weighty palate. Ripe tannins are well balanced with sweet baked fruit.*	**£12.00**	WTS	B
L'AVENIR PINOTAGE 1997, L'AVENIR ESTATE Stellenbosch	*Plump fruits and beautiful wood leans on a cherry ripe palate of great depth with a clean finish.*	**£12.10**	WIN NYW BPW	S
BOUCHARD FINLAYSON GALPIN PEAK PINOT NOIR 1997, BOUCHARD FINLAYSON Walker Bay	*Strawberries with light vegetal aromas, soft, well rounded tannins and very good length.*	**£12.60**	BWL FUL WTS NYW	S

Wine	Description	Price	Stockists	Award
KANONKOP CABERNET SAUVIGNON 1995, KANONKOP ESTATE Stellenbosch	*Oaky nose - classic and young. Ripe, full-bodied palate with iron grip of tannins.*	**£12.70**	VLW RSS	B
HAUTES CABRIÈRE PINOT NOIR 1997, CABRIÈRE ESTATE Franschhoek	*Green pea, vegetal nose with ripe, vibrant berry fruit characters on the palate. Good length.*	**£14.20**	NYW ENO	B
MEERLUST RUBICON 1994, MEERLUST ESTATE Stellenbosch	*A lovely minty nose surrounded by ripe fruit meets a well balanced palate.*	**£16.00**	RBS GSH MMD	B
AGUSTA COUNT AGUSTA CABERNET SAUVIGNON 1997, COUNT AUGUSTA Paarl	*Lovely full flavoured cherry fruit on the nose with a hint of boiled sweet, a fullsome palate and lengthy finish.*	**£16.40**	NYW LIB	B
HAMILTON RUSSELL PINOT NOIR 1997, HAMILTON RUSSELL Walker Bay	*Amazing depth of flavour, stewed strawberries, earthy mushrooms and feral aromas flow to the supple palate.*	**£17.00**	Widely Available	B

SOUTH AFRICA • SPARKLING

Wine	Description	Price	Stockists	Award
PONGCRAZ SPARKLING METHODE CAPE CLASSIC NV, BERGKELDER Western Cape	*A gorgeous bouquet with toasty slightly burnt also floral aromas and classy complexity on the palate.*	**£9.00**	PFC	B
PIERRE JOURDAN BLANC DE BLANCS NV, CABRIERE ESTATE Paarl	*Yeasty aromas with minty citrus fruit on the nose and palate and a clean acid tail.*	**£13.00**	RBS ENO	B

SOUTH AFRICA • SWEET

Vin de Constance 1993, Klein Constantia Constantia	*Lovely fresh rose petals and marmalade, appealing viscosity in the mouth with crisp acid and good length.*	**£17.00**	MZC	(B)

SOUTH AFRICA • WHITE

Pacific Wines Cape Chardonnay 1998, Pacific Wines Stellenbosch	*Soft, creamy characters with pleasant lime fruit and a very clean and crisp finish.*	**£4.50**	UNS	(B)
Sable View Chardonnay 1998, SFW Stellenbosch	*A very perfumed nose of flowers and cream follow on to a well balanced palate.*	**£4.50**	CEN DIO SLM CAX	(B)
Tesco Robertson Chardonnay Colombard NV, John Worontschak Stellenbosch	*Ripe tropical fruits are joined by herbal nuances on the nose, palate shows balanced oak and finishes cleanly.*	**£4.50**	TOS EHL	(B)
Spar South African Classic White NV, Madeba Robertson	*Citrus fruit with hints of gooseberries on the nose, the palate is clean and soft.*	**£4.60**	SPR	(S)
Longridge Bay View Chenin Blanc Chardonnay 1998, Longridge Winery Western Cape	*Lovely ripe soft fruit driven palate with some grip and complexity, clean on the finish.*	**£4.70**	QWW SPR NEG	(B)

Wine	Description	Price	Stockists	Award
KLEINE ZALZE CHENIN BLANC BARREL FERMENTED 1998, KLEINE ZALZE Stellenbosch	*Earthy fuller style wine with big ripe fruit, quite a lot of oak and soft acidity.*	**£4.80**	NYW GRA	B
PINNACLE CHENIN BLANC 1998, STELLENBOSCH VINEYARDS Stellenbosch	*Lovely herby, green apples on the nose travel well through the fresh crisp palate.*	**£5.00**	TOS IWS	S
LONGRIDGE BAY VIEW CHENIN BLANC CHARDONNAY 1997, LONGRIDGE WINERY Western Cape	*Depth, weight and complexity plus herbal overtones make for an interesting wine.*	**£5.40**	SPR	B
KLEINE ZALZE CHARDONNAY BARREL FERMENTED 1998, KLEINE ZALZE Stellenbosch	*Ripe tropical fruit on the nose trumpets generous vanilla oak characters and a decisive finish.*	**£5.50**	GRA FRT	B
NEDERBURG CHARDONNAY 1998, SFW Paarl	*Perfumed lime and citrus nose with light clean fresh fruit and slightly vegetal notes on the palate.*	**£5.50**	CDE CAP SOA VWE CAX	B
FAIRVIEW CHARDONNAY 1998, CHARLES BACK Paarl	*Candied citrus nose with peppery fruit and vanilla overtones introduce mouthfillling fruit characters with a fine oak veil.*	**£6.00**	UNS CWS TOS CHN	S
HERCULES PARAGON SEMILLON 1998, SIMONSVLEI CO-OP WINERY Coastal Region	*Rich guava and pineapples with fresh cream are apparent, the palate is balanced with drying oak.*	**£6.00**	WST	B
SAINSBURY SOUTH AFRICAN RESERVE SELECTION CHARDONNAY 1998, SAINSBURY'S Coastal Region	*Oak dominated with fresh fruit buttery nose and rounded palate leading to a clean fruit finish.*	**£6.00**	HBR JSM	B

Wine	Tasting note	Price	Stockists	Award
WELTEVREDE GEWÜRZTRAMINER 1998, WELTEVREDE Robertson	*A very unusual bouquet offering notes of soft vanilla ice cream flavours rising from a vinous palate with steely notes.*	£6.20	RBS NYW FEN AVB HOH	S
CONSTANTIA UITSIG CHARDONNAY 1998, CONSTANTIA UITSIG Constantia	*A lemony, minerally nose signal a crisp, well balanced palate with nice acidity and fruit flavours.*	£6.30	GSH BPW	B
BRAMPTON CHARDONNAY 1997, RUSTENBERG Constantia	*Lovely structured honeysuckle and vanilla tones sit happily in a crisp casing and offer good length.*	£6.50	MZC	B
CONSTANTIA UITSIG SAUVIGNON BLANC 1998, CONSTANTIA UITSIG Constantia	*Nice fragrant, sweet, herbal fruit here, good balance of acid and fruit sweetness, finishing long.*	£6.50	BPW	B
VERGELEGEN SAUVIGNON BLANC 1998, VERGELEGEN Coastal Region	*Attractive florals and asparagus to start, with a minerally, citric palate evolving with character.*	£6.50	TOS AMF	B
FAIRVIEW CYRIL BACK SEMILLON 1998, FAIRVIEW Paarl	*Citrus and tropical fruit mix with new oak on the nose and nice warmth and length on the palate.*	£7.00	CHN	B
SAXENBERG SAUVIGNON BLANC 1998, SAXENBERG ESTATE Stellenbosch	*Green beans and asparagus, very rich almost fat in the mouth leading to a concentrated finish.*	£7.00	FWM BBR	S
THANDI ELGIN CHARDONNAY 1998, LEBANON FARM Elgin	*Subtle oak characters from this rounded and soft wine offering a clean citrus finish.*	£7.00	VNF	B

Wine	Description	Price	Stockists	Award
Backsberg Chardonnay 1998, Backsberg Paarl	*Bold oak on the nose and palate. Sweet round fruit with good acid and finish.*	£7.30	HOF CHH SOA ECA	B
L'Avenir Chenin Blanc 1998, L'Avenir Estate Stellenbosch	*A flinty nose leads to a full round fruit palate with very pleasant integrated acidity and impressive length.*	£7.40	UNS GSH NYW BPW	S
Simonsig Stellenbosch Chardonnay 1997, Simonsig Estate Stellenbosch	*Remarkably complex fruit characters float over a biscuity gingerbread oak palate wih a clean mineral finish.*	£7.60	WCR NYW SEL SOA CAP PAR LAW	G
Jordan Blanc Fumé 1998, Jordan Winery Stellenbosch	*Nice fresh, smokey, aromatics showing grapefruit with a nutty, leesy overlay. Quality oak with crisp acidity.*	£7.70	GGW AUS	S
Dewetsshof Estate Chardonnay d'Honneur 1998, Dewetshof Estate Robertson	*Exotic honey aromas, lime fruit characters and firm acidity in harmony with balanced oak, wonderful lime finish.*	£8.00	VLW RSS	S
Glen Carlou Chardonnay 1998, Glen Carlou Paarl	*Subtle oranges and lemon on the nose. Dried fruit characters with buttery oak on the palate.*	£8.00	AUS	B
Spier Block Chardonnay 1998, Spier South Africa	*Citrus driven nose with touches of vanilla stem from a palate of peardrop and lychee characters.*	£8.00	PLB	S
Constantia Uitsig Chardonnay Reserve 1997, Constantia Uitsig Constantia	*Aromas of melon and creamy vanilla oak, the palate consists of lovely fleshy tropical fruit.*	£8.10	WCR NYW BPW	G

SOUTH AFRICA • WHITE

Klein Constantia Sauvignon Blanc 1998, Klein Constantia Constantia	*Honeyed goosberries, cut grass and nettles, very complex with superb fruit grip and excellent follow through.*	**£8.20**	NYW VWC L&W TAN CAC MZC	G
Klein Constantia Estate Chardonnay 1998, Klein Constantia Constantia	*Plenty of upfront ripe fruit here with lovely melon and gooesberry notes. A subtle oak palate leads to a pleasant finish.*	**£8.30**	UNS MSF WFL SOA CAC MZC	S
Jordan Chardonnay 1997, Jordon Winery Stellenbosch	*Creamy oak and delicate fruit aromas dance from a palate of subtle fruit and well integrated oak.*	**£8.50**	UNS CTH GGW WTS	B
Jordon Chardonnay 1998, Jordon Winery Stellenbosch	*Apple, peach and pineapple follow on to the palate with additional lime and lemon characters.*	**£8.70**	UNS CTH GGW NYW AUS	S
Rustenberg Chardonnay 1998, Rustenberg Stellenbosch	*Honeyed fruit and earth characteristics lead to a palate with plenty of fresh, green fruit, and a zippy finish.*	**£8.70**	NYW MZC	S
Boschendal Chardonnay Reserve 1997, Boschendal Paarl	*Rich, creamy aromas and flavours of pineapples, mangoes and melons with vanilla and zippy lime.*	**£8.80**	Widely Available	S
Agusta Chardonnay Reserve 1998, Agusta Coastal Region	*Lemon and buttery toasty oak on the nose, creamy vanilla palate with tropical fruit characters.*	**£9.00**	LIB	S
Plaisir de Merle Chardonnay 1997, SFW Paarl	*Hints of pepper and spice on the nose with lots of ripe tropical fruit and well integrated oak.*	**£9.00**	CAP MWW TOS CAX	B

Wine	Description	Price	Stockists	Award
VERGELEGEN SAUVIGNON BLANC RESERVE 1998, VERGELEGEN Stellenbosch	*Powerful gooseberry with subtle grassy aromas, flinty and tight follow through on the palate.*	**£9.00**	AMF	B
HAMILTON RUSSELL CHARDONNAY 1998, HAMILTON RUSSELL Walker Bay	*Lovely lemon scented fruit salad leading to supportive oak and crisp acid to the balanced end.*	**£9.10**	Widely Available	S
HARTENBERG CHARDONNAY 1997, HARTENBERG Stellenbosch	*Cream and fruits on the nose lead to mouthfilling melon and peach flavours.*	**£9.80**	FWM BBR	S
VERGELEGEN CHARDONNAY RESERVE 1997, VERGELEGEN Stellenbosch	*Grapefruit with hints of cut grass on the nose. Fresh citrus palate, moderate acidity with good length.*	**£10.00**	TOS AMF	S
BOUCHARD FINLAYSON CHARDONNAY 1996, BOUCHARD FINLAYSON Walker Bay	*Rich sweet toasty aromas lead to a rich fruit palate of pineapples and melons.*	**£10.30**	BWL SAF	B
GLEN CARLOU CHARDONNAY RESERVE 1997, GLEN CARLOU Paarl	*Lovely charred nose leads to zingy, lively acidity with lime fruit and integrated mild oak on the palate.*	**£11.50**	AUS	B
HAMILTON RUSSELL CHARDONNAY 1997, HAMILTON RUSSELL Walker Bay	*Cashews and exotic honeyed notes provide the lead up to the zesty palate of taut structure.*	**£11.90**	Widely Available	S
COUNT AGUSTA CHARDONNAY 1998, AGUSTA Paarl	*Rich ripe fruit and nutty characters on the nose, palate of medium weight with a pleasant finish.*	**£13.00**	LIB	B

Spain

Spain is surging ahead with an enviable blend of the traditional, the unique, and the truly post-modern, reflected in a range of wine styles seldom found in any other wine producing country. This year, while Rioja's, La Mancha's and Valdepeñas put on their usual show stopping performances, hidden secrets such as those wines from Rias Baixas and the previously underrated Priorato's, are gaining vinous respect and appreciation faster than the approach of the new millenium. Search them out, Salud!

SPAIN • FORTIFIED

Wine	Description	Price	Stockists	Award
Tio Mateo Fino, Real Tesoro Jerez	*Bright, fresh, zesty, rich flor approach with the palate reminiscent of candied lemon peel and salted cashews.*	**£3.00**	THS TOS PLB	S
Sainsbury Palo Cortado, Francisco Gonzalez Fernandez Jerez	*Dry austere, nutty nose, good, clean and fresh. Slightly spirited and more commercial in style.*	**£3.50**	JSM	B
Moscatel Oro de Muller, De Muller Tarragona	*Elegant and light caramalised orange flavours on a fairly simple but incredibly enjoyable palate.*	**£3.60**	VLW COC JOB L&S	B
Cabrera Cream Sherry NV, D G Gordon Jerez	*Soft, quite rich figgy and oxidised aromas flowing to an uncomplicated palate and enjoyable finish.*	**£4.40**	WRT	B
Somerfield Cream Sherry, Espinosa de los Monteros Jerez	*Deep fragrant almond-toffee nose with a hint of vanilla and rancio. A popular cream style.*	**£4.40**	SMF	S

Wine	Description	Price	Stockists	Award
Tesco Palo Cortado Sherry, Sanchez Romate Jerez	*Caramel and interesting slightly leafy nose and array of palate flavours. Nicely balanced finish.*	**£5.00**	TOS	S
Dry Sack, Williams & Humbert Jerez	*Caramel and toffee on the nose, palate is not quite dry but has nice weight.*	**£5.50**	TOS BLN EHL	B
La Concha, Gonzalez Byass Jerez	*A very rich style offering exotic mineral characters with an incredibly cleansing palate of remarkable length.*	**£5.90**	UNS VLW SMF FDB	S
Pando Fino, Williams & Humbert Jerez	*Quite nutty nose with a light,tangy, salty palate showing good weight and length.*	**£6.20**	NYW WTS	B
Findlaters Dry Fly, Hidalgo Jerez	*Rich nuts and honey gliding into a long clean palate of sweet toffee, concluding crisply.*	**£6.30**	WTS	B
Harveys Club Classic, John Harvey Jerez	*Nutty nose. The palate is soft and smooth, quite sweet but pleasant, an easy drinking style.*	**£6.30**	Widely Available	S
Pedro Ximenez Cream Of Creams, Manuel de Argueso Jerez	*Rancio, huge sweet fruit and coffee creams, very sweet but balanced by ripe figgy fruit.*	**£6.30**	HWL SVT BEL DBY	S
NPU Amontillado, Sanchez Romate Jerez	*Roasted hazelnuts and butterscotch with a smidge of acetone. Palate shows good rancio and huge power.*	**£6.60**	EHL	S

Wine	Tasting note	Price	Stockists	Award
IBERIA CREAM, SANCHEZ ROMATE Jerez	*Nice coffee, walnut cake and figgy aromas, showing good structure and balance and an intriguing finish.*	£7.20	EHL	S
WAITROSE FINO SHERRY, LUIS CABALLERO Jerez	*Attractive nutty flor nose, palate showing characteristic zest and tang, well balanced, finishes well.*	£7.20	WTS	B
TIO PEPE, GONZALEZ BYASS Jerez	*Wow! Intense ripe flor with tangy lemon with moreish nutty oiliness leading to a refreshing finish.*	£7.80	UNS WAC VLW SMF MHV CWS FDB	G
OLOROSO ANADA 1918 ALMACENISTA PILAR ARANDA, EMILIO LUSTAU Jerez	*Lovely elegant nutty richness, dry and austere with fresh acidity and good palate weight.*	£7.80	NYW PHI PTR M&V	B
ALFONSO, GONZALEZ BYASS Jerez	*Smoky, nutty, dry caramel on nose, palate is spicy and dry with a quite fine finish.*	£7.90	VLW FDB	B
OLOROSSO VIEJO DE JEREZ ALMACENISTA BORREGO, EMILIO LUSTAU Jerez	*Spicey Christmas pudding on the nose, quite dry with good breadth, rather nicely done.*	£8.10	RBS NYW F&M M&V	B
MANZANILLA AMONTILLADO ALMACENISTA CUEVOS JURADO, EMILIO LUSTAU Jerez	*Inviting caramel nose, the palate shows some elegance and a little complexity, not for everyone.*	£8.20	RBS BDR NYW PTR PHI M&V	B
LOS ARCOS DRY AMONTILLADO, EMILIO LUSTAU Jerez	*Spicey raisins and sweet rancio aromas, the palate is a little burnt with a light dry finish.*	£8.30	M&V SHB NYW WWT F&M M&V	B

Wine	Tasting note	Price	Stockists	Award
Amontillado del Puerto Almacenista Obregon, Emilio Lustau Jerez	*Butterscotch and dried fruits, palate showing good hazelnuts and acid balance with a salty conclusion.*	£8.40	BDR NYW BTH SOM BOL LNL M&V	B
Palo Cortado Almacenista Vides, Emilio Lustau Jerez	*Nice, crisp ripe dried fruit and lovely creamy caramel, shows bold flavours and finishes cleanly.*	£8.40	RBS M&V F&M DBY	S
Capataz Andres Deluxe Cream, Emilio Lustau Jerez	*Lovely sweet sugared almonds and light rancio with a sniff of new oak, nice finish.*	£8.50	M&V DBY TPE MOR	B
Manzanilla Pasada de Sanlucar, Emilio Lustau Jerez	*Delicate nose of lemon blossom and tangy flor, refreshing palate with a hint of sweetness.*	£8.50	RDW WHI F&M GRT RBS M&V	B
Old East India, Emilio Lustau Jerez	*Dense smoky,nutty and orange nose. Excellent depth and structure with balance, fantastic acidity and length.*	£9.00	NYW F&M GRT DBY EVI MOR M&V	S
Oloroso Viejo, Manuel de Argueso Jerez	*Fantastic stewed prunes, plums and mature oloroso characters, elegant grip. Bursting with character, utterly delicious.*	£9.50	SVT EBA RIC HWL	G
Sandeman Royal Corregidor, House Of Sandeman Jerez	*Very rich nuttiness and sweet spirit aromas. The palate comes in waves of powerful pungent fruitcakey characters.*	£9.60	RBS ODD F&M HAR ROD SEA	S
Dos Cortados, Williams & Humbert Jerez	*Lovely allspice, almonds and dried peel with complexing aldehydes. Mind blowing depth, who said sherry was dying??*	£9.70	UNS BDR NYW WTS BLN EHL	G

SPAIN • FORTIFIED

Wine	Description	Price	Stockists	Award
Barbadillo Reliquia, Antonio Barbadillo Jerez	*An incredibly complex nose displaying layers of phenolics, VA and perfumed fruits. An awesome, challenging wine.*	£10.00	NYW JEF	S
Oloroso Cream "Vina el Alamo", Pedro Romero Jerez	*Toffee, treacle and rich dried fruit on the nose, good mid-palate, nice warm and long.*	£10.00	EBC	B
Oloroso Dry "Vina el Alamo", Pedro Romero Jerez	*Lovely coffee bean, caramel and nutty approach, palate is pleasingly dry, well balanced finishing long.*	£10.00	EBC	S
San Emilio Pedro Ximinez, Emilio Lustau Jerez	*Rich, intense fresh fig and prune nose, palate showing nice rancio and caramel richness, good length.*	£10.70	NYW MFS BTH DBY JUS M&V	B
Domecq Amontillado 51-1A NV, Domecq Jerez	*Golden brown with caramel and toffee nose, palate has nice saltiness with a good nutty finish.*	£15.00	ADD	B
Domecq Sibarita NV, Domecq Jerez	*Lovely mixed nuts and dried fruit, layers of complex, intense flavours offering very sensual mouthfeel.*	£15.00	ADD	G TROPH WIN
Sandeman Royal Ambrosante, House Of Sandeman Jerez	*Warm creme brulee, raisins, figs and toffee, gorgeously unctuous with a very clean finish, simply delicious.*	£15.00	TBA SEA	G
Matusalem Oloroso Dulce Muy Viejo, Gonzalez Byass Jerez	*Big powerful raisins flowing to a rich palate of nutty caramel and molasses. Brilliant, and sweet.*	£15.10	UNS VLW WTS	G

Wine	Description	Price	Stockists	Medal
Apostoles Palo Cortado Muy Viejo, Gonzalez Byass Jerez	*Buckets of raisins, orange zest and prunes on the intense nose. Rich nutty layered palate. Yum!*	**£17.10**	RBS VLW WTS FDB	S
Barbadillo Principe, Antonio Barbadillo Jerez	*Soft, loose sweetness on the nose but the palate tightens displaying attractive cashews, attractive finish.*	**£20.00**	JEF RSW POP JEF	B
Noë Muy Viejo, Gonzalez Byass Jerez	*Liquid Christmas pudding! Showing lovely depth and balance, like a ball bearing of flavour in the mouth.*	**£20.00**	VLW FDB	S
Del Duque Amontillado, Gonzalez Byass Jerez	*Light fruit cake covered in warm caramel, nice palate with cutting acidity and a drying finish.*	**£20.50**	RBS VLW FDB	B
Cardinal Cisnero - PX, Sanchez Romate Jerez	*Awesome rancio and raisins with burnt toffee, balanced sweetness and waves of flavour.*	**£20.90**	EHL	G
Palo Cortado Solera Pap, Bodegas Osborne Jerez	*Very fresh, sharp, pungent nose displaying caramel coated nuts. Well made with a very pleasant finish.*	**£22.00**	HBJ	S
Prestige Palo Cortado Hijo de Pedro Romero, Pedro Romero Jerez	*Remarkable wine of great complexity and depth showing notes of almonds and marzipan.*	**£40.00**	EBC	S

Pinpoint who sells the wine you wish to buy by turning to the stockist codes. If you know the name of the wine you want to buy, use the alphabetical index. If the price is your motivation, refer to the invaluable price guide index; red and white wines under £5, sparkling wines under £12 and Champagne under £16. Happy hunting!

SPAIN • RED

Wine	Description	Price	Stockists	Award
Gandia Co-op Tempranillo Oak Aged NV, Vicente Gandia Utiel-Requena	*A perplexing nose with a fleshy texture and notes of plum, damson and rhubarb.*	**£3.50**	CWS	B
Don Darias NV, Bodegas Victorianas Vino de Mesa	*A jammy, floral nose with a hint of herb and nice vanilla flavoured tannins.*	**£3.80**	UNS SMF SAF TOS WRC PLB	B
Covinca Venturoso Tempranillo Garnacha 1998, Co-Op Covinca Cariñena	*Concentrated blackberry fruits with a good dose of raspberry and vanilla give rise to a happy tail.*	**£4.00**	IWS	S
Fuente del Ritmo 1997, Boedgas Centro Espanolas La Mancha	*Plum colour with evolving berry fruit on the nose and a drying sweetish fruit finish.*	**£4.00**	WTS FUL WST	B
Phoenix Old Vine Garnacha 1998, Castell Bel Art Terra Alta	*Perfumed sweet plums and cherries joined by a waft of spice. Well balanced with soft tannins.*	**£4.00**	TOS PLB	S
Remonte Cabernet Sauvignon Crianza 1996, Co-Op Vinicola Murchantina Navarra	*Plenty of up front fruit and some developed leafy characters and smooth tannins leading to a memorable finish.*	**£4.00**	BUP MRN THS BGL	S
Viña Fuerte Garnacha 1998, Bodega San Gregorio Calatayud	*Heady perfumed berry and raspberry notes seep into a full bodied palate with great length and finesse.*	**£4.00**	WTS	S

Wine	Description	Price	Stockists	Award
SIERRA ALTA TEMPRANILLO 1998, MOTA DEL CUERVO La Mancha	*A very spicey nose with a hint of spinach leads to a fruity palate with good length.*	**£4.30**	SMF EHL	B
VIÑA ALBALI RESERVA 1993, VINA ALBALI Valdepeñas	*Sweet chewy oak and a clean finish of fresh apples and pears.*	**£4.40**	Widely Available	B
BODEGAS PIRENOS ESPIRAL CABERNET SAUVIGNON TEMPRANILLO 1997, BODEGAS PIRENOS Somontano	*Pecan nuts and tight fruit on the nose introduce a nicely structured palate with firm tannins.*	**£4.50**	IWS WTS	S
SAFEWAY CASTILLO DE SIERRA RIOJA NV, VINEDOS DE ALDEANUEVA Rioja	*Soft, ripe fruit well balanced with good acidity and a lovely finish.*	**£4.50**	SAF	B
LOMASOL TINTO GRAN RESERVA 1989, BODEGAS MIGUEL CALATAYUD Valdepeñas	*Lots of oak with a plum edge on the nose announce a nice long oak palate.*	**£4.60**	SPR BKI	B
CASTAÑO CASARIO CRIANZA 1996, BODEGAS CASTANO Yecla	*Nice ripe fruit with balancing tannins and a splash of damson in the mouth.*	**£4.70**	EHL	B
ESPIRAL MORISTEL TEMPRANILLO 1998, BODEGAS PIRINEOS Somontano	*Ripe fruit with good concentration and very firm tannins and a pleasant fruit acid finish.*	**£4.80**	TOS IWS	S
MARCO REAL GARNACHA CRIANZA 1996, BODEGAS MARCO REAL Navarra	*Blackcurrant, cassis and winegums with warm fruits on the palate and a pleasant finish.*	**£4.80**	TOS PLB	B

SPAIN • RED

Wine	Description	Price	Stockists	Award
Baso 1998, Cia de Vinos de la Granja Navarra	*Clean,fresh fruit with medium level acidity and a pleasant bubble gum finish.*	£5.00	ADN THS JNW HAS	B
Castaño Viña Montana Monastrel Merlot 1998, Bodegas Castano Yecla	*Dried fruits and figs with a big dose of vanilla cream on the palate. Super tannins to balance.*	£5.00	SMF TOS EHL	G
Fuente del Ritmo Reserva 1994, Bodegas Centro Espanolas La Mancha	*Vivacious plummy berry fruit leading to well balanced tannins and a soulful finish.*	£5.00	WST	B
Mota del Cuervo Viniberia Sierra Alta Premium Tempranillo 1998, Viniberia La Mancha	*Blackberry blue with deep blackcurrant pastilles on the nose and a wash of cherry.*	£5.00	SOM EHL	B
Pere Ventura Tempranillo 1994, Pere Ventura Penedès	*Cherry leather nose with ripe fruit and good depth. Well balanced and soft in the mouth.*	£5.00	CDT WAV	B
Berberana "Dragon" Tempranillo 1997, Bodegas Berberana Rioja	*Rounded inviting nose of damson and vanilla flows nicely onto the palate to meet firm tannins.*	£5.10	SMF CWS BWC TOS D&D	S
Lar de Barros 1996, Bodegas Inviosa Riberio del Guadiana	*Well integrated fruit and oak nose with a good dousing of coffee and tar.*	£5.20	WAW ADN BEN NYW HAS	S
Gandia Reserva Cabernet Sauvignon 1995, Vicente Gandia Utiel Requena	*Ripe red fruits and mint flow on to the palate where grainy tannins lead to a neat finish.*	£5.30	PLB	B

Wine	Description	Price	Stockists	Award
Miguel Torres Sangredetoro 1996, Miguel Torres Penedès	*Jammy fruits with vanillin oak introduce a firm palate with savoury notes before dovetailing into a clean acid finish.*	**£5.30**	THS EUR FEN MOR MRN TOS	G
Señorio de los Llanos Reserva 1995, Bodegas los Llanos Valdepeñas	*Wood dominant with some jam treats in this big wine showing a firm palate and neat tail.*	**£5.30**	RBS VLW TOS SAN LAY L&S	B
Masia Bach Merlot 1996, Masia Bach Penedès	*Ripe, red fruit on the nose follows on to the palate with nice body and firm tannins.*	**£5.40**	SAF FRT GSJ	B
Orobio Tempranillo Rioja 1998, Cosecheros Alaveses Rioja	*Classic style with bright plum and cherry fruits with a rich vein of vanillin oak.*	**£5.50**	TOS VTS	B
Viñas del Vero Cabernet Sauvignon 1997, Viñas del Vero Somontano	*Intense minty cassis nose lead to a dry, spicy, minty palate with well-defined fruit and soft tannins.*	**£5.50**	UNS DWS	B
Capcanes Mas Collet 1997, Capcanes Tarragona	*Forward violet and vanilla style. Chunky fruits fill the firm well structured palate.*	**£5.60**	JNW	S
Guelbenzu Jardin Garnacha 1998, Bodegas Guelbenzu Navarra	*Big mouthful of rich slightly tart fruit with complexing nuttiness good structure finishing with drying tannins.*	**£5.60**	RBS JNW NYW WSO GRT MOR	B
Miguel Torres Coronas 1997, Miguel Torres Penedès	*Ripe, rich fruit with vanilla notes breathe through a palate layered with savoury, gamey and plummy flavours.*	**£5.80**	TOS	S

Wine	Tasting note	Price	Stockists	Award
VALLFORMOSA RESERVA 1994, MASIA VALLFORMOSA Penedès	*A nice vegetal nose with dried fruits. Mature and welcoming with very soft tannins .*	**£5.80**	FTH	B
GANDIA HOYA DE CADENAS TINTO RESERVA 1994, VICENTE GANDIA Utiel-Requena	*Stylish with complex spicey fruit on the nose and a saucy palate with a neat acid tail.*	**£6.00**	PLB	B
HUGE JUICY RED 1998, COOPERATIVA SAN GREGORIO Calatayud	*Fruit jam and violets with plenty of red fruit on the palate and a nice clean acid finish.*	**£6.00**	TOS IWS	B
JOAN D'ANGUERA 1998, CELLERS JOAN D'ANGUERA Tarragona	*Warm, ripe and spicey with subtle notes of mild, cooked black fruits and biscuits.*	**£6.00**	VLW BOO RAM LAY L&S	S
LOMASOL TINTO RESERVA 1993, BODEGAS MIGUEL CALATAYUD Valdepeñas	*Spicey with a hint of warmth and a palate of chewy tannins with a pleasant finish.*	**£6.00**	SPR BKI	B
MARQUÉS DE GRIÑON 1997, ARCO BODEGAS UNIDAS Rioja	*Spicey oak notes on a black cherry nose with rich fruit plate with integrated, firm tannins.*	**£6.00**	RBS WCR BWC D&D	S
VIA AURELIA MASIA LES COMES 1995, CONCAVINS Conca de Barbera	*Ripe, complex vanilla and orange peel nose. Fruity and tannic on the palate with a good finish.*	**£6.00**	HWL	B
VIÑA ALBALI TINTO GRAN RESERVA 1991, VINA ALBALI Valdepeñas	*Pleasant sweet fruit nose with chocolate notes and a nice tannin tail.*	**£6.00**	JMC CEL FUL WCR ASD PEC	B

Wine	Description	Price	Stockists	Award
Viña Albali Crianza 1995, Bodegas Felix Solis Valdepeñas	*A lighter style showing fragrant vanillin notes and a hint of milk chocolate.*	£6.10	PEC	B
Albet I Noya Lignum 1997, Albet I Noya Penedès	*Concentrated black fruits meet spicey oak on the nose and the palate shines with meaty tannins and fruity acidity.*	£6.50	VRT	G
Beronia Rioja Elaboracion Especial 1997, Bodegas Beronia Rioja	*A lighter style with a plum nose and sweetish, oaked finish. Clean and well balanced.*	£6.50	GBI GCF	B
Glorioso Rioja 1996, Bodegas Palacio Rioja	*Warm, ripe plummy fruits with a raisiny overtone. Lovely definition and length.*	£6.50	OHI	B
Miguel Torres Gran Sangre de Toro Reserva 1996, Miguel Torres Penedès	*Redcurrant and spices hang in an earthy air and join toasty oak on the palate.*	£6.50	MOR UNS JSM ROD GRO B&B SCA	S
Montecillo Viña Cumbrero Tinto 1996, Bodegas Montecillo Rioja	*Pleasant nose of ripe cherries and plums. Light weight palate with a long and clean finish.*	£6.50	HBJ	S
Pata Negra Gran Reserva 1991, Bodegas Los Llanos Valdepeñas	*Mature red with brown rim offers an intriguing nose of oak with a fragrant edge.*	£6.50	VLW LAY C&B SAN HWL L&S	S
Enate Rosado 1998, Enate Somontano	*Round, deep and long, a clean fruity wine with good acidity, warmth and mineral characters.*	£6.70	AVB SEL HOH	S

Wine	Description	Price	Stockists	Award
Monjardín Tinto Crianza 1995, Bodegas Castillo de Monjardin Navarra	*Floral nose with mulberry notes leads to a fleshy palate of fine fruity tannins and nicely balanced acidity.*	**£6.70**	VLW FSW SEL LAY L&S	S
Cosme Palacio y Hermanos Rioja 1996, Bodegas Palacio Rioja	*Rounded, ripe and mellow wine. Ready now with fruity pastilles and vanillin notes.*	**£6.90**	WCR UNS	B
Agapito Rico Carchello Shiraz 1998, Agapito Rico Jumilla	*Excellent young fruit and oak flows gracefully onto a bed of fine grained vanillin flavoured tannins.*	**£7.00**	FUL EHL	S
Cosme Palacio y Hermanos 1997, Bodegas Palacio Rioja	*A coconut and berry scented nose. Nice palate weight and chalky tannins lead to a pleasing fruit finish.*	**£7.00**	OHI	S
Enate Crianza 1996, Enate Somontano	*A gamey and plummy nose and a delicate palate of fresh fruits with fine tannins.*	**£7.00**	ODD WCR CFN A&N SEL HOH	B
Lagunilla Reserva 1994, Arco Bodegas Unidas Rioja	*Rich, warm and spicy nose showing coconut cream and toasty oak cascade onto a funky, fruit palate .*	**£7.00**	D&D	G
Marqués del Puerto Reserva 1994, Marqués del Puerto Rioja	*Sweet fruit with rustic tones meet a finely textured palate of some length.*	**£7.00**	CDT WAV	B
Miguel Torres Atrium 1998, Miguel Torres Penedès	*Complex and ripe showing fruits of the forest. Judicial use of oak creates a well balanced wine.*	**£7.00**	TOS	S

Wine	Description	Price	Stockists	Award
Señoria de Nava 1997, Pechiney Ribera del Duero	*Attractive spicey nose with a nice medium body and good mouthfeel leading to clean fruit finish.*	**£7.00**	UNS SPR	B
Señorio de Nava Tinto Cosecha 1997, Señorio de Nava Ribera del Duero	*Lovely herbaceous nose with underlying fruitcake characters, this is well structured and has the potential to travel.*	**£7.00**	PEC	S
Vicente Gandia Ceremonia 1996, Vicente Gandia Utiel-Requena	*Good ripe, hearty fruits with a firm tannin base, very powerful wine.*	**£7.00**	PLB	B
Dominio de Montalvo Tinto do Rioja 1996, Bodegas Campo Viejo Rioja	*Bright, beaming crimson colour offering a berry fruit and jammy nose with some spice.*	**£7.10**	WCR MAR VWE THS WSO BPW	B
Miralmonte Crianza 1996, Bodegas Frutos Villar Toro	*A burst of red action on the nose with groovy balance and hard rockin tannins.*	**£7.10**	L&S VLW LAY	B
Bodegas Agrosol Pers Tempranillo 1997, Bodegas Agrosol Almeria	*A lustrous purple colour with a chocolatey nose, a rich inky vein and porty characters*	**£7.20**	C&D	S
Campo Dorado Rioja Reserva 1995, Bodegas Olarra Rioja	*A medium weight style with a nice firm palate with a tangy cherry finsh.*	**£7.20**	MHV	B
Castaño Monastrel Tempranillo 1998, Bodegas Castano Yecla	*Nice struttin fruit with a fine tannin balance and generous finish.*	**£7.30**	EHL	B

Wine	Description	Price	Stockists	Award
Berberana Reserva 1994, Arco Bodegas Unidas Rioja	*Great vegetal nose with hints of cinnamon and cloves and an underlying fruit vein meet fine grained tannins.*	**£7.50**	NYW D&D	G
Campillo Rioja Crianza 1996, Bodegas Campillo Rioja	*A lovely burst of fruit with a nudge of vanilla oak flows onto the palate to meet firm tannins.*	**£7.50**	ASD VWC PLB	B
Campo Viejo Reserva 1994, Bodegas Campo Viejo Rioja	*A light and spicey style with hints of pepper. Palate is well structured and finishes cleanly.*	**£7.50**	Widely Available	B
Bodegas Ochoa Tempranillo Crianza 1996, Bodegas Ochoa Navarra	*Fantastic colour with lovely vanilla, woody notes and a soft, spicey palate with some meaty tannins and nice acidity.*	**£7.60**	WAW UNS L&W CAC DWS	B
Cosme Palacio y Hermanos Rioja 1996, Bodegas Palacio Rioja	*Inviting nose of plums and berries flow on to a jammy palate to mix with nicely integrated wood.*	**£7.60**	NIC	B
Baron de Ley Reserva 1995, Baron de Ley Rioja	*Rich smoky, gamey nose meets a mouthfilling palate of vanilla and plums.*	**£7.80**	CWS WRC BUP MAR THS GGW SKW ASD	S
Altun Rioja 1996, Monje Amestoy Rioja	*Concentrated vanillin and coconut cream nose. Good palate weight and a long finish.*	**£8.00**	BLN EHL	B
Artadi Viñas de Gain Crianza 1995, Cosecheros Anavesas Rioja	*Country stew with farmyardy and stable characters. Good middle palate with excellent length.*	**£8.00**	TOS VTS MWW	B

Wine	Tasting note	Price	Stockists	Award
LAN RESERVA 1995, BODEGAS LAN Rioja	*A light and elegant style showing vanilla oak and fruit on the nose and lovely follow through.*	**£8.00**	ABY	B
LAR DE LARES GRAN RESERVA 1994, BODEGAS INVIOSA Riberio del Guadiana	*Savoury popcorn oak nose with a broad mouth coating texture and full flavoured finish.*	**£8.00**	ADN PFT DBY HAS	B
ONDARRE RESERVA RIOJA 1995, BODEGAS ONDARRE Rioja	*Classic ripe Tempranillo fruit. Full bodied and ripe with great structure and balance.*	**£8.00**	WCR FEN AVB HOH	S
SEÑORIO DE NAVA CRIANZA 1996, SEÑORIO DE NAVA Ribera del Duero	*Enourmous structure with spice, prunes, tobacco and leather coming through. Nice length.*	**£8.00**	MHV PEC	B
BODEGAS AGROSOL PERS MONESTRAL 1997, BODEGAS AGROSOL Almeria	*A gamey, savoury nose signals a wine of wonderful complexity with notes of ripe berries and a smooth palate.*	**£8.10**	C&D	B
COTO DE IMAZ RESERVA 1994, EL COTO DE RIOJA Rioja	*Lively mint nose with summer fruits introduces a mid weight finely tuned palate with good length.*	**£8.30**	GGW CKB	S
MONTECILLO RESERVA 1994, BODEGAS MONTECILLO Rioja	*A lighter style but quite complex with clove, cinnamon and cherry aromas. A clean, lengthy finish.*	**£8.50**	HBJ	B
MONTECILLO RIOJA GRAN RESERVA 1991, BODEGAS MONTECILLO Rioja	*An old blockbuster with wonderful licorice and truffle complexities flow onto the palate with ease. Enjoy now.*	**£8.50**	HBJ	G

Wine	Description	Price	Stockists	Award
Palacio de la Vega Reserva 1995, PR Larios Navarra	*Smoky, meaty, gamey flavours with blackberry fruit offering smooth tannins.*	£8.50	CWS EPO ODD CAX	B
Sainsbury Classic Selection Rioja Reserva 1994, La Rioja Alta Rioja	*Rich aromatic berry fruits on the nose. Quite complex with nice use of oak, Interesting wine.*	£8.50	JSM	B
Solagüen Crianza 1996, Unión de Cosecheros Labastida Rioja	*Big soft fruits with plenth of earth. A nicely balanced wine with a sweet fruit palate.*	£8.50	TOS	B
Castell del Remei Merlot 1996, Castell del Remei Costers del Segre	*Some tar on the nose with mint aromas leading to soft oak and big berry and plum flavours.*	£8.70	MOR	B
Finca L'Argata 1997, Joan d'Anguera Tarragona	*Leathery, tarry notes before big fruit cake flavours and ripe, juicy tannins.*	£8.90	VLW NYW PHI SEL CEB LAY L&S	B
Marqués de Griñon Reserva 1994, Arco Bodegas Unidas Rioja	*Smoky savoury characters and stewed fruits meet spice and vanilla on a complex palate.*	£8.90	BWC NYW D&D	S
Marqués de Riscal Reserva 1995, Marqués de Riscal Rioja	*Rich, curranty oaky nose and a pleasant well balanced fruit and oak palate. Nice length.*	£9.00	UNS WAC GRT LPD	B
Marqués del Puerto Gran Reserva 1989, Marqués del Puerto Rioja	*A rich nose of pepper and spice, light in the mouth and with a pleasant finish.*	£9.00	CDT WAV	B

Wine	Description	Price	Stockists	Medal
Viña Alcorta Reserva 1994, Bodegas Campo Viejo Rioja	*Rich, leathery fruity nose. Cherries and strawberries emerge on the palate and finishes clean and dry.*	**£9.00**	BPW	B
Pinord Chateldon Gran Reserva 1993, Bodegas Pinord Penedès	*Earthy, spicey style with nudges of jam and red fruit on the palate. Nice dry finish.*	**£9.20**	VIM	B
Berberana Reserva Rioja 1989, Berberana Rioja	*Seductive aged aromas of spicey caramel and berry pie with excellent fruit intensity and a spicey tail.*	**£9.30**	CWS BDR	S
Doce Linajes 1998, Bodegas Gormaz Ribera del Duero	*Fanatastic leathery nose with classic fruit tannins and elegant poise and length. Well made.*	**£9.30**	C&D	B
Marqués de Vitoria Reserva 1994, Bodegas Marqués de Vitoria Rioja	*Oaky, fruity nose with a vanillin vein. Well balanced with firm tannins and a smooth texture.*	**£9.50**	PLB	S
Marques de Griñon Cabernet Sauvignon 1996, Arco Bodegas Unidas Penedès	*Deep and dark with attractive berry fruits and soft rich oak. A full bodied palate with good length.*	**£9.80**	BWC D&D	B
Navajas Tinto Reserva 1994, Bodegas Navajas Rioja	*Black, jammy fruits with a hint of vanilla and a warm tannin palate with nice structure and length.*	**£10.00**	GRO NYW MOR	B
Cune Reserva 1995, Cune Rioja	*Nice rounded style with quite pronounced fruits and walnut and coconut characters.*	**£10.10**	WAW GRT BUP DWS	B

SPAIN • RED				
Albet I Noya Syrah Colleccion 1997, Albet I Noya Penedès	*Massive atttack of plums leads to a firm bed of tannins with meaty notes and a tangy tail.*	**£10.50**	VRT	S
Campillo Reserva 1992, Bodegas Campillo Rioja	*Sweet fruits still shining among developed barn-yard and stable char-caters. Good palate weight.*	**£10.50**	TOS	B
Marqués de Griñon Domino de Valdespusa Petit Verdot 1996, Arco Bodegas Unidas La Mancha	*A tight, tarry nose before a smooth, sweet-middled, berry fruited entry with ripe violets and blackber-ries on the finish.*	**£10.80**	NYW D&D	G
Marqués de Griñon Syrah 1996, Arco Bodegas Unidas Penedès	*Sappy pepper, superb fruit and soft vanillin oak flavours with firm tannins and a psychedel-ic finish.*	**£10.80**	BWC D&D	G
Campo Viejo Gran Reserva 1991, Bodegas Campo Viejo Rioja	*Black and red fruits combine with pepper on the nose and lead to a full bodied palate.*	**£11.00**	MAR ODD THS VWE BPW	B
Enate Reserva 1995, Enate Somontano	*Perky strawberry nose with a dry, ripe and con-centrated palate. Fine tannins and a pleasant finish.*	**£11.00**	WCR ODD CFN AVB HOH	B
Marqués de Velilla Crianza 1996, Grandes Bodegas Ribera del Duero	*Concentrated cassis and spice on the nose with great depth of sweet fruits, pruny raisins and impressive length.*	**£11.00**	NYW MOR	S
Pago de Carraovejas Crianza 1996, Pago de Carraovejas Ribera del Duero	*A more mature spicy nose with hints of san-dalwood, stewed rhubarb and a plummy punch.*	**£11.00**	Widely Available	S

Wine	Tasting note	Price	Stockists	Award
Raimat Cabernet Sauvignon Reserva 1987, Raimat Costers del Segre	*A delightful wine with subtle fruits on the nose with a hint of herb and some pronounced mint.*	**£11.00**	TOS PLB CON	G
Riberal Crianza 1996, Bodegas Santa Eualia Ribera del Duero	*A little closed on the nose but with opulent concentrated fruits on the palate leading to a lush finish.*	**£11.00**	VLW LAY L&S	B
Abadia Retuerta 1996, Abadia Reteurta Ribera del Duero	*A mellow yet intense fruit nose with vanilla and malt notes. Nice rounded berry fruits in the mouth.*	**£11.40**	MAR VWE GGW EUW	S
Viña Herminia Reserva 1994, Vinedos de Aldeaneua Rioja	*Sweet oak and ripe berry fruits meet soft ripe tannins in the mouth and finish cleanly.*	**£11.80**	TOS PLB	B
Scala dei Tinto Crianza 1993, Scala Dei Priorato	*Subtle fruit aromas with a light weight palate of summer fruits and a concise finish.*	**£11.90**	RBS WSO MOR	B
Marqués de Murrieta YGAY Reserva Especial Tinto 1994, Marqués de Murrieta Rioja	*Lovely colour with sweet raisiny fruit and a well balanced fruity palate. Drinks well now.*	**£12.10**	RBS JNW MMD	B
Faustino I Gran Reserva 1992, Faustino Rioja	*Big blackcherry nose with savoury characters and peppery palate with a sweet fruit finish.*	**£12.20**	UNS WAC MHV ODD HDB	B
Marqués de Vitoria Gran Reserva 1992, Bodegas Marqués de Vitoria Rioja	*Cherry fruit and blackberry on the nose spiced with cloves and a dose of vanillin on the palate.*	**£12.50**	PLB	S

Wine	Description	Price	Stockists	Award
ALLENDE TINTO 1996, BODEGAS ALLENDE Rioja	*Chunky fruit and olive tones on the nose meld with plummy, raisiny flavours on the palate.*	£13.00	NYW MOR	S
GUELBENZU EVO 1996, BODEGAS GUELBENZU Navarra	*Densely flavoured with cedary oak and rich currant veins. Good balance and length.*	£13.00	WSO MFS MOR	B
LA VICALANDA RESERVA 1995, BODEGAS BILBAINAS Rioja	*Lovely raisiny fruit comes on to the palate to meet coconut cream and toasty oak flavours.*	£13.00	CON FRT	B
VALDUERO RESERVA 1995, BODEGAS VALDUERO Ribera del Duero	*Really meaty on the nose with mature spice flavours flowing onto well balanced palate.*	£13.50	VLW LAY HAR FSW PHI L&S	S
COSTERS DEL SIURANA USATGES 1996, COSTERS DEL SIURANA Priorato	*A lighter style with a soft cherry nose and medium weight dried fruit palate. Pleasant.*	£13.80	VLW NYW L&S	B
FINCA VALPIEDRA RESERVA 1994, MARTINEZ BUJANDA Rioja	*Great depth of earthy, savoury characters which follow through onto the palate with a cherry splash .*	£13.90	UNS VEX BDR JNW	S
MARQUÉS DE ALELLA TIONIO 1997, MARQUES DE ALELLA Ribera del Duero	*Lovely, smoky cassis and pepper nose with warm sweet coffee tones cascading onto the oaky palate with finesse.*	£14.00	HNW SAN MOR	S
ALBET I NOYA RESERVA MARTI 1995, ALBET I NOYA Penedès	*Bright fruit aromas with vanilla notes lead to an oasis of jelly fruits and savouries, immersed in spicey firm tannins.*	£14.50	VRT	G

Wine	Tasting note	Price	Stockists	Award
Teofilo Reyes 1996, Bodegas Reyes Ribera del Duero	*Attractive young wine with a smoky, leathery and blackfruit nose has a pleasant mouthfeel and good length.*	**£14.80**	NYW WRW HAR BBR VLW LAY L&S	B
Mayor de Ondarre Reserva 1994, Bodegas Ondarre Rioja	*Hot jam and savouries with a hint of herbs, lay on a bed of vanillin laced chalky tannins.*	**£16.00**	AVB HOH	G
Masia Barril Classico 1987, Masia Barril Priorato	*Sweet and complex nose with an inviting muddiness introduce a soft and rounded damson and plum dominated palate.*	**£17.00**	MOR GRO NYW BTH WSO	S
Rotllan I Torra Balandra 1996, Rotllan I Torra Priorato	*Oak and plump fruit on the nose hint at the basket of vanillan drenched blackfruits to come.*	**£17.00**	NYW GRO MOR	S
Castell del Remei '1780' 1996, Castell del Remei Costers del Segre	*Coconut cream nose over blackfruits bursts in the mouth with extra vanilla flavour before a luxurious finish.*	**£18.00**	MOR	S
Mas Igneus FA112 1997, Mas Igneus Priorato	*Very ripe fruit and a velvety texture in the mouth lead to a very fine fruit and nut finish.*	**£19.00**	VRT	S
Raimat Cabernet Sauvignon Mas Castell 1994, Raimat Costers del Segre	*An amalgam of developed fruit cake like characters on the nose lead to a superbly fruit focussed palate.*	**£20.00**	FRT CON	G
La Rioja Alta Gran Reserva 904 1989, La Rioja Alta Rioja	*A warm, inviting nicely developed nose of cooked vegetal aromas and a lovely sweet fruit finish.*	**£20.30**	Widely Available	S

SPAIN • RED

Wine	Description	Price	Stockists	Award
Rotllan I Torra Amadis 1996, Rotllan I Torra Priorato	*Clean, ripe fruit with firm tannins and nice acid is set to go the distance.*	**£22.00**	NYW GRO MOR	B
Costers del Siurana Miserere 1996, Costers del Siurana Priorato	*Encouraging youthful appearance with toasty aromas and sun drenched fruit. Will shine.*	**£22.40**	VLW LAY FSW DBY HCK L&S	B
Valduero Primium Reserva Especial 1994, Bodegas Valduero Ribera del Duero	*Warm and spicey raisins on the nose with a textured palate showing velvety fruits with vanilla notes.*	**£22.90**	LAY L&S	S
Scala Dei Catoixa 1996, Scala Dei Priorato	*Green vegies, spice and pudding characters precede a hefty palate of tannins finishing very dry. Not for the faint hearted.*	**£25.00**	MOR	S
Cuvee el Palomar 1996, Abadia Reteurta Sardon del Duoro	*Rich and opulent wine offers dense fruit with leathery tones on a well structured tannin palate.*	**£25.80**	GGW EUW	S
Costers del Siurana Clos de l'Obac 1996, Costers del Siurana Priorato	*Accentuated fruit on the nose with earthy tones leads to a palate of firm tannins with clean balancing acidity.*	**£27.70**	VLW L&W NYW LAY FSW TAN HAR L&S	S
Valduero Gran Reserva 1990, Bodegas Valduero Ribera del Duero	*Savoury notes spiked with vanilla flow onto the palate where they meet firm, silky tannins.*	**£28.60**	HAR HCK LAY VLW L&S	S
Cuvee el Campanario 1996, Abadia Reteurta Sardon del Duoro	*Very herbal on the nose with toasty notes and a touch of vanillin oak on the palate.*	**£29.10**	GGW EUW	B

SANTA CATARINA PINOT NOIR 1996, SANTA CATARINA Mallorca	*Ripe cherry fruit and new oak in excellent balance. Firm tannins lead to vanilla tones on the finish.*	£30.00	LIB NFF	S

SPAIN • SPARKLING

COOPERATIVE CAVA BRUT NV, CODORNIU Penedès	*A clean nose of pears and apples preceded a spritzy palate of good length with a crisp finish.*	£5.00	CWS PLB CRS	B
PARXET CUVEE 21 NV, PARXET Cava	*Up front lemon and limes lead to a lively mousse palate with a clean finish.*	£6.00	MOR	B
TORRE ORIA CAVA NV, TORRE ORIA WINERY Requena	*Slightly closed on the nose but the palate is showing full creamy fruit with balanced acidity.*	£6.60	MOR BKI	B
BONAVAL BRUT CAVA NV, BOGEGAS INVIOSA Riberio	*Creamy biscuity notes on the nose with a lightweight, soft, bubbling, delicate fruit palate.*	£7.00	ADN SHB DBY HAS	B
SANDORA CAVA NV, CAVAS NAVARAN Cava	*Pale yellow in colour with soft sherberty characters on the nose and a lean slightly acidic palate.*	£7.00	VWE SEA	B
TORRE ORIA BRUT RESERVE NV, TORRE ORIA WINERY Requena	*Green apple and citrus fruit flavours joined with blue cheese and delicately yeasty nose.*	£7.00	MOR BKI	B

SPAIN • SPARKLING

RAVENTOS I BLANC CAVA L'HEREU NV, JOSEP MARIA Cava	*A little ray of sunshine with light zesty fruit on the palate and warm biscuity aromas.*	**£7.30**	P&R WAW	(B)
PARXET BRUT RESERVA NV, PARXET Cava	*Lovely yeasty aromas on a streamlined palate with moderate acidity and slightly short finish.*	**£7.50**	MOR	(B)
RAIMAT CAVA CHARDONNAY BRUT NATURE NV, RAIMAT Costers del Segre	*Juicy ripe fruit on the nose leads to a fine beaded palate and green apple acid finish.*	**£8.50**	CON FRT PLB	(B)

SPAIN • WHITE

MARQUÉS DE RISCAL RUEDA 1998, MARQUÉS DE RISCAL Rueda	*Light floral characters with flinty notes and mineral nuances, good acidity providing length and structure.*	**£5.70**	UNS LPD	(B)
CON CLASS SAUVIGNON BLANC 1998, BODEGAS CON CLASS Rueda	*Good, fresh and clean fruit salad and lemons at the fore, warm and quite ripe.*	**£6.00**	GRT POR P&R MOR	(B)
MARQUÉS DE RISCAL SAUVIGNON 1998, MARQUÉS DE RISCAL Rueda	*Spicey vegetal fruit with asparagus notes lead to a soft tropical palate and herbaceous finish.*	**£6.00**	LPD	(S)
MIGUEL TORRES GRAN VIÑA SOL CHARDONNAY 1998, MIGUEL TORRES Penedès	*Attractive blossom and nectarines lead to a medium weight palate with well measured oak.*	**£6.30**	EUR SEL SAF BUP WRC HAR HVN	(B)

Wine	Description	Price	Stockists	Award
Marques de Alella Clasico 1998, Marques de Alella Alella	*Off dry style with zingy citrus fruit with hints of spice and balanced acidity and nice length.*	**£6.60**	RBS	B
Navajas Blanco Crianza 1993, Bodegas Navajas Rioja	*Showing nice bottle age development with vanilla and blanched almonds. Good oak support with lovely character.*	**£7.00**	NYW MOR GRO WAW	S
Palacio de Bornos 1998, Bodegas de Crianza Castilla la Vieja Rueda	*Green apples combined with soft floral fruit and herbs with nice weight and balanced acidity.*	**£7.20**	C&D	B
Monjardín Chardonnay Reserva 1996, Bodegas Castillo de Monjardin Navarra	*Light fruit with a neat oak lacing and wonderful mouthfeel concludes a refined acid finish.*	**£8.40**	VLW FSW LAY L&S	B
Lagar de Cervera 1998, Lagar de Fornelos Rias Baixas	*Delicate citrus fruit aromas combined with a surprisingly full bodied ripe fruit palate.*	**£9.50**	RBS FSW HAR VLW WRW LAY L&S	S
Miguel Torres Fransola 1997, Miguel Torres Penedès	*Clean ripe fruit on the developing nose leads to a lemony palate showing good use of wood.*	**£10.30**	MOR POR ROD COK ICL	B
Miguel Torres Milmanda 1997, Miguel Torres Conco de Barberà	*Citrus fruit with a hint of apple and marzipan are the start of the myriad of flavours you will enjoy.*	**£18.30**	SEL	S

Pinpoint who sells the wine you wish to buy by turning to the stockist codes. If you know the name of the wine you want to buy, use the alphabetical index. If the price is your motivation, refer to the invaluable price guide index; red and white wines under £5, sparkling wines under £12 and Champagne under £16. Happy hunting!

REDS • £5 AND UNDER

MontGras Carmenere Reserva 1998	£ 3.50	S
Ramada 1998	£ 3.50	S
California Mountain Genache Cabernet 1997	£ 3.70	S
Andre Daguin Côtes de St Mont 1997	£ 3.80	S
Joanis VdP de Vauclause 1997	£ 3.80	S
Safeway Claret NV	£ 3.80	S
Barrelaia 1997	£ 4.00	S
Cecchi Sangiovese di Toscana 1997	£ 4.00	S
Covinca Venturoso Tempranillo Garnacha 1998	£ 4.00	S
Phoenix Old Vine Garnacha 1998	£ 4.00	S
Remonte Cabernet Sauvignon Crianza 1996	£ 4.00	S
Viña Fuerte Garnacha 1998	£ 4.00	S
MHV Australian Shiraz NV	£ 4.20	S
Vendange Red 1997	£ 4.30	S
Briccolo 1997	£ 4.40	S
Pedras do Monte 1998	£ 4.40	S
Bodegas Pirenos Espiral Cabernet Sauvignon Tempranillo 1997	£ 4.50	S
Domaine Jeune VdP du Gard 1998	£ 4.50	S
Merum Primitivo 1998	£ 4.50	S
Safeway Australian Shiraz 1998	£ 4.50	S
Two Oceans Cabernet Merlot 1998	£ 4.70	S
Chiaro di Luna Montepulciano d'Abruzzo Oak Aged 1998	£ 4.80	S
Espiral Moristel Tempranillo 1998	£ 4.80	S
Château Saint Benoit Minervois 1997	£ 4.90	S
Hardys Stamp Of Australia Shiraz Cabernet 1998	£ 4.90	S
Santiago Graffigna Cabernet Sauvignon Syrah 1998	£ 4.90	S
Vista Andes Cabernet Sauvignon Reserva 1997	£ 2.70	B
Badgers Creek Australian Shiraz Cabernet 1998	£ 3.00	B
Castillo de Molina Reserva Pinot Noir 1998	£ 3.00	B
Safeway Bulgarian Country Red 1998	£ 3.00	B
Etchart Rio de Plata Malbec 1996	£ 3.20	B
Asda Karalta Oak Aged Dry Red 1998	£ 3.30	B
Castillo de Molina Reserva Merlot 1997	£ 3.40	B
Cantine & Palme Rosso di Puglia NV	£ 3.50	B
Co-op Veneto Merlot NV	£ 3.50	B
Gandia Co-op Tempranillo Oak Aged NV	£ 3.50	B
Safeway Bulgarian Cabernet Sauvignon Reserve 1995	£ 3.70	B
Casa Girelli Canaletto Merlot del Veneto 1998	£ 3.80	B
De Neuville Cabernet Sauvignon 1997	£ 3.80	B

REDS • £5 AND UNDER

Diemersdal Shiraz 1998	£ 3.80	B
Don Darias NV	£ 3.80	B
Foncalieu Syrah Special 1998	£ 3.80	B
Idlerock Romanian Pinot Noir 1998	£ 3.80	B
Alain Brumont Tannat VdP des Côtes de Gascogne 1998	£ 3.90	B
Angove's Nanya Vineyard Malbec Ruby Cabernet 1997	£ 4.00	B
Bellefontaine Syrah 1998	£ 4.00	B
Big Franks Red Minervois 1997	£ 4.00	B
Boyar Oriachovitza Cabernet Sauvignon Reserve 1995	£ 4.00	B
Cape Piper Cinsault Pinotage 1998	£ 4.00	B
Co-op Chilean Old Vines Carignan 1998	£ 4.00	B
Co-op Los Pampas Cabernet Malbec 1998	£ 4.00	B
Domaine Sainte Bauzille Cab. Sauv., Syrah VdP d'Oc 1997	£ 4.00	B
Foncalieu Syrah Top 1998	£ 4.00	B
Foral Douro Reserva Red 1997	£ 4.00	B
Fuente del Ritmo 1997	£ 4.00	B
La Tour du Prévot 1998	£ 4.00	B
Lovico Suhindol Merlot Reserve 1995	£ 4.00	B
Lovico Suhindol Merlot Reserve 1995	£ 4.00	B
Marcus James Cabernet Sauvignon 1996	£ 4.00	B
Rio de Plata Tempranillo Malbec 1998	£ 4.00	B
"Top" Cabernet Sauvignon 1998	£ 4.00	B
Two Tribes Red NV	£ 4.00	B
Banrock Station Mataro Grenache Shiraz 1998	£ 4.10	B
Portada 1997	£ 4.10	B
Safeway Australian Shiraz Cabernet 1998	£ 4.20	B
Trivento Syrah 1998	£ 4.20	B
Segada Baga-Trincadeira 1997	£ 4.30	B
Sierra Alta Tempranillo 1998	£ 4.30	B
Tesco Reserve Claret 1997	£ 4.30	B
Villa Icona Sangiovese 1998	£ 4.40	B
Viña Albali Reserva 1993	£ 4.40	B
Balbi Vineyard Malbec 1998	£ 4.50	B
Barbera d'Asti Superiore le Croci 1996	£ 4.50	B
Black Ridge Carignan Grenache 1997	£ 4.50	B
L'Abbé de Breyac Cotes du Marmandais 1998	£ 4.50	B
Domaine Boyar Premium Cuvée Cabernet Sauvignon 1998	£ 4.50	B
Domaine de Madame Costières de Nîmes 1997	£ 4.50	B
LA Cetto Nebbiolo 1995	£ 4.50	B
LA Cetto Zinfandel 1998	£ 4.50	B
Safeway Castillo de Sierra Rioja NV	£ 4.50	B
Tesco Australian Red Wine NV	£ 4.50	B
Trilogie VdP d'Oc 1997	£ 4.50	B
Lomasol Tinto Gran Reserva 1989	£ 4.60	B

Spice Trail Red 1997	£ 4.60	B
Bright Brothers Atlantic Vines Baga 1998	£ 4.70	B
Castaño Casario Crianza 1996	£ 4.70	B
Co-op Australian Cabernet Sauvignon 1997	£ 4.70	B
Tesco McLaren Vale Shiraz 1997	£ 4.70	B
Alianca Dão Reserva Red 1997	£ 4.80	B
Canepa Private Reserve Cabernet Sauvignon Merlot 1995	£ 4.80	B
Herdade do Esporao Monte Velho 1997	£ 4.80	B
Kouros Nemea 1996	£ 4.80	B
Marco Real Garnacha Crianza 1996	£ 4.80	B
Palmela Castelao 1997	£ 4.80	B
Plantation Ruby Cabernet 1998	£ 4.80	B
Basilicata Rosso 1998	£ 4.90	B
Côtes du Rhône Rouge Cuvée Speciale 1998	£ 4.90	B
Foncalieu Ceps du Sud Old Vine Grenache 1997	£ 4.90	B
Oak Village Cabernet Sauvignon 1996	£ 4.90	B

WHITES • £5 AND UNDER

Banrock Station Chardonnay 1998	£ 4.00	G
Castillo de Molina Reserva Chardonnay 1997	£ 2.80	S
Safeway Mátra Mountain Oaked Chardonnay 1998	£ 3.70	S
Vinprom Rousse Reserve Chardonnay 1997	£ 3.70	S
Hungarian Private Reserve Gewürztraminer 1997	£ 3.80	S
Safeway Matra Mountain Unoaked Pinot Grigio 1998	£ 3.80	S
Hilltop 2000 1998	£ 4.00	S
Lindemans Cawarra Unoaked Chardonnay 1998	£ 4.60	S
Spar South African Classic White NV	£ 4.60	S
Lawson's Dry Hills Gewürztraminer 1998	£ 4.70	S
Samos Vin Doux Greek Muscat NV	£ 3.00	B
VdP du Jardin de la France Sauvignon Blanc NV	£ 3.30	B
Reh Kendermann Bend In The River 1998	£ 3.50	B
La Croix Blanc 1998	£ 3.60	B
Asda Private Reserve Sauvignon Blanc 1998	£ 3.80	B
Hilltop Castle Ridge Sauvignon Blanc 1998	£ 3.90	B
Verdicchio Classico Inanfora 1998	£ 3.90	B
Argenta Chenin Blanc Chardonnay 1998	£ 4.00	B
Bellefontaine Terret Sauvignon VdP d'Oc 1998	£ 4.00	B
California Mountain Vineyards Chardonnay 1997	£ 4.00	B
Gioacchino Garofoli Verdicchio Classico CLASSICO 1998	£ 4.00	B
Hilltop Neszmély River Duna Chardonnay Barrique 1997	£ 4.00	B
Hilltop Neszmély Tolusi Oaked Chardonnay 1997	£ 4.00	B
Hilltop Sauvignon Blanc 1998	£ 4.00	B
Kohi Point Sauvignon Blanc Semillon 1998	£ 4.00	B
Safeway Chilean Semillon Chardonnay 1998	£ 4.00	B
Safeway Mátra Mountain Sauvignon Blanc 1998	£ 4.00	B
Spice Trail White 1998	£ 4.00	B
Verdicchio dei Castelli di Jesi Classico 1998	£ 4.00	B
Vivian Ducorneau Vdp Côtes de Gascogne 1997	£ 4.00	B
Wyndham 1828 Semillon Chardonnay 1998	£ 4.00	B
Frascati Superiore Selezione Satinata 1997	£ 4.10	B
Casa Leona Chardonnay 1998	£ 4.20	B
Jarrah Ridge Dry White 1998	£ 4.20	B
MHV Frascati Superiore 1998	£ 4.20	B
Canaletto Garsanesa del Veneto Pinot Grigio 1998	£ 4.30	B
Chapel Down Summerhill Oaked NV	£ 4.30	B
Reserve St Marc Sauvignon Blanc 1998	£ 4.30	B
Domaine du Tariquet 1998	£ 4.40	B

WHITES • £5 AND UNDER

Foncalieu Ceps du Sud Old Vine Vermentino 1998	£ 4.40	B
Domaine du Haut Rauly Monbazillac 1997	£ 4.50	B
Foncalieu Ceps du Sud Muscat Sec 1998	£ 4.50	B
Fortant de France VdP d'Oc Chardonnay 1998	£ 4.50	B
Four Corners Bordeaux Sauvignon Blanc 1998	£ 4.50	B
Hardys Stamp Of Australia Semillon Chardonnay 1998	£ 4.50	B
Les Frères Scaramouche VdP d'Oc Chardonnay 1998	£ 4.50	B
Miranda Pioneers Raisined Muscat 1998	£ 4.50	B
Pacific Wines Cape Chardonnay 1998	£ 4.50	B
Penfolds Bin 381 Semillon 1998	£ 4.50	B
Sable View Chardonnay 1998	£ 4.50	B
Soleca Semillon Chardonnay 1997	£ 4.50	B
Tesco Robertson Chardonnay Colombard NV	£ 4.50	B
Falerio dei Colli Ascolani Saladini Pilastri 1998	£ 4.60	B
35 Sur Chardonnay 1998	£ 4.70	B
Jacob's Creek Dry Riesling 1998	£ 4.70	B
Longridge Bay View Chenin Blanc Chardonnay 1998	£ 4.70	B
Santa Amalia Sauvignon Blanc 1998	£ 4.70	B
Valdivieso Chardonnay 1998	£ 4.70	B
Herdade do Esporao Monte Velho 1998	£ 4.80	B
Hilltop Bin AK 28 Sauvignon Blanc 1997	£ 4.80	B
Kleine Zalze Chenin Blanc Barrel Fermented 1998	£ 4.80	B
Viña Alamosa Semillon 1998	£ 4.80	B
French Connection Chardonnay Viognier 1998	£ 4.90	B
JP Branco NV	£ 4.90	B
Lawson's Dry Hills Chardonnay 1997	£ 4.90	B

SPARKLING • £12 AND UNDER

Cockatoo Ridge Black NV	£7.20	G
Seppelt Show Sparkling Shiraz 1987	£11.20	G
Sparkling Chenin Brut NV	£4.50	S
Somerfield Asti Spumante NV	£4.80	S
d'Arenberg The Peppermint Paddock Sparkling Chambourcin 1997	£6.50	S
Jacob's Creek Sparkling Chardonnay Pinot Noir NV	£7.00	S
Seaview Pinot Noir Chardonnay Brut 1995	£7.70	S
Yellowglen Vintage 1995	£10.00	S
Green Point Brut Vintage 1995	£11.50	S
Clairette de Die NV	£3.50	B
Safeway Asti Spumante NV	£4.80	B
Cooperative Cava Brut NV	£5.00	B
Rialto Asti Spumante 1998	£5.00	B
Martini d'Asti Spumante NV	£5.80	B
Carrington Brut Rose NV	£6.00	B
Parxet Cuvee 21 NV	£6.00	B
Seaview Brut NV	£6.60	B
Torre Oria Cava NV	£6.60	B
Bonaval Brut Cava NV	£7.00	B
Hardys Nottage Hill Sparkling Chardonnay 1997	£7.00	B
Safeway Cremant de Bourgogne Brut NV	£7.00	B
Sandora Cava NV	£7.00	B
Torre Oria Brut Reserve NV	£7.00	B
Raventos I Blanc Cava l'Hereu NV	£7.30	B
Parxet Brut Reserva NV	£7.50	B
Raimat Cava Chardonnay Brut Nature NV	£8.50	B
Orlando Trilogy Brut NV	£9.00	B
Pongcraz Sparkling Methode Cape Classic NV	£9.00	B
Seppelt Sparkling Shiraz 1994	£9.10	B
Berrys' Australian Sparkling Wine NV	£10.80	B
Cuvée Napa by Mumm Rose NV	£10.90	B
Deutz Marlborough Cuvée NV	£11.10	B

CHAMPAGNE • £16 AND UNDER

Le Brun de Neuville Cuvee Selection Brut NV	£ 15.80	G
Champagne Bernard Brémont Brut Grand Cru Rosé NV	£ 15.50	S
Champagne Drappier Rose Val des Demoiselles NV	£ 15.30	S
Champagne A Margaine Rosé Brut NV	£ 14.90	S
Drappier Carte d'0r 1991	£ 14.60	S
Champagne Jean Moutardier Carte d'Or Brut NV	£ 14.00	S
MHV The House Brut Champagne NV	£ 13.80	S
Alexandre Bonnet Brut NV	£ 10.00	S
Mansard Blanc de Blancs Grand Cru 1992	£ 15.50	B
Ayala Brut NV	£ 14.80	B
Marne et Champagne Jean de Braieux Brut NV	£ 14.00	B
Albert Etienne Brut NV	£ 13.50	B
Champagne J F Bourgeois Brut	£ 12.50	B
André Simon Champagne Brut NV	£ 12.50	B

STOCKISTS

Every wine in the guide has one or more stockist codes beside its entry, identifying where the wine can be bought. The list below translates the code into the company name, with a telephone number for you to make enquiries.

Where the stockists are stated as Widely Available there are more than 10 outlets who stock this wine. In these cases you should be able to find the wine in most good wine retailers. Every effort has been made to list all the stockists with their relevant wines. Should you encounter any problems with finding a wine listed in this guide, then please write to:
The International WINE Challenge, Quest Magazines, Wilmington Publishing, 6-8 Underwood Street, London N1 7JQ

3DW	3D Wines	01205 820745
4PL	Four Plus	01892 525733
A&A	A & A Wines	01483 274666
A&N	Army & Navy	0171 834 1234
ABA	Adam Bancroft Associates	0171 793 1902
ABO	Anthony Borges	01932 853453
ABY	Anthony Byrne Wine Agencies	01487 814555
ACH	Andrew Chapman Fine Wines	01235 550707
ADD	Allied Domecq Spirits & Wine	0117 978 5216
ADE	Adel (UK) Ltd	0181 994 3960
ADG	Adgestone Vineyard Ltd	01983 402 503
ADI	Allders International	01703 644599
ADN	Adnams Wine Merchants	01502 727222
ADS	Alldays Stores Ltd	01703 645000
ADW	Andrew Darwin	01544 230534
AFI	Alfie Fiandaca Ltd	0181 752 1222
AGM	Avontaur Wines U.K.	01483 456671
AGM	Avontaur Wines U.K.	01483 456671
AGR	Agrimar Ltd	01959 540000
AGS	Amazing Grapes	0181 202 2631
AHW	A. H. Wines Ltd	01935 850116

AIS	Austrian Trade Commission	0171 584 4411
ALA	Australian Premium Wines Ltd	0171 801 9583
ALD	Aldi Stores Ltd	01827 710 871
ALE	Alexander Wines	0141 882 0039
ALI	Alivini Compa ny Ltd	0181 880 2525
ALL	Alliance Wine Company Ltd	01505 506060
ALO	Alouette Wines	0151 346 1107
ALR	Alvear (UK)	01584 811333
ALZ	Allez Vins!	0385 264445
AMA	Amathus Wines Ltd	0181 886 3787
AMF	Anglo- American Farms (UK) Ltd	01844 201947
AMU	Antu Mapu U.K.	01531 670743
AMW	Amey's Wines	01787 377144
ANT	Anthony & Son	0171 403 4669
APC	Arthur Purchase	01243 783144
AQU	Aquitaine Wines	01347 6612
ARL	Auriol Wines	01252 843190
ARM	Arthur Rackham	01483 458700
ARP	A R Parker & Son	01322 525231
ARR	Arrowfield Wines	01494 678971
ASD	Asda Stores Ltd	0113 241 9169
ASH	Ashley Scott	01244 520655
ASN	André Simon	0171 388 5080
AST	Astley Vineyards	01299 822907
ASW	Ashdown Wine	0181 841 4134
AUC	The Australian Wine Club	01753 544546
AUE	Australian Estates	01438 820955
AUR	Auriga Brands International	01256 880611
AUS	Australian Wineries (UK) Ltd	01780 755810
AVB	Averys of Bristol	01275 811100
AVI	Arlington Vintners Int. Ltd	0181 670 0601
AWB	Australian Wine Bureau	0171 887 5259
AWC	Anthony Wine Cellars	0171 722 8576
AWL	Adriatic Wine Ltd	0191 233 2700
AWM	Albert Wharf Wine Co Ltd	0171 223 8283
AWS	Albion Wine Shippers	0171 242 0873
B&B	Bottle & Basket	0181 341 7018
B&S	Brown & Strauss	01582 834224
BAB	Bablake Wines	01203 228272
BAC	Backsberg Estate	01491 577707

BAD	Bad'ner Wein-Cabinet UK	01932 241443
BAG	Bacchus Gallery	01798 342844
BAK	Barkham Manor Vineyard	01825 722103
BAL	Ballantynes of Cowbridge	01446 774840
BAM	Blenheim Asset Management Ltd	01892 861 444
BAS	The Black Sea Wine Company	0171 404 4554
BAT	Battersea Wine Co	0171 924 3631
BBB	Barnsbury Bottle & Basket	0171 713 0427
BBL	Bat & Bottle Wine Merchants	01785 284495
BBO	Barrels & Bottles	0114 276 9666
BBR	Berry Bros & Rudd	0171 396 9600
BBS	Barton Brownsdon Sadler	01892 824024
BBU	Bruce Burlington	01268 562224
BBV	Breaky Bottom Vineyard	01273 476427
BCK	Beck Marketing	0171 582 8811
BCL	Best Cellars	01364 652546
BCW	Brian Coad Fine Wines	01752 896545
BDG	Bodega Off Sales	0150 553031
BDI	Bordeaux Wine Information Centre	0171 833 5544
BDM	Bodenham Wine	01568 797483
BDR	Bordeaux Direct	0118 903 0903
BDT	Benedict's	01983 529596
BEC	Beaconsfield Wine Cellars	01494 675545
BEL	Bentalls of Kingston	0181 546 1001
BEN	Bennetts	01386 840392
BES	Bestway Cash & Carry Ltd	0181 453 1234
BET	Bethany Wines (UK)	0114 272 1167
BEX	Bitter Experience	0181 852 8819
BFI	Bedford Fine Wines	01234 721153
BFV	Baron Freidrich von Wrede Ltd	01823 451228
BFW	Bellefrance Wines Ltd	0171 706 3462
BGD	Bottle Green Drinks Co.	01453 872882
BGL	Bottle Green Ltd	0113 257 7545
BHW	B H Wines	01228 576711
BID	Biddenden Vineyards Ltd	01580 291 726
BIL	Billecart-Salmon (UK) Ltd	01932 840515
BIN	Bin 89 Wine Warehouse	0114 275 5889
BIS	Bishopsmead Wine Co	01306 76713
BKC	Berkeley Wines (Cheshire)	01925 444555
BKI	Kingsland Wine & Spirits	0161 333 4300

BKR	Bergkelder Distribution Europe	01895 672100
BKT	Bucktrout	01481 724444
BLA	Blakes & Co Ltd	01292 264880
BLG	Communications Plus	0171 978 4132
BLN	Belloni & Company	0171 704 8812
BLS	Balls Brothers of London	0171 739 6466
BLV	Bacchus Les Vignobles	0181 675 9007
BLW	Blayneys	0191 548 3083
BNC	Bottlenecks (London)	0181 520 2737
BNE	Bin Ends (Rotherham)	01709 367771
BNK	Bottleneck (Broadstairs)	01843 861095
BNS	The Benevolent Society	0171 248 1343
BOB	Booze Brothers	01284 811203
BOD	Bodegas Direct	01243 773474
BOH	La Boheme (London) Ltd	0181 656 7383
BOL	Bacchus of Olney	01234 711140
BOO	Booths of Stockport	0161 432 3309
BOR	De Bortoli Wines UK Ltd	01725 518646
BOS	Boschendal Estate	01491 577707
BOU	Bouteilles en Fete	0151 346 1107
BOW	Bodega Wine Company	0181 551 9521
BOX	The Boxford Wine Co	01787 210187
BOZ	Boze Down Vineyard	0118 9844031
BPR	Baron Philippe de Rothschild	0171 584 6417
BPW	Boutinot Wines	0161 477 1171
BRB	Brown Brothers (Europe) Ltd	01628 776446
BRF	Brown-Forman Wines International	0171 323 9332
BRI	Bordeaux Index	0171 250 1982
BRU	Bruisyard Wines	01728 638 281
BRW	Breckland Wines	01953 881592
BSC	Ben Shaw's Wine Cellar	01484 516624
BSD	Boisdale Wines	0171 730 6922
BSN	Benson Fine Wines	0181 673 4439
BSS	Besos (UK) Ltd	01243 575454
BSV	Bearsted Vineyard	01622 736974
BTB	Bottlebank	01865 821564
BTH	Booths Supermarkets	01772 251701
BUA	Burridges of Arlington Street	01293 530151
BUC	Buckingham Vintners	01753 521336
BUD	International Brands Ltd	01892 723096

STOCKISTS

BUG	Burgundy Growers Ltd	01306 881062
BUP	Bottoms Up	01707 328244
BUT	The Butlers Wine Cellar	01273 698724
BVC	The Bulgarian Vintners Co Ltd	0171 841 6500
BVI	Bishops Waltham Vineyard	01489 896803
BWC	Berkmann Wine Cellars	0171 609 4711
BWH	Bermondsey Wine Warehouse	0171 231 0457
BWL	Bibendum Wine Ltd	0171 722 5577
C&B	Corney & Barrow	0171 251 4051
C&D	C & D Wines Ltd	0181 778 1711
C&H	Cairns & Hickey	0113 267 3746
C&W	Carley & Webb Ltd	017128 723503
CAM	Cambridge Wine Merchants	01223 568 991
CAN	Canandaigua Wine Co.	0181 296 1868
CAP	Cape Province Wines	01784 451860
CAR	C A Rookes	01789 297777
CAT	Cantino Augusto	0171 242 3246
CAU	Cauldron Snout	0034932123
CAX	Caxton Tower Wines Ltd	0181 758 4500
CBW	City of Belfast Warehousing	01232 746274
CCC	Cave Cru Classé Ltd	0171 378 8579
CCI	Chiswick Cellars	0181 994 7989
CCW	Cachet Wine	0148 2581792
CDC	Casa Cortes de Cima Ltda	+ 351 84 463119
CDE	Cote d'Or	0181 998 0144
CDH	Champagne Dehours	01730 816044
CDI	Carpe Diem Communications Ltd	0181 969 6444
CDL	California Direct	0171 207 1944
CDM	Caves de la Madeleine	0171 736 6145
CDN	Chiddingstone Vineyards	01892 870 277
CDO	Chapel Down Wines Ltd	01580 763033
CDT	Waverley Vintners Limited	01738 472024
CEB	Croque-en-Bouche	01684 565612
CED	Cellars Direct (London)	0171 378 1109
CEL	Cellar 5	01925 444555
CEN	Centurion Vintners	01453 763223
CER	Cellar 28	01484 717914
CES	Cellar Select Ltd/ Winefinds	01722 716100
CFI	Wine Institute of California	0171 630 9101
CFN	Carringtons Fine Wines	0161 446 2546

CFP	Perfect Partners	01580 712633
CFT	The Clifton Cellars	0117 973 0287
CFW	Christchurch Fine Wine	01202 473255
CGA	Champagne Granier	0161 941 5038
CGI	Casa Girelli	01584 811333
CGP	The Cellar Group Ltd	0181 785 7419
CGW	The Cote Green Wine Company	0161 426 0155
CHC	Churchill Vintners	0121 4141719
CHF	Chippendale Fine Wines	01943 850633
CHH	Charles Hennings	01798 872485
CHI	Chilford Hundred Limited	01223 892641
CHL	Château Lascombes	01283 512777
CHN	Charles Hawkins	01572 823030
CHS	Quellyn Roberts (Wine Merchants) Ltd	01244 310455
CHV	Champagne de Venoge (UK) Ltd	0171 834 2092
CIB	Ciborio Limited	0181 578 4388
CKB	Cockburn & Campbell	0181 875 7008
CLA	Classic Wines and Spirits Ltd	01244 288444
CLD	Caledonian Wines	01228 43172
CLI	Le Cellier	01670 737825
CLP	La Reserve	0171 978 5601
CLR	Castle Growers Ltd	01603 250515
CLW	Percy Fox & Co.	01279 633541
CMI	Charles Mitchell Wines Ltd	0161 775 1626
CML	Chateau Musar (UK) Ltd	0181 941 8311
CMM	Communications +	0171 978 4132
CNF	Champagne Nicolas Feuillatte UK	01794 507115
CNL	Connolly's	0121 236 9269
COC	Corks of Cotham	0117 973 1620
COD	Coddington Vineyard	01531 640668
COE	Coe of Ilford	0181 551 4966
COG	Conghurst Vineyard	01580 752634
COK	Corkscrew Wines	01228 543033
CON	Codorniu	0181 410 4480
COT	Cotswold Wine Company	01242 678880
CPD	Food Brands Group	0171 978 5300
CPS	C P A's Wine Ltd	01792 360707
CPW	Christopher Piper Wines Ltd	01404 814139
CRL	Wine Centre/ Charles Stevenson Wines	01822 615985
CRM	Craven's Wine Merchants	0171 723 0252

CRS	The Co operative Society	01706 891628
CST	The County Stores (Somerset) Ltd	01823 272235
CSW	Chislehurst Wines	0181 467 4340
CTH	Charterhouse Wine Co Ltd	0171 587 1302
CTL	Continental Wine & Food	01484 538333
CTV	Carr Taylor Vineyards	01424 752501
CVP	Patrice Calvet UK Ltd	01730 816044
CVR	Celtic Vintner	01633 430055
CVW	Chiltern Valley Wines	01491 638330
CVY	Chanctonbury Vineyard	01903 892721
CWA	Cheviot Wine Agencies	01327 860 548
CWD	Cellarworld International	01252 703857
cwg	Chalone Wine Group	+707 254 4200
CWI	A Case of Wine	01558 650671
CWS	CWS Ltd	0161 834 1212
CYP	Cyprus Trade Centre	0171 629 6288
D&D	D & D Wines International Ltd	01565 650952
D&F	D & F Wine Shippers Ltd	0181 838 4399
DAV	Dartmouth Vintners	01803 832602
DBO	Domaine Boyar Ltd	0171 537 3707
DBS	Denbies Wine Estate	01306 876616
DBW	David Baker Wines	01656 650732
DBY	D Byrne & Co	01200 423152
DDT	Domaine Direct	0171 837 1142
DEL	Delegat's Wine Estate (UK) Ltd	0181 892 6999
DEN	Dennhofer Wines	0191 232 73242
DIC	Dickinson's Wines Ltd.	01432 353720
DIO	Dionysus	0181 874 2739
DIR	Direct Wine Shipments	01232 238700
DLA	Daniel Lambert Wine Agenices	01222 666128
DLG	Dulong UK	01584 811333
DNC	Deinhard & Co Ltd	0171 208 2520
DNL	Dunell's Ltd	01534 736418
DOU	Dourthe UK	0171 258 3010
DOW	Downers Vineyard	01273 857670
DRD	Dr Demuth	01584 811333
DVD	Davisons Direct	0181 681 3222
DVL	De Vine Legs Wine Company Ltd	01580 291186
DVP	Davenport Vineyards	01892 852380
DVX	Devaux UK	01584 811333

DVY	Davy & Co Ltd	0171 407 9670
DWI	Dedicated Wine Importers Ltd	01865 400330
DWL	Darlington Wines Ltd	0181 453 0202
DWS	Freixenet (DWS) Ltd	01344 758 500
E&B	E&B Wines	01732 355988
E&J	Ernest & Julio Gallo Winery	01895 813444
EBA	Ben Ellis Wines	01737 842160
EBC	The Exclusive Brandy Club	0169 773744
ECA	Edward Cavendish & Sons Ltd	01794 516102
ECK	Eckington Wines	01246 433213
EDC	Edencroft	01270 625302
EGG	Ernst Gorge (Wine Shippers) Ltd	01235 538006
EHL	Ehrmanns Ltd	0171 359 7466
EIA	Enoteca Italiana	0171 251 8732
ELL	Ellingham Wines Ltd	0181 892 9599
ELV	El Vino Company Ltd	0171 353 5384
ENO	Enotria Winecellars Ltd	0181 961 4411
EOO	Everton's of Ombersley	01905 620282
EOR	Ellis of Richmond Ltd	0181 943 4033
EPO	Eldridge Pope	01305 258347
ESL	Edward Sheldon Ltd.	01608 661409
EST	Estramadura Wines	0181 932 3370
ETM	Elliot & Tatham	0171 349 0884
ETV	Eton Vintners	01753 790188
EUR	Europa Foods Ltd	0181 845 1255
EUW	Eurowines	0181 994 7658
EVE	Everymans	01743 362466
EVI	Evington's Wine Merchants	0116 254 2702
EWC	English Wine Centre	01323 870164
EWD	Euro World Wines	0141 649 3735
F&M	Fortnum & Mason	0171 734 8040
FAB	Fabat UK Ltd	0171 636 7640
FAR	Farr Vintners	0171 828 1960
FBG	Food Brands Group Ltd	0171 978 5300
FCA	Fraser Crameri Assoc.	01580 200 304
FCC	The Fine Champagne Company Co	01923 774053
FCV	France Vin	01494 680857
FDB	First Drinks Brands Ltd	01703 312000
FDL	Findlater Mackie Todd	01344 825900
FEN	Fenwick Ltd	0191 232 5100

FES	Fransican Estates	01707 963 7112
FFE	First Fine Wine (London) plc	01494 450696
FJJ	Rioja Traders Ltd	0171 266 5463
FLC	First London Corporation	0171 436 3234
FLM	Ferrers le Mesurier	01832 732660
FLW	For the Love of Wine	01359 270377
FNS	A. K. Finch Noyes & Co	01476 585288
FNZ	Fine Wines of New Zealand	0171 482 0093
FOC	Focus PR	0171 823 5533
FPR	Freddy Price	0181 997 7889
FRI	Friarwood	0171 736 2628
FRN	Frenmart	01384 892941
FRV	The Four Vintners	0171 739 7335
FRW	Fraser Williamson Fine Wines	01580 200 304
FSA	Francis Stickney Agencies	0181 201 9096
FSW	Frank Stainton Wines	01539 731886
FTH	Forth Wines Ltd	01577 863668
FTP	Four Throws Post Office	01580 753210
FUL	Fuller Smith & Turner	0181 996 2000
FVM	FVM International Ltd	01453 860881
FWC	Four Walls Wine Company	01243 535 219
FWL	Fine & Rare Wines Limited	0181 960 1995
FWM	Fields Wine Merchants	0171 589 5753
FWW	FWW Wines (UK) Ltd	0181 786 8161
G&G	Godwin & Godwin	01225 337081
G&M	Gordon & Macphail	01343 545111
G2W	Grape 2 Wine Limited	01531 670100
GAG	Grape & Grain	0181 426 1562
GAR	Garland Wine Cellar	01372 275247
GBA	Georges Barbier	0181 852 5801
GBl	Gonzalez Byass (UK) Ltd	01279 633632
GBY	Elizabeth Gabay & Partners	0181 883 9331
GCF	Les Grands Chais de France	01962 622 067
GCl	Graingers Ltd.	0114 221 0888
GDA	Giada Ltd	01904 691 628
GDM	Giles de Mare	01985 844695
GDS	Garrards Wine Merchants	01900 823592
GEL	Gelston Castle	01556 503012
GEN	Gentilini U.K.	0171 580 6491
GFF	Giffords Hall Vineyard	01284 830464

STOCKISTS

GFO	Gardners Folly	01453 731 509
GFT	Guild of French Traditional Wines	01886 832696
GGW	The Great Gaddesden Wine Company Ltd	01582 840001
GHC	Goedhuis & Company	0171 793 7900
GHL	George Hill of Loughborough	01509 212717
GIE	German Wine Information Service	0171 331 8800
GIR	Gironde Wines	01494 672305
GLO	Global Wines	0121 429 1662
GLY	Gallery Wines	01504 48762
GMV	G M Vintners	01392 218166
GNW	Great Northern Wine Co	0113 246 1200
GON	Gauntleys of Nottingham	0115 911 0555
GOY	Goyt Wines	01663 734214
GPA	Grapevine (Andover)	01264 737658
GRA	Geoffrey Roberts Agencies	01275 890740
GRO	Grog Blossom	0171 794 7808
GRT	Great Western Wine Company Ltd	01225 322800
GSH	The Grape Shop	0171 924 3638
GSJ	Grants of St James	01275 890283
GSl	Gerrard Seel Ltd	01925 819695
GTA	Grands Terriors Associés	0171 258 3010
GWB	Greek Embassy Commercial Section	0171 727 8860
GWC	Greek Wine Centre Ltd	01743 364636
GWF	Gilbey Wine Club	01491 411567
GWI	The General Wine & Liquor Company	01428 722201
GYW	Guy Anderson Wines	01460 241043
H&B	H&B Wines Ltd	0171 924 2506
H&D	Hicks & Don	01258 456040
H&H	H & H Fine Wines Ltd	01480 411599
H&W	Hall & Woodhouse Ltd	01258 452141
HAC	Hailsham Cellars	01323 441212
HAE	Halewood International Ltd	0151 480 8800
HAG	The Hanwood Group Ltd	01455 556161
HAL	Hall & Batson	01603 415115
HAM	Hampden Wine Co	01844 201641
HAR	Harrods	0171 730 1234
HAS	Haughton Agencies	01502 727 288
HAW	The Hantone Wine Company	0171 978 5920
HAY	Hayward Bros. (Wines) Ltd	0171 237 0567
HBJ	Heyman, Barwell Jones Ltd	01473 232322

HBR	BRL Hardy Wine Company Ltd	01372 738200
HBW	H and B Wines Limited	0171 924 2506
HBY	Hall & Bramley	0151 525 8283
HCK	Pierre Henck Wines	01902 751022
HDB	Highland Distillers Brands (UK) Ltd	01753 752600
HDL	Alexander Hadleigh	01489 885959
HDM	H&D Marketing	01438 820955
HDY	Hollywood & Donnelly	01232 799335
HEV	Horton Estate Vineyard	01258 840258
HEW	Hein Wines	0171 730 1099
HEY	Heyman, Barwell Jones Ltd.	0171 881 0052
HFI	Hill International Wines (UK) Ltd	01283 217703
HHC	Haynes Hanson & Clark	0171 259 0102
HHF	H&H Fine Wines	01480 411599
HLV	Halves	01588 673040
HMA	Hatch Mansfield Agencies Ltd	01753 621126
HMS	HMS Wines Agency	01275 849703
HMW	Hemisphere Wines Ltd	0171 736 3350
HNS	H. Needham & Sons (Wines)	01732 740422
HOB	Hobson and Friends Too Ltd	0181 780 3323
HOH	Hallgarten Wines Ltd	01582 722538
HOL	Holland Park Wine Co	0171 221 9614
HOP	Hopton Wines	01299 270734
HOT	House of Townend	01482 326891
HOU	Hoults Wine Merchants	01484 510700
HPD	Harpenden Wines	01923 2527180
HRF	Howard Ripley Fine French Wines	0181 360 8904
HRQ	Henriques & Henriques	01730 825860
HRV	Harrison Vintners	0171 236 7716
HSL	Hanslope Wines	01908 510262
HSN	Hannesen (UK)	01584 811333
HST	La Réserve, Hampstead	0171 435 6845
HSV	Hidden Spring Vineyard	01435 812640
HUG	Hughenden Cellars	01494 446557
HVB	John Harvey & Sons	0117 927 5010
HVD	Harbourne Vineyard	01797 270420
HVN	Harvey Nichols	0171 235 5000
HVV	Hale Valley Vineyards	0171 269 5545
HVW	Helen Verdcourt Wines	01628 25577
HWA	Heritage Wines & Charles de Cazanove	01454 294099

HWB	Howells of Bristol	01454 294085
HWL	Hedley Wright & Co Ltd	01279 506512
HWM	Harvest Wine Group	01734 344290
HWW	High Weald Winery	01622 850637
HYP	Hyperama Plc	0115 9851301
HZW	Hazeley Wines Ltd	01244 332 008
ICL	Italian Continental Food & Wine	01628 770110
IGH	Ian G. Howe Wine Merchant	01636 704366
IHD	Inver House Distillers Ltd	01236 769377
IRI	Guinness Northern Ireland	01232 661611
IRV	Irvine Robertson	0131 553 3521
ISW	Isis Wines	01628 771199
ITE	Italian Trade Centre	0171 734 2412
ITI	Italvini	01494 680857
IVV	Inverarity Vaults	01899 220234
IVY	Ivy Wines	01243 377883
IWS	International Wine Services	01494 680857
J&B	Justerini & Brooks	0171 493 8721
J&F	Jacques & Francois Lurton	01494 814 804
JAG	J. A . Glass	01592 651850
JAK	James Aitken & Son	01382 221197
JAR	John Armit Wines	0171 727 6846
JAS	Jascots Wine Merchants Ltd	0181 749 0022
JAV	John Arkell Vintners	0119 382 3026
JBF	Julian Baker Fine Wines	01206 262 358
JBR	Eldridge Pope Fine Wines	01305 258249
JBV	Julian Bidwell Vintner	0181 874 9388
JCB	J C Broadbent	01534 23356
JCK	J C Karn & Son Ltd.	01242 513265
JCP	Palmers Brewery	01308 422396
JEF	John E Fells	01442 870900
JEH	J E Hogg	0131 556 4025
JER	J. E. Ridlington & Son	01205 364747
JFE	James Fearon Wines	01248 370200
JFR	John Frazier	0121 704 3415
JHJ	J. H. Jaffe & Co Ltd.	01534 25241
JHL	J H Logan	0131 667 2855
JIN	Jinro Scotland Ltd	0141 959 881
JLW	John Lay Wines	01206 713525
JMC	James E McCabe	01762 333102

STOCKISTS

JNW	James Nicholson Wine Merchant	01396 830091
JOB	Jeroboams	0171 235 1612
JOV	Jolly Vintner	01884 255644
JPL	John & Pascalis Ltd	0181 452 0707
JSM	Sainsbury Supermarkets Ltd	0171 695 6000
JSS	John Stephenson & Sons	01282 698827
JUS	Just-in-Case	01489 892969
JWW	Whittaker Wines (Stockport)	0181 878 2302
K&B	King & Barnes Ltd	01403 270470
KAT	Roberts Estate	0181 773 0296
KDA	K D Abigail Ltd	0171 930 9947
KME	Kendal Milne	0161 832 3414
KOC	Kelly of Cults	01224 867596
KWI	Kwik Save Stores Ltd	01745 887111
KWS	The Winery	0161 333 4317
L&S	Laymont & Shaw Ltd	0181 543 2854
L&T	Lane & Tatham	01380 720123
L&W	Lay & Wheeler Ltd	01206 764446
LAH	Lamberhurst Vineyards	01892 890286
LAS	Havern Wholesales (formerly Liquid Assets)	0116 276 8471
LAU	Lauriston Wines Ltd	01372 459270
LAV	Les Amis du Vin	0181 451 0469
LAW	Chalié, Richards & Co Ltd	01403 250500
LAY	Laytons Wine Merchants Ltd	0171 388 4567
LCC	Landmark Cash & Carry	0181 863 5511
LCD	Cochonnet Wines	01326 340332
LEA	Lea & Sandeman	0171 376 4767
LEF	Le Fleming Wines	01582 760125
LFD	Battle Wine Estate	01424 773183
LHP	Laurence Hayward & Partners	01892 784333
LHZ	Lost Horizons	01923 852820
LIB	Liberty Wines	0171 720 5350
LLV	Lakeland Vintners	01539 821999
LLY	Luciana C Lynch	01428 606619
LME	Laurent Mentge	0171 337 9440
LMN	Luxmanor Ltd	0116 2709918
LNR	Le Nez Rouge	0171 609 4711
LOH	Larners of Holt	01263 712323
LOL	Louis Latour Ltd	0171 409 7276
LPD	Laurent-Perrier Distribution	01628 475404

LSH	Laurence Smith	0131 667 3327
LTW	Littlewoods Organisation plc	0151 235 2222
LUC	Luckins Wines	01371 872839
LUD	Luigi's Deli	0171 352 7739
LUS	Emilio Lustau	01932 223598
LUV	Lovico International Ltd	01494 511234
LVF	Les Producteurs & Vignerons de France Ltd	01273 730277
LVN	La Vigneronne	0171 589 6113
LWE	London Wine Emporium	0171 587 1302
M&M	M&M Imports UK	01235 813815
M&S	Marks & Spencer plc	0171 268 3825
M&V	Morris & Verdin	0171 357 8866
MAC	Makro Self Service	0161 707 1585
MAK	c/o Makro Self Service	01372 468571
MAR	Marco's Wines	0181 875 1900
MAS	Macs Neighbourhood Centres Ltd.	01707 663366
MAY	F & E May Ltd	0171 405 6249
MBO	Morrison Bowmore Distillers Ltd	0141 558 9011
MCD	Marne & Champagne Ltd	0171 499 0070
MCL	McLeod's	01507 601094
MCO	Malcolm Cowen	0181 965 1937
MCS	Mauler & Cie SA	0181 392 9900
MCT	Matthew Clark Wholesale Ltd.	01275 890283
MDA	Michael Druitt Agencies	0171 403 9191
MDL	Macedonian Drinks Ltd	01273 489043
MFS	Martinez Fine Wine	01422 320022
MFW	Marcus Fyfe Wines	01546 603646
MFZ	Morgan Furze	01279 626 801
MGN	Michael Morgan Wines	0171 407 3466
MHU	Moet Hennessy UK Ltd	0171 235 9411
MHV	Booker Belmont Wholesale Ltd	01933 371363
MHW	Merchant Vintners	01482 329443
MII	Mitchells of Lancaster	01524 63773
MIS	Mistral Wines	0171 262 5437
MJW	Michael Jobling Wines	0191 261 5298
MKV	McKinley Vintners	0171 928 7300
MMD	Maisons Marques et Domaines	0181 332 2223
MMW	Michael Menzel Wines	0114 268 3557
MON	Mondial Wine Ltd	0181 335 3455
MOO	Moorlynch Vineyard	01458 210393

MOR	Moreno Wine Importers	0171 723 6897
MPE	Michael Peace MW	0171 937 9345
MRF	Mark Reynier Fine Wines	0171 589 2020
MRN	Morrison Supermarkets	01924 875234
MSA	Mersea Vineyard	01733 270318
MSF	Milton Sanford Wines	01628 829 449
MTB	Martyn T Barker UK	01279 414808
MTC	Manningtree Wine Cellar	01206 395095
MTL	Mitchells Wine Merchants	0114 274 0311
MTR	Charles Taylor Wines Ltd	0171 928 8151
MTW	Montana Wines Ltd	0181 250 1325
MUK	Monteadria (UK) Ltd	0171 935 3433
MVG	Mille Vignes	0171 633 0278
MVN	Merchant Vintners Company	01482 329443
MVV	Meon Valley Vineyard	01489 890180
MWS	Midhurst Wine Shippers	01730 812222
MWW	Majestic Wine Warehouses Ltd	01923 298200
MYL	Myliko International (Wines) Litd	01204 392222
MZC	Mentzendorff & Co Ltd	0171 415 3200
N&P	Nickolls & Perks	01384 394518
NAD	Nadder Wines Ltd.	01722 325418
NAP	Napa Valley Vintners Association	0171 223 7683
NBV	Nutbourne Manor Vineyards	0171 627 3800
NEG	Negociants International UK Ltd	01582 462859
NEI	R & I Neish Ltd	01779 472721
NET	Nethergate Wines	01787 277244
NEV	Neve Agencies	01730 816044
NFF	New Forest Fare Ltd	01702 467224
NGB	Newglobal Business Centre ldt	0171 6364610
NGS	The South African Wine Centre	0171 224 1994
NHC	N H Creber	01822 612266
NHV	New Hall Vineyards	01621 828343
NIC	Nicolas UK Ltd	0171 436 9338
NOB	Noblesource Ltd	01780 450 490
NOW	Nick Oakley Wines	01787 223196
NRM	Norman's Ltd	01772 51701
NRW	Noble Rot Wine Warehouses Ltd	01527 575606
NSV	Northbrook Springs Vineyard	01489 892659
NUM	Vinum Austria	01234 343 202
NUR	Nurdin & Peacock	0181 971 1638

NYE	Nyetimber Vineyard	01798 813989
NYW	Noel Young Wines	01223 566 744
NZW	Wine Institute of New Zealand	0171 973 8079
OAT	Oatley Vineyard	01278 671 340
ODD	Oddbins	0181 944 4400
ODF	Oddbins Fine Wine	0181 944 4400
OFL	Oldacre-Field Ltd	0161 928 4898
OHI	Oakhouse Wine Co	01584 811747
OLS	Old St Wine Co	0171 729 1768
ORB	Orbital Wines Ltd	01858570600
ORG	The Organic Wine Co (High Wycombe)	01494 446557
ORL	Orlando Wines	0181 758 4539
OSW	Old School Wines	01886 821613
P&R	Peckham & Rye	0141 334 4312
PAC	Pacific Wines	01494 680857
PAG	Pagendam Pratt	01937 844711
PAL	Pallant Wines	01903 882288
PAR	Partridges	0171 730 0651
PAT	Patriarche Père et Fils Ltd	0171 381 4016
PAV	The Pavilion Wine Company Ltd	0171 628 8224
PBC	Premium Brand Corporation Ltd	0171 495 2187
PDG	Peter Gilding & Co Ltd	0151 548 7070
PDN	Portal, Dingwall and Norris	01243 377883
PEA	Peake Wine Assocs	01329 822733
PEC	Pechiney UK Ltd	01753 522800
PEF	Southcorp Wines Pty Ltd	0181 334 2000
PES	Penshurst Vineyard	01892 870255
PEY	Phillip Eyres Wine Merchant	01494 433823
PFC	Percy Fox & Co	01279 626801
PFT	Parfrements	01203 503646
PGA	Portugalia Wines (UK) Ltd	0181 368 8899
PGM	Pengethley Manor	01989 730211
PGR	Patrick Grubb Selections	01869 340229
PGS	Page & Sons	01843 591214
PHI	Philglas & Swiggot	0171 924 4494
PHP	Phil Parrish	01377 252373
PIC	La Reserve	0171 402 6920
PIM	Pimlico Dozen Ltd	0171 834 3647
PJN	Pierre Jean	01372 468571
PLA	Playford Ros Ltd	01845 526777

 STOCKISTS

PLB	Private Liquor Brands	01342 318282
PLE	Peter Lehmann Wines (UK) Ltd	01227 731353
PMA	Perry Mill Associates	01256 880611
PMN	Phillip Morgan	01222 231570
PMV	Pilton Manor Vineyard	01749 890325
PNA	Phillips Newman Agencies	01322 627581
PNW	Partnership Wines Ltd	0118 9320281
POL	Pol Roger Ltd	01432 262800
POM	Pomona Wines	01634 235658
PON	Peter Osborne	01491 612311
POP	The Pipe of Port	01702 614606
POR	Portland Wine Company (Manchester)	0161 962 8752
POT	Le Pont de la Tour	0171 403 2403
POU	Growers & Chateaux	01737 214957
PRB	Public Relations Business	0171 323 2121
PRC	P R Connection	0171 233 5400
PRG	Paragon Vintners Ltd	0171 887 1800
PRS	Prestige Wines	01294 602409
PST	Penn Street	01494 715376
PSW	Pat Simon Wines	0181 455 4255
PTC	Peretti Communications	0171 496 4909
PTR	Peter Green	0131 229 5925
PVS	Prestige Vintners	01264 335586
PVY	Partridge Vineyards	01258 452596
PWI	Portland Wine Cellar (Southport)	01704 534299
PWW	Peter Watts Wines	01376 561130
PWY	Peter Wylie Fine Wines	01884 277555
QRW	Quellyn Roberts Wine Merchants	01244 310455
QWW	Quay West Wines	01392 410866
R&R	R&R Teamwork	0171 349 9044
RAC	Rackham's Dept Store	0121 236 3333
RAE	Raeburn Fine Wine & Foods	0131 343 1159
RAM	Ramsbottom Victuallers	01706 825070
RAV	Ravensbourne Wine	0181 692 9655
RAW	Richard Ambridge Wines	01903 820143
RBA	Rodrigues Bartholomew	0385 940786
RBS	Roberson Wine Merchants	0171 371 2121
RBW	Rothbury Wines (Europe) Ltd	01483 224477
RDS	Reid Wines	01761 452645
REM	Remy & Associates (UK) Ltd	01753 752600

STOCKISTS

REN	Renvic Wines Ltd	01763 852470
RES	La Reserve	0171 589 2020
REW	La Reserva Wines	0171 978 5601
REY	Raymond Reynolds Ltd	01663 742 230
RGW	The Rogers Wine Company	01473 748464
RHC	Reh Wine Group	01295 760000
RHV	Richard Harvey Wines Ltd.	01929 481437
RIC	Richard Granger	0191 281 5000
RKW	Rickwood of Bearstead Green	01622 737130
RMA	Richard Mulcaster Associates	0171 331 8888
RML	Richard Mallinson	01256 770397
RNS	Rex Norris	01444 454756
ROB	T M Robertson	0131 229 4522
ROD	Rodney Densem Wines	01270 623665
ROG	Roger Harris Wines	01603 880171
ROI	Robin Oxford International	01844 213822
ROS	Rosemount Estate Wines Ltd	01483 211466
ROZ	Rozès UK	0181 742 2391
RS2	Richardson & Sons	01946 65334
RSN	Richard Speirs Wines	01483 537605
RSS	Raisin Social Ltd	0181 686 8500
RSW	R S Wines	0117 963 1780
RTB	Italian Wine Brands Ltd	01992 561888
RTW	The Rose Tree Wine Company	01242 583732
RUK	Ruinart Champagne UK Ltd	0171 416 0592
RVA	Randalls (Jersey)	01534 887788
RWD	Richards Walford	01780 460 451
RWL	Richmonde Wines Ltd	01562 822777
RWR	R W Randall (Guernsey)	01780 460451
RYW	Hugh Ryman	01629 640133
S&D	Saltmarsh & Druce	01993 703721
SAC	La Reserve	0171 381 6930
SAF	Safeway Stores Plc	0181 848 8744
SAN	Sandiway Wine Co	01606 882101
SBS	Sainsbury Brothers	01225 460981
SCA	Scatchard	0151 236 6468
SCK	Seckford Wines Ltd.	01394 446622
SCL	Stephan's Cellar Ltd	01873 850 668
SEA	Seagram UK Ltd	0181 250 1018
SEB	Sebastopol Wines	01235 850471

STOCKISTS

SEL	Selfridges Ltd	0171 318 3730
SEN	Sensible Wine Services Ltd	01622 832640
SER	Serenus International Ltd	0171 535 0361
SGL	Stevens Garnier Ltd	01865 263300
SHA	Shawsgate Vineyard	01728 724060
SHB	Shaws of Beaumaris	01248 810328
SHG	Wine Shop on the Green	01437 766864
SHJ	S H Jones & Company	01295 251179
SHR	Sharpham Vineyard	01803 732203
SIP	Peter A Sichel	01580 715341
SKA	Skalli Fortant de France	0171 610 2898
SKW	Stokes Fine Wines Ltd	0181 944 5979
SLM	Salamis & Co Ltd	0171 609 1133
SMF	Somerfield Stores Ltd	0117 935 9359
SNO	Snowdonia Wine Warehouse	01492 870567
SNP	S.N. Paul Sapin	01603 880171
SOM	Sommelier Wine Co	01481 721677
SPR	Spar Landmark	0181 863 5511
SPS	Sapsford Wines	01920 421492
SPW	Specialist Wine Importers Ltd	01483 283115
SSV	St Sampson Vineyard	01726 833707
STA	Staple Vineyard	01304 812 571
STB	Stokes Brothers (UK) Ltd	01303 252178
STE	Stephane Auriol Wines	01252 843190
STG	Tony Stebbings	01372 468571
STH	Styria Wine Hamer	0181 296 0770
STP	Staplecombe Vineyards	01823 451217
STT	Santat Wines	01483 450494
STW	Stewarts Wine Barrels	01232 704434
SVT	Smedley Vintners	01462 768214
SWA	Swiss Wine Exporters Assoc	0171 287 6117
SWB	Satchells	01328 738272
SWI	Sherston Wine Co (St Albans)	01727 858841
SWN	S Wines	0171 351 1990
SWS	Stratfords Wine Shippers & Merchants Ltd	01628 810606
SYI	Sherry Institute of Spain	0171 486 0101
SYM	Symington Port & Madeira Shippers	0171 385 9896
T&T	Thierry's Wine Services	01794 507100
T&W	T&W Wines	01842 765646
TAN	Tanners Wines Ltd	01743 234500

 STOCKISTS

TAN	Tavern Group Ltd	0161 864 5000
TBS	Thomas Baty & Son	0151 236 1601
TBW	T B Watson (Dumfries)	01387 720505
TCV	Three Choirs Vineyards Ltd	01531 890555
TCW	T C Wines	0151 931 3390
TGW	Good Wine Company (London)	0181 858 5577
THC	The Haselmere Cellar	01428 645081
THP	Thos Peatling	01284 755948
THR	Throwley Vineyard	01795 890276
THS	Thresher	01707 328244
THV	Thwaites Vintners	01254 54431
THW	Southern Wine Brands Ltd	01484 608898
TIB	Talbot Wines	01926 484386
TLC	Valdivieso UK	01494 678 971
TMS	Thames Wine Sellers Ltd	0171 928 8253
TMW	Moffat Wine Shop	01683 220554
TNI	The Nobody Inn	01647 252394
TOS	Tesco Stores Ltd	01992 632222
TOU	Toucan Wines	01232 790909
TPA	The Wine Warehouse	01666 503088
TPE	Terry Platt Wines	01492 592971
TPW	Topsham Wines	01392 874501
TRO	Trout Wines	01264 781472
TRV	Transit Vin Ltd	0181 674 6344
TVD	Tenterden Vineyard	01580 763033
TVN	The Vintner Ltd	01483 765470
TVV	Valley Vineyard	0118 934 0176
TVW	Turville Valley Wines	01494 868818
TWB	The Wine Bank	01892 514343
TWC	Wine Cellar (Fareham)	01329 822733
UBC	Ubiquitous Chip	0141 334 5007
UDV	UDV UK Ltd	01279 626 801
UNS	Unwins Ltd	01322 272711
UPC	The Upper Crust	01483 284757
UWM	United Wine Merchants	01232 231231
V&C	Valvona & Crolla	0131 556 6066
V&V	Vino Vino	0403 436 949
VAU	Vaux Breweries	0191 567 6277
VBB	Vinedos y Bodegas Bella Union SA	598 2 507 3023
VCV	Viña Carta Vieja de Chile	01737 222 585

 STOCKISTS

VDA	Ets Vitivinicolas Dante Irurtia SA	598 2 9004019
VDO	Val D'Orbieu Wines Ltd	0171 736 3350
VDP	Vinhos de Portugal Ltd	01865 263305
VDT	Vins Direct	01534 483160
VDV	Vin du Van Wine Merchants	01233 758727
VEC	Vin Ecosse	01368 864800
VEN	Venue International Wines	01636 708761
VER	Vinceremos Wines	0113 257 7545
VEX	Vinexports Ltd	01584 811333
VHW	Victor Hugo Wines	01534 32225
VIC	Vica Wines Ltd	01273 477132
VIL	Village Wines	01322 558772
VIM	Vinimpo	01737 842763
VIN	Vinum	0181 840 4070
VIW	Vintage Wines	0115 947 6565
VLW	Villeneuve Wines	01721 722500
VNF	Vinfruco Ltd	01753 712432
VNO	Vinoceros (UK)Ltd	01209 314711
VNP	Vinoceros (Australia)	01209 314 711
VRL	Verulam Vintners	01784 421822
VRS	Veritaus Co	01428 607233
VRT	Vintage Roots	0118 976 1999
VSC	Victory Spirit Co. Ltd	01732 834 146
VTl	Vine Trail	0117 942 3946
VTS	Vinities UK	0171 924 4974
VTT	Vinopolis	0171 645 3700
VWC	Victoria Wine Cellars	01483 715066
VWE	Victoria Wine	01483 715066
VXL	Vinexcel Ltd	0161 485 4592
W&V	Wine & The Vine	0973 753928
WAC	Waters of Coventry Ltd	01926 888889
WAF	Wines of South Africa	0171 349 8820
WAV	Waverley Vintners Ltd	01738 629621
WAW	Waterloo Wine Co	0171 403 7967
WBL	Westbury Blake	0171 404 5575
WBM	Wine Byre Merchants	01334 653215
WBR	Wadebridge Wines	01208 812692
WBU	Wine Bureau	01403 256446
WCK	Wickham Wines	01237 473292
WCL	Wines of Chile	0171 222 2073

WCR	Wine Cellar Ltd (Parisa)	01925 444555
WCS	The Wine Cellar (Sanderstead)	0181 657 6936
WDI	Wine Direct Ltd	01932 820490
WDM	Waddesdon Manor	01296 651282
WEK	Wine Emporium/Cockburns	0131 346 1113
WEP	Welshpool Wine Company	01938 553243
WER	Wine Cellar (Douglas)	01624 611793
WES	Wessex Wines	01308 427177
WET	Westbay Distributors Ltd	01703 635 252
WEX	Wine Experience	01949 851499
WFB	Mildara Blass (UK) Ltd	0181 947 4312
WFD	Wine Finds	01584 875582
WFL	Winefare Ltd	01483 458700
WFM	World Fresh Marketing	0181 390 1444
WFS	Wines from Spain	0171 486 0101
WGA	Winegrowers Agencies Ltd	01954 230176
WGS	William Grant & Sons International Ltd	0181 332 1188
WGW	Woodgate Wines	01229 885637
WHG	Wines of Hungary	01751 473933
WHS	Wine House	0171 737 0242
WIC	Jolly's Drinks	01237 473292
WIL	Willoughby's of Manchester	0161 834 6850
WIM	Wimbledon Wine Cellar	0181 540 9979
WIN	The Winery	0171 286 6475
WKM	Wickham Vineyard	01329 834042
WKV	Wyken Vineyards	01359 250257
WLI	Winelink Ltd International	01280 824120
WLL	Williams Winesellers	0181 374 1462
WLM	William's Winesellers	0181 374 1462
WMK	Winemark	01232 746274
WNC	Winchcombe Wines	01242 604313
WNS	Winos	0161 652 9396
WOA	Wallaces of Ayr	01292 262330
WOC	Whitesides of Clitheroe	01200 422 281
WOI	Wines of Interest Ltd	01473 215752
WON	Weavers of Nottingham	0115 958 0922
WOO	Wooldings Vineyard & Winery	01256 895200
WOP	Wines of Portugal	0171 828 7029
WOW	Wines of Westhorpe	01283 820285
WPL	The Wine Portfolio Ltd	01225 852484

 STOCKISTS

WRC	Wine Rack (First Quench)	01707 328244
WRI	Wrightson Wines	01325 374134
WRK	Wine Raks	01224 311460
WRO	Wroxeter Roman Vineyard	01743 761888
WRT	Winerite Ltd	0113 283 7654
WRU	William Rush Wines	Ex Directory
WRW	The Wright Wine Co	01756 700886
WSA	Wineshare Ltd	01306 742164
WSC	Winesource	01225 783007
WSG	Walter S Siegel Ltd	01256 701101
WSO	The Wine Society Ltd	01438 741177
WSP	Wine Schoppen Ltd	0114 255 3301
WST	Western Wines Ltd	01746 789411
WTA	Winetraders	0165 251 851
WTD	Waitrose Direct	01344 824694
WTH	Withers Agencies Ltd	01273 477132
WTL	Whittalls Wines	01922 36161
WTR	The Wine Treasury Ltd	0171 793 9999
WTS	Waitrose Ltd	01344 424680
WVV	Wylye Valley Vineyard	01985 211337
WWC	Walmer Wine Company	01472 240558
WWD	Wineworld	01923 264718
WWG	Wingara Wine Group	0181 542 8101
WWI	Woodhouse Wines	01258 452141
WWS	Windermere Wine Stores	01539 446891
WWT	Whitebridge Wines	01785 817229
WYW	Wychwood Wines	01932 855323
YAL	Yalumba	01582 462859
YAP	Yapp Brothers	01747 860423
YOB	Young & Co	0181 875 7007
YVM	Tony Stebbings / Yvon Mau	01372 468571
YWL	Yates Brothers Ltd	01204 391777
ZON	Zonin UK	01372 818000

INDEX

INDEX

INDEX

INDEX

INDEX

INDEX

INDEX

INDEX

INDEX

INDEX

INDEX

INDEX

INDEX

INDEX

INDEX

INDEX

INDEX

INDEX

INDEX

INDEX

INDEX

INDEX

INDEX

INDEX

INDEX

NOTES ON STOCKISTS AND WINES

WINE NAME
STOCKIST
TASTING NOTE

WINE NAME
STOCKIST
TASTING NOTE

WINE NAME
STOCKIST
TASTING NOTE

WINE NAME
STOCKIST
TASTING NOTE

WINE NAME
STOCKIST
TASTING NOTE

WINE NAME
STOCKIST
TASTING NOTE

WINE NAME
STOCKIST
TASTING NOTE

WINE NAME
STOCKIST
TASTING NOTE

WINE NAME
STOCKIST
TASTING NOTE

WINE NAME
STOCKIST
TASTING NOTE

WINE NAME
STOCKIST
TASTING NOTE

WINE NAME
STOCKIST
TASTING NOTE

NOTES ON STOCKISTS AND WINES

WINE NAME
STOCKIST
TASTING NOTE

WINE NAME
STOCKIST
TASTING NOTE

WINE NAME
STOCKIST
TASTING NOTE

WINE NAME
STOCKIST
TASTING NOTE

WINE NAME
STOCKIST
TASTING NOTE

WINE NAME
STOCKIST
TASTING NOTE

NOTES ON STOCKISTS AND WINES

WINE NAME
STOCKIST
TASTING NOTE

WINE NAME
STOCKIST
TASTING NOTE

WINE NAME
STOCKIST
TASTING NOTE

WINE NAME
STOCKIST
TASTING NOTE

WINE NAME
STOCKIST
TASTING NOTE

WINE NAME
STOCKIST
TASTING NOTE

NOTES ON STOCKISTS AND WINES

WINE NAME
STOCKIST
TASTING NOTE

WINE NAME
STOCKIST
TASTING NOTE

WINE NAME
STOCKIST
TASTING NOTE

WINE NAME
STOCKIST
TASTING NOTE

WINE NAME
STOCKIST
TASTING NOTE

WINE NAME
STOCKIST
TASTING NOTE

NOTES ON STOCKISTS AND WINES

WINE NAME
STOCKIST
TASTING NOTE

WINE NAME
STOCKIST
TASTING NOTE

WINE NAME
STOCKIST
TASTING NOTE

WINE NAME
STOCKIST
TASTING NOTE

WINE NAME
STOCKIST
TASTING NOTE

WINE NAME
STOCKIST
TASTING NOTE

NOTES ON STOCKISTS AND WINES

WINE NAME
STOCKIST
TASTING NOTE

WINE NAME
STOCKIST
TASTING NOTE

WINE NAME
STOCKIST
TASTING NOTE

WINE NAME
STOCKIST
TASTING NOTE

WINE NAME
STOCKIST
TASTING NOTE

WINE NAME
STOCKIST
TASTING NOTE

NOTES ON STOCKISTS AND WINES

WINE NAME
STOCKIST
TASTING NOTE

WINE NAME
STOCKIST
TASTING NOTE

WINE NAME
STOCKIST
TASTING NOTE

WINE NAME
STOCKIST
TASTING NOTE

WINE NAME
STOCKIST
TASTING NOTE

WINE NAME
STOCKIST
TASTING NOTE

NOTES ON STOCKISTS AND WINES

WINE NAME

STOCKIST

TASTING NOTE

WINE NAME

STOCKIST

TASTING NOTE

WINE NAME

STOCKIST

TASTING NOTE

WINE NAME

STOCKIST

TASTING NOTE

WINE NAME

STOCKIST

TASTING NOTE

WINE NAME

STOCKIST

TASTING NOTE

NOTES ON STOCKISTS AND WINES

WINE NAME
STOCKIST
TASTING NOTE

WINE NAME
STOCKIST
TASTING NOTE

WINE NAME
STOCKIST
TASTING NOTE

WINE NAME
STOCKIST
TASTING NOTE

WINE NAME
STOCKIST
TASTING NOTE

WINE NAME
STOCKIST
TASTING NOTE

NOTES ON STOCKISTS AND WINES

WINE NAME
STOCKIST
TASTING NOTE

WINE NAME
STOCKIST
TASTING NOTE

WINE NAME
STOCKIST
TASTING NOTE

WINE NAME
STOCKIST
TASTING NOTE

WINE NAME
STOCKIST
TASTING NOTE

WINE NAME
STOCKIST
TASTING NOTE

WINE NAME
STOCKIST
TASTING NOTE

WINE NAME
STOCKIST
TASTING NOTE

WINE NAME
STOCKIST
TASTING NOTE

WINE NAME
STOCKIST
TASTING NOTE

WINE NAME
STOCKIST
TASTING NOTE

WINE NAME
STOCKIST
TASTING NOTE

WINE NAME
STOCKIST
TASTING NOTE

WINE NAME
STOCKIST
TASTING NOTE

WINE NAME
STOCKIST
TASTING NOTE

WINE NAME
STOCKIST
TASTING NOTE

WINE NAME
STOCKIST
TASTING NOTE

WINE NAME
STOCKIST
TASTING NOTE

ACKNOWLEDGMENTS

The End...Year on year we have tried to give an insight into the International WINE Challenge, the exhilaration and the fatigue. This year, however, I would simply ask you to empathise by gaining as much pleasure from hunting down and drnking these wines as we have in putting the results together. For this we have the following people to thank:

• **the International WINE Challenge team** – for their dedication and good humour and for performing so well under pressure, especially the computer boffins and the hand–writing decipherers. We hope your full recovery and integration back into society is both speedy and painless. Thanks, also, to all the tasters who gave their time and expertise to help us, Sega Fredo for provision of a complete coffee bar, Samual Adams and Hoegaarden for the beer at the end of the day, Riedel for the glasswear and Carrs Water Biscuits for keeping the tasters' mouths fresh.

• **from WINE magazine** – Robert Joseph, Charles Metcalfe, Kirsty Bridge and Georgina Severs.

• **for subbing and database management** – the editorial team of Tracey (**TJ**) Binnie, Nick (**Bummer**) James-Martin and Peter (**Rabbit**) Keeghan.

Finally, thanks go to **editor** James Gabbani for his ability to extract every inch of energy and the infamous 'Gabbani dozen's' - just a dozen more to go guys. Yeah right.

HOW YOU CAN HELP US

If you have any ideas about how we can improve the format of the **WINE Magazine Pocket Wine Buyer's Guide** then please write to:

James Gabbani, WINE PWBG, Wilmington Publishing,
6-8 Underwood Street, London N1 7JQ

The type of subjects we would particularly like to hear about are:

- **Do you prefer to have countries sub-divided by region or grape variety?**
- **Do you find the £5 and Under guides useful?**
- **Would food and wine pairing suggestions be useful?**
- **How else might you like to see the wines sorted or divided?**
- **What other information regarding wines and stockists would be of interest?**
- **Would you prefer the Guide to be ring-bound or loose leafed?**